D0291574

___EIGHTH EDITION___

Daytrips

NEW YORK

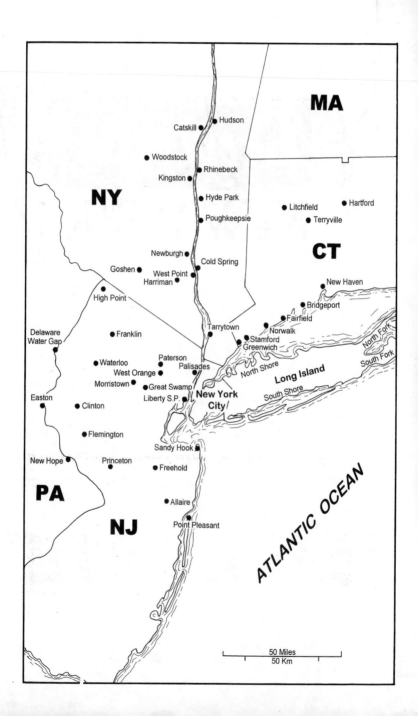

EIGHTH EDITION

Daytrips

NEW YORK

50 *one day adventures in New York City and nearby New York State, Connecticut, New Jersey and Pennsylvania*

EARL STEINBICKER

HASTINGS HOUSE
Book Publishers
Fern Park, Florida

ISBN: 0-8038-2021-6

All photos by the author except as otherwise credited.

Cover design and book layout by Mark Salore, Digital Design Services

Printed in the United States of America
10 9 8 7 6 5 4 3 2 1

Comments? Ideas?

We'd love to hear from you. Ideas from our readers have resulted in many improvements in the past, and will continue to do so. And, if your suggestions are used, we'll gladly send you a complimentary copy of any book in the series. Please send your thoughts to Hastings House, Book Publishers, 2601 Wells Ave., Fern Park, FL 32730, or fax us at 407-339-5900, or e-mail to Hhousebks@aol.com. Visit us at www.DaytripsBooks.com

Contents

	Introduction	7
Section I	**Daytrip Strategies**	**9**
	New York City As Your Base	10
	Choosing Destinations	13
	Getting Around	13
	Food and Drink	13
	Practicalities	14
	Suggested Tours	15
	Tourist Information	16
Section II	**Daytrips Within New York City**	**17**
	Getting Around NYC	18
	Shopping	21
	Festivities	22
	Safety	23
	Local Tourist Information	24
	1. Lower Manhattan	25
	2. Chinatown, Little Italy, and the Lower East Side	37
	3. TriBeCa, SoHo, and Greenwich Village	44
	4. West Midtown to Chelsea	56
	5. Fifth Avenue and the East Side	66
	6. Central Park and the Museum Mile	75
	7. Upper Manhattan	86
	8. Brooklyn Heights to Prospect Park	93
	9. Northern Staten Island	99
	10. Staten Island South of the Expressway	104
Section III	**Daytrips in the Hudson Valley**	**107**
	11. Sunnyside to Tarrytown	109
	12. More Treats at Tarrytown	112
	13. Garrison, Boscobel, and Cold Spring	115
	14. Poughkeepsie and Hyde Park	120
	15. Rhinebeck	126
	16. Columbia County	131
	17. West Point and the Hudson Highlands	137
	18. Bear Mountain and Harriman State Parks	142
	19. Newburgh	147
	20. Central Orange County	152
	21. Kingston	156
	22. Scenic Drives in the Catskills	161

6   CONTENTS

Section IV   **Touring on Long Island**   168
    23. The North Shore   170
    24. The North Fork   178
    25. The South Shore   182
    26. The South Fork: Through the Hamptons
        to Montauk   189
Section V   **Daytrips to Connecticut**   197
    27. Greenwich and Stamford   198
    28. Ridgefield and Norwalk   204
    29. Fairfield, Bridgeport and Stratford   209
    30. New Haven   215
    31. The Litchfield Hills   221
    32. Terryville to Wethersfield   228
    33. Hartford   234
Section VI   **Daytrips to New Jersey and Pennsylvania**   243
    34. The Palisades   244
    35. Liberty State Park, the Statue of Liberty,
        and Ellis Island   250
    36. Northern Monmouth County   255
    37. Southeastern Monmouth County   259
    38. The Jersey Shore: Barnegat Peninsula   263
    39. Flemington   268
    40. Princeton   272
    41. West Orange and Montclair   277
    42. The Great Swamp   282
    43. Morristown   287
    44. Clinton   293
    45. Paterson   297
    46. The Village of Waterloo   301
    47. New Jersey's Northwest Skylands   305
    48. Delaware Water Gap   310
    49. New Hope   314
    50. The Two Rivers and Their Canals   319
Index   324

Introduction

After the horrific events of September 11 2001, it becomes essential to reestablish a normal American way of life. To do otherwise would hand victory to the terrorists.

Not only do New Yorkers enjoy living in what is arguably the world's most fabulous city, but they are also within easy striking distance of other highly attractive destinations, as well as several relatively unknown but intriguing byways. Many of these lie within 50 miles of Times Square, and the overwhelming majority are less than 100 miles away. Although it stretches the daytrip concept just a tad, a few destinations are so compelling that they've also been included even though they are located as far as 130 miles from the Big Apple.

For both residents and visitors alike, daytrips are the ideal way to probe this compact, treasure-filled region. And, if you have a weekend or more at your disposal, why not combine several daytrips into a mini-vacation?

New York City is, of course, one of the world's great destinations in itself. To help you enjoy its wonders, this book opens with eight one-day walking tours that explore the most interesting corners of town, ranging from the tip of Manhattan to its very top, and even venturing over into Brooklyn. You won't need a car for these short excursions, as all of them can easily be reached by subway, bus, cab, or even on foot. There are also two tours of Staten Island, reached by ferry boat and traveled by bus or car.

The scenic Hudson Valley is next, with 12 daytrip destinations ranging from nearby Tarrytown to as far away as the Catskills. Nearly half of these are within 50 miles of the city, and some can even be reached by public transportation.

Long Island follows, with visits to Teddy Roosevelt's family home, to the Planting Fields Arboretum, to ritzy Old Westbury Gardens, to the Vanderbilt Mansion, to Jones Beach and Fire Island, to the North Fork vineyards, to the fabulous Hamptons, and finally all the way to Montauk Point. And a lot more, besides.

The western part of Connecticut is included as it lies within comfortable daytrip range, and features such sights as the Aquarium at Norwalk, the Yale campus at New Haven, historic sites in Hartford, and the lovely rural splendors of the Litchfield Hills.

Finally, the last section deals with New Jersey and even a touch of Pennsylvania. From the Palisades just across the Hudson and Liberty State Park by the Statue of Liberty and Ellis Island to the Jersey Shore, from

Edison's lab at West Orange to the Great Swamp and the Revolutionary War battlefield at Morristown, there is a great deal of nature and history to explore. The trips also include the beautiful Ivy League campus at Princeton, the bargain shopping at Flemington, a re-created Indian village and a restored canal town at Waterloo, underground mines at Sterling Hill, the natural splendors of Delaware Water Gap, and the artists' colony of New Hope — plus much more.

Wherever practical, the daytrips have been arranged as walking tours following a carefully-tested route on the accompanying map. This works well in larger towns and cities, and sometimes even in historic villages. In other cases, however, the attractions are just too far apart to see on foot, so their descriptions are arranged in a driving sequence from which you can pick and choose, matching site numbers with those on the trip's road map. A few of the daytrips, such as that to Connecticut's Litchfield Hills, are designed for the sheer pleasure of driving, with just a few attractions that you might want to see along the way.

Dining well is a vital element in any travel experience. For this reason, a selection of particularly enjoyable restaurants has been included for each of the daytrips. These are price-keyed, with an emphasis on the medium-to-low range, regional cooking, and local atmosphere. Their concise location descriptions make them easy to find.

Time and weather considerations are important, and they've been included under the "Practicalities" section of each trip. These let you know, among other things, on which days the sights are closed, when some special events occur, and which places to avoid in bad weather. The location, telephone number, and (when applicable) Internet site of the local tourist information office is also given in case you have questions.

Please remember that places have a way of changing without warning, and that errors do creep into print. If your heart is absolutely set on a particular sight, you should check first to make sure that it's open, and that the times are still valid. Phone numbers and, where applicable, Internet sites for this purpose are given for each of the attractions, or you could contact the local tourist office.

One last thought: It isn't really necessary to see everything at any given destination. Be selective. Your one-day adventures both in and around New York City should be fun, not an endurance test. If they start becoming that, just find your way to the nearest refreshment stop and enjoy yourself while soaking up local atmosphere. There will always be another day.

Happy Daytripping!

Section I

DAYTRIP STRATEGIES

The word "Daytrip" may not have made it into dictionaries yet, but for experienced independent travelers it represents the easiest, most natural, and often the least expensive approach to exploring many of the world's most interesting areas. This strategy, in which you base yourself in a central city (or its suburbs) and probe the surrounding region on a series of one-day excursions, is especially effective in the case of New York City and its surrounding region.

ADVANTAGES:
  While not the answer to every travel situation, daytrips have significant advantages over point-to-point touring following a set itinerary. Here are ten good reasons for considering the daytrip approach:
1. Freedom from the constraints of a fixed itinerary. You can go wherever you feel like going whenever the mood strikes you.
2. Freedom from the burden of luggage. Your bags remain in your hotel while you run around with only a guidebook and camera.
3. Freedom from the anxiety of reservation foul-ups. You don't have to worry each day about whether that night's lodging will actually materialize.
4. The flexibility of making last-minute changes to allow for unexpected weather, serendipitous discoveries, changing interests, new-found passions, and so on.
5. The flexibility to take breaks from sightseeing whenever you feel tired or bored, without upsetting a planned itinerary. Why not sleep late in your base city for a change?

6. The opportunity to sample different travel experiences without committing more than a day to them.
7. The opportunity to become a "temporary resident" of your base city. By staying there for a while you can get to know it in depth, becoming familiar with the local restaurants, shops, theaters, night life, and other attractions - enjoying them as a native would.
8. The convenience of not having to pack and unpack your bags each day. Your clothes can hang in a closet where they belong, or even be sent out for cleaning.
9. The convenience (and security!) of having a fixed address in your base city, where friends, relatives, and business associates can reach you in an emergency.
10. The economy of staying at one hotel on a discounted longer-term basis, especially in conjunction with package plans. You can make advance reservations for your base city without sacrificing any flexibility at all.

And, of course, for those who actually live in or around New York City, daytrips are the key to discovering one of America's most fascinating regions — one day at a time.

NEW YORK CITY
AS YOUR BASE

GETTING THERE:

By Air: Most of the world's major airlines, along with numerous small carriers, fly in and out of at least one of New York's three airports. **John F. Kennedy International Airport** (JFK), in southeastern Queens some 15 miles east of Manhattan, is the largest and handles mostly international and long-distance flights. It is connected to Manhattan by a cheap but very tedious subway ride, direct commercial buses to various midtown locations, an expensive cab ride, or limousine service. A light rail link with connections to the Long Island Rail Road, subways, and city buses is supposed to be operational by 2003. ☎ 718-244-4444, Internet: www.panynj.gov/aviation. **LaGuardia Airport** (LGA), in northern Queens about eight miles from midtown, handles domestic and commuter flights, including shuttle service to Boston and Washington D.C. It connects to midtown Manhattan via a cheap-but-tedious bus-and-subway combination, commercial buses to various locations, cabs, limousine services, and the Delta Water Shuttle ferry to East 34th Street and to Wall Street. ☎ 718-533- 3400, Internet: www.panynj.gov/aviation. **Newark International Airport** (EWR), some 15 miles southwest of Manhattan in New Jersey, offers both international, domestic, and commuter flights from a wide range of carriers. It is linked to midtown Manhattan by airport bus to Newark, then NJ

Transit or PATH trains to Manhattan — an inexpensive and not-too-bad option — direct commercial buses to midtown locations, and limousine services. Cabs are also available but as it's an interstate trip you'll have to negotiate a price first. A monorail connecting all the terminals with the Northeast Corridor rail line near Newark is under construction. ☎ 201-961-2000, Internet: www.panynj.gov/aviation. **All three airports** are served by two van services offering convenient service at fair prices: **Gray Line Air Shuttle**, ☎ 1-800-451-0455, Internet: www.graylinenewyork.com; and **SuperShuttle**, ☎ 1-800-258-3826, Internet: www.supershuttle.com.

By Rail: Amtrak provides fast, very frequent service along the Northeast Corridor south to Philadelphia, Wilmington, Baltimore, and Washington, and north to New Haven, Providence, and Boston. These routes feature the new premium high-speed **Acela Express** trains along with regular expresses. They also offer somewhat more leisurely rides to upstate New York, Canada, the South, and points west. ☎ 1-800 USA-RAIL, Internet: www.amtrak.com and www.acela.com.

By Commuter Train: Four commuter railroads operate in and out of New York City. **Metro North**, using Grand Central Terminal as its base, provides very frequent service to and from the Hudson Valley, Westchester, Putnam, and Dutchess counties, and much of Connecticut as far as New Haven. ☎ 212-532-4900 or 1-800-METRO-INFO, Internet: www.mta.nyc.ny.us. The **Long Island Rail Road**, using a part of Pennsylvania Station as its base, offers frequent service to virtually all of Long Island. ☎ 212-217- 5477, Internet: www.mta.nyc.ny.us. **New Jersey Transit** connects Pennsylvania Station with most of New Jersey, with economical connections to Philadelphia and Wilmington. ☎ 973-762-5100 or 1- 800-626-7433, Internet: www.njtransit.state.nj.us. **PATH** trains, operated by the Port Authority, provide frequent low-cost (if somewhat uncomfortable) service from Midtown Manhattan (33rd, 23rd, and 14th streets under Sixth Ave. plus Greenwich Village) to Hoboken, Jersey City, and Newark. ☎ 1-800-234-PATH, Internet: www.panynj.gov.

By Bus: The enormous Port Authority Bus Terminal at Eighth Avenue and 42nd Street, the nation's largest and most modern, provides bus service to practically anywhere in the continental United States, Canada, or Mexico, either directly or via connections. There are also frequent services to the three major airports, leaving from the terminal's north wing. ☎ 212-564- 8484. While slower than planes or trains, intercity bus travel has the decided advantage of being much cheaper.

By Car: Parking is the major reason to avoid driving in Manhattan. While traffic is manageable and the street layouts make finding your way around fairly easy, curbside parking is virtually non-existent and commercial parking lots exorbitantly expensive. You'll need a car for most of the out-of-town daytrips described in this book, but within the city you're better off sticking to public transportation.

ACCOMMODATIONS:

Unless you live in or around New York City, you'll need a place to stay. Although the metropolis has a seemingly infinite number of hotels, they're often booked solid, making advance **reservations** essential. Discount package deals that combine transportation with hotel rooms are offered by several airlines as well as by Amtrak. Many hotels offer deeply discounted **weekend packages**; check your travel agent about this. The city levies a 13.25% **room tax** plus a $2 per-room-per-night occupancy tax on all accommodations, which must be figured into your budget. Some recommended booking agencies include: **Accommodations Express,** ☎ 1-800-991-7666, Internet: www.accommodationsexpress.com; **Express Hotel Reservations,** ☎ 1-800-356-1123, Internet: www.express- res.com; **Hotel Con-X-ions,** ☎ 1-800-522-9991, Internet: www.hotelconxions.com; **Hotel Reservations Network,** ☎ 1-800-964-6835, Internet: www.hoteldiscount.com; and **Quickbook,** ☎ 1-800-789-9887. There are three **YMCAs** in Manhattan as well as one in Queens, which are considerably less expensive than hotels. Some are co-ed. For information and reservations contact the **Y's Way,** ☎ 212-308-2899. Manhattan also has a **HI-AYH Hostel** at 891 Amsterdam Ave., ☎ 212-932-2300, Internet: www.hinewyork.org.

For adventurous travelers, **Bed & Breakfast** stays in New York City are becoming an increasingly popular way of cutting costs while enjoying a much more personalized service. If you'd like to try this alternative, there are several booking agencies that can give you information and make arrangements. Some of these are: **Bed & Breakfast of New York,** ☎ 212-645-8134; **Urban Ventures,** ☎ 212-594-5650; and **New World Bed & Breakfast,** ☎ 212-675-5600 or 1-800-553-3800. A somewhat similar arrangement is to rent a **furnished apartment** for a week or longer. One agency handling this option is **Oxbridge Property Services,** ☎ 212-348-8100.

NEARBY ALTERNATIVES:

Staying in the **outer boroughs** is a good way to save money, and may actually be more convenient for the out-of-town daytrips. As for visiting Manhattan itself, you can always take a subway there or, in the case of Staten Island, a ferry ride. Because it is home to both JFK International and LaGuardia airports, Queens has a particularly good selection of medium-price motels with good parking facilities and nearby subways. Similarly, nearby New Jersey has many motels along the highways going into the city; some of these have bus or train connections into Manhattan. Other options are Westchester County, just north of the city, and Nassau County, just beyond Queens on Long Island. Both have numerous motels, easy parking, and convenient public transportation into Manhattan. State and local tourist information offices (see page 16) will gladly tell you all about them.

CHOOSING DESTINATIONS

With 50 trips from which to choose, and several attractions for each trip, deciding which are the most enjoyable for you and yours might be problematic. You could, of course, read through the whole book and mark the most appealing spots, but there's an easier way to at least start. Just turn to the index and scan it, looking out for the special-interest categories set in **BOLD FACE** type. These will immediately lead you to choices under such headings as Art Museums, Restored Historic Villages, Revolutionary War Sites, Boat Trips, Children's Activities, Railfan Interest, and many others.

The elements of one trip can often be combined with another to create a custom itinerary, using the book maps as a rough guide and a good road map for the final routing.

Some of the trips, listed in the index as **SCENIC DRIVES**, are just that — they are primarily designed for the pure pleasure of driving, with just enough attractions along the way to keep things lively. These are especially enjoyable if you are blessed with a car that's fun to drive.

GETTING AROUND

The driving directions for each trip assume that you're leaving from Manhattan in New York City. Chances are, however, that you live (or are staying) elsewhere in the outer boroughs, Westchester or Nassau counties, or in New Jersey, so you'll need to modify the routes a bit.

The route **maps** scattered throughout the book show you approximately where the sites are, and which main roads lead to them. In many cases, however, you'll still need a good, up-to-date road map. An excellent choice for a single-sheet map that covers nearly all of the destinations is the *75-Mile Radius Map From New York City,* published by Hagstrom. The free maps distributed by state tourist offices vary greatly in quality, so if the one they give you isn't clear enough, head for your bookstore and look over their selection.

The majority of daytrips in this book are designed to be made by car, and do not really lend themselves to public transportation. If you've arrived in New York City without wheels, you'll have to rent, borrow, buy, or steal a vehicle; or else limit yourself to those trips that can be done easily by subway, ferry, train, or bus.

Specific information about transportation within New York City itself will be found in Section II. In addition, each daytrip has a "Getting There" section outlining the most practical routes and, when applicable, public transportation services.

FOOD AND DRINK

Several choice restaurants that make sense for daytrippers are listed for each destination in this book. Most of these are long-time favorites of experienced travelers, are open for lunch, are on or near the suggested tour route, and provide some atmosphere. Their approximate price range is shown as:

$ -   Inexpensive.
$$ -   Reasonable.
$$$ -   Luxurious and expensive.
X: -   Days closed.

If you're really serious about dining you should consult an up-to-date restaurant and hotel guide such as the annual *Zagat Survey Guide for New York,* or the various *Tour Books* available free to members of the AAA.

Fast-food outlets are, of course, nearly everywhere, and have the advantage of not taking up much of your sightseeing time. In warm weather, why not consider a picnic? Many of the attractions have picnic facilities that you can use; these are indicated in the practical information for those sites.

PRACTICALITIES

WEATHER:

New York City can be hot and humid in July and August, and bitterly cold in January and February. If you're coming then, be prepared to spend most of your time indoors, such as in museums, theaters, or shopping — or in mid-summer making daytrips to the cooler countryside.

Spring, early summer, and fall are the best seasons for the entire region, and therefore the most crowded. This is a good time to explore the less-famous attractions in the surrounding states.

OPENING TIMES, FEES, and FACILITIES:

When planning a daytrip, be sure to note carefully the **opening times** of the various sites — these can sometimes be rather quirky. Anything unusual that you should know before starting, such as "don't make this trip on a Monday," is summarized in the "Practicalities" section of each trip.

Entrance fees listed in the text are, naturally, subject to change — and they rarely go down. For the most part, admissions are reasonable considering the cost of maintaining the sites, although a few attractions in Manhattan might strike you as exorbitant. Places with free entry, especially those not operated by governments, are usually staffed with unpaid volunteers and have a donation box to help keep the wolves from the door. Please put something in it.

Any special facilities that a site may offer are listed in the italicized information for that site, along with the address, phone number, and web site. These often include restaurants or cafeterias, cafés, information counters, gift shops, tours, shows, picnic facilities, and so on.

TELEPHONE NUMBERS:

Telephone numbers are indicated with a ☎; relevant area codes are indicated by the first three digits. In some areas the area code must be dialed for all calls, including purely local ones, as several "area codes" sometimes serve the same locale. In these cases it is not necessary to add the prefix numeral "1" for local calls. This 10-digit "overlay" dialing will surely spread to other areas as well. Calling ahead, always a good idea, is especially convenient if your car or pocket is equipped with a cell phone.

HANDICAPPED TRAVELERS:

Access varies with each individual's needs and abilities, so no firm statement can be made about any site. Those that are generally accessible without much difficulty are indicated with the symbol ⅙, but when in doubt it is always best to phone ahead.

GROUP TRAVEL:

If you're planning a group outing, always call ahead. Most sites require advance reservations and offer special discounts for groups, often at a substantial saving over the regular admission fee. Some sites will open specially or remain open beyond their scheduled hours to accommodate groups; some have tours, demonstrations, lectures, and so on available only to groups; and some have facilities for rental to groups.

SUGGESTED TOURS

Two different methods of organizing daytrips are used in this book, depending on local circumstances. Some are based on **structured itineraries** such as walking tours and scenic drives that follow a suggested route, while others just describe the **local attractions** from which you can choose. In either case, a town or area map always shows where things are, so you're not likely to get lost. Circled numbers in the text refer to the numbers on the appropriate map.

Major attractions are described in one or more paragraphs each, beginning with practical information for a visit. **Additional sites** are worked into the text, along with some practical information in italics. All are arranged in a logical geographic sequence, although you may want to make changes to suit your preferences.

Walking tours, where used, follow routes shown by heavy broken lines on the accompanying map. You can estimate the amount of time that any segment of a walking tour will take by looking at the scaled map and figuring that the average person covers about 100 yards a minute.

Trying to see everything at any given destination could easily lead to an exhausting marathon. You will certainly enjoy yourself more by being selective and passing up anything that doesn't catch your fancy, and perhaps planning a repeat visit at some other time.

Practical information, such as opening times and admission fees, is as accurate as was possible at the time of writing, but will certainly change. You should always check with the sites themselves if seeing a particular one is crucially important to you. It is best to do this by phone, as their web sites are not always up-to-date.

*OUTSTANDING ATTRACTIONS:

An *asterisk before any attraction, be it an entire daytrip or just one exhibit in a museum, denotes a special treat that in the author's opinion should not be missed.

TOURIST INFORMATION

The addresses, phone numbers, and Internet sites of local and regional tourist offices as well as major sights are given in the text whenever appropriate. These are usually your best source for specific information and current brochures, always bearing in mind that they are often commercial operations intent on getting your business. On a wider scale, state tourist offices offer free "vacation planning kits," maps, and brochures that are often useful. You can contact them at:

New York State Department of Economic Development
Division of Tourism, P.O. Box 2603, Albany, NY 12220-0603
☎ 518-474-4116 or 1-800-225-5697
Internet: www.iloveny.state.ny.us

Connecticut Division of Tourism
865 Brook St., Rocky Hill, CT 06067
☎ 860-270-8080 or 1-800-282-6863
Internet: www.ctbound.org

New Jersey Commerce and Economic Growth Commission
Office of Travel and Tourism
20 West State St., Trenton, NJ 08625-0820
☎ 609-777-0885 or 1-800-VISIT NJ
Internet: www.visitnj.org

Pennsylvania Visitors Bureau
450 Forum Bldg., Harrisburg, PA 17120
☎ 717-787-5453 or 1-800-847-4872
Internet: www.state.pa.us/visit

Section II

DAYTRIPS WITHIN
NEW YORK CITY

Some of the practical information about New York City attractions, especially those in Lower Manhattan, is subject to change as a result of the terrorist attack on the World Trade Center and the subsequent cleanup and reconstruction. Please check with the tourist information offices at the end of this chapter for up-to-date information.

Before heading off on daytrips to the Hudson Valley, Long Island, Connecticut, New Jersey, or Pennsylvania, you'll certainly want to explore the Big Apple itself. The ten self-guided tours described in this section can guide you to both the most famous sites and also to some rather obscure attractions — always by way of enjoyable routes, both on foot and by public transportation. The walks average a bit under four miles in length and should take about four hours or so to complete, assuming that you visit some of the museums and other attractions along the way.

New York City was originally called New Amsterdam, and was first settled by the Dutch in the early 1600s. Nearly a century before that, in 1524, Giovanni da Verrazano, an Italian working for King François I of France, was the first European to discover Manhattan Island. It was again explored in 1609 by Henry Hudson while on a mission for the Dutch East India Company. The first permanent settlement, a fort and 30 houses, began in 1625 and quickly grew into a town with over 300 houses. Dutch rule ended in 1664, after which England took over, changing the name to New York in honor of the Duke of York, King Charles II's brother. Unlike other European colonies in North America, New York was founded for commercial rather than religious reasons, and its inhabitants never really cared who ruled them as long as they could make lots of money. That attitude still prevails.

New York City is divided into five boroughs, each of which is a county in its own right, and all of which are under one joint municipal government. The **Bronx** (Bronx County) is the only borough on the U.S. mainland; all of the others are on islands. **Manhattan** (New York County) is the center of just about everything and features nearly all of the tourist attractions, hotels, and amenities. **Queens** (Queen's County) and **Brooklyn** (King's County) occupy the western end of Long Island, and are largely residential with some light industry. **Staten Island** (Richmond County), anchored off the New Jersey coast, is almost completely residential although it does boast a few important sights.

GETTING AROUND
NEW YORK CITY

Although most of the tours are designed for walking, you'll still need to use some form of transportation to get to their starting points, and then back home. Here are the options:

BY SUBWAY:

New York's subway system is in many ways both the best and the worst in the world. The best because it is fast, efficient, goes just about everywhere, and operates 24 hours a day, seven days a week. Some three and a half million people ride its hundreds of route miles every day, making it the greatest system on Earth. The worst because despite recent improvements, it is noisy, old (opened in 1904), confusing, and — to some — more than a little intimidating. Still, it is the most effective way to travel longer distances, so get up your courage, descend into one of its 468 stations, and take advantage of this modern marvel. Nothing else will make you feel more like a real New Yorker.

Be sure to pick up a free copy of **The Map**, a comprehensive folding diagram that clearly shows all of the routes, stations, and connections. These are available — free — at stations and at tourist information offices and kiosks. *The Map* also shows bus connections, ferry routes, commuter rails throughout the entire region, and other transportation options, and does it in nine languages. The subway portion of this map is also posted in every subway car.

You may often hear the various lines referred to as being part of either the BMT, IND, or IRT systems. That nomenclature dates from the days when New York had three independent subway operating companies, a situation that ended in 1940 although New Yorkers have yet to acknowledge that. What can you expect of people who still refer to the Avenue of the Americas as Sixth Avenue, when that name was changed over 50 years ago?

Routes are identified by numbers (former IRT lines) or letters (former BMT or IND lines), NOT by their color on the map. Final destinations are also marked. Not all trains on the same route go all the way to the final stop. Check.

Unlike other subway systems, New York's has both **express** and **local** trains, operating on parallel tracks. This can get you around much faster or leave you off miles beyond your intended stop. Make certain that you're going to an express stop before boarding an express train — otherwise take the local and be safe.

Fares are $1.50 per ride, regardless of distance. You could, in fact, pay one fare and ride the system for ever, traveling all over the city again and again, presumably living on hot dogs from station snack bars. Seriously, though, the system is a bargain if you know how to use it. Although tokens are still available and still in use, you are better off purchasing a **MetroCard**, a plastic stored-value card that operates the subway turnstiles, gets you on buses, and allows free transfers between subway/bus, bus/subway, and bus/bus within a two-hour period. There are two kinds: **Pay-per-Ride**, sold in denominations from $3 to $80 with a 10% bonus for amounts of $15 or more, in which the fare is electronically subtracted from the card every time you use it and which can be recharged at machines or booths in the stations, and **Unlimited Rides** — $4 for 1 day, $17 for seven days, or $63 for 30 days. The one- or seven-day cards are a **terrific bargain** for tourists making more than two subway or bus rides a day. The cards are sold in stations and at many stores, newsstands, and the like displaying the MetroCard logo. Seniors over 65 and disabled persons qualify for reduced fares, ☎ 718-243-4999 for details. *For card information ☎ 212-METROCARD or 1-800- METROCARD. For all transit information ☎ 718-330-1234, Internet: www.mta.nyc.ny.us.*

For your own **safety**, avoid using subways between midnight and the morning rush hours; if you must travel then, use only the well-marked "off hours" part of the platforms and stick to center cars on the train. Don't stand too close to the edge of the platform, where some nut can push you onto the tracks. At all times, **avoid standing or sitting next to exit doors** — sneak thieves can relieve you of your possessions and disappear into station crowds just as the doors close and the train starts moving. For your own **comfort**, try to avoid rush hours (7:30-9:30 a.m. and 5-6:30 p.m.), when the trains can be extremely crowded.

BY BUS:

Buses are the best way to travel shorter distances, especially for crosstown trips. Although they are often mired in traffic, they do allow you to see where you're going while enjoying the sights. They are also cleaner, safer, and less irritating to the nerves. Sometimes they are even to be preferred for long trips, such as the Route M-4 for the Uptown Manhattan trip (see page 86) — where the views are well worth the slow pace.

Bus stops are indicated by a blue sign with the route numbers that stop there along with a not-to-be-relied-on schedule; sometimes there is even a convenient shelter to keep the raindrops away. Most buses stop every two or three blocks, or every block on crosstown routes, but "limited" buses make fewer stops. "Express" buses go to outlying districts, run mostly during rush hours only, and charge a higher fare. Be sure to check the **final destination** on the front of the bus as some do not go all the way to the end of the route. If in doubt just ask the driver.

Fares are $1.50, payable by coins (not pennies or half- dollars and no paper money), subway tokens, or the **MetroCard** (see *By Subway,* above). Board through the front door only. Handicapped persons may use the wheelchair lift by the center door. Signal your stop about a block ahead of time by pressing the tape strip above the windows. Exit through the rear door by pushing on it when a green light above the door is lit. Most buses have automatic doors that open when you press the tape strip on the door. **Route maps** for each borough are available free at some subway stations and from tourist information centers and kiosks.

TAXIS:

Taxis are a somewhat expensive but otherwise reasonable way to get around New York City, especially when several people are traveling together. Cabs carry up to four passengers, and it's all on the same fare, even if some get off before the final destination. Only **yellow cabs** may legally pick up fares that were not arranged in advance. These may be hailed in the streets, except when their "off duty" light is on. **Fares** are complex, but count on at least five dollars for a typical ride of about a mile. A tip of at least 15–20% is expected. Make sure you know where you're going so you don't get taken for a "ride" — some unscrupulous drivers have been known to go miles out of the way to run up a larger fare. If you do feel cheated, note the driver's number (on the dashboard) and cab number (on the roof) and report it to the **Taxi Commission,** ☎ 212-221-8294. Use the same number to trace lost articles left in cabs. That said, most drivers are perfectly honest and want to give you good service. The only problem you may encounter is language; many drivers are recent immigrants with an imperfect command of English — and of the city's geography.

BY CAR:

Avoid driving in Manhattan any more than you absolutely have to. While the traffic is not really too horrendous most of the time, and the logical street layout easy to follow, parking will prove your undoing. There is simply virtually no free street parking available, parking lots are usually not in prime locations, and the prices they charge are nothing short of exorbitant. Expect anything left in a car to be stolen — if not the car itself. Be wise and stick to public transportation.

BY BICYCLE:

Pedaling your way through Manhattan may be an enjoyable exercise on weekends and holidays, but doing it on a normal business day is a risk to life and limb. If you feel the urge to bike, do so in Central Park, where it's safer and bikes can be rented.

ON FOOT:

Walking is the best way to see Manhattan, and often the fastest way as well. When you get tired, just hop on a bus or take a taxi to the next destination; if that's far away, take a subway. Be sure to wear comfortable walking shoes or sneakers — after all, you're enjoying the sights, not going to a business meeting.

ORIENTATION:

The map on page 17 gives a general idea of where things are, while the individual walking-tour maps for each trip show all of the sites and major streets in the relevant neighborhoods. Most of Manhattan north of Houston Street and Greenwich Village follows a simple grid pattern, with **numbered streets** running east to west and numbered or named **avenues** running north to south. Crosstown numbered streets are designated as either "east" or "west," with Fifth Avenue being the dividing line. Heading uptown or downtown, 20 numbered blocks equals one mile; the distance between avenues varies but is considerably longer. Note that there is no Fourth Avenue, its name was changed to **Park Avenue** a long time ago. Also note that there is no Sixth Avenue as it was renamed **Avenue of the Americas** some fifty years back; despite this, virtually all New Yorkers still call it by its former name and will direct you to addresses there, as does this book. Defying the grid, **Broadway** meanders its way at an angle, from the tip of Manhattan to its very top — and beyond.

SHOPPING

If you can imagine it, and really want it, you can certainly buy it in New York. This is surely the world's greatest shopping mecca. Anything — *anything* — your heart desires can be found here for a price. Just wandering around the prime shopping neighborhoods can be an adventure in itself. Where to start?

Fifth Avenue from 59th Street south to around 48th Street, and its intersecting **57th Street** from Lexington Avenue to Sixth Avenue (Avenue of the Americas) is prime hunting territory, with one elegant shop following another.

Madison Avenue, from 42nd Street all the way to 79th Street, just gets classier and classier as you head uptown, especially above 59th Street.

Herald Square, Broadway at 34th Street, is home to the gigantic original Macy's, a vast emporium selling a far greater variety than their suburban branches, and to two indoor vertical shopping centers, the Herald Center and the Manhattan Mall.

Chelsea, from 18th to 23rd streets, mostly around Sixth Avenue, features unusual shops along with a variety of discounters.

Greenwich Village, in particular 8th Street between Second Avenue and Sixth Avenue (Avenue of the Americas), attracts younger buyers with its trendy offerings.

SoHo, from Canal Street north to Houston, from West Broadway east to Broadway, is home to all manner of boutiques and galleries. Canal Street is lined with junk shops where real gems can sometimes be found.

These were just a sampling; as you wander around you'll come across the unexpected just about everywhere. Be sure to bring your credit card or lots of money — or just window shop.

FESTIVITIES

It seems there is always something special going on in New York, events that can enhance your visit if they happen to be of interest to you — or even possibly to avoid if they're not. A current, complete list of these is available from the Convention & Visitors Bureau (below), either in their free *Official NYC Guide* booklet or on their web site. Some of the more important recurring events include:

Chinese New Year, mid-January to early February, Chinatown. Two weeks of dragons and fireworks.

Saint Patrick's Day Parade, mid-March, Fifth Avenue from 44th to 86th streets. America's oldest and most tumultuous parade celebrates everything about being Irish.

Memorial Day Celebration, South Street Seaport, late May.

Salute to Israel Parade, first Sunday in June, on Fifth Avenue from 57th to 79th streets. ☎ 212-245-8200, x255.

Puerto Rican Day Parade, second Sunday in June, on Fifth Avenue from 44th to 86th streets.

Museum Mile Festival, mid-June, Fifth Avenue from 82nd to 105th streets. This street fair features art, entertainment, food, and free admission to the museums. ☎ 212-606-2296.

Gay and Lesbian Pride March, late June, Fifth Avenue from 52nd Street down to Washington Square. ☎ 212-807-7433.

Festival of San Gennaro, Mulberry Street in Little Italy, mid- to late September. An Italian celebration of life, with food, rides, entertainments, and a religious procession. ☎ 212- 768-9320.

German-American Steuben Parade, mid-September, Fifth Avenue from 63rd to 86th streets. Traditional German culture comes alive with bands and floats, some from the Old Country. ☎ 516-239- 0741.

General Casimir Pulaski Day Parade, first Sunday in October, Fifth Avenue from 26th to 52nd streets. Commemorates the Polish hero of the American Revolution. ☎ 887-4-PULASKI.

Hispanic Day Parade, second Sunday in October, Fifth Avenue from 44th to 72nd streets. ☎ 212-242-2360.

Columbus Day Parade, early October, Fifth Avenue from 44th to 86th streets, then east to Third Avenue. ☎ 212-249-9923.

Village Halloween Parade, on Halloween in late October, Sixth Avenue from Spring to 22nd streets. A wildly fanciful event noted for its outrageous costumes. ☎ 914-758-5519.

New York City Marathon, first Sunday in November, goes up First Avenue from 59th Street to The Bronx, swings around and ends in Central Park. ☎ 212-860-4455.

Veterans' Day Parade, early November, Fifth Avenue from 42nd to 23rd streets. ☎ 212-693-1475.

Thanksgiving Day Parade, from Central Park West at 77th Street down Broadway to 34th Street and Seventh Avenue. Macy's annual extravaganza, a real treat for children. ☎ 212-494-4495.

Christmas Tree Lighting, Rockefeller Center, early December. ☎ 212-332-6868.

New Year's Eve in Times Square. Watch the famous ball drop, and beware the drunks. ☎ 212-768-1560.

These were just for starters. There are many, many, other festivities, both perennial favorites and one-time events. Check the tourist office for current listings.

SAFETY

New York City is much safer than its reputation suggests. Actually, in recent years its crime rate has never been as high as in many other American cities, or even some of their suburbs. Still, being careful and using a few street smarts can save you much grief. First, avoid looking too much like a tourist — they are easy marks, easily distracted and unaware of their surroundings. Second, don't display expensive jewelry, cameras, and the like; and don't count the money in your wallet in public. Third, keep your wallet in a safe place, not the hip pocket. Don't let other valuables out of your grasp — they vanish easily into thin air. Fourth, avoid dark or deserted streets — or the lonely end of a subway platform. Fifth, if you are actually mugged (a very remote chance), give them what they want — your life is worth more than your wallet.

Visitors are actually more likely to fall victim to con artists than to muggers. Beware the three-card monte tricksters who dupe otherwise sensible people into thinking that they can actually win at this phony sidewalk card game. The guy you see winning is actually an accomplice. And *his* accomplice is a pickpocket working the crowd. Also beware of anyone who approaches you with a hard-luck story and needs just a few dollars to get home to his dying mother. He probably grosses more than you do.

LOCAL TOURIST INFORMATION

Your best source for all manner of local tourist information is to visit the **NYC & Company Convention & Visitors Bureau Visitor Center** at 810 Seventh Avenue, between 52nd and 53rd streets, just north of Times Square, ☎ 212-484-1200 or 1-800-NYC-VISIT, Internet: www.nycvisit.com. Offering a plethora of services as well as many free maps and brochures, they are open on Mondays through Fridays 8:30–6, and on Saturdays and Sundays 9–5. Another helpful source is the **Times Square Visitors Center** at 1560 Broadway, between 46th and 47th streets, ☎ 212-768-1560, Internet: www.timessquarebid.org.

South Street Seaport, Lower Manhattan

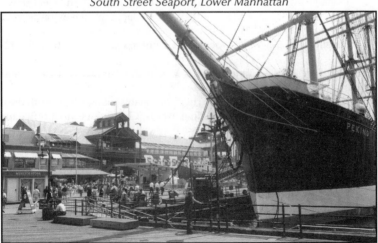

*Lower Manhattan

When this daytrip was written in summer, 2001, it included a visit to the World Trade Center. Then, on September 11 2001—just as people were going to their offices and this book was going to press—two hijacked airliners crashed into that symbol of American enterprise, killing thousands of innocent men, women, and children in an act of unspeakable evil.

The walking route on this trip has since been modified, as little as possible, to take you within sight of the ruins where you can reflect on that horrible event before moving on to happier places. Access to various streets will vary as the cleanup and subsequent reconstruction progresses, so you may have to vary the suggested route a bit.

Where better to begin exploring New York City than where it all began? When the first Dutch settlers arrived here in the early 1600s they could never have imagined the scene that stretches before you today. Time permitting, you can arrive by boat too, by starting your day with a free cruise on the Staten Island ferry. Heading north from the ferry terminal there are, snuggled down between the office towers, a few reminders of the past, including the tavern where George Washington took leave of his officers after the Revolutionary War was over, and the very spot where he was sworn in as the infant republic's first president.

Wall Street, that bastion of capitalism, is a fascinating place to explore — even if you don't take the free tour of the Stock Exchange. The walk continues with a stroll down Broadway to an unlikely outpost of the Smithsonian Institution, then across the ancient Bowling Green to a surviving fortress from the War of 1812. From here an utterly delightful riverside trail, offering panoramic views of the busy harbor, leads north to the dazzling World Financial Center with its impressive yacht basin.

Just a block from all this modernity is a remarkable Colonial-era church, an early skyscraper that many consider to be the most beautiful ever built, and the historic City Hall.

What may be the most famous span in the world — the Brooklyn Bridge — beckons, and you'll just have to take a stroll across it, at least part of the way, on the pedestrian walkway high above the traffic.

For a finale, there's the South Street Seaport, a preserved bit of 19th-century New York complete with historic sailing ships, a museum, fun-filled boat rides, atmospheric restaurants and cafés, and an upscale shopping mall built on top of an old pier on the East River. What a way to end the day!

GETTING THERE:

See page 18 for general transit information.

By Subway, the best connection is to take the number 1 or 9 *(IRT Broadway/Seventh Ave. local)* line to its southern terminus, South Ferry. Alternatively, you can take the number 4 or 5 *(IRT Lexington Ave. express)* to Bowling Green, or the N or R *(BMT Broadway local)* to Whitehall St./South Ferry. These last choices might be more convenient for you, but they involve a few more blocks of walking.

By Bus, you can take the M-1 *(Fifth Ave., weekdays only)*, M-6 *(Seventh Ave.)* or M-15 *(Second Ave.)* all the way down to South Ferry. Make sure the bus is marked "South Ferry" as some don't go that far. Buses are much slower than subways, but they do offer sights along the way.

By Taxi, ask the driver for South Ferry. You might have to point this out on a map.

PRACTICALITIES:

Lower Manhattan comes to life on **weekdays** from 9 to 5, when the streets pulsate with energy. On weekends and holidays it is practically deserted — except for the tourists. Pleasant weather will greatly enhance this largely out-of-doors walk, which is approximately 3.5 miles long, not counting a stroll across the Brooklyn Bridge or any side trips. There are a great many sights to experience, so be sure to get off to any early start. Alternatively, you might split it into two walks. For **tourist information** see page 24, or ask at one of the kiosks of the Alliance for Downtown New York, ☎ 212-566-6700, Internet: www.DowntownNY.com.

FOOD AND DRINK:

Lower Manhattan abounds in places to eat, from street vendors to fast-food joints to some of New York's premier establishments. Here are just a few choices:

Fraunces Tavern (54 Pearl St. at Broad St.) Traditional Colonial and other American dishes, in an historic building. ☎ 212-269-0144. $$

Yankee Clipper (170 John St., at the South Street Seaport) A wide variety of fresh seafood dishes, along with a few landlubber choices. ☎ 212-344-5959. $$

Zigolini's (66 Pearl St., near Coenties Slip) Pastas, foccacias, and sandwiches; all with an Italian touch — indoors or out. ☎ 212-425-7171. X: weekends. $

Ellen's Café (270 Broadway, a block north of City Hall) This unusually good coffee shop is a favorite with local politicians. ☎ 212-962-1257. $

North Star Pub (93 South St., at Fulton St.) An English-style pub with the usual grub, plus a wide choice of beers. ☎ 212-509-6757. $

SUGGESTED TOUR:

Circled numbers in text correspond to numbers on the map.

A nice way to begin your day, if you have the time, is to take a short cruise on the *Staten Island Ferry ❶, departing from the terminal opposite the South Ferry subway and bus stops. This will give you an unsurpassed *view of lower Manhattan, the busy harbor, Governors Island, the Statue of Liberty, Ellis Island, Brooklyn, and even New Jersey. The round trip, assuming you do not linger on Staten Island, takes a bit over an hour, and the best views are from the lower deck openings at either end of the boat. Best of all, this wonderful, breezy treat is **absolutely free**, courtesy of the city taxpayers! ☎ *718-390-5253, Internet: www.siferry.com. Operates daily, all day long, every 15 minutes during rush hours, every half-hour most of the day, and hourly late at night. Snack bar on board. Passengers free, cars $3.*

Back on dry land, cross State Street to see a few survivors from New York's almost-forgotten past. There, amid the towers of commerce, is the James Watson House of 1792, now serving as the **Shrine of St. Elizabeth Seton ❷**. Born here in New York, Elizabeth Ann Seton (1774–1821) was canonized as the first US-born saint in 1975. Drop inside to see the peaceful chapel. ☎ *212-269-6865. Donation.* At the rear of the courtyard adjacent to the church is a small exhibition of urban archaeology called **New York Unearthed**. Much of today's Lower Manhattan is actually landfill dating from Colonial days, so every time a new building goes up all sorts of treasures are revealed in the muck below. Some of the best of yesterday's trash is on display, and visitors can watch archaeologists sifting through the stuff as well as take a video journey through the bowels of the Earth. ☎ *212-748- 8628. Open April–Dec., Mon.–Sat. noon–6; Jan.–March, Mon.–Fri. noon–6. Free.*

A right on Pearl Street takes you to another reminder of the past — this one a skillful 1907 reconstruction of the historic **Fraunces Tavern ❸**, where George Washington bade goodbye to his officers in 1783 following the successful end of the Revolutionary War. The original structure dated from 1719 and was later owned by one Samuel Fraunces, believed to be an African-American originally from the French West Indies. It is still an attractive pub and restaurant, serving three meals a day on Mondays through Fridays. Upstairs is the small **Fraunces Tavern Museum** of early American history, with a few period rooms and changing exhibitions of artifacts. ☎ *212-425-1778. Open Mon.–Fri. 10–4:45, Sat.–Sun. noon–4. Closed major holidays except July 4. Adults $2.50, seniors, students, and children $1. Gift shop.*

Continue east on Pearl Street, the principal street of Nieuw Amsterdam in the early 17th century and once its waterfront, named for the shells found along the banks. In one block, turn right at Coenties Slip, a dock in Dutch Colonial days, to the **Vietnam Veterans' Memorial** across Water Street, which has sadly seen better days. Just steps northeast of this, at 55 Water Street, is a raised plaza with great **views** across the East River to

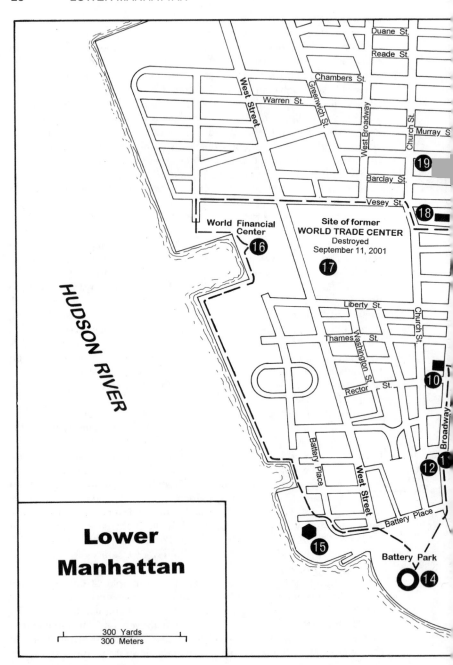

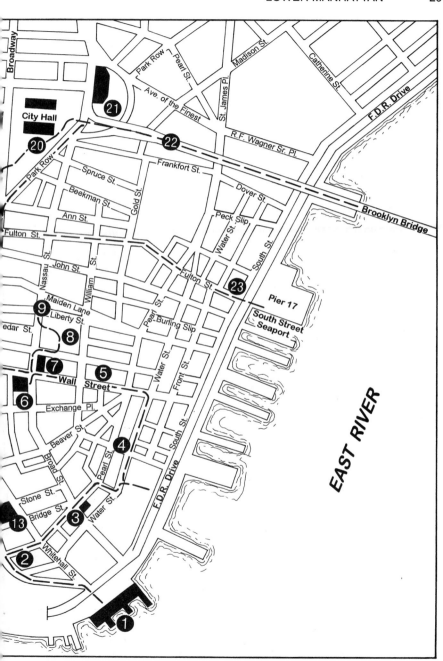

Brooklyn Heights. You can access it by escalator.

Continue on to **Hanover Square** ❹, home of the Italianate India House of 1837, once a bank, then a cotton exchange, and later a club. Today it's a restaurant. Hanover Square was also the site of New York's first newspaper, in 1725, and earlier the home of one Captain William Kidd, the notorious pirate who was hung in England in 1701. Just up from this is a delightful little park at 77 Water Street, where you can rest amid the fountains and sculptures.

Turn left into the world center of capitalism, **Wall Street**, which got its name from the protective town wall that extended along here from the Hudson River to the East River, erected in 1653 and marking the northern boundary of Dutch Nieuw Amsterdam. The Brits tore it down in 1664. Since then, so many tall buildings were erected without regard to the street below that it is really a dark, narrow canyon, usually devoid of sunlight.

One of the few really outstanding pieces of architecture along here is the **J.P. Morgan Bank Headquarters** ❺ at 60 Wall Street. Built in 1988, and reaching up some 47 stories, it has an inviting lobby with greenery, tables, and chairs that is open to the public.

Continue straight ahead to the massive **New York Stock Exchange** ❻ of 1903. It is possible to take a self-guided tour through parts of this, looking down on the floor action from an enclosed gallery. An exhibition explains the workings of the market, conveniently downplaying its excesses such as the infamous crash of 1929. ☎ *212-656-5165, Internet: www.nyse.com. Open Mon.–Fri. 9–4:30, closed major holidays. Free. Tickets distributed outside on a first-come basis; they are often all gone by noon. After obtaining a ticket visitors wait in line for admission.* ⅄.

Just across Wall Street stands a most impressive structure, the:

FEDERAL HALL NATIONAL MEMORIAL ❼, 26 Wall St., ☎ 212-825-6888, Internet: www.nps.gov/feha. *Open year-round Mon.–Fri. 9–5. Closed federal holidays. Free.* ⅄.

What is now known as Federal Hall was erected as a customs house in 1842 on the site of the first U.S. Capitol, where George Washington took the oath of office as the first president in 1789. George, or at least a handsome statue of him, is still there, overlooking the entire scene and perhaps wondering what to make of all the financial goings-on across the street. Inside, you can see the very Bible used in that historic inauguration, along with other important artifacts including those pertaining to the Zenger trial held here in 1735, which did much to advance the concept of free speech. The building itself, a masterpiece of the Greek Revival style, deserves a careful examination.

From here you can make a little **side trip** north to some other notable financial institutions. Head up Nassau Street for one block, turning right on Pine Street. Opening to the left are the sunken Japanese **gardens** designed by Isamu Noguchi in 1964, and a wonderful 1972 sculpture by Jean Dubuffet. Rising high above this is the headquarters of the **Chase Manhattan Bank** ❽, a towering edifice designed in the early 1960s by Skidmore, Owings & Merrill.

Continuing up Nassau Street for another block brings you to the **Federal Reserve Bank** ❾, on the right. What is noteworthy about this building is not the structure, but what's in it. Here resides, safely locked away in underground vaults, the gold reserves of some 80 foreign nations; probably the greatest such accumulation on Earth. As countries pay each other their debts, the bars are simply moved from one vault to the next. Why here and not in, say, Zurich? Most of it was brought to this safe haven during World War II to escape the ravages of that conflict. Yes, you can take a peek, but only if you make reservations at least a week in advance. ☎ 212-720-6130, Internet: www.nyfed.org. Tours   Mon.–Fri. at 9:30, 10:30, 11:30, 1:30, and 2:30. Free. ♿.

Back on Wall Street, you'll notice, at its western end (and looking monumentally out of place), the Gothic spire of:

TRINITY CHURCH ❿, Broadway at Wall St., ☎ 212-602-0872, Internet: www.trinitywallstreet.org. *Open Mon.–Fri. 7 a.m.–6 p.m., Sat. 8–4, Sun. 7–4. Museum open Mon.–Fri. 9–11:45 and 1–3:45, Sat. 10–3:45, Sun. 1–3:45. Guided tours daily at 2. Donation. Gift shop. Rest rooms. ♿.*

This was once the tallest building in New York. The first church on this site, partially financed by Captain Kidd (of piracy fame), was chartered by King William III and erected in 1698. It burned down in 1776, and its replacement collapsed in 1839. The present structure dates from 1846. Its bronze doors, facing Broadway, were designed by Richard Morris Hunt and recall, in their depiction of Biblical scenes, those of the Baptistery in Florence. Step inside to see its wonderful **stained-glass windows**, reredos, and high altar. The **Museum**, to the left of the sanctuary, contains gifts from King William III, Queen Anne, and King George III. What is most attractive about Trinity Church, however, is the very English-style ***Churchyard**, where several notables are buried. See if you can find the graves of Alexander Hamilton and Robert Fulton.

Amble down Broadway, perhaps stopping at the statue of the charging bull to visit the **Museum of American Financial History** ⓫ in the former Standard Oil Building of 1922. Displays here are concerned with the story of Wall Street finance and include antique stock tickers, an actual stock exchange seat, and various memorabilia. The museum is an affiliate of the Smithsonian Institution. ☎ 212-908-4519 or 1-877-98-FINANCE, Internet: www.financialhistory.org. *Open Tues.–Fri. 10–4. Closed major holidays. Suggested donation $2. Museum shop.*

Across Broadway stands the former **Cunard Building** ⓬ of 1921, once the splendidly ornate ticket office for the great steamship company, and now a post office. Some of the fabulous decor is still there, so drop in for a peek. This is also the new home of the **New York City Police Museum**, filled with ingenious weaponry used by notorious criminals of the past and present, as well as with more mundane police matters. ☎ *212-301-4440, Internet: www.nycpolicemuseum.org. Open Tues.–Fri. 10–6, Sat. 10–4. Closed major holidays. Free.*

Broadway ends at **Bowling Green**, the city's first park. Originally this was a cattle market, then a parade ground, and finally in 1733 it became a place for the outdoor game of bowls. A statue of King George III stood here, but when the Declaration of Independence was read here on July 9, 1776, it was torn down, broken into bits, shipped to Connecticut, and made into musket balls to fire at the hated British. To the south of this — on the site of the original Dutch fortress — rises a most magnificent structure, the former **U.S. Custom House** of 1907, designed in the Beaux-Arts tradition by Cass Gilbert. After years of disuse, it now houses the New York branch of the Smithsonian Institution's:

NATIONAL MUSEUM OF THE AMERICAN INDIAN ⑬, ☎ 212-514-3700 or 1-800-242-NMAI, Internet: www.si.edu/nmai. *Open daily 10–5, closed Christmas. Free. Gift shops.* ⟁.

You are now standing at the very spot where Peter Minuit, first commander of Nieuw Amsterdam, in 1626 purchased Manhattan from some passing Indians for trinkets worth about 60 guilders ($24 in today's currency). Unfortunately, the Indians probably were not locals and did not "own" the land they sold. Before entering, take a look at the four **sculptures** by Daniel Chester French, creator of the Lincoln Monument in Washington, D.C. These depict the four continents of the trading world, and their races, in terms that today would make the politically correct shudder.

Inside, the George Gustav Heye Center of the museum focuses on Native American art, culture, and lifestyles, from the ancient past right up to the present. The innovative exhibitions here are constantly changing, and represent native peoples from both North and South America. The major part of the museum is scheduled to open in 2003 on The Mall in Washington, D.C.

A stroll through **Battery Park** affords marvelous panoramic views. Until a mid-19th-century landfill this was all water — and the round structure you see straight ahead was actually some 200 feet offshore. Now known as **Castle Clinton** ⑭, the fortress was built in 1811 as the West Battery, one of several gun positions defending New York harbor. It was never used for that purpose, and in 1824 — renamed Castle Garden — it became a place of entertainment for the next 30 years before being again transformed. Its next use was as a processing station for immigrants before Ellis Island was completed in 1890, after which it was an aquarium until 1941. Now named for De Witt Clinton, the great governor of New York State in the 19th century, it was taken over by the National Park

Service as an historic site. Inside, there is a visitor center, a small exhibition, and the ticket office for the **Statue of Liberty Ferry.** A trip out to the statue — and nearby Ellis Island — requires at least half a day and is better saved for later, or visited from New Jersey. See page 000 for details. *Castle Clinton National Monument,* ☎ *212- 344-7220. Open daily 8:30–3:30, closed Dec. 25. Free. Bookstore.* ♿.

From here, a thoroughly enjoyable path heads north along the water's edge, offering wonderful views of the busy harbor, the Statue of Liberty, and New Jersey. Near the beginning of this, to the right on Battery Place, is the modern **Museum of Jewish Heritage — A Living Memorial to the Holocaust ⓯**. Its six sides symbolize the points of the Star of David, as well as the six million Jews who perished in the Holocaust. The Jewish experience throughout the 20th century is brought to life with artifacts, photos, and videotaped narratives. Although there is a strong emphasis on the horrors of the Nazi era, the overall message is one of hope. ☎ *212-509-6130, Internet: www.mjhnyc.org. Open mid-April through mid-Sept.; Sun.–Wed. 9–5, Thurs. 9–8, Fri. and eve of Jewish holidays 9–3; rest of year Sun.–Wed. 9-5, Thurs. 9–8, Fri. and eve of Jewish holidays 9–2. Last admission one hour before closing. Closed Jewish holidays and Thanksgiving. Adults $7, seniors and students $5, under 5 free. Museum shop. Kosher café.* ♿.

Continue along the riverside pathway, passing South Cove, parks, and contemporary upscale residences to the yacht-filled North Cove and the sumptuous **World Financial Center ⓰**. Several of the nation's most prestigious financial firms are headquartered within its four copper-roofed towers of glass and granite. For visitors, the chief draw is the elegant ***Winter Garden**, a glass-enclosed, sun-filled gallery of luxurious shops and restaurants, complete with palm trees, a white marble staircase, a various free entertainments. ☎ *212-945-0505, Internet: www.worldfinancialcenter.com. Free.*

Directly to the east, across West Street, lies the site of the former **World Trade Center ⓱**, utterly and totally destroyed by terrorists flying two hijacked jetliners on September 11, 2001. This tragic event, the worst in American history, claimed the lives of over six thousand innocent men, women, and children in a cowardly act of inconceivable horror. Weep a bit, say a prayer, and reflect on man's inhumanity to man as you survey the scene.

The route at this pont becomes tenuous as reconstruction progresses, but you should be able to pick your way over to the nearby **St. Paul's Chapel ⓲**, the oldest public building in continuous use in Manhattan. Built in 1766 and modeled after London's Church of St. Martin-in-the-Fields, it is flanked by a picturesque **graveyard.** Step inside to see the pew from which George Washington worshiped just after becoming the first president, and the wonderful altar attributed to Pierre Charles L'Enfant, the man who basically designed Washington, D.C. Above the pulpit is the symbol of the Prince of Wales, testimony to the fact that this was a royal church back in Colonial days. ☎ *212-602-0874, Internet: www.trinitywall street.org. Open Mon.–Fri. 9–3, Sun. 7–3. Closed holidays. Donation. Concerts at noon on Mon. and at 1 on Thurs., admission $2.* ♿.

A block or so to the north on Broadway stands another skyscraper, this one far more attractive than the sterile World Trade Center. When it was erected in 1913, the **Woolworth Building** ⓳ was also the tallest building on Earth, a distinction it held for 17 years. Rising to a height of 792 feet, it is completely done in the Gothic style of Old-World cathedrals, and suitably embellished with gargoyles, flying buttresses, finials, and the like — a handsome sight indeed. Step inside to witness the stupendous *lobby, positively dripping with mosaics and frescoes. There's a real sense of playfulness in this "Cathedral of Commerce," what with a carving of its owner, dime-store magnate F.W. Woolworth, counting his coins, and of the architect, Cass Gilbert, grasping a model of the building.

Cross Broadway to **City Hall** ⓴, set in a delightful little park. Seemingly small for the vast metropolis it governs, this cross between a French château and a Georgian mansion serves as both the mayor's office and the seat of the city council. The **Governor's Room**, which may be visited, contains a small museum of historic paintings and furnishings. ☎ *212-788-4636, Internet: www.council.nyc.ny.us. Usually open Mon.–Fri. 10–3:30. May be closed for security reasons. Free.* ♿.

Immediately north of City Hall is the **Tweed Courthouse** of 1872, whose history is a classic study in municipal corruption of the worst kind. "Boss" William Marcy Tweed was the ruthless head of the Democratic Party's Tammany Hall, which ruled the city for quite some time. Of the $14 million that was spent on this one structure — an extravagant amount at the time — an estimated $10 million wound up in the pocket of "Boss" Tweed through kickbacks. Unhappily for him, a political satirist named Thomas Nast revealed all, and Tweed went to jail, where he died in 1878 at the age of 55. Despite its unsavory connection, this is a handsome building, and it features in its lobby some of those increasingly rare WPA murals.

To the right of this rises the gloriously overblown, marvelously ostentatious hulk of the huge **Municipal Building** ㉑ of 1914. Inside resides much of the city's bureaucracy, along with the civic wedding office, where over 10,000 couples a year get legally hitched for next to nothing.

Now for a real treat, if you're up to some extra walking. Just a block southeast of the Municipal Building is the entrance ramp to that most famous of spans — the magnificent *Brooklyn Bridge ㉒. A pedestrian — and bicycle — path, high above the traffic, crosses this, offering some of the very best **views** of Lower Manhattan, as well as being an experience in itself. You don't have to stroll all the way across to Brooklyn; even a short amble out on the structure will prove highly rewarding. Don't miss this.

Until 1883, the only way to get across the East River was by boat. On the other side was Brooklyn, then one of the largest cities in America, and not yet a part of New York City. The challenge of building such a bridge was formidable. Swift and constantly changing currents in the river —

which is not really a river at all, but a tidal estuary — required a suspension span of a length previously unattempted, as did the passing of tall sailing ships below. The designing engineer, John Augustus Roebling, suffered a tragic accident when taking initial measurements, and died soon afterwards. His son, Washington Roebling, took over, only to be crippled by the bends in an underwater caisson. In all, the project took some 14 years to complete and cost the lives of 20 workers. At the time it was the largest suspension bridge in the world, the first to use steel cables, and for decades after that featured the longest single span on Earth. Probably no other bridge has ever inspired as much passion, or burned as deeply in the imaginations of man.

Return to the Manhattan end of the bridge and turn left on Park Row, then left again on Broadway. In just one block make another left onto Fulton Street, named after the inventor of the steamboat, who operated a ferry to Brooklyn from the foot of the street. Narrow and crowded, this largely pedestrianized street is lined with discount shops and inexpensive places to eat. At its end is the perfect finale to your day's walk, the marvelous:

*SOUTH STREET SEAPORT ㉓, ☎ 212-748-8600, Internet: www.southstreet seaport.com. *Shops open Mon.–Sat. 10 a.m. to 9 p.m., Sun. 11–8. Restaurants and bars open later. Museum open April–Sept., daily 10–6, remaining open until 8 on Thurs.; rest of year Wed.–Mon. 10–5. Historic streets, piers, and shopping malls free. Museum and historic ships: Adults $6, seniors $5, students $4, ages 2–11 $3. Various boat rides extra. Shops. Restaurants. Pubs. Cafés. Partially &.*

This entire neighborhood, once a rough and decaying area of docks, fish markets, prostitution, and general debauchery, was restored, deodorized, and polished during the 1980s as a first-rate attraction for visitors and New Yorkers alike. With cobblestone streets and buildings dating back as far as 1811, historic tall ships at the docks, restored shops, boat rides, a museum, many upscale shops, and plenty of places to eat and drink, this is the best possible spot to relax after hiking through the canyons of Lower Manhattan.

Among the attractions are the **Museum Block** bordered by Fulton, Water, Beekman, and Front streets. The **Visitor Center** at 12 Fulton is the place to begin, where you can find out about the day's activities, see some exhibits, and purchase museum tickets. Stroll over to the re-created Printing Shop, the restored Chandlery, and the Gallery.

Extending along Fulton Street from Front to South streets is the picturesque **Schermerhorn Row**, a group of early 19th-century buildings that were beautifully preserved and now house shops, galleries, and the like. Opposite this is the **Fulton Market Building**, a 1983 structure that blends in well with its historic surroundings. It is filled with all manner of shops and eateries, and has several attractive outdoor cafés in good weather.

Cross South Street and go under the elevated highway to the docks.

To your far left is the **Fulton Fish Market**, still there after all these years, and still (as of this writing) functioning in the wee hours of the morning.

Straight ahead is **Pier 17**, a glitzy multi-level shopping mall and restaurant complex built atop an old pier in the East River. Just beyond the food court on the upper level is an open area with chairs, where you can relax and take in the scene for free. A variety of **boat trips** of varying length are offered near the entrance to the pier.

Historic ships berthed at piers 15 and 16 include the *Peking*, a four-masted barque of 1911 that ranks among the largest sailing vessels ever launched, the *Wavertree*, a square-rigger of 1885, and the *Ambrose*, a light-ship that once guided seafarers toward New York harbor. All of these may be boarded with your museum ticket, or for a separate admission. There are usually some other vessels here as well, some of which can be visited.

Wander around the streets here, relax, stop for refreshments, and perhaps have dinner at one of the many restaurants.

South Street Seaport

Chinatown, Little Italy, and the Lower East Side

I f Lower Manhattan is characterized by historical sites, stunning architecture, and spectacular vistas, the low-lying area just north of it is a world of intimate details revealing a kaleidoscopic mixture of cultures. Chinatown, one of the largest and most vibrant Chinese communities outside of Asia, spills over remnants of a colorful Italian neighborhood, practically next door to the old Jewish immigrant *shtetl* known as the Lower East Side. Each preserves much of its original flavor — something that is to be all the more treasured in an increasingly homogenized world.

This was, and to a large extent still is, a community of poor immigrants getting their first start in America. You won't see any grand buildings along this walk, but you will encounter a lot of life, wonderful ethnic foods, unfamiliar customs and beliefs, and even some great shopping opportunities amid the old tenements and narrow streets. And, best of all, you can gain an understanding of the immigrant experience that contributed so much to the development of this nation.

GETTING THERE:
See page 18 for general transit information.

By Subway, the best connection from midtown is to take the number 4 or 5 *(IRT Lexington Ave. express)* or number 6 *(IRT Lexington Ave. local)* line to the **Brooklyn Bridge/City Hall** station. From Brooklyn or Queens, take the J or Z *(BMT express)*, or M *(BMT local)* line to Chambers Street.

By Bus, you can take the M-1 *(Fifth Ave., weekdays only, make sure the bus goes that far)* to **Chambers Street**. Other choices are the M-103 *(Lexington/Third avenues, daily)* or the M-15 *(First/Second avenues, weekdays only, must be marked for Park Row)* to Park Row/City Hall.

By Taxi, ask the driver for **Foley Square**.

PRACTICALITIES:
Chinatown is always alive and may be visited on any day. The Lower East Side Tenement Museum, a major attraction, is closed on Mondays. Many shops and restaurants in the Lower East Side are closed on the Sabbath (sundown Friday to sundown Saturday). Two special events of

enormous interest are the **Chinese New Year** in early January, when Chinatown goes wild, and the **Feast of San Gennaro** in mid-September, when Little Italy does the same. For **tourist information**, see page 24.

FOOD AND DRINK:

Chinatown and Little Italy abound in restaurants, several of which are overpriced tourist traps. The Lower East Side, despite a changing population, retains a few of its renowned Jewish eateries. Some reliable choices in all three neighborhoods are:

Il Cortile (125 Mulberry St. in Little Italy) Superb Italian cuisine in an indoor garden setting. ☎ 212-226-6060. $$ and $$$

Canton (45 Division St., just east of Chatham Sq. and Bowery) Exceptional Cantonese cuisine with a bit of style. ☎ 212-226-4441. X: Mon., Tues., mid-July to mid-Aug. $$

Ristorante S.P.Q.R. (133 Mulberry St. in Little Italy) Traditional Italian dishes in an old-fashioned dining room. ☎ 212-925-3120. $$

Ratner's (138 Delancey St., 4 blocks northeast of the Tenement Museum) The classic old-fashioned Jewish dairy restaurant — huge, always busy, and totally kosher. ☎ 212-677- 5588. X: Fri. eve., Sat. $$

Puglia Restaurant (189 Hester St. at Mulberry, in Little Italy) Communal dining, huge servings, and a noisy crowd make this a fun place for southern Italian cooking. ☎ 212-966-6006. $ and $$

Katz's Deli (205 East Houston St., 4 blocks north of the Tenement Museum) World famous for its authentic Jewish deli food since 1888. Both cafeteria style and full service seating is offered, at different prices. ☎ 212-254-2246. $ and $$

Wong Kee (113 Mott St., a block north of the Buddhist Temple in Chinatown) Good Cantonese fare at bargain prices. ☎ 212-966-1160. $

House of Vegetarian (24 Pell St. in Chinatown) Healthy Chinese veggie dishes, cleverly disguised as meat. ☎ 212-226-6572. $

Little Szechuan (5 East Broadway at Chatham Sq.) A good value in the spicy cuisine of Szechuan. ☎ 212-732-0796. $

Nice Restaurant (35 East Broadway, a block east of Chatham Sq. in Chinatown) This huge, modern Hong Kong-style eatery serves Cantonese specialties, and is renowned for its dim sum. ☎ 212-406-9510. $

SUGGESTED TOUR:

Circled numbers in text correspond to numbers on the map.

As a matter of transportation convenience, the walk begins in **Foley Square ❶**, which has little to do with the Lower East Side. This large, open area is lined on all sides with a plethora of court houses — federal, state, and local. To the right, in the southeast corner, is the **United States Courthouse**, an unusual temple-like Classical Revival structure of 1936 surmounted by a strange 32-story tower with a pyramidal top. Just northeast of it stands the **New York State Supreme Court** of 1927. Another Classical Revival edifice fronted with Corinthian columns, this one is worth a quick visit for its stunning rotunda lined with those wonderful WPA murals of the 1930's. Visitors are welcome to drop in, and even to attend a trial.

Foley Square, once the Collect Pond of Colonial days, was drained in 1808 by a canal, since filled in and named Canal Street. Several other courthouses line all sides, of which the most noticeable — and ugliest — is the **Criminal Courts Building** in the northeast corner at 100 Centre Street. Built in the 1930s, this three-block-long Art Deco monstrosity replaced the former Tombs, a notoriously overcrowded prison of 1835 that was famed for both its squalor and its frequent hangings.

Enough of all that. Follow the map through St. Andrews Place, around the rear of the U.S. and New York State courthouses, and then right on Worth Street to **Columbus Park ❷**. Chinatown's only park was created in the 1890s on the site of the city's worst slum, at that time largely inhabited by recently-arrived Italian immigrants. The first Chinese arrived in the mid- 19th century, but were hardly welcome — especially after the rise of the notorious tong gangs and the resulting violence. The Exclusion Acts of 1882, 1888, 1902, and 1924 kept their numbers low until repeal in 1943, and the abolition of racial quotas in 1965. Where once Chinatown encompassed only a few square blocks and a population of perhaps 10,000, it is now home to over 100,000 Chinese, and has spread far to the north and east, overtaking much of Little Italy and the Lower East Side.

Stroll through the park and turn right on Bayard Street. On the northeast corner, well hidden above commercial shops, is the **Museum of Chinese in the Americas ❸**. Though tiny, this museum has a lot to tell about the Chinese-American experience. *70 Mulberry St.,* ☎ *212-619-4785. Open Tues.–Sat., noon–5. Adults $3, seniors and students $1.*

Amble east on Bayard Street, turning south on Mott Street. This is the very heart of Chinatown, where the first immigrants settled in the 1850s, and where the first Chinese grocery store was opened in 1878. At number 25 is the **Church of the Transfiguration**, built by the Lutherans in 1801 and sold to the Roman Catholics in 1853. In its time it has served various waves of immigrants, first the Irish, then the Italians, and later the Chinese. Today's services are conducted in Mandarin, Cantonese, and English.

Turn left on Pell Street, then right on Doyers Street. This is the infamous **Bloody Angle**, once among the most crime-ridden alleys in America, where tong gangs fought for control of the opium and gambling rackets until at least the 1940s. It still looks a bit sinister. Follow it around to **Chatham Square ❹**, a.k.a. Kim Lau Square. First named for an English noble who supported the American colonists in their 1776 dispute with the king, it also celebrates a Chinese-American hero of World War II. Just south of his memorial arch is the **First Shearith Israel Cemetery**, begun in 1683 as a place of burial for the Jews of Colonial New York.

Head north on Bowery and make a left on Bayard Street, following this back to Mott Street. To your right, at 64 Mott, is the **Eastern States Buddhist Temple of America ❺**. Visitors are more than welcome to step inside and examine the ornate interior, perhaps learning a bit about the

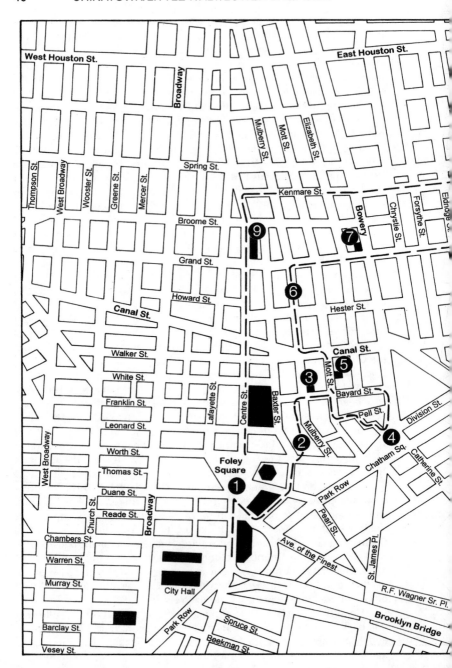

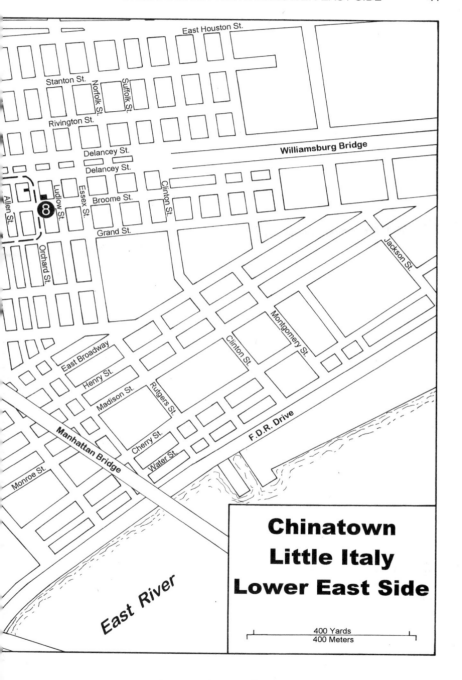

Chinatown
Little Italy
Lower East Side

400 Yards
400 Meters

Buddhist faith at the same time. ☎ *212-699-6229*. Continue north on Mott to Canal Street and turn left. This major thoroughfare runs from river to river, linking the Holland Tunnel to New Jersey with the Manhattan Bridge to Brooklyn. It also was the traditional border between Chinatown and Little Italy, but as Chinese immigration continues and many Italians have long since moved to the suburbs, that has all changed.

Fortunately, some parts of **Little Italy** still exist, and even thrive, if only on the tourist trade. Cross Canal Street and stroll north on **Mulberry Street** ❻. This could almost be a scene right out of Naples, what with the noisy crowds, wall-to-wall Italian restaurants, caffès, tiny shops, and generally festive air. The street really comes to life during the **Feast of San Gennaro**, a fun-filled 10-day-long festival honoring the patron saint of Naples and commencing on the second Thursday in September.

Turn right on Grand Street to The Bowery, passing the splendid **Bowery Savings Bank** ❼ building of 1894, perhaps the only sign of architectural elegance along this entire tour. **The Bowery** is actually a southern extension of Park Avenue, but is worlds apart in character. Once a trail leading to Peter Stuyvesant's farm (*bouwerie* in Dutch) in the mid-17th century, by the mid-19th century it became home to numerous lowbrow theaters with their bawdy productions, and eventually slipped downward into a poverty-ridden dark world of flophouses, alcoholism, and despair. All of that is rapidly changing now, and the seedy old Bowery is actually becoming a bit gentrified.

Continue on Grand Street, crossing Sara Delano Roosevelt Park, and in three more blocks turn north on Orchard Street to the major attraction on this tour, the:

*LOWER EAST SIDE TENEMENT MUSEUM ❽, Visitor Center at 90 Orchard St. at Broome St., ☎ 212-431-0233, Internet: www.tenement.org. *Open Tues.–Sun. 11–5. Tours Tues.–Fri. at 1, 1:30, 2, 2:30, 3, and 4; Sat.–Sun. every half-hour from 11–4:30. Confino Apartment by reservation. Neighborhood walking tours on Sat.–Sun. at 1 and 2:30. Tenement tours: Adults $9, seniors and students $7, neighborhood walking tours: Adults $9, seniors and students $7. Tours are limited to 15 persons; tickets are sold on first-come, first-served basis, so arrive as early as possible or make advance reservations. There are interesting exhibits and videos to watch while you wait at the visitors center. Gift shop. The tenements are not handicapped-accessible.*

Your journey into the Lower East Side immigrant experience of the late 19th and early 20th centuries begins at the **Visitor Center**, where you purchase tickets for a tour of the nearby 1863 Tenement House. While waiting for the next tour, you can watch videos on immigrant life, examine the various displays and artifacts of tenement life, look over the gift shop, or go out to lunch.

The **1863 Tenement House** at 97 Orchard Street was condemned as unsafe and vacated in the late 1930s. Somehow, it escaped the wreckers' ball — probably because the land was worth so little — and remained boarded up until 1988, when it was rescued as a testament to the hardships of immigrant life. For about fifty years it remained untouched and abandoned. Right here in Manhattan! What you see today is exactly as it was during the 70-odd years of occupancy; a dark, dingy, oppressive, airless, and practically windowless home to poor immigrants. The lives of three families who lived there in three different decades — the Gumpertzes in the 1870s, the Rogarshevskys in 1910s, and the Baldizzis in the 1930s — are celebrated with photos, letters, furniture, and artifacts miraculously gathered from their descendants. This is truly an experience more powerful even than a visit to Ellis Island (see page 254).

On weekends, by advance reservation, the museum offers "living history" tours of the **Confino Family apartment** of 1916 in which costumed interpreters acting as family members welcome visitors as though they were newly arrived immigrants themselves. Here you can touch everything, try on the period clothes, and even use the wind-up Victrola. Also offered on weekends are the **Lower East Side Walking Tours.**

Orchard Street and the surrounding neighborhood is more than just tenements. Bargain hunters will relish the **cheap shopping** in hundreds of tiny discount stores, especially if they are skilled at haggling over the already-low prices. All kinds of merchandise is peddled here, from "designer" clothes to housewares to computers. Sunday is by far the best day to come, although the stores are also open from Mondays until early afternoon on Fridays. They close for the Sabbath, sundown Friday until Sunday morning.

Turn west on Delancey Street, named after one James de Lancey, a New York Supreme Court judge from 1731 to 1760. At Bowery, this becomes Kenmare Street. Continue on it, turning south on Centre Street. One block to the south is the incredibly ornate former **Police Headquarters** ❾ of 1909, now housing luxury apartments. From here you can either amble back down through Little Italy or Chinatown, perhaps for dinner, or catch a subway at Canal Street.

Trip 3
New York City

TriBeCa, SoHo, and Greenwich Village

O ne of New York's most fascinating — and enjoyable — areas lies between downtown and midtown, encompassing the colorful neighborhoods of TriBeCa, SoHo, the East Village, and Greenwich Village. There are no skyscrapers here as this part of town developed in the mid-19th century atop land that could not support tall buildings. What you will find instead are narrow, often meandering, streets lined with old warehouses and commercial structures now reborn as fashionable housing, galleries, boutiques, chic eateries, and the like. This is New York's center of art and creativity.

TriBeCa, an acronym for the TRIangle BElow CAnal, once a rundown 19th-century industrial quarter, is now among the city's most desirable residential neighborhoods. Its ancient warehouses have been converted into that greatest of New York rarities — spacious living arrangements.

SoHo is a flourishing west side area whose name is derived from its location, SOuth of HOuston. Houston Street, that is — the great dividing line stretching from river to river.

The East Village, an eastward extension of Greenwich Village, has a distinct character all its own. The counterculture of the 1960's thrived here; its remnants still do. Although many of its streets are a bit scruffy, they are also alive with an honest mix of down-to-earth creativity and more-recent immigrant vitality. This walk takes you through the best parts, a changing section that is becoming quite fashionable in certain circles.

Finally, to end the day, there is good old Greenwich Village, long a center of artistic activity. While no longer the haunt of starving artists, its well-off residents do relish the rather tame bohemian life amid the cute restored buildings and narrow, twisting streets. This is also the home of New York University, Washington Square Park, numerous off-Broadway theaters, jazz clubs, galleries, boutiques, and many, many restaurants.

GETTING THERE:
See page 18 for general transit information.

By Subway, the best connection is to take the number 2 or 3 *(IRT Broadway/Seventh Ave. express)* or the number 1 or 9 *(IRT Broadway/Seventh Ave. local)* line to **Chambers Street**. Alternatively, you can take the A train *(IND 8th Ave. express)* or C train *(IND 8th Ave. local)* to Chambers Street.

For the return trip, numerous subways make stops along Broadway, Sixth Avenue, and Seventh Avenue in Greenwich Village.

By Bus, you can take the M-20 *(Seventh Ave.)* or the M-6 *(Seventh Ave./Broadway)* to **Chambers Street**.

By Taxi, ask the driver for **Chambers and Greenwich streets**.

PRACTICALITIES:

This trip can be taken at any time, but note that the various small art museums and galleries usually close one or two days each week. These closings are on Sundays, Mondays, Tuesdays, or even Wednesdays; be sure to check the individual listings if contemporary art is of interest to you.

Good weather is essential, as nearly all of the trip is out of doors.

Taken all the way, this walk is about five miles long, but that can be considerably reduced by eliminating the east or west village portions and ending at Washington Square Park. Or by dividing it into two separate trips: TriBeCa/SoHo and East Village/Greenwich Village. For **tourist information** see page 24.

FOOD AND DRINK:

There are plenty of places to eat — in all price ranges — along the entire length of the walk. Just a few suggestions for lunch along the way are:

In TriBeCa and SoHo:

TriBeCa Grill (375 Greenwich St., at Franklin St., in TriBeCa) Superb, sophisticated American cuisine is featured in this casual restaurant — a favorite haunt of celebrities. Reservations needed. ☎ 212-941-3900. X: Sat. lunch, holidays. $$$

Chanterelle (2 Harrison St. at Hudson St., TriBeCa) Innovative French cuisine of the highest order, impeccably served in elegant surroundings. Dress well and reserve. ☎ 212-966-6960. X: Sun., Mon. lunch. $$$

L'École — French Culinary Institute (462 Broadway at Grand St., SoHo) Student chefs prepare fine Nouvelle French cuisine, served with elegance. An especially good value at lunch. ☎ 212-219-3300. X: Sun., holidays. $$ and $$$

Balthazar (80 Spring St., between Broadway and Lafayette St., SoHo) Many celebrities are attracted to this casual, traditional French brasserie — so reserve. ☎ 212-965-1414. $$ and $$$

Rosemarie's (145 Duane St., between West Broadway and Church St., TriBeCa) Creative, homemade Northern Italian specialties, in comfortable surroundings. ☎ 212-285-2610. X: Sun., holidays. $$

Jerry's (101 Prince St., between Mercer and Greene sts., SoHo) An upscale, trendy diner with an eclectic selection of dishes. ☎ 212-966-9464. X: weekends. $ and $$

Moondance Diner (80 Sixth Ave., between Grand and Canal sts., SoHo) A real, old-fashioned diner with excellent sandwiches, burgers, omelettes, and the like. ☎ 212-226-1191. $

Lupe's East L.A. Kitchen (110 Sixth Ave. at Watts St., SoHo) Tasty Mexican fare in a simple, down-to-earth *cantina.* ☎ 212- 966-1326. $

In the East Village:

Dojo's (24 St. Mark's Pl., just east of Cooper Union) Healthy vegetarian and Japanese cuisine at bargain prices. Outdoor tables in season. ☎ 212-674-9821. $

Khyber Pass (34 St. Mark's Pl., between 2nd and 3rd avenues) Afghani and other Middle Eastern dishes, with many vegetarian options. ☎ 212-473-0989. $

Kiev (117 Second Ave. at 7th St.) Eastern European comfort foods at any time of the day. ☎ 212-674-4040. $

Second Avenue Deli (156 Second Ave., at 10th St.) This classic Jewish deli is a long-time favorite. Kosher, of course. ☎ 212-677-0606. $

In Greenwich Village:

Il Mulino (86 West 3rd St., a block south of Washington Square Park) Renowned Italian cuisine in a small, lovely setting. Dress well and reserve. ☎ 212-673-3783. X: Sat. lunch, Sun., holidays. $$ and $$$

Gotham Bar & Grill (12 East 12th St., between 5th Ave. and University Pl.) Creative contemporary American cuisine in a smart, sleek setting. ☎ 212-620-4020. X: Sat. lunch, Sun. lunch. $$ and $$$

Rincón de España (226 Thompson St., between Bleecker and West 3rd sts.) A long-time neighborhood favorite for quality Spanish cuisine, in an Old World setting. ☎ 212-260-4950. $$

The Pink Teacup (42 Grove St., between Bleecker and Bedford sts.) A tiny restaurant serving Southern soul food; a bargain at lunch. ☎ 212-807-6755. $ and $$

Monte's Trattoria (97 MacDougal St., between Bleeker and West 3rd sts.) Homemade traditional Italian cuisine in a friendly setting. ☎ 212-228-9194. X: Tues. $ and $$

Cucina Stagionale (275 Bleecker St. at Jones St.) Extremely popular for its good-value Italian dishes. BYOB. ☎ 212-924-2707. $

John's Pizzeria (278 Bleecker St., between 6th and 7th aves.) Considered by some to be New York's best pizza. ☎ 212- 942-7288. $

SUGGESTED TOUR:

Circled numbers in text correspond to numbers on the maps.

Begin this tour at **City Hall** ❶   (see page 34) and stroll west on Chambers Street. At the northwest corner of Greenwich and Chambers is the pleasant **Washington Market Park** ❷, an oasis of greenery in a sometimes desolate urban landscape. This was once the site of New York's first real fruit and vegetable market.

You are now entering the heart of **TriBeCa**, the **Tri**angle **Be**low **Ca**nal, an area of 19th-century warehouses and early 20th-century commercial buildings reborn into one of New York's trendiest residential and creative centers. As business, and especially shipping from Hudson River piers,

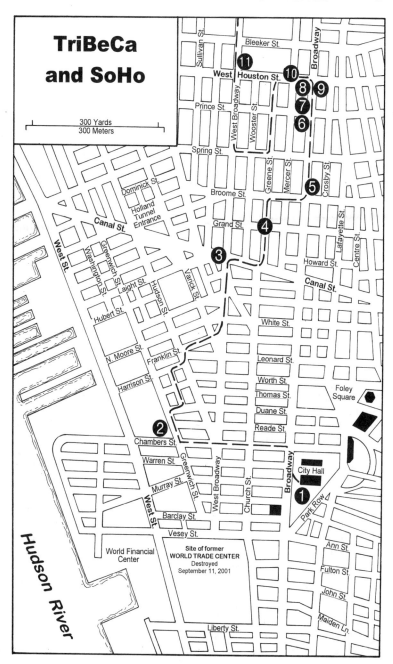

moved elsewhere, these aging lofts became vacant. But not for long. Artists need space — lots of cheap space — and could no longer afford the increasingly high rents in Greenwich Village and SoHo. So they moved south, snapping up the bargain spaces and creating a whole new environment, a thriving community now filled with great restaurants, cafés, and art galleries. This is a place to wander around, soaking up the atmosphere and poking your head into narrow byways. The route on the map gives a good overview, but you should really try other streets as well.

Canal Street ❸ is the main traffic link between the Holland Tunnel to New Jersey and the Manhattan Bridge to Brooklyn. For many years it has also been the venue of dingy discount shops spilling their wares onto the sidewalks, a veritable flea market of odds and ends. Today this is slowly changing as chic new establishments such as the Grand Hotel at West Broadway and Grand Street attract an international, art-oriented clientele.

Cross Canal Street, at one time actually a canal, and step into **SoHo** — the area **So**uth of **Ho**uston Street. Once devoted largely to manufacturing, this neighborhood has become New York's trendiest — and in a way — most fashionable. Beginning in the 1960s, artists flocked here to take over the vacant commercial lofts with their spacious interiors, high ceilings, and dirt cheap rents. Alas, the artists were soon followed by galleries, wealthy collectors, newly-rich stockbrokers looking for a more bohemian way of life, luxury restaurants, and finally by fashion boutiques. Rents soared. No longer able to afford them, the creative people who brought the place to life were now forced to move south into TriBeCa, or the East Village, Brooklyn, or even New Jersey's Hoboken. But their patrons carry on, enjoying a vibrant community of only slightly alternative lifestyles.

SoHo is the center of the **Cast Iron Historic District ❹**, a unique architectural heritage of 19th-century commercial structures built of prefabricated cast-iron sections. Developed in the 1840s as an inexpensive way to erect rather fancy buildings almost overnight, the durable cast-iron structures remained popular until the 1890s, after which taller buildings with steel framing and elevators came into vogue.

Some of the best of these structures can be seen along **Greene Street**, especially the two blocks from Canal to Broome streets. An outstanding example stands at **numbers 28-30**, a six-story masterpiece in the Second Empire style erected in 1872. Designed by Isaac F. Duckworth, it is noted for its mansard roof, dormers, and central bay. Just north of it, at the southeast corner of Grand Street, are what appear to be two stone townhouses, but which in reality are actually made of cast iron made to look like masonry in 1869. On the southwest corner of Broome Street is the Gunther Building of 1871, elegantly fitted with curved plate-glass windows.

Turn right on Broome Street and head east for two blocks. Rising before you, on the northeast corner of Broome Street and Broadway, is the truly magnificent **Haughwout Building ❺** of 1857. Not only is this cast-iron wonder a work of beauty, it is also historically important as the oldest existing structure of its type in New York and the first building in America to feature a safety passenger elevator — a steam-powered convenience installed during construction by Mr. Otis himself. Vaguely reminiscent of a Venetian palace, the intricately-detailed five-story building has a remarkable amount of window space and is today in fine shape, even down to the clock above the Broadway entrance. Its design, fifty years ahead of its time, foreshadowed the light-filled curtain-wall buildings of the modern era.

Head north on Broadway, passing the **Little Singer Building** of 1904, an early "skyscraper" of unusual elegance rising at the southwest corner of Prince Street. Just across that street is the:

*GUGGENHEIM   MUSEUM   SOHO   ❻,   ☎   212-423-3500,   Internet: www.guggenheim.org. *Open Thurs.–Mon., 11–6. Closed Tues.–Wed., Thanksgiving, Christmas, New Year's Day. Free. Museum store open Mon.–Sat. 10:30–7, Sun. 11–6; free admission.* ﾖ.

New York's current art scene — what's really new and exciting — is always on display at this downtown branch of the world-famous Solomon R. Guggenheim Museum (see page 81). Housed in an historic structure of 1882, the spacious, airy museum provides a valuable link between the official art world of uptown and the creative spirit of downtown. Well worth a visit, especially for anyone interested in contemporary works.

Just a few steps up Broadway brings you to the **New Museum of Contemporary Art ❼**, specializing in risky, offbeat works that are too far out for even the Guggenheim. Its recently expanded and renovated interior welcomes visitors to experience conceptual ideas through novel approaches. *583 Broadway.* ☎ *212-219-1222, Internet: www.new museum.org. Open Thurs.–Sat. noon–8, Wed. and Sun. noon–6. Closed Mon.–Tues. Adults $6, seniors and students $3. Bookstore.* ﾖ.

Continue a few steps north to the **Museum for African Art ❽**. Changing exhibits here focus on the entire sweep of African art and culture, from all over the continent and from ancient times right up to the present. *593 Broadway.* ☎ *212-966-1313, Internet: www.africanart.org. Open Tues.–Fri. 10:30–5:30, Sat.–Sun. noon–6. Closed Mon. Adults $5, seniors, students, children $2.50. Gift shop.* ﾖ.

Across Broadway is the **Alternative Museum ❾**, which of late has been turning itself into a Internet-based virtual museum accessed through its web site. This is where you'll encounter fresh works by emerging talents, often politically oriented, multi-cultural, and highly unusual. *594 Broadway, 4th floor.* ☎ *212-966-4444, Internet: www.alternative museum.org. Open Tues.–Sat. 11–6. Closed Sun.–Mon. and Aug. Suggested donation $3.*

Follow the map through the lively old streets of SoHo, taking in the ever-changing scene of galleries, boutiques, restaurants, and cafés. West Broadway is particularly interesting, leading north to **West Houston Street**

❿. This is the dividing line between SoHo and Greenwich Village. It is also the dividing line between real New Yorkers, who correctly pronounce it as *HOW-ston*, and visitors, who think it had something to do with that man from Texas. It doesn't.

La Guardia Place ⓫ is the entrance into Greenwich Village, but shares little of its atmosphere. On your right you'll pass a statue of the "Little Flower" himself, Fiorello La Guardia (1882–1947), who served as New York's best and most colorful mayor from 1934 to 1945. Continue on to Washington Square Park ⓱, which you'll be visiting later after sampling a bit of the East Village.

The many buildings of **New York University ⓬**, America's largest private university, completely dominate this area — bringing a youthful vitality to its urban mix. Founded in 1831, NYU has over 45,000 students spread between this main campus and several other locations throughout the city. Their **Information Center** at 50 West 4th Street can tell you all about it. A block north of this, at 29 Washington Place East, is the site of the infamous Triangle Shirtwaist Company, which burned down in 1911, killing 145 employees who were locked in to prevent their taking breaks. Public outcry at this atrocity eventually led to worker safety laws, although the responsible employer was acquitted of any crime. There is nothing to see here today other than a small memorial plaque.

Stroll east on 4th Street, passing the **Merchant's House Museum ⓭**. This Greek Revival row house of 1832 was home to a prosperous merchant named Seabury Tredwell, and remained with his descendants for nearly a hundred years. Practically unchanged over that time, and still sporting its original furnishings, this is the most intact 19th-century house in Manhattan, offering a good chance to glimpse the lifestyle of that era and social class. *29 E. 4th St. ☎ 212-777-1089, Internet: www.merchants house.com. Open Thurs.–Mon., 1–5. Adults $5, seniors and students $3, children free. Gift shop.*

You are now entering the **East Village**, a lively — if often seedy — district that was once home to the Beat Generation, then to the hippies of the 1960's, and to every counterculture group since. Although there has been some of the inevitable gentrification, the neighborhood still retains much of its non-conformist atmosphere despite the trendy restaurants and galleries. Turn north on Bowery to Cooper Square and **Astor Place ⓮**. The elaborate subway entrance here is a wonderful 1985 reconstruction of the 1904 original, while down below the beaver bas-reliefs still celebrate John Jacob Astor's role in the 19th-century fur trade. Near the entrance is the "Alamo," a big black cube balanced on one corner, that can allegedly be rotated if you push hard enough.

In the center of the square stands the **Cooper Union**, a massive brownstone structure of 1859 that houses the nation's first coeducational and racially integrated college, founded by the great 19th-century inventor, industrialist, and philanthropist Peter Cooper (1791–1883). This is also the oldest existing steel-framed building in America. Many famous people have delivered speeches in its Great Hall, including the 1860 oration that won the Republican Party presidential nomination for Abraham Lincoln. Head south for one block on Third Avenue, turning left on 7th Street. If you're feeling thirsty by now, you might want to stop at **McSorley's Old Ale House** at 15 East 7th. Established in 1854 and hardly changed since, the historic pub serves its own ale, and only its own ale, light or dark, two mugs at a time. Around 1970 McSorley's finally opened its doors to women, but only after a court decision forced it to. Before that this was always an all-male hangout, often frequented by writers, artists, politicians, and the like.

Stroll north on Second Avenue to the corner of 10th Street and **St. Mark's in the Bowery Church ⓯**. Looking wildly out of place in its almost rural setting, St. Mark's is an architectural mélange including the main structure of 1799, a Greek Revival steeple of 1828, and an Italianate porch of 1854. Many events are held here, ranging from farmers' markets to poetry readings. The graveyard is allegedly haunted by the ghost of Peter Stuyvesant, the Dutch Colonial dictator of *Nieuw Amsterdam,* as New York City was called at the time, from 1647 until 1664. This land was part of his 600-acre farm, or *bouwerie,* and this is where he's buried.

Now follow East 10th Street west all the way to Fifth Avenue, reentering **Greenwich Village**. A little side trip can be made by heading north on Fifth Avenue for two blocks to the:

*FORBES MAGAZINE GALLERIES ⓰, 62 Fifth Ave., ☎ 212-206-5548. *Open Tues.–Sat. 10–4; Thurs. reserved for groups. Closed Sun. and Mon. Admission limited to 900 persons per day; first come, first served. Children under 16 must be accompanied. Admission free.* ♿.

The late Malcolm Forbes, publisher of Forbes Magazine, was a collector of the strange and wonderful, the eclectic and the truly unique. From the elaborate **Fabergé** Imperial Easter eggs of Czarist Russia to the hundreds of **toy boats** from the 1870s to the 1950s, from the thousands of **toy soldiers** to the very first versions of **Monopoly**, from **presidential papers** to **bizarre trophies** — there's enough here to keep your eyes amazed for the better part of an hour. Best of all, this treat is free.

Heading south on Fifth Avenue, take a look at **Washington Mews**, a block-long cobblestoned alley on the left below 8th Street. The charming little houses lining it, now highly desirable properties, were once stables and servants' quarters for the wealthy of Washington Square North. Fifth Avenue ends at ***Washington Square Park ⓱**, the very heart of Greenwich Village. This is where everyone, but everyone, in the Village gathers, and consequently just about the best people-watching place in New York. Take a stroll along its shady lanes, dodging the skateboarders, listening to impromptu musicians, and taking in the whole lively scene. It is also a great place to just sit down on one of the abundant park benches, perhaps enjoying a snack from one of the many vendors. Strangely, this happy

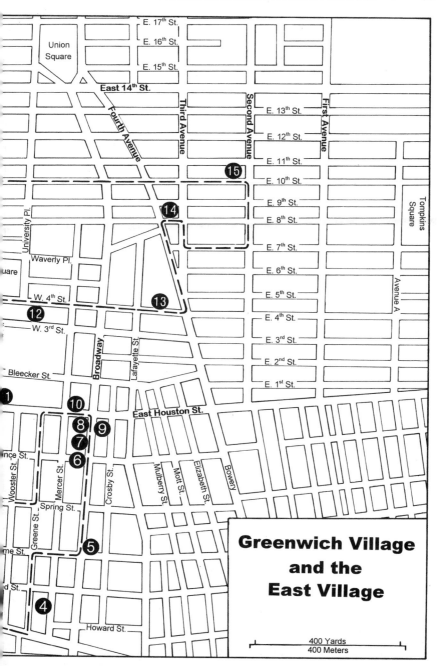

Greenwich Village and the East Village

400 Yards
400 Meters

place sits atop what was a potter's field in the 18th century, and a place for public executions during the Revolutionary War.

At the north entrance to the park stands **Washington Arch**, a 77-foot-high marble memorial to President George Washington, who is depicted on the north side as both a soldier and a civilian. Erected in 1892, it replaced a temporary wooden arch commemorating the centennial of Washington's first inauguration in 1789, also held in New York (see page 30).

If you have any energy left, you might want to take a pleasant stroll through the more colorful streets and back lanes of the Village. A particularly engaging route, shown on the map, is to exit the park at its northwest corner, heading north on MacDougal Street. To the right is **MacDougal Alley**, a delightful little passage lit by gas lamps and lined with tiny row houses and stables.

Turn left on West 8th Street, the Village's main shopping venue, a busy thoroughfare with some rather unusual shops. At its end is what true New Yorkers still call **Sixth Avenue**, despite all the signs proclaiming it as the Avenue of the Americas. This dual identity has been going on for over half a century, and only serves to confuse out-of-towners. To the right, across Village Square, rises a strange red-brick castle festooned with pointy roofs, turrets, and an odd clock tower. A masterpiece of the Victorian Gothic style, now known as the **Jefferson Market Library** ⓲, it was built in 1877 as a courthouse and nearly demolished in the 1960s as an eyesore. Public outcry saved it and put it to good use sheltering books instead of judges.

Head down Christopher Street to **Christopher Park** ⓳. Just across the street is the site of the original Stonewall Inn, remembered for the Stonewall Riots of 1969 in which a group of gay men battled police who were harassing them, an event that led to the gay-rights movement. It is commemorated by a George Segal sculpture of two ghostly couples, one male and the other female, standing and sitting in the park.

Cross Seventh Avenue and continue west on Grove Street. Just beyond Bedford Street, on your left, is **Grove Court**, a pretty little cul-de-sac lined with Federal-style houses from the 1850's. On the far side of Hudson Street stands the **Church of St. Luke in the Fields** ⓴, the third-oldest church in Manhattan. Erected in 1821 when this was indeed "in the fields," the church has a delightful little garden that is open to the public and accessed through a gate between the church and its school.

Re-cross Hudson Street and follow the map down Barrow, Commerce, and Bedford streets. Along the way you'll pass the **Cherry Lane Theater**, a pioneer in off-Broadway productions ever since the 1920s. Its founder, the author Edna St. Vincent Millay, lived in the extremely narrow house around the corner at 75-1/2 Bedford Street.

Escape the Seventh Avenue traffic by heading down Morton Street, turning left on Hudson and left again on St. Luke's Place. Now cross Seventh and follow Leroy Street to Bleecker Street, which still retains some of its old-time immigrant atmosphere. Dodge the traffic on Sixth Avenue (OK, Avenue of the Americas) and cross over to Minetta Street, leading to Minetta Lane and the historic Minetta Tavern. From here, taking MacDougal Street north for two blocks returns you to Washington Square Park ⓱, the end of the walk.

Jefferson Market Library

West Midtown
to Chelsea

Manhattan's West Midtown offers some of the city's premier tourist sights along with a wide range of experiences. Glitzy Times Square, the "Crossroads of the World," has been cleaned up in recent years, but still retains all of its sensory excitement despite creeping multinational, sanitized commercialism. Even Disney could not undo the decades of decadent fun these streets have offered the world.

A few blocks north through the neon canyons takes you to Carnegie Hall, America's most prestigious concert venue, where you might want to take a tour. From here, a side trip by bus to the Hudson River offers a choice of marvelous attractions — the Intrepid Sea-Air-Space Museum, mostly on board a World War II aircraft carrier; or a three-hour cruise completely around the island of Manhattan.

A bus ride across 42nd Street drops you off at Fifth Avenue for a visit inside the magnificent New York Public Library and its fascinating exhibits, all free. Following that, the route continues on foot or by bus to the Empire State Building, the very symbol of the city, where you can enjoy an unsurpassed view of the entire metropolitan region from its observatory. At this point, you might opt for a side trip to the many shopping opportunities around Herald Square, or just continue south to explore the revitalized, newly fashionable district of Chelsea.

GETTING THERE:

See page 18 for general transit information.

By Subway, take the number 2 or 3 *(IRT Seventh Ave. express)* or number 1 or 9 *(IRT Broadway/Seventh Ave. local)* line to Times Square. Another choice is the N or R *(BMT Broadway local)* train, also to Times Square. Those coming from East Midtown might use the S *(Shuttle)* train from Grand Central, or the number 7 *(IRT Flushing express or local)* line from Queens.

By Bus, take the M-20 *(7th and 8th Avenues)* or M-104 *(Broadway)* routes to 42nd Street and Broadway. Crosstown, use the M-42 *(42nd St.)* route.

By Taxi, ask the driver for 42nd Street and Broadway.

On Foot, chances are that Times Square is within walking distance of your hotel.

PRACTICALITIES:

This trip can be taken on any day, but note that the Intrepid Sea-Air-Space Museum is closed on Mondays and Tuesdays from October through April, as well as on New Year's Day, Thanksgiving, and Christmas. Fine weather is essential as nearly all of the trip is out of doors.

Taken in its entirety, including side trips, this route is some six miles long — level all the way. Fortunately, there are frequent buses along nearly all of the route, so you can hop on and off and save your feet. An economical and convenient way to do this is to purchase a one-day Metro Card, which allows unlimited rides for less than the price of three rides. Full information about this bargain is given on page 19.

The **Times Square Visitors Center** on Broadway between 46th and 47th streets provides free information and a multitude of essential tourist service. *1560 Broadway,* ☎ *212-869-5453. Open daily 9–6.* For additional tourist information see page 24.

FOOD AND DRINK:

There are hundreds — possibly thousands — of eateries in this area. Out of such an abundance, here are just a few choices:

Sardi's (234 West 44th St., between Broadway and 8th Ave.) The quintessential Broadway Theater restaurant, long a haunt of the stars. Continental cuisine; reservations needed. ☎ 212-221-8440. X: Mon. $$ and $$$

Trattoria dell' Arte (900 Seventh Ave., between 56th and 57th sts.) Northern Italian cuisine in an arty setting; convenient to Carnegie Hall. ☎ 212-245-9800. $$ and $$$

Barbetta (321 West 46th St., between 8th and 9th avenues) A traditional Northern Italian restaurant, with classical elegance and a romantic garden. ☎ 212-246-9171. X: Sun., holidays. $$ and $$$

Virgil's Real Barbecue (152 West 44th St., between Broadway and 6th Ave.) Southern-style pork barbecue, ribs, catfish, chicken and the like, in a roadhouse setting. ☎ 212-921-9494. $$

Joe Allen (326 West 46th St., between 8th and 9th avenues) American comfort food is served in this famous old pub, long a favorite of the theater crowd. Reservations advised. ☎ 212-581-6464. $$

Uncle Nick's (747 9th Ave., between 50th and 51st streets) This favorite Greek restaurant specializes in seafood, but offers meat dishes as well. ☎ 212-245-7992. $$

Victor's Café (236 West 52nd St., between Broadway and 8th Ave.) Cuban and South American cuisine; especially noted for its steaks. ☎ 212-586-7714. $$

Carnegie Deli (854 Seventh Ave. at 55th St.) This famous New York deli has been a landmark since 1937. Overstuffed sandwiches, matzo ball soup, and don't forget the cheesecake. ☎ 212-757-2245. $ and $$

Siam Inn Too (854 Eighth Ave., between 51st and 52nd streets) Authentic Thai cuisine in a relaxed setting. ☎ 212-757-4006. X: weekend lunches. $ and $$

Uncle Vanya Café (315 West 54th St., between 8th and 9th avenues) A delightful place serving traditional Russian dishes at reasonable prices. ☎ 212-262-0542. X: Sun. lunch. $ and $$

Zen Palate (663 Ninth Ave. at 46th St.) Healthy vegetarian dishes with an Asian influence, served in a relaxed setting. ☎ 212-582-1669. $

Café Europa (205 West 57th St. at 7th Ave.) A simple but energetic place for sandwiches, pizza, pasta, and salads — and especially for desserts. ☎ 212-977-4030. $

SUGGESTED TOUR:

Circled numbers in text correspond to numbers on the map.

Begin at the corner of **42nd Street and Broadway ❶**, strolling north into **Times Square**. There are several attractions in this immediate area that might interest you, or that you might want to come back to later. One such establishment with a particularly broad appeal is **Madame Tussaud's**, a wax-works experience with over 175 realistic figures of celebrities, movers and shakers in themed environments. *42nd St. & Broadway, ☎ 1-800-246-8872, Internet: www.madame-tussauds.com. Open Sun.–Thurs. 10–6, Fri.–Sat. 10–8. Combined experience: Adults $21.95, seniors (60+) 19.95, children (4–12) $17.95. Food service. Gift shop. ⓑ.* Sports fans may be attracted to the **ESPN Zone**, where they can eat, drink, watch, and play at the ultimate sports dining and entertainment experience. *1472 Broadway at 42nd St., ☎ 212-921-ESPN.* Investors should head to the **MarketSite**, Nasdaq's high-tech tower, broadcast facility, and public interactive exhibit. Outside, its eight-story-high video screen (the largest in the world) provides financial news from around the globe. Also visible from the street is the financial TV studio used by major cable networks. Inside, the **MarketSite Experience** brings the stock market to life with the latest interactive techniques. *4 Times Sq., corner of Broadway and 43rd St. Experience open Sun. 10–8, Mon.–Fri. 9–8, Sat. 10–10. Time-dated tickets $7, advance purchase recommended. ☎ 1-877-Nasdaq-1, Internet: www.nasdaq.com. ⓑ.*

Times Square was once known as Longacre Square, and in the 19th century was the center of New York's horse business, with stables, black-smiths, carriage shops, and horse auctions. This all changed in 1904 when The New York Times moved into the triangular building between Broadway and Seventh Avenue, from 42nd to 43rd streets. Badly remod-eled, this once-elegant structure is still there, and its famous ball still drops at the stroke of midnight on New Year's Eve, but the Times has long since moved around the corner to 229 West 43rd Street.

Early in the 20th century Times Square became America's center for theater, a distinction it still retains, with dozens of landmark theaters lin-ing the side streets surrounding the square. By the 1960s, however, its future was clouded by sleazy sex joints, porn shops, drug dealers, and flourishing crime. Efforts at cleaning up the mess have finally paid off, and the only danger facing the square today is that of over-gentrification, what with Disney and like organizations having recently set up shop. Still, much of the atmosphere remains, enhanced by an endless sea of neon and the bustle of the crowded streets.

Turn west on 44th Street to **Shubert Alley ❷**, the very heart of the Theater District. Linking 44th and 45th streets, this narrow pedestrian thoroughfare is actually a required fire exit for some of the theaters, and a busy place during intermissions. Pass through and turn right on 45th Street, crossing Broadway and turning north on Seventh Avenue. At 47th Street, on a tiny island between the main streets, is the famed **TKTS booth**, where same-day tickets to Broadway shows are sold at greatly reduced prices. A posted sign lists the available tickets, so join the line if you spot a bargain. ☎ *212-768-1818. Open Mon.–Sat. 3–8 for evening shows; Wed. and Sat. 10–2 for matinees, and Sun. 11–7 for both. Cash or travelers checks only.*

Continue up Seventh Avenue, drinking in the scene and possibly stopping at the **Times Square Visitors Center**. *1560 Broadway, between 46th and 47th streets,* ☎ *212-768-1560, Internet: www.timesquarebid.org.* Another similar stop is the **New York Convention and Visitors Bureau Center**. *810 Seventh Avenue, between 52nd and 53rd streets,* ☎ *212-484-1200, Internet: www.nycvisit.com.*

Remaining on Seventh Avenue all the way to 57th Street brings you to the renowned **Carnegie Hall ❸**, built in 1891 by philanthropist Andrew Carnegie as America's most prestigious concert hall. Just about every musical star since then has performed here, from classical to jazz to rock, as have numerous lecturers from Winston Churchill to Martin Luther King Jr. The hall has always been noted for its near-perfect acoustics, possibly the best anywhere in the world. Nearly demolished to make way for yet another office tower in the 1950s, Carnegie Hall was saved by concerned citizens, and in 1985 given a complete, 50-million-dollar, restoration. *154 W. 57th St.,* ☎ *212-247-7800. Tours Jan.–June and Sept.–Dec., Mon., Tues., Thurs., Fri. at 11:30, 2 and 3. Adults $6, seniors and students $5, children (under 12) $3.* ♿.

Stroll west on 57th Street and turn south on Broadway, heading back into Times Square. A particularly enjoyable **side trip** can be made by boarding at 49th street a west-bound M-50 bus to either of two riverside attractions, or taking a cab, or hiking all the way over to the Hudson River. However you get there, don't miss the:

*INTREPID SEA-AIR-SPACE MUSEUM ❹, Pier 86, W. 46th St. at 12th Ave., New York, NY 10036, ☎ 212-245-0072, Internet: www.intrepidmuseum.org. *Open April–Sept., Mon.–Fri. 10–5, Sat.–Sun. 10–6, holidays 10–7; rest of year Tues.–Sun. 10–5. Closed Thanksgiving, Christmas, New Year's Day. Last admission one hour before closing. Adults $12, seniors (64+) and youths (12–17) $9, children (6–11) $6. Paid admissions (age 12 and older) include use of Acoustiguide audio tour device. Cafeteria. Museum store. Mostly* ♿.

Docked at Pier 86 are three proud warships that have served the

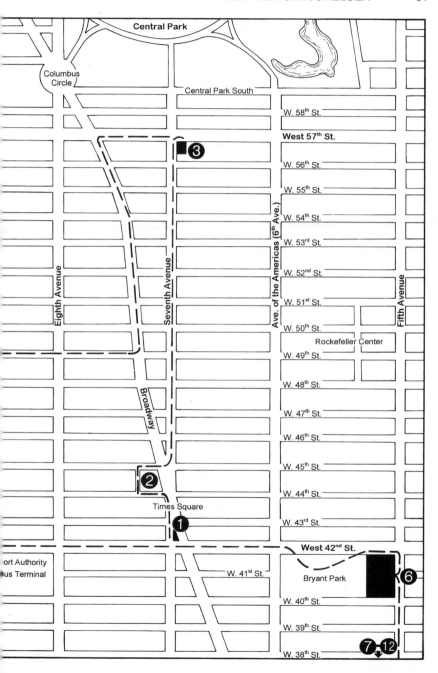

nation well. The largest of these, the USS *Intrepid*, an Essex Class aircraft carrier launched in 1943, fought in several major campaigns during World War II, surviving kamikaze, bomb, and torpedo attacks. In the 1960s she served as a prime recovery vessel for NASA, and continued as an anti-submarine carrier through the Vietnam conflict, ending her naval career in 1974. In 1982 she was rescued from the scrap yard and transformed into a floating museum. Her **Flight Deck** is lined with historic warplanes, both American and foreign, including the incredible **A-12 Blackbird**, a spy plane used by the CIA as the world's fastest jet. Beneath this, the cavernous **Hanger Deck** has been fitted out as a museum chronicling the history of naval aviation and sea, air, and space technology. There are many hands-on, interactive displays, and even an action-packed **flight simulator** that you can try out for a small extra fee.

Also docked at the museum is the **USS *Growler***, the only guided-missile submarine in the world that is open to the public. It may be seen on guided tours included in the admission price. Behind this is the **USS *Edson***, a Vietnam-era destroyer that can be explored on your own or on a guided tour. Other ships from around the world frequently visit the museum, and are usually open for free tours.

Just a few blocks south of the Intrepid is Pier 83, departure point for the:

*CIRCLE LINE SIGHTSEEING CRUISES ❺, West 42nd St. and Hudson River, New York, NY 10036, ☎ 212-563-3200, Internet: www.circleline.com. *Operates early May to early Sept., daily 10–4:30; rest of year at reduced schedule. 3-hour cruise: Adults $24, seniors $20, under 12 $12. 30-minute, 1- and 2-hour cruises also available. Snacks & beverages available. ᕫ.*

Circle Line's classic three-hour circumnavigation of Manhattan Island, a 35-mile narrated trip that points out numerous sights along the way, is a delightful way to spend a lazy afternoon well away from any cultural pursuits. Just sit back and enjoy the passing scenery along with the cooling breezes. Other shorter or specialized tours are also offered. Reservations are not necessary, just join the line and board the boat.

Board the M-42 eastbound bus and ride it to Fifth Avenue. Those who did not take the side trip (above) can board this same bus at the corner of 42nd Street and Broadway, just below Times Square, or walk the short distance.

Amble down Fifth Avenue. On your right is the magnificent **New York Public Library ❻**, whose entrance is flanked by two marble lions named Patience and Fortitude. Surely one of the greatest libraries on Earth, it was built in the Beaux-Arts style in 1911 on the site of a former water reservoir. Its impressive interior is well worth a visit, especially the recently-renovated **Main Reading Room** and the various exhibition halls. Don't try to borrow a book here, though, as this main branch is strictly for research. ☎ *212-930-0800, Internet: www.nypl.org. Open Mon., Thurs.–Sat. 10–6,*

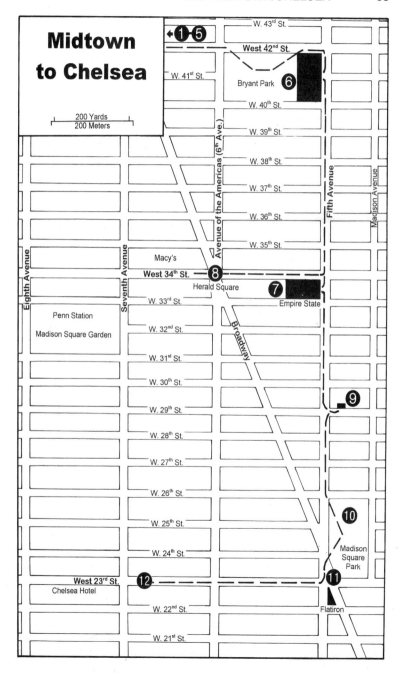

Midtown to Chelsea

200 Yards
200 Meters

Tues.–Wed. 11–7:30. Closed Sun. and major holidays. Guided tours Mon.–Sat. at 11 and 2. Free. Gift shop. &. Behind the library stretches **Bryant Park**, an exceptionally pleasant place to relax before pressing on.

Continue down Fifth Avenue for eight blocks, passing the elegant **Lord & Taylor** store, to 34th Street. If your feet hurt, you could take a bus instead. The numbers M-2, M-3, M-4, M-5, and Q-32 all follow this route. However you got there, you are now facing what is arguably New York's most renowned structure, the:

*EMPIRE STATE BUILDING ❼, 350 Fifth Ave., New York, NY 10118, ☎ 212-736-3100, Internet: www.esbnyc.com. *Observatory open daily 9:30 a.m. to 11:30 p.m. Adults $9, seniors and military personnel $7, children (5–11) $4, under 5 free. Skyride open daily 10 a.m. to 10 p.m. Adults $11.50, seniors and children (4–12) $8.50. Combination ticket: Adults $14, seniors and children $9. Snack bar. Gift shop.* &.

Even though it has been eclipsed in height by other structures in Chicago and Kuala Lumpur, the Empire State Building remains the quintessential skyscraper in the minds of just about everyone because it just looks as tall as it really is. This Art Deco masterpiece, completed in 1931, stands alone on its site — unchallenged by any neighbor.

The ***view** from the Observatory levels on the top — on a clear day — is simply the best you'll find anywhere in New York. Check the visibility level on the sign by the ticket desk; if it's perfect you'll see for 80 miles in every direction, if it's as low as five miles you'll still see the harbor, but if it's zero you won't see a thing. The ***86th Floor Observatory** level offers both indoor and outdoor viewing decks, and from here you can continue up into the spire to the **102nd Floor Enclosed Viewing Area**. This part of the tower was originally designed as a mooring mast for transatlantic Zeppelins, but was never used as such due to the incredible danger of an airship disaster high above the city. Today it serves as a TV and radio transmission antenna.

The Empire State Building has another attraction as well; this one down on the second floor. The **New York Skyride** is a simulated thrill ride that plunges over, under, and through some of the city's most famous sights.

At this point you might want to make a little **side trip** to nearby **Herald Square ❽**, just one long block to the west. This is home to the original **Macy's**, once the world's largest store and still a mighty impressive one. Many other retail establishments are crowded around here, and there are two multi-storied indoor shopping malls to explore.

Back on Fifth Avenue, continue south to 29th Street, turning left to the **Little Church Around the Corner ❾**, officially known as the Church of the Transfiguration. Looking more like a scene out of a quaint English village, this mid-19th-century Episcopal church set in a charming garden acquired its popular name in 1870 when a more proper church, refusing to hold funeral services for such low-lifes as actors, referred them to this humble parish. The church has been a favorite with theatrical folk ever since, as you'll discover when you check out its stained-glass windows. ☎ *212-684-6770, Internet: www.littlechurch.org. Open daily 8–6. Free.* &.

Continue south on Fifth Avenue to **Madison Square Park** ❿, beginning at 26th Street. Originally this was swampy land, used as the site of New York's first baseball games, and transformed in 1847 into a military parade ground. The first **Madison Square Garden**, built at the end of the century at the northeast corner, was torn down in 1925 to make room for the New York Life Insurance Building. The "Garden" was then moved to West 49th Street, and later to its current location above Pennsylvania Station. Today, the park provides a welcome relief from the city's bustle; a place to sit down and gather your thoughts.

Towering over the southern end of the park, at 23rd Street and Fifth Avenue, is the historic **Flatiron Building** ⓫ of 1902. At 20 stories in height, this was once the world's tallest "skyscraper." Its name, actually a nickname, derives from its strange triangular shape, dictated by the intersection of Broadway and Fifth Avenue. The same shape creates unusual wind currents, which back in the early 1900s caused women's skirts to raise, providing endless entertainment for passing gents. Despite its age, the Flatiron Building remains an architectural triumph in a dramatic setting.

If you have any energy left, you might want to head west on 23rd Street into fashionable **Chelsea** ⓬, a burgeoning area filled with art galleries, trendy cafés, unusual shops, and alternative lifestyles. Crossing Sixth (OK, the sign says Avenue of the Americas) and then Seventh avenues, you'll soon come to the notorious **Chelsea Hotel** of 1884, long a home to writers, artists, and musicians. Eighth Avenue is more-or-less the main drag of Chelsea, and if you wander far enough west you'll eventually come to the Hudson River and the **Chelsea Piers**, a redeveloped waterfront project with a wide range of sports facilities.

No matter how far west you've roamed, the number M-23 bus can return you to the center of town, with subway connections at Eighth and Sixth avenues, Broadway, and Park Avenue South.

Trip 5
New York City

Fifth Avenue and the East Side

N o visit to New York City is complete without a stroll down Fifth Avenue, arguably the most prestigious shopping venue on Earth. Whether you purchase anything or not, the window shopping along this thoroughfare just can't be beat. On a less materialistic note, the route offers the world's premier museum of modern art, the hidden delights of Paley and Greenacre parks, such architectural triumphs as Rockefeller Center, Saint Patrick's Cathedral, Saint Bartholomew's Church, the Chrysler Building, and CitiCorp Center, visits to a major broadcaster, a train station to end all train stations, and a tour of the United Nations.

GETTING THERE:

See page 18 for general transit information.

By Subway, the closest service is to take the N or R *(BMT Broadway local)* train to the Fifth Avenue stop. Alternatively, you might take the B or Q *(IND Sixth Avenue express)* train to 57th Street, or the numbers 4 or 5 *(IRT Lexington Avenue express)* or number 6 *(IRT Lexington Avenue local)* to 59th Street.

By Bus, the start of this walk is served by the number M-1, M-2, M-3, M-4, or M-5 buses to 59th Street, or the Q-32 to Fifth Avenue, or the crosstown M-31 or M-57 to Fifth Avenue at 57th Street.

By Taxi, ask the driver for Fifth Avenue and 59th Street.

On Foot, chances are that Grand Army Plaza is within walking distance of your hotel.

PRACTICALITIES:

This trip can be taken on any day, noting that the Museum of Modern Art is closed on Wednesdays. Decent weather is essential as much of the trip is out of doors. The streets are more alive on normal working days.

Taken all the way and making all the stops, this walk is some four miles long, practically level all the way. There are frequent buses along nearly all of the route, so you can hop on and off to save your feet. An economical and convenient way to do this is to purchase a one-day Metro Card, which allows unlimited bus and subway rides for less than the cost of three rides. Full information about this bargain is given on page 19.

For **tourist information** see page 24.

FOOD AND DRINK:

Countless eateries of every description line the streets of this walking tour; here are a few choices:

Café Centro (200 Park Ave. on 45th St.) French and Mediterranean dishes, with a truly Parisian atmosphere. Reserve. ☎ 212-818-1222. X: Sat. lunch, Sun., major holidays. $$ and $$$

Oyster Bar (lower level, Grand Central Terminal) New York's classic seafood restaurant offers an old-time experience along with great food. ☎ 212-490-6650. X: weekends. $$ and $$$

Shun Lee Palace (155 East 55th St., between Third and Lexington avenues) Szechwan and Cantonese specialties in a friendly setting. ☎ 212-371-8844. $$ and $$$

Bombay Palace (30 West 52nd St., off Fifth Ave.) Authentic Indian cuisine, including an all-you-can-eat buffet. ☎ 212-541-7777. $$

La Bonne Soupe (48 West 55th St., off Fifth Ave.) A variety of healthy soups plus salads, breads, and desserts. ☎ 212-586- 7650. $

Dosanko (433 Madison Ave., between 48th and 49th streets) Tasty Japanese dumpling and noodle dishes at quite reasonable prices. ☎ 212-688-8575. $

Cucina & Co. (200 Park Ave. on 45th St.) Sandwiches, salads, and pastas — all with an Italian flair. ☎ 212-682-2700. $

Ess-A-Bagel (831 3rd Ave., between 50th and 51st streets) Real New York bagels, with a wide choice of spreads. ☎ 212-980-1010. $

Those in a hurry, or wanting to save money, might opt for an alfresco sandwich at Paley Park or Greenacre Park — or stop by one of the many sidewalk vendors around Fifth Avenue.

SUGGESTED TOUR:

Circled numbers in text correspond to numbers on the map.

Begin your day at **Grand Army Plaza** ❶, the intersection of Fifth Avenue and 59th Street. To the north stretches **Central Park**, the subject of the next chapter. Facing the square is the renowned **Plaza Hotel**, a National Historic Landmark opened in 1907 and still one of the city's most impressive structures. Step inside the lobby to witness real opulence or perhaps have a drink in the fabled Oak Room. Just across Fifth Avenue, and possibly more affordable, is that ultimate toy emporium, **F.A.O. Schwarz**, a mecca for the inner child in everyone.

Stroll down Fifth Avenue, passing what may be the most luxurious clothing store in the world, **Bergdorf-Goodman**. Cater-corner from it, at 57th Street, are the intriguing window displays of **Tiffany & Co.**, the jewelry store par excellence. Some of its offerings are not quite as expensive as you might imagine — so step inside and take a look. For really conspicuous consumption that staggers the imagination, the shops in **Trump Tower**, just a few steps down the avenue, are hard to beat. This indoor shopping

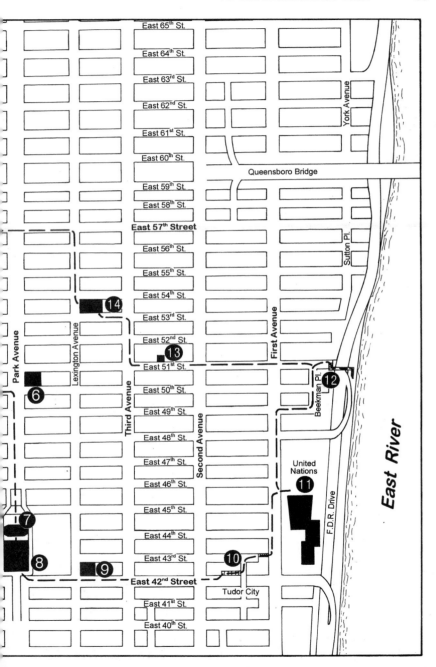

mall features a six-story atrium with its own waterfall, pink marble walls, glitzy brass details, and boutiques whose prices would frighten a billionaire.

Continue down Fifth past more world-renowned shops and hotels to 53rd Street. A half-block to the right is the:

*MUSEUM OF MODERN ART ❷, 11 W. 53rd St., New York, NY 10019, ☎ 212-708-9400, Internet: www.moma.org. *Open Thurs.–Tues., 10:30–5:45, remaining open until 8:15 on Fri. Closed Wed., Thanksgiving, Christmas. Adults $10, seniors (65+) and students with ID $6.50, children under 16 accompanied by adults are free. Admission on Fri. from 4:30–8:15 is pay as you wish. Restaurant. Café. Design store. Bookshop.* ♿.

Anyone who loves modern art — or who would just like to understand it — should definitely not miss an opportunity to visit this world-renowned institution. MoMA, as it's known to afficionados, is regarded by many as the most comprehensive survey of twentieth-century art anywhere on Earth. Opened just 10 days after the stock-market crash of 1929 with an exhibition of then-unknown painters named Cézanne, Gauguin, Seurat, and van Gogh, the museum expanded into the fields of photography, architecture, film, and industrial design before moving to its present address in 1939. Since then the premises have been greatly enlarged with new structures and an outdoor sculpture garden. A new expansion and renovation project, to be completed in 2005 at a cost of 650 million dollars, will again enhance this masterful collection.

Return to Fifth Avenue, cross it, and amble east a few yards on 53rd Street to **Paley Park ❸**. This tiny oasis of calm in the middle of Manhattan's bustle features a waterfall, trees, and outdoor tables where you can bring your own lunch or purchase sandwiches, snacks, and drinks from the kiosk. This is a great place for a rest stop.

Continue down Fifth and, just past 50th Street, turn west down a promenade into the heart of **Rockefeller Center ❹**. Stretching from 47th to 52nd streets, and from Fifth Avenue to west of Sixth, this marvelous urban complex consists of some 19 harmonious buildings erected between the 1930s and 70s, all connected by an underground concourse complete with shops and restaurants. Put simply, this is probably the finest example of urban planning anywhere. The 22-acre site, once a fashionable residential neighborhood, had declined by the early 20th century, largely due to the noisy (and long-departed) Sixth Avenue elevated railroad. In 1928, the land was leased from its owner, Columbia University, by John D. Rockefeller Jr. for a cultural project to include a new opera house. The Great Depression of 1929 put an end to that plan, and instead Rockefeller built a vast commercial center around the new RCA Building of 1933. Construction on the other buildings continued until 1940, and resumed after World War II, with the last added in 1973.

The most dramatic entrance into the complex is via the ***Channel**

Gardens, a long, sloping promenade that separates the low-lying **British Empire Building** from its twin, **La Maison Française**, as the real English Channel separates those two nations. At its end is a **sunken plaza** rimmed by colorful flags representing the countries of the United Nations. During the winter this becomes a skating rink, and in the summer an outdoor café. Overlooking the scene is the golden statue of **Prometheus**, and above it the towering majesty of the ***GE Building**, formerly the RCA Building — the name changed in 1990. Step inside the lobby for a look at the **murals** depicting man's progress, which quickly replaced the original murals by Diego Rivera showing a triumphant Lenin leading the proletariat as they take over the world — an image that did not sit well with the Rockefellers. The offending pictures were quickly destroyed. Stop at the information desk for a free self-guided tour map to the entire complex. You might also ask about **guided tours** of the **NBC Studios**, where many favorite TV broadcasts take place. These depart from the **NBC Experience Store** at Rockefeller Plaza and 49th Street, last a bit over one hour, and cover the network's history since 1926, two or three studios, a demonstration control room, and the new HDTV Theater of new TV technology. ☎ *212-664-3700, Internet: www.nbc.com/store. Open Mon.–Sat., 8:30 to 5:30, 6:30, or 8, depending on season; Sun. 9:30 to 4:30 or 7. Adults $17.50, seniors and children (6–16) $15. Under 6 not admitted.* &.

    Radio City Music Hall, another part of the complex, sits on the corner of 50th Street and Sixth Avenue (officially called the Avenue of the Americas, but not by New Yorkers). Opened in 1932 as the largest indoor theater in the world, it soon shifted from variety shows to movies, and is now best known for its spectacular stage extravaganzas. In 1979 the Music Hall was saved from demolition by a huge public outcry, and its wonderful Art Deco interior has been fully restored in recent years. Behind-the-scene guided tours, lasting about one hour, are offered. ☎ *212-307-7171 or Internet: www.radiocity.com for reservations. Tours Mon.–Sat. 10–5, Sun. 11–5. Adults $16, children under 12 $10.*

    Return to Fifth Avenue and cross it, passing the exclusive **Saks Fifth Avenue** department store. Between 50th and 51st streets rises:

***ST. PATRICK'S CATHEDRAL ❺**, ☎ 212-753-2261. *Open daily 6:30 a.m. to 8:45 p.m. Free. Tours by appointment.*

    This Gothic Revival structure, built between 1858 and 1879, is New York City's major Roman Catholic cathedral, and represents the success of the Irish immigrants in a nation that was often hostile to them. Designed by the renowned architect James Renwick (of Smithsonian fame), it compares favorably with the great cathedrals of Europe and follows their cruciform layout. Deeply sculpted bronze doors open into a large nave lit by stained-glass windows from France. Of special note inside is the lovely baldachin over the high altar, and the Lady Chapel in the apse.

    The cathedral is also the focus point of the annual **St. Patrick's Day Parade**, a massive event that totally dominates Fifth Avenue from 44th to

86th streets on one boisterous day in mid-March.

Turn east on 50th Street, passing the **Villard Houses** of 1885 on the corner of Madison Avenue. Originally, these were a group of six mansions grouped around a U-shaped courtyard, but they now serve as the public rooms of the New York Palace Hotel. In another block you'll come to **Park Avenue** and **St. Bartholomew's Church** ❻. Completed in 1919 in the Romanesque style with predominantly Byzantine details, this Episcopal church is famed for its multi-colored dome, terraced garden, sculpted bronze doors, Aeolian organ, and the mosaic of the Transfiguration in the apse. Besides its spiritual offerings, the church has a delightful outdoor café, a great place to relax. ☎ *212-378-0200. Open daily 8–6. Free. Gift shop.* ♿.

Just south of St. Bart's is the luxurious **Waldorf-Astoria Hotel** of 1931. Take a look at its opulent lobby, then continue south for three blocks to where Park Avenue seems to end. Actually, it doesn't. Traffic winds its way uphill through the ornate **Helmsley Building** of 1929, built as the headquarters of the former New York Central Railroad. You may hear the rumbling of passing trains here as Park Avenue and the surrounding area for a block in either direction (and all the way up to 96th Street) is built on top of railroad yards servicing Grand Central Terminal.

Take the open passageway through the building to the front of the former **Pan Am Building** ❼, now known as the **Met Life Building** following the demise of the once-great airline. This 59-story behemoth (only the Pentagon has more office space) of 1963 was designed in part by the great Bauhaus master, Walter Gropius, and shaped to suggest an aircraft wing. It has had a strange history. The flat roof was actually a heliport for shuttling airline passengers to and from JFK International Airport, a service that was suspended due to complaints about the noise. Later resumed using quieter helicopters, the service came to a disastrous end in the late 1970s when a copter went out of control, killed several people, and dropped much of its remains into the crowded streets below.

Enter the building and stroll through its immense lobby to the south end, where you'll descend on escalators into the heart of *Grand Central Terminal* ❽. Recently restored, this gleaming Beaux-Arts masterpiece was built in 1913 to replace an earlier depot of 1871. Electrification of the line allowed the tracks, yards, and platforms to be buried in two levels under the streets and surrounding buildings, and accessed via an amazing network of corridors and tunnels. You can easily get lost in its bowels. Its *Main Concourse*, at the bottom of the escalators, is one of the world's grandest interior spaces. Look up at the ceiling, some 125 feet above your head, on which is re-created a winter night sky with thousands of luminous stars. Corridors lined with shops run off in all directions, and there are several places to stop for a drink or a snack. Although long-distance trains no longer stop here, every working day sees about 500 trains disgorge some 200,000 commuters from the northern suburbs and

Connecticut. ☎ *212-340-2345, Internet: www.grandcentralterminal.com. Free guided tours are offered on Wed. at 12:30, departing from the information booth in the center of the main concourse, ☎ 212-935-3960. Another free tour is held on Fri. at 12:30, departing from 42nd St. in front of the Phillip Morris Building on the west side of Park Ave., ☎ 212-697-1245.*

Exit onto 42nd Street and turn left. The familiar structure at the corner of Lexington Avenue is that triumph of the Art Deco style, the renowned *Chrysler Building ❾ of 1930. As it neared completion, it was the second-tallest building on Earth — but then the architect pulled his surprise and hoisted the hidden stainless-steel spire through the crown and up into the sky to capture the world's-tallest title. Alas, its moment of glory was short lived — the Empire State Building topped it the very next year. Look up at the marvelous gargoyles and other details depicting in steel the motifs of period automobiles. Although the Chrysler Corporation has long since moved out, the building is well maintained and its elaborate lobby is still a place of beauty. Pop in for a look.

Continue east on 42nd Street. Beyond Second Avenue a bridge leaps across this. If you don't mind climbing a few steps to the upper level, you can explore **Tudor City ❿**, a strange residential neighborhood that lies within the big city but seems far removed from it in spirit. Another staircase in line with 43rd Street leads down to the next attraction, which can also be reached at street level by instead staying on 42nd Street and turning left on First Avenue. However you get there, you are now facing the:

*UNITED NATIONS HEADQUARTERS ⓫, First Ave. at 46th St., New York, NY 10017, ☎ 212-963-8687, Internet: www.un.org. *Guided tours leave the visitor's entrance at 46th St. frequently from 9:15–4:45, daily except weekends in Jan. and Feb. Tours: Adults $7.50, seniors (60+) $6, students $5, children (grades 1–8) $4, disabled 20% discount. Children under 5 not admitted. Special exhibits. Gift shop. Bookstore. Restaurant. &.*

When you step beyond the entrance gate, you have left the jurisdiction of the United States and entered international territory, where American laws do not apply. The only way to see the interior is to take a 45-minute **guided tour**, which includes a visit to the General Assembly along with other highlights. The extent to which you might enjoy this tour depends to a great extent on your attitude toward the U.N. and your interest in their activities. When finished, you might visit the rose garden and statuary park, which offers fine views of the East River.

Back on American soil, or concrete, amble up First Avenue to 49th Street and turn right on Mitchell Place. In another block make a left onto **Beekman Place ⓬**, a somewhat hidden little residential street that has long been home to celebrities and billionaires seeking a quiet spot of their own. During the Revolutionary War the British headquarters was located here, and it was here that they tried Nathan Hale as a spy, and hung him. Turn right at the street's end, 51st Street, where you'll find steps leading down to the East River. The climb down — and back up — is somewhat steep, but the views compensate.

Head west on 51st Street to **Greenacre Park** ⓭, a well-hidden little oasis halfway between Second and Third avenues. Like Paley Park off Fifth Avenue, this secluded gem — open to the public — includes a waterfall, benches and tables, and a snack bar offering sandwiches, drinks, and the like — a great place for a rest stop.

Continue to Third Avenue and turn north for two blocks, then left on 53rd Street to Lexington Avenue. Above you towers the shining expanse of **Citicorp Center** ⓮, a highly unusual skyscraper of 1978 that stands on four stilts above its indoor courtyard and attached church. Its sloping roof was intended to provide power by collecting the sun's rays, but that never worked out. A dynamic device called a Tuned Mass Damper balances the structure against winds and movements in the earth. Despite this, the tower had a close brush with disaster when, shortly after completion, someone noticed a fatal flaw in the engineering. Corrections were immediately undertaken, but before they could be installed the city received a hurricane warning. Fearful of the whole thing being blown over, officials prepared an evacuation plan for the entire neighborhood. Fortunately, the hurricane turned out to sea, and the modifications were completed. Be sure to explore its inner courtyard, lined with shops and eateries; and don't miss the attached **St. Peter's Lutheran Church**, a strikingly modern sanctuary noted for its jazz concerts.

Head up Lexington Avenue, passing the **Central Synagogue** of 1870, and turn left on swanky **East 57th Street**. Lined with the poshest of antique shops, art galleries, and boutiques, this is one of the most elegant thoroughfares in America. Cross Park Avenue and continue across Madison Avenue. On the left is the **IBM Building** ⓯, which sports an unusually attractive public atrium with comfortable seats and a snack bar. The same building also houses, on its Madison Avenue side, the **Newseum/NY**, a public exhibition of news gathering and media affairs. ☎ *212-317-7596, Internet: www.mediastudies.org. Open Mon.–Sat. 10–5:30. Free.* ♿.

Immediately south of this is the **Sony Wonder Technology Lab** ⓰ in the Sony Building. Here you can try out all sorts of electronic marvels and techno wizardry. ☎ *212-833-8100, Internet: www.sonywondertechlab.com. Open Tues.–Sat. 10–6, Sun. noon–6. Free.* ♿.

You are now only two blocks from your starting point.

*Central Park and the Museum Mile

You'll never exhaust all of the treats along this one-day walking tour — not in a day, not in a week, not in a year, maybe not even in a lifetime. So, you'll have to carefully choose which of the many renowned museums along the route interest you most, and which of the countless gems within them to head for. As a double treat, most of the route takes you through what is surely one of the world's greatest urban parks, a delightful place whose features are as varied as the museums along its perimeter.

For many New Yorkers, the very best thing about their city is Central Park. Over two miles long by a half-mile wide, this oasis encompasses everything from the most genteel of diversions to near-wilderness areas. The need for an urban retreat became apparent as early as the 1840s. At that time this was a swampy wasteland, occupied by squatters and pigs. By the 1850s public interest had been aroused, the land acquired, and landscape architects Frederick Law Olmsted and Calvert Vaux chosen to design the project. Work began in 1857, continuing for nearly 20 years as the "ugly and repulsive wasteland" was transformed into a picturesque, romantic 19th-century concept of idealized "nature," complete with lakes, ponds, pastoral meadows, and formal gardens.

Several of the world's greatest art museums line this route. If you intend to visit more than one of them, you should beware of the infamous Stendhal Syndrome, a quasi-medical condition in which the poor victim is reduced to utter fatigue from the ecstasies of too much culture at one time. Go easy, visit only one museum, and then only the parts of it that really interest you. You can always come back for more on another day.

GETTING THERE:

See page 18 for general transit information.

By Subway, the closest service is to take the N or R *(BMT Broadway local)* train to the Fifth Avenue stop. Alternatively, you might take the B or Q *(IND Sixth Avenue express)* train to 57th Street, or the numbers 4 or 5 *(IRT Lexington Avenue express)* or number 6 *(IRT Lexington Avenue local)* to 59th Street.

By Bus, the start of this walk is served by the number M-1, M-2, M-3, M-4, or M-5 buses to 59th Street, or the Q-32 to Fifth Avenue, or the crosstown M-31 or M-57 to Fifth Avenue at 57th Street.

By Taxi, ask the driver for Fifth Avenue and 59th Street.

On Foot, chances are that the Grand Army Plaza entrance to the park is within walking distance of your hotel.

PRACTICALITIES:

Good weather is absolutely essential for an enjoyable stroll through the park, although not for the museums. Be sure to check the closing days for the museums you're interested in as they vary quite a bit.

Taken all the way, this walk is between four and five miles in length, nearly level all the way and with many places to stop for a rest. By studying the map and eliminating a few sites you could cut the distance down to two or three miles. Be sure to wear appropriate shoes.

Despite stories to the contrary, Central Park is a safe place to visit as long as you stick to populated areas. Those exploring the Ramble or some of the northern sections should remain alert, and everyone should avoid the park at night — except when there are special events going on. Remember that there is always safety in numbers.

Information concerning Central Park can be had from the Reception Center at The Dairy, south of 65th Street and just west of the zoo, ☎ 212-794-6564, Internet: www.centralparknyc.org. For general tourist information see page 24.

FOOD AND DRINK:

Some good choices for lunch in and around Central Park include:

Tavern on the Green (just inside the park at West 67th Street) American cuisine in a wonderland setting, with outdoor dining in season. Reservations suggested, ☎ 212-873-3200. $$$

Boathouse Café (at the boathouse on the lake opposite East 74th Street) A wide range of contemporary American dishes right on the water's edge. Reservations suggested, ☎ 212-517-2233. $$$

Café des Artistes (1 West 67th Street) Dress nicely and reserve for this romantic French getaway, a longtime favorite. ☎ 212-877-3500. $$ and $$$

Shun Lee (43 West 65th Street) Hunan and Szechwan cuisine in a busy, friendly setting. ☎ 212-595-8895. $$

Metropolitan Museum Restaurant and Café (in the Metropolitan Museum of Art, 1st floor) A convenient, lively and attractive place for lunch. Reservations recommended for the full-serve restaurant, which also features Sunday brunch. The adjoining cafeteria has much the same offerings at lower prices. There are also cafés scattered all over the museum. ☎ 212-570-3711. X: Mon. $, $$, and $$$

Sarabeth's at the Whitney (in the Whitney Museum) Lunches and weekend brunches overlooking the sculpture garden. X: Mon., evenings. ☎ 212-570-3670. $$

Museum Café (in the Guggenheim Museum) Light meals and desserts in a setting designed by Frank Lloyd Wright. X: Sun., evenings from

Mon.–Thurs. ☎ 212-423-3500. $

In addition, Central Park has numerous push-cart food vendors, especially in the southern parts, as well as cafés around the Zoo, the Conservancy Water, and The Lake. You might even bring your own picnic lunch.

SUGGESTED TOUR:

Circled numbers in text correspond to numbers on the map.

Like the previous trip, this one begins at **Grand Army Plaza ❶**, an elegant square bordered by prestigious shops, the sumptuous Plaza Hotel, and Central Park. Horse-drawn **carriage rides** through lower portions of the park are available here; if you are tempted to take this romantic option be sure to settle on the price first, as they are quite expensive. Those continuing on foot should enter the park through the **Scholar's Gate** at Fifth Avenue and 59th Street. From here stroll down the pleasant promenade, passing some of the 8,968 benches that provide welcome relief for footsore pedestrians all over the park. Just beyond the cafeteria and gift shop is the delightful:

*CENTRAL PARK WILDLIFE CENTER ❷, 830 Fifth Ave. at 64th St., ☎ 212-861-6030, Internet: www.wcs.org/zoos. *Open daily 10–5. Adults $3.50, seniors (65+) $1.25, children (3–12) 50¢. Café. Gift shop.* ♿.

Formerly known as the **Central Park Zoo**, this venerable institution has in recent years gone through a vast transformation for the better. Gone are the cages, gone are the larger animals. Today the zoo focuses on small, naturalistic environments grouped into three climatic regions: the Tropic Zone, the Temperate Territory, and the Polar Circle. Visitors get quite close to the animals, separated from them by glass walls. While this is not a great, comprehensive zoo, it is an enjoyable — and enlightening — experience well worth making.

Directly opposite the zoo, facing Fifth Avenue, is the ivy-covered **Arsenal**, an early 19th-century military structure that today houses park offices and a free exhibition relating to the park. Just north of it you will pass under the charming **Delacorte Clock**, a mechanical musical affair featuring an hourly parade of bronze animals. Beyond this, on the right, is the **Children's Zoo ❸**, where kids can pet domestic animals. After the underpass, bear left and follow the map. As you amble along you'll notice many large rock outcroppings. These are no ordinary rocks. *Manhattan schist,* as it's called, is the very foundation of Manhattan Island — the stuff that holds up its skyscrapers. Dig a deep enough hole anywhere on the island and this is what you'll hit.

Continue on to **The Mall ❹**, a long, formal promenade lined with stately elms and statues of famous writers. Today this is a favorite venue for rollerbladers, who show off their skills to appreciative crowds. At the far end, cross the 72nd Street Transverse and descend the staircase to the

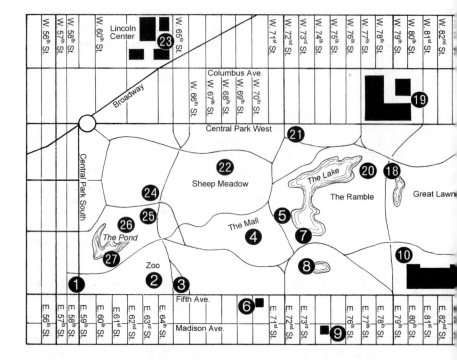

ornate ***Bethesda Fountain** ❺ with its famous *Angel of the Waters* statue of 1868. Behind this spreads **The Lake**, a meandering body of water used by rowboats and the occasional Venetian gondola. A particularly lovely bridge leads to the woods beyond, but skip that for now as you'll be coming back this way.

At this point, lovers of classical art might want to make a little **sidetrip** over to Fifth Avenue and the:

***FRICK COLLECTION** ❻, 1 East 70th Street, ☎ 212-288-0700, Internet: www.frick.org. *Open Tues.–Sat. 10–6, Sun. 10–6. Closed Mon., New Year's Day, July 4, Election Day, Thanksgiving, Dec. 24–25. Adults $10, seniors (61+) and students with ID $5. Children under 10 not admitted, ages 11–15 must be accompanied by an adult.* ♿.

This is no ordinary art museum; rather it is a magnificent mansion built in 1914 for the industrialist Henry Clay Frick (1849–1919), who made a vast fortune in coal and steel. Despite his brutal business tactics, Frick had impeccable taste and collected only the very finest examples of European art from the early Renaissance to the late 19th century. The 40-room residence has been kept pretty much as it was when the Fricks lived there. Besides the many paintings adorning the various rooms, there are classic

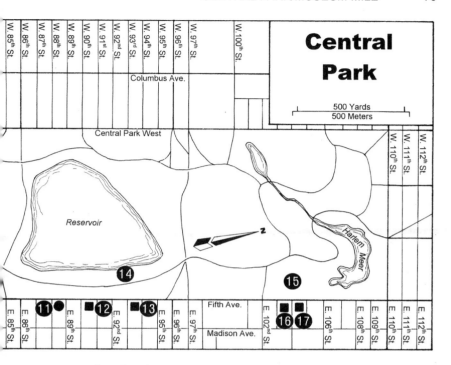

Central Park

500 Yards
500 Meters

examples of sculpture and the decorative arts. Among the talents represented are Rembrandt, Titian, Vermeer, Fragonard, Holbein, Gainsborough, Turner, Constable, Whistler, Bellini, Veronese, El Greco, Goya, Velasquez, van Eyck, Corot, Boucher, and Renoir. What a treat — and what a place to view them in! When your eyes tire of all that richness, you can always step out into the serene *Garden Court with its greenery, pool and fountain.

This part of Fifth Avenue is a good spot for enjoying one of New York's colorful festivities, such as the Saint Patrick's Day Parade, the Salute to Israel Parade, the Puerto Rican Day Parade, the German-American Steuben Parade, and the Columbus Day Parade. For details, see page 22.

Back in Central Park, follow a path to the Loeb Boathouse ❼, where you can rent a rowboat or a bicycle for exploring under your own muscle power. The boathouse also has a snack bar as well as an upscale restaurant.

Now stroll on over to the Conservatory Water ❽, a rather formal pond used by model boat enthusiasts. On its west side is a favorite spot for New York's children, the statue of *Hans Christian Andersen,* where on Saturday mornings storytellers often entertain the little ones. Kids also love the statue of *Alice in Wonderland,* which they can climb all over, at the pond's northern end. Along the eastern side is the **Ice Cream Café** with its out-door tables, a welcome source of refreshment by now. Also here (in season) is a cart from which you can rent radio-controlled model boats and join in the fun.

From here, both Fifth and Madison avenues are lined with some of the world's major art museums, extending north for about a mile, and known as **Museum Mile**. You might consider making a sidetrip to one — or even two — of them, or come back and enjoy them more leisurely on another day. They are the:

WHITNEY MUSEUM OF AMERICAN ART ❾, 945 Madison Ave. at 75th St., ☎ 212-570-3676, advance tickets 1-877-WHITNEY, Internet: www.whitney.org. *Open Tues.–Thurs. 11–6, Fri. 1–9, Sat.–Sun. 11–6. Closed Mon., New Year's Day, Thanksgiving, Christmas. Adults $10, seniors (over 62) and students with ID $8. Children under 12 free. Restaurant. Museum shop. &.*

For living American artists, this is the most important museum on Earth. Have just one of your works exhibited here and your reputation (and income) soars. From the outside, the Whitney looks like a brutal concrete fortress, brooding heavily over Madison Avenue and approached only by a bridge over what appears to be a sunken moat. Designed by the noted architect Marcel Breuer, the cantilevered structure was built in 1966 and enlarged in 1997. Inside, however, is an ingeniously designed museum filled with contemporary American works, including many by famous artists who were alive when Gertrude Vanderbilt Whitney began the collection in 1930 but who have since passed on. As important as the permanent collection most surely is, the museum is equally noted for its **Whitney Biennial**, a often-controversial presentation of what's happening in the American art scene. This is held from March to June in odd-numbered years, and you'd best get reserved tickets well in advance.

*THE METROPOLITAN MUSEUM OF ART ❿, Fifth Ave. at 82nd St., ☎ 212-535-7710, Internet: www.metmuseum.org. *Open Tues.–Thurs. 9:30–5:30, Fri.–Sat. 9:30–9, Sun. 9:30–5:30. Closed Mon., New Year's Day, Thanksgiving, Christmas. Suggested admission: Adults $10, seniors (over 64) and students with ID $5, accompanied children under 12 free. Admission includes The Cloisters (see page 91). Concerts. Lectures. Tours. Restaurant. Cafeteria. Cafés. Bookshop. Gift shops. Audio guide rentals in six languages, $5. &, wheelchairs available.*

New Yorkers never tire of the Met, coming back time and again to rejoice in what is probably the world's greatest collection of art in all its forms. And not only New Yorkers — after all, this is the city's number one tourist attraction. It would take you weeks to see everything on display here, so the best plan of attack is to decide on what interests you most and come back at another time when you can devote the better part of a day to it. Barring that, even a short visit of just a few hours is certainly worthwhile.

Spanning a time frame of over five thousand years and encompassing the whole world, the collections include superb examples of just about anything that can be considered art — from Egyptian mummies and African masks to clocks, guns, and musical instruments. And yes — there are paintings and sculptures, thousands and thousands of them — along with costumes, photographs, architecture, furniture, a Chinese garden, Islamic art, and much, much more.

Stop at the information desk just inside the main entrance to pick up a free floor plan of the collections, possibly taking one of the free introductory tours to help you decide what to focus on. Alternatively, you might just stroll around, serendipitously chancing on unexpected treasures. Either way, you'll have a great time.

SOLOMON R. GUGGENHEIM MUSEUM ⓫, 1071 Fifth Ave. at 89th St., ☎ 212-423-3500, Internet: www.guggenheim.org. *Open Sun.–Wed. 9–6, Fri.–Sat. 9–8. Closed Thurs., Christmas, New Year's Day. Adults $12, seniors (over 64) and students with ID $8, children under 12 free. Café. Museum store.* ♿.

Once controversial, Frank Lloyd Wright's bold white spiral of a building seems tame compared to some of the world's latest museum creations. In fact, this 1959 structure has already achieved official landmark status — and Fifth Avenue would look odd without it. Its main exhibition space is a downward spiral of galleries, where the floor always slopes just a little, putting visitors ever so slightly off balance. In 1992 this was augmented with a ten-story skylit tower, effectively doubling the exhibition space. While the Guggenheim is most noted for its temporary exhibitions of modern art, its permanent collection contains stunning works by such artists as Brancusi, Braque, Calder, Chagall, Delaunay, Giacometti, Kandinsky, Klee, Léger, Miró, Picasso, and van Gogh.

COOPER–HEWITT NATIONAL DESIGN MUSEUM ⓬, 2 East 91st St. at Fifth Ave., ☎ 212-849-8400, Internet: www.si.edu/ndm. *Open Tues. 10–9, Wed.–Sat. 10–5., Sun. noon–5. Closed Mon., New Year's Day, July 4, Thanksgiving, Christmas. Adults $8, seniors and students with ID $5, children under 12 free. Bookstore. Gift shop.* ♿.

This outpost of the Smithsonian Institution is devoted to both design and the decorative arts and is housed in a fabulous 64-room mansion built in 1901 for industrialist Andrew Carnegie. Although the museum is most noted for its **temporary exhibitions**, it does have a very extensive **permanent collection** of metalwork, woodwork, jewelry, ceramics, textiles, wallpaper, ornamental and architectural drawings, and other examples of the decorative arts spanning some 3,000 years of world history. The mansion itself is a great attraction, as is its romantic garden.

THE JEWISH MUSEUM ⓭, 1109 Fifth Ave. at 92nd St., ☎ 212-423-3200,

Internet: www.thejewishmuseum.org. *Open Sun.–Mon. and Wed.–Thurs. 11–5:45, Tues. 11–8. Closed Fri., Sat., Jewish holidays. Adults $8, seniors (over 64) and students with ID $5.50, under 12 free. Café. Gift shop.* ♿.

Yet another grand mansion houses the magnificent Jewish Museum, the largest in the nation devoted to Jewish history and culture. Exhibits here take visitors on a 4,000-year journey through the Jewish experience, brought to life with rare artifacts from Biblical to modern times. There are also works by leading contemporary artists and changing exhibitions on Jewish matters.

If you skipped the museums, you can just wander up Fifth Avenue to the next destination. However you get there, re-enter the park at 90th Street. Straight ahead, slightly elevated, is the **Jacqueline Kennedy Onassis Reservoir** ⑭, a functioning part of New York's water supply system and a favorite venue for runners, joggers, and just plain walkers. A pathway completely circles this body of water, and provides access to some charming vistas. Climb up to the path and turn right, heading north.

If you're really ambitious, you could return to Fifth Avenue at 96th Street and make another **sidetrip**, hiking north for about a half mile to 104th Street and the **Conservatory Garden** ⑮. From late spring through early fall, these delightfully romantic gardens are in full bloom, with hidden little pathways leading to secret corners.

Just across Fifth Avenue from the garden are two museums that might interest you:

MUSEUM OF THE CITY OF NEW YORK ⑯, 1220 Fifth Ave. at 103rd St., ☎ 212-534-1672, Internet: www.mcny.org. *Open Wed.–Sat. 10–5, Sun. noon–5. Closed Mon.–Tues., Jan. 1, Thanksgiving, Dec. 25. Suggested contribution: Adults $7, seniors (over 64), students with ID, and children $4. Gift shop.* ♿.

The whole long history of the city is chronicled with artifacts, prints, photos, maps, costumes, videos, furniture, art, and actual room settings. There are also excellent temporary exhibitions on city-related matters.

EL MUSEO DEL BARRIO ⑰, 1230 Fifth Ave. at 104th St., ☎ 212-831-7272, Internet: www.elmuseo.org. *Open Wed.–Sun. 11–5. Closed Mon.–Tues. Suggested contribution: Adults $5, seniors and students $3, children free.* ♿.

Latino culture, both Caribbean and Latin American, is celebrated through changing exhibitions, art, photography, film, video, and other media. Of special note are the collections of pre-Columbian art and *Santos de Palo* (carved figures of saints).

Back at the north end of the Reservoir, continue strolling westward on the waterside jogging trail. Just beyond a stone structure by the water's edge, the splendidly ornate **Gothic Bridge** leaps across a bridle path and its occasional equestrian traffic. The jogging trail now turns south, with nice views to either side. When you reach the southern end of the Reservoir, make a right turn over a bridge and continue south past the **Great Lawn**, a wide open space used for concerts, softball, touch football, soccer, and the like.

You will soon come to the **Delacorte Theater**, where outdoor performances of Shakespearean plays are given in summer. Behind the stage is a small lake, and rising above that, the incredible visage of *Belvedere Castle ⑱. Built in 1869 in the style of a small, medieval Scottish castle, this fanciful folly is a scene right out of a fairy tale. For a long time it was used as a weather station; it now sees service as an information and learning center. Be sure to climb up to it for the very best view from the park, then continue south on a path through the **Shakespeare Garden**, where you can enjoy every plant and herb mentioned in the Bard's works.

From here it is possible to make a short **sidetrip** to Central Park West and the:

*AMERICAN MUSEUM OF NATURAL HISTORY ⑲, Central Park West at 79th Street, ☎ 212-769-5100, Internet: www.amnh.org. *Open Sun.–Thurs. 10–5:45, Fri.–Sat. 10–8:45. Closed Thanksgiving and Christmas. Suggested admission: Adults $10, seniors and students with ID $7.50, children (under 12) $6; additional admissions for IMAX theater and Planetarium, combo tickets available. Cafeteria. Gift shop. Tours.* ♿.

Founded in 1869 and occupying the present premises since 1877, this stupendous museum has in recent years been thoroughly refurbished and brought into the 21st century with new thinking and state-of-the-art displays. Kids absolutely adore it, and even grownups will have a wonderful time exploring everything from dinosaurs to outer space. Still, as one of the largest — if not *the* largest — museums on Earth, it can wear you down with a tiring trek through miles of corridors and millions of displays. Be selective, study a diagram of the layout, and decide on what you want to see — leaving the rest for a later day.

Pride of place in the museum of course goes to the *Dinosaur Halls, where the prehistoric creatures have been imaginatively rearranged in dramatic action settings; a far cry from the musty displays of yesteryear. Other particularly outstanding exhibits include the **Hall of African Mammals**, the **Hall of African Peoples**, the **Hall of Asian Peoples**, the **Pacific Northwest Hall**, the **Hall of Human Biology and Evolution**, and the **Hall of Meteorites**. And, of course, there's the ever-popular **IMAX Theater** and the renowned **Hayden Planetarium**; both with a separate admission.

Back in the park via the Hunter's Gate at 79th Street, cross the bridge spanning the 79th Street Transverse and bear left, finding your way through a wooded area called **The Ramble** ⑳. You'll probably get lost here, but eventually find your way out of the twisting paths. The Ramble is probably the closest thing to a real wilderness to be found in Manhattan, and a popular spot for bird watching and other nature pursuits. Be careful, though — this is no area to visit after dark or when there are few other people around. If in doubt, just follow the path alongside the roadway instead.

At the bottom of The Ramble is the gorgeous *Bow Bridge** of 1879, crossing a narrow part of The Lake. Once across, bear right, following the water's edge around to its southern end and continuing west to Central Park West and 72nd Street. On the northwest corner here is **The Dakota**, a massive apartment building built in 1884, when this part of town was considered to be "as remote as the Dakota Territory." Many famous personalities have lived here, and still do, but one event in particular stands out. On December 8, 1980, former Beatle and Dakota resident John Lennon was murdered on the sidewalk outside the building by a disturbed fan. Lennon's wife, Yoko Ono, later petitioned City Hall for a living memorial just inside the park from the scene of the crime. This three-acre oasis of quiet and reflection is known as **Strawberry Fields** ㉑ and is adorned with a mosaic spelling out the word *Imagine*. Numerous fans still gather here to remember Lennon, and perhaps their own youth.

Heading southeast through the park brings you to the vast **Sheep Meadow** ㉒, where sheep actually grazed as late as 1934. On any fine day, especially on a summer weekend, this rolling lawn is literally covered with people out to catch a few rays. You are now very close to another attraction, one that is best left for another day. However, if you want to take a peep now, just make a **sidetrip** to the corner of West 64th Street and Columbus Avenue (one block west of the park), to visit:

LINCOLN CENTER FOR THE PERFORMING ARTS ㉓, Broadway at 64th St., ☎ 212-LINCOLN for general info or 212-875-5350 for tours, Internet: www.lincolncenter.org. *One-hour tours conducted daily at 10:30, 12:30, 2:30, and 4:30 from the concourse level beneath the Metropolitan Opera House; adults $9.50, seniors (65+) and students with ID $8, children (3–12) $4.75. Reservations strongly recommended. Other specialized tours also available. No tours on Jan. 1, July 4, Thanksgiving, Dec. 25.* ♿.

Until the late 1950s, the 14 acres that now make up Lincoln Center — as well as the surrounding area west of Broadway — were part of a run-down neighborhood best known as the setting for the film *West Side Story*. Thousands of people were evicted from their humble dwellings, and hundreds of buildings demolished, to make way for this vast center for the performing arts. At that time, both Carnegie Hall and the old Metropolitan Opera were considered to be no longer suitable for a city as culturally significant as New York, and the idea emerged of consolidating concerts, opera, ballet, and other performing arts into one grandiose complex — while at the same time revitalizing the West Side.

Arranged around a central court with its signature fountain are the major buildings of the center, all in the same architectural style of the 1960s and all looking perhaps a wee bit dated today. The most impressive, straight ahead, is the **Metropolitan Opera**, whose lobby features murals by

Marc Chagall, a marvelous double staircase, and brilliant chandeliers. To your right is **Avery Fisher Hall**, home of the New York Philharmonic. To the left is the **New York State Theater**, which houses both the New York City Opera and the New York City Ballet. Off to the sides are other theaters, a music school, a library, and Damrosch Park, where outdoor concerts are held in summer.

Back in the park, continue south through the Sheep Meadow to the **Carousel** ㉔, a classic century-old merry-go-round that still provides fun for kids and even for adults. ☎ 212-879-0244. *Operates daily from mid-March to Thanksgiving, then on weekends only. Rides $1.* To the east of this, just beyond the roadway, is the **Dairy** ㉕, a 19th-century structure that once provided fresh milk for poor children. Today it houses the park's information center as well as some exhibitions.

Directly south of here is the **Wollman Rink** ㉖, a place to ice skate in winter and roller skate in summer. Now follow the path alongside **The Pond** ㉗, bordered on the west by a bird sanctuary. Get your camera ready, because you're passing one of the classic ***views** of New York, with the buildings of Central Park South reflected in the water, framed by an arched bridge. This is especially lovely at twilight in winter, just after a fresh snowfall. In only a few more steps you'll be back where you started this walk.

The Wollman Rink in Central Park

Upper Manhattan

Often overlooked by visitors, the upper reaches of Manhattan are home to such diverse attractions as the (surprise!) world's largest cathedral, one of the nation's major universities, an interdenominational church with the greatest carillon on Earth and a fabulous view to go with it, the elaborate tomb of a U.S. president, an unusual grouping of small museums, one of the greatest bridges anywhere, and a fortified medieval cloister complex transplanted to the New World and stuffed with art treasures. All along the way are magnificent panoramic vistas across Manhattan and the Hudson Valley, and closeup views of colorful ethnic enclaves. Perhaps best of all, there is very little walking involved as nearly all of this trip can be made by bus.

GETTING THERE:

Bus is definitely the way to go on this trip. Arm yourself with an unlimited-ride MetroCard (see page 19) and board a northbound M-4 bus, which runs from Pennsylvania Station, east across 32nd Street, then north on Madison Avenue and west on 110th Street (Central Park North, becoming Cathedral Parkway). Get off at the corner of Amsterdam Avenue and Cathedral Parkway. This same bus route takes you to all of the destinations, so you'll be hopping on and off it several times. Allow plenty of time as there's a long distance to cover, passing through diverse neighborhoods.

By Subway is faster but less enjoyable, and involves more walking. Take the number 1 or 9 *(IRT Broadway/Seventh Ave. local)* train to Cathedral Parkway (110th St.) and walk east one block OR the B *(IND Sixth Ave. express)* or C *(IND Eighth Ave. local)* train to Cathedral Parkway and walk west three blocks. After seeing the cathedral, campus, church, and tomb you should really travel by bus to the other destinations.

PRACTICALITIES:

Bear in mind that the Cloisters are closed on Mondays, and some other sights on a few major holidays. Otherwise, this trip can be made on any day in good weather. Again, since you'll be taking several rides on public transportation, you should use the economical and convenient unlimited-use **MetroCard** (see page 19). For general **tourist information** see page 24.

FOOD AND DRINK:

The area around Columbia University abounds in unusual, casual, inexpensive eateries; with a wide variety of ethnic cuisines as well as standard fare available. Beyond that the pickings get mighty slim. A few choices are:

Obaa Koryoe (3143 Broadway, south of 125th St.) Authentic, tasty West African dishes in a comfortable setting. ☎ 212-316- 2950. $$

Zula Café (1260 Amsterdam Ave. at 122nd St.) Excellent Ethiopian cuisine, popular with Columbia students. ☎ 212-663- 1670. $$

Mill Korean Restaurant (2895 Broadway at 112th St.) A wide variety of traditional Korean dishes at modest prices. ☎ 212- 666-7653. $ and $$

Tom's (2880 Broadway at 112th St.) A typical diner with typical diner food, made famous on the *Seinfeld* TV series. ☎ 212-864-6137. $

Amir's Falafel (2911A Broadway, between 113th and 114th streets) *Falafel, shwarma, baba ghanoush, musakaa,* and other Middle Eastern treats; all at very low prices. Nothing fancy. ☎ 212-749-7500. $

Hungarian Pastry Shop (1030 Amsterdam Ave. at 111th St.) Great pastries and coffees in a moody, bohemian setting — or out on the sidewalk. The strudel is fabulous. ☎ 212-866-4230. $

SUGGESTED TOUR:

Circled numbers in text correspond to numbers on the map.

Begin you tour at the corner of Cathedral Parkway and Amsterdam Avenue, where the M-4 bus stops and within an easy walk of two subway lines. Head uphill north for two blocks to the:

*CATHEDRAL OF ST. JOHN THE DIVINE ❶, 1047 Amsterdam Ave., ☎ 212-316-7540, Internet: www.stjohndivine.org. *Open Mon.–Sat. 7–6, Sun. 7–8. Suggested donation $2. Tours on Tues.–Sat. at 11, Sun. at 1, $3. Vertical tours (on foot) to the top on 1st and 3rd Sat. of each month at noon and 2, reservations and $10 advance payment required,* ☎ *212-932-7347. Gift shop.* &.

It may seem strange that the world's largest cathedral is right here in New York, not in Rome or Paris or London. This Gothic masterpiece was begun way back in 1892 and is still under construction, still a long way from completion. Much of the work is being done in the tradition of the Middle Ages, with local stonemasons working as they would have centuries ago, and without the benefits of a steel frame. Current estimates call for completion of the structure sometime in the middle of the 21st century.

When finished, the west front will have two Gothic towers soaring to a height of 266 feet. Between them is the magnificent, already-completed ***Portal of Paradise** with its double set of bronze doors depicting scenes from the Old and New Testaments. A statue of St. John the Divine separates the doors, and above the portal is a tympanum showing *Christ in Majesty.*

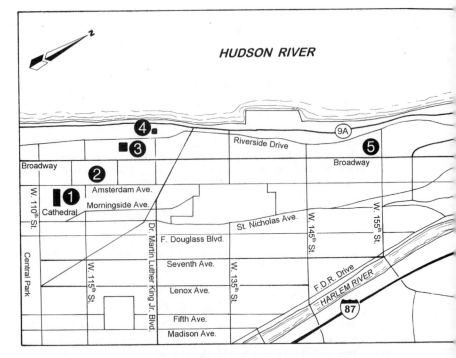

Enter through the narthex into the enormous *nave, itself the size of two football fields. Running down either side of this are chapels, several of which reflect the church's commitment to contemporary social problems such as racism or AIDS. From the crossing on, the Gothic style gives way to the earlier Romanesque of the original 1888 design, which was scrapped in 1907. The transepts are still under construction. Beyond here lies the choir, the high altar, and the ambulatory; and to the north the **baptistry**, decorated with figures from the early history of New York. Be sure to visit the extensive gift shop just off the north aisle at the crossing.

Besides its normal Episcopal services, the cathedral is noted for many special events, such as the Blessing of the Animals on St. Francis of Assisi's feast day in October, and the winter solstice celebration of contemporary world music. It also houses numerous works of art ranging from Raphael to Keith Haring, and is the venue for lectures, poetry readings, dance, drama, art exhibitions, and other secular happenings.

Outside, on the cathedral grounds, is a Biblical Garden, a Rose Garden, a Peace Fountain, and other delightful finds as well as an opportunity to observe medieval-style construction in progress.

Stroll north on Amsterdam Avenue to West 114th Street and turn left. On your right are steps leading onto the campus of **Columbia University**

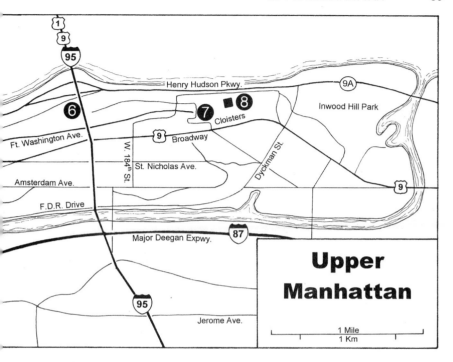

❷, a leading Ivy League school founded in 1754 as King's College by a charter from King George II of England. Originally located in lower Manhattan, it was the *alma mater* of such early luminaries as Alexander Hamilton and Chief Justice John Jay. Renamed Columbia College following the American Revolution, it moved first to Madison Avenue at 49th Street and later, in 1897, to this location, occupying the site of a former insane asylum. Straight ahead, dominating the formal Beaux-Arts layout is the elegant ***Low Memorial Library** of 1898. Modeled after the Pantheon in Rome, this is now used for administrative offices and also houses the **Visitors Center.** *Walking tours of the main campus are available,* ☎ *212-854-4900 to make arrangements. A virtual tour can be taken on the Internet at www.columbia.edu.*

Right in front of the library is the grand 1903 statue of *Alma Mater* by Daniel Chester French, who also did the famous likeness of a seated Lincoln in Washington. In 1968 this was the focus of student riots protesting the war in Vietnam. Take a few steps to the right to see another famous statue, a casting in bronze of *The Thinker* by Rodin, located in front of Philosophy Hall. As you wander around the 36-acre campus you'll encounter other notable sculptures by Lipchitz, Henry Moore, and others. Follow the map north, taking the steps down to West 120th Street. Turn left and walk three blocks to Riverside Drive and the renowned:

RIVERSIDE CHURCH ❸, 490 Riverside Drive, ☎ 212-870-6700, Internet: www.theriversidechurchny.org. *Bell tower open Tues.– Sat. 11–4, Sun. 12:30–4. Bell tower visits $2, seniors and students $1. Gift shop. Partially* ♿.

Built in the late 1920s and inspired by the great Cathedral of Chartres in France, Riverside Church is an interdenominational, interracial, and international Christian community with a strong focus on contemporary social issues. Pass through the west portal, whose columns are carved with figures from the Old and New Testaments. Above this is a figure of *Christ in Majesty*. Inside, at the far end of the narthex (vestibule), are two 16th-century ***stained-glass windows** originally made for the Cathedral of Bruges in Belgium. A stairway here leads down to the Visitor Center, where you can purchase tickets for the Bell Tower. Near this is a door leading to an outdoor garden with its *Madonna and Child* sculpture by Sir Jacob Epstein.

Also at this level is the elevator that whisks you up 20 stories to begin your visit to the ***Bell Tower** and its world-famous ***carillon**. From the top of the elevator you climb 147 steps past the carillon mechanism, on what becomes a narrow staircase winding its way through the 74 bells. The magnificent ***view** from the top, spreading across the city, the bay, Long Island, and up the Hudson River makes the strenuous climb all worthwhile.

Return to the ground floor and visit the Gothic-style **nave**, which seats 2,500 worshipers. The **clerestory windows** here are duplicates of those in Chartres, while the capitals of the supporting columns tell the story of the prophet Jeremiah. In the rear, at the gallery level, is a golden *Christ in Majesty* **sculpture** by Epstein. The **pulpit**, made of limestone, is carved with the façades of ten European cathedrals. Beyond this, on the chancel floor, is a miniature replica of the medieval labyrinth at Chartres.

Exit the church and stroll a few steps over to:

GRANT'S TOMB ❹, Riverside Drive at 122nd St., ☎ 212-666-1640, Internet: www.nps.gov/gegr. *Open daily 9–5. Closed Jan. 1, Thanksgiving, Christmas. Free.*

Operated by the National Park Service, this white granite mausoleum is more than just a tomb; it also celebrates the life of the Civil War hero and 18th U.S. President Ulysses S. Grant (1822–85) with displays and artifacts. Long neglected — and covered with graffiti — the tomb was restored in 1996 and is now in fine condition. Just behind the structure are some very strange park benches, obviously inspired by the creations of Antonio Gaudí at Parc Güell in Barcelona.

Head east on West 122nd Street, cross Broadway, and there board the northbound M-4 bus, first making sure that it is marked Ft. Tryon/Cloisters. This ride takes you through a variety of colorful ethnic neighborhoods, so get a window seat and enjoy the sights. Along the way are two other attractions that you might want to stop for, the first being **Audubon Terrace ❺** at West 155th Street. This was once part of the estate of John James Audubon (1785–1851), the famous ornithologist. Since the early 20th century it has been home to a few minor museums built on an impressive terrace that was intended to help gentrify this out-of-the-way neighborhood. It failed to do that, and its institutions remain rather isolated but still worthwhile if their subjects interest you. The *Hispanic Society of America**, devoted to the cultures of Spain and Portugal, has a wonderful collection of art by such masters as El Greco, Goya, and Velázquez. Covering a time span from pre-Roman days to the present, the museum takes a sweeping view of the life and times of the Iberian peninsula. ☎ 212-926-2234, Internet: www.hispanicsociety.org. Open Tues.–Sat. 10–4:30, Sun. 1–4. Free. In the same grouping, the **American Numismatic Society** traces the history of coinage (and money in general) from ancient to modern times, with one of the world's leading collections on display. ☎ 212-234-3130. Open Tues.–Fri. 9–4:30. Free. Lastly, there is the **American Academy of Arts and Letters**, which is open only during special exhibitions. ☎ 212-368-5900 for current schedules.

Continuing uptown on the M-4 bus, at 178th Street you'll pass the *George Washington Bridge** ❻. When it opened in 1931, this was the world's longest suspension span, and is still the only one with 14 lanes of traffic. Much of its beauty is due to the fact that it was never really completed. The original plans called for it to be sheathed in stone, but the Great Depression put a stop to such extravagance, leaving the open steel framework as an elegant expression of the modern age. You can actually walk across the bridge to New Jersey, which you might want to consider for the trip beginning on page 244.

At West 190th Street the bus reaches **Fort Tryon Park** ❼, the end of the line for those buses not marked "Cloisters." The park offers ruins of Fort Tryon, one of the last defensives to fall to the British in 1776. There are also superb views across the Hudson River. It is entirely possible to walk from here to the next destination, but you're better off taking the bus. However you get there, don't miss:

*THE CLOISTERS** ❽, Fort Tryon Park, ☎ 212-923-3700, Internet: www.met museum.org. Open March–Oct., Tues.–Sun. 9:30–5:15; Nov.–Feb., Tues.–Sun. 9:30–4:45. Suggested admission: Adults $10, seniors (over 64) and students with ID $5, accompanied children under 12 free. Guided tours March–Oct., Tues.–Fri. at 3, Sun. at noon. Admission includes same-day visit to the Metropolitan Museum of Art (see page 80). Museum shop. Partially ♿.

In a serene setting high atop a hill overlooking the Hudson Valley, the marvelously medieval Cloisters is home to much of the Metropolitan Museum's vast collection of art from the Middle Ages. Even if this does not thrill you, the complex of buildings, the stunning views, and the tranquil atmosphere of the place surely will. Five medieval cloisters were brought here from France, stone-by-stone, reassembled as parts of an earlier museum, and moved to this location in the late 1930s through the generosity of billionaire John D. Rockefeller Jr. To these were added modern reproductions of monasteries in the Romanesque and Gothic styles. Among the treasures on display are the renowned *Unicorn Tapestries, woven in Brussels around 1500, the *Nine Heroes Tapestries* of 1385, and exquisite German stained glass from the 15th century. There are, of course, the delightful cloisters themselves, especially the intimate **Trie Cloister**. Be sure to stroll out into the gardens to enjoy their fragrance along with the river views.

Return to midtown Manhattan via the M-4 bus, which stops just out-side the entrance. This is a very slow ride during peak traffic periods. If you're in a hurry, get off at the bottom of Fort Tryon Park and take the A train subway *(IND 8th Avenue Express)* from West 190th Street, which goes down the length of Manhattan's West Side, through Brooklyn, and out beyond JFK Airport.

In The Cloisters

Brooklyn Heights to Prospect Park

One of the most enjoyable — and relaxing — daytrips you can make within the city is to amble across the marvelous Brooklyn Bridge, explore the old waterfront area, drink in the charm of Brooklyn Heights, delight in the stupendous views from its Promenade, visit a few minor museums, and possibly continue on by bus to the famous (and sometimes infamous) Brooklyn Museum, the Brooklyn Botanic Garden, and Prospect Park.

GETTING THERE:

By Subway via a walk across the Brooklyn Bridge: Take the number 4 or 5 *(IRT Lexington Avenue express)* or the number 6 *(IRT Lexington Ave. local)* train to Brooklyn Bridge/City Hall, **OR** the A *(IND Eighth Avenue express)* or C *(IND Eighth Avenue local)* to Fulton Street and walk north a few blocks.

By Subway direct to Brooklyn: Take the F train *(IND Sixth Avenue local)* to York Street and walk west a few blocks, **OR** the A *(IND Eighth Avenue express)* or C *(IND Eighth Avenue local)* to High Street, **OR** the number 2 or 3 *(IRT Seventh Avenue express)* to Clark Street. In every case these are the first stops in Brooklyn. If you end you trip in the Heights you will probably want to return from one of these stops instead of walking back across the bridge.

By Bus: Your only option is to take the B-51 bus from City Hall/Park Row in lower Manhattan, which crosses the Manhattan Bridge.

By Cab: Ask the driver for Cadman Plaza in Brooklyn Heights, and have a map handy to show him.

PRACTICALITIES:

This trip can be enjoyed on any day in fine weather, but if you intend to visit the Brooklyn Museum you should avoid Mondays and Tuesdays. For general **tourist information** see page 24.

FOOD AND DRINK:

There are many eateries in the Heights, especially around Montague Street. Just south of this, Atlantic Avenue is lined with Middle Eastern restaurants. Some choices are:

The River Café (1 Water St., base of Brooklyn Bridge) Brooklyn's renowned River Café offers a fabulous view of Manhattan along with its innovative American cuisine. Dress well and reserve, ☎ 718-522-5200. $$$+

Gage & Tollner (372 Fulton St. at Jay St., near the Transit Museum) This classic old-time restaurant has been around since 1879, serving steaks and seafood with a Southern touch. ☎ 718-875-5181. X: Sun. $$

Caravan (193 Atlantic Ave., between Court and Clinton streets) Middle Eastern cuisine in a neighborhood that's famous for it. ☎ 718-488-7111. $ and $$

Petite Crevette (127 Atlantic Ave., between Henry and Clinton streets) An inexpensive place for simple seafood dishes, with some choices for landlubbers. ☎ 718-858-6660. $

Junior's (386 Flatbush Ave. at DeKalb, east of the Fulton Mall) Exceptionally tasty diner fare, and world-famous for its cheesecake. ☎ 718-852-5257. $

SUGGESTED TOUR:

Circled numbers in text correspond to numbers on the map.

What better way to approach Brooklyn than to walk across the famous ***Brooklyn Bridge** ❶? You could, of course, get to the Heights by subway, but a stroll across this span is an experience you'll remember for a long time. Enjoy the views. A description and history of this most famous of bridges can be found on page 34.

At the Brooklyn end, follow a pedestrian ramp to Cadman Plaza, stroll through the park, and turn right to Old Fulton Street. Paralleling the base of the bridge, this leads west under the Brooklyn-Queens Expressway and into the historic **Fulton Ferry Terminal area** ❷. A ferry service connecting Brooklyn, then a separate city, with Manhattan operated from here between the late 18th century and the opening of the bridge in 1883. Shortly thereafter, Brooklyn lost its independence and in 1898 became a part of New York City. The old warehouses lining these narrow streets have largely been converted into art galleries, performance spaces, desirable residences, upscale restaurants, and the like. One that remains itself is the **Watchtower Building**, world headquarters of the fundamentalist Jehovah's Witnesses faith. Stroll under the bridge to explore **Fulton Ferry Park**, then return to Old Fulton Street.

Now follow the map south on Columbia Heights, turning right onto the **Promenade** ❸, a pedestrian walkway offering unparalleled, breathtaking ***views** of Lower Manhattan and the entire Upper Bay. The houses to your left, set well back from the walkway, are among the most sought-after residences in town. Continue south to Montague Street and step down into the narrow lanes of Brooklyn Heights.

Heading north on Willow Street takes you past rows of 19th-century houses dating back as far as 1825. Turn right on Orange Street to the **Plymouth Church of the Pilgrims** ❹. Built in 1846, this Congregational

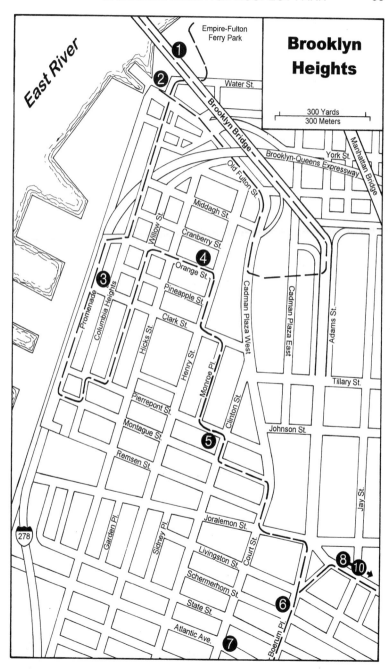

Brooklyn
Heights

300 Yards
300 Meters

East River

Empire-Fulton
Ferry Park

Water St.

Brooklyn Bridge

York St.

Manhattan Bridge

Brooklyn-Queens Expressway

Old Fulton St.

Middagh St.

Willow St.

Cranberry St.

Orange St.

Pineapple St.

Cadman Plaza West

Cadman Plaza East

Adams St.

Promenade

Columbia Heights

Hicks St.

Clark St.

Henry St.

Monroe Pl.

Clinton St.

Tillary St.

Pierrepont St.

Montague St.

Johnson St.

Remsen St.

Jay St.

Garden Pl.

Sidney Pl.

Joralemon St.

Livingston St.

Court St.

278

Schermerhorn St.

State St.

Boerum Pl.

Atlantic Ave.

church was from 1847 until 1887 the preaching base for Henry Ward Beecher, remembered for his anti-slavery and women's rights oratory as well as for being the brother of Harriet Beecher Stowe, author of *Uncle Tom's Cabin*. Among the people who were attracted to his sermons here were Abraham Lincoln, Mark Twain, and Horace Greeley.

Turn south on Henry Street, passing the venerable **Saint George Hotel**, once the largest in New York. It has since been converted to housing. Go east on Clark Street for one block, then south on Monroe Place and east on Pierrepont Street. At number 128 is the **Brooklyn Historical Society ❺**, with displays on the colorful past of the borough. Along with early history, these cover the construction of the bridge, the social impact of Coney Island, and the much-loved and much-missed Brooklyn Dodgers baseball team. ☎ *718-624-0890, Internet: www.brooklynhistory.org. Open Mon. and Thurs.–Sat., noon–5. Adults $2.50, seniors (64+) and children (1–12) $1.*

A block south on Clinton Street stands the **St. Ann and the Holy Trinity Church**, noted for its vast expanse of stained glass as well as for its involvement in the performing arts. Take Montague Street east to Court to Court Street, there turning south to Joralemon Street and the impressive **Brooklyn Borough Hall** of 1851. Now follow the map for three more blocks to the **New York Transit Museum ❻**, hidden away in an abandoned subway station. Mass transit is what makes New York function; without it all would come to a grinding halt. The entire history of this marvelous system is recalled with documents, photos, artifacts, and a collection of vintage subway cars of various ages that you can stroll through. ☎ *718-243-8601, Internet: www.mta.nyc.ny.us/museum. Open Tues.–Fri. 10–4, Sat.–Sun. noon–5. Adults $3, seniors and children $1.50. ♿, call ahead.*

Atlantic Avenue ❼ is just two blocks south of here, and if you're hungry you might want to stroll down it. This is the center of New York's vibrant Middle Eastern community, with many inexpensive restaurants featuring Lebanese, Yemeni, and similar cuisines. There are also colorful ethnic groceries, bakeries, and even antique shops.

Return to Joralemon Street and head east past Borough Hall on Fulton Street. This pedestrianized thoroughfare, known as the Fulton Mall, is a major shopping venue and a lively place to wander through. Continue on it to Flatbush Avenue and there board a southbound B-41 bus to the:

*BROOKLYN MUSEUM OF ART ❽, 200 Eastern Parkway at Washington Ave., ☎ 718-638-5000, Internet: www.brooklynart.org. *Open Wed.–Fri. 10–5, Sat.–Sun. 11–6. Closed Mon., Tues., Jan. 1, Thanksgiving, Christmas. Suggested donation: Adults $6, seniors and students $3, under 12 free. Gift shop. Café. ♿.*

New York's other great museum spanning the entire scope of art is right here in Brooklyn, where its location makes it much quieter and less crowded than Manhattan's Metropolitan (see page 80). Its special exhibitions have of late sometimes been more daring, more avant-garde, and certainly more controversial than its rival across the river. In fact, a recent

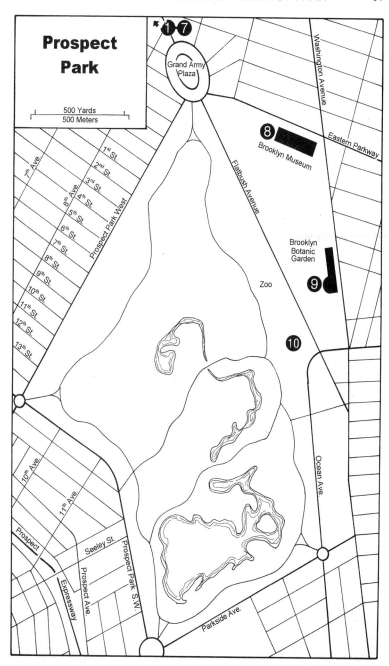

Prospect
Park

500 Yards
500 Meters

Grand Army Plaza

Washington Avenue

Eastern Parkway

Brooklyn Museum

Flatbush Avenue

Brooklyn
Botanic
Garden

Zoo

7th Ave.

1st St.
2nd St.
3rd St.
4th St.
5th St.
6th St.
7th St.
8th St.
9th St.
10th St.
11th St.
12th St.
13th St.

8th Ave.

Prospect Park West

10th Ave.

11th Ave.

Prospect
Expressway

Seeley St.

Prospect Ave.

Prospect Park S.W.

Parkside Ave.

Ocean Ave.

show raised such a fuss that the mayor threatened to close down the entire museum. That aside, the regular permanent collections include one of the world's greatest gatherings of Egyptian artifacts, wonderful Middle Eastern, Greek, and Roman antiquities, primitive art from around the world, Asian galleries, European art from medieval to modern, and vast holdings of major American art. You'll surely come across some surprises here, and wonder why more visitors don't make it this far.

Immediately south of the museum is the *Brooklyn Botanic Garden 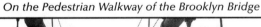, one of the finest in the nation and a must-visit for anyone with a green thumb. Established in 1910 and spreading over 52 acres, it has a series of specialized gardens for all tastes. ☎ *718-622-4433, Internet: www.bbg.org. Open April–Sept. Tues.–Fri. 8–6, Sat.–Sun. and holidays 10–6; Oct.–March, Tues.–Fri. 8–4:30, Sat.–Sun. and holidays 10–4:30. Adults $3, seniors and students $1.50, children under 16 free. Gift shop. Café. ♿.*

Stretching to the south of here is the vast 526-acre **Prospect Park**, an urban oasis of civilization brought to you by the same folks who built Manhattan's Central Park. You might want to go for a stroll before returning to Manhattan via the number 2 or 3 subway train from the museum, the D train from the Botanic Garden, or the F train from the west side of the park.

On the Pedestrian Walkway of the Brooklyn Bridge

Northern Staten Island

Yes, this is still New York City, even though you may think you're just about anywhere else. Staten Island, 14 miles long and 8 miles wide, is New York's forgotten borough; a place that periodically attempts to secede but has not yet succeeded in doing so. First discovered by the Italian explorer Giovanni da Verrazano in 1524, it was given the name *Staaten Eyelandt* by Henry Hudson in 1609 while on a business trip for the Dutch East India Company. The island remained an isolated backwater, more attuned to nearby New Jersey than to far-off Manhattan, and reachable only by boat. Then, in 1964, the Verrazano Narrows Bridge, the world's second-longest suspension span, opened to traffic, bringing an Interstate highway in its wake.

Despite its sleepy history, Staten Island does have some surprisingly good attractions; enough in fact to warrant two daytrips. This excursion covers the area north of the expressway, the following one some real gems to the south. As a bonus, those coming by ferry get to experience one of the very best half-hour voyages anywhere.

GETTING THERE:

By Public Transportation: A short half-hour voyage on the Staten Island Ferry is surely the most enjoyable way to reach this outpost of N.Y.C. It leaves from the southern tip of Manhattan, and it's free. See page 27 for details. From the terminal you can take public buses to the various attractions.

By Car, take I-278 via the Verrazano Narrows Bridge (from Brooklyn) or the Goethals Bridge (from New Jersey) to Staten Island, then head north on Bay St. Follow around past the ferry terminal to the Snug Harbor Cultural Center on Richmond Terrace. The Zoo is about a mile south of this, on Broadway. The Austen House is at the north end of Hylan Blvd., near the expressway, and the Garibaldi-Meucci Museum nearby on Tompkins Ave. Return to the ferry terminal, close to which is the Staten Island Institute of Arts & Sciences. Note that it is also possible to bring your car over on the ferry, for which there is a charge.

PRACTICALITIES:

The Children's Museum, Alice Austen House, and Garibaldi-Meucci Museum are closed on Mondays, and the Austen House also on Tuesdays.

Clear weather will insure good views of New York harbor and the skyline. Those traveling around by bus rather than private car should invest in a one-day **Metro Card** (see page 19). For further information contact the **Staten Island Tourism Council**, One Edgewater Plaza, Whitehall and South streets, Staten Island 10305, ☎ 718-442-4356 or 1-800-573-SINY, Internet: www.ci.nyc.ny.us/statenislandtourism.

FOOD AND DRINK:

Other than the usual fast-food outlets and chain restaurants, there are precious few places to eat in this part of Staten Island. Here is a suggestion:

Melville's Café (in the Snug Harbor Cultural Center) Light lunches, soups, sandwiches, and the like. ☎ 718-816-0011. X: evenings, weekends. $

LOCAL ATTRACTIONS:

Circled numbers in text correspond to numbers on the map.

Begin at the **St. George Ferry Terminal** ❶, arrival point for the renowned Staten Island Ferry, departure point for the island's buses, northern terminus of the Staten Island Railway, and location of a huge commuter parking lot. The present rather dingy terminal is to be completely rebuilt in the near future, and will include a new waterfront museum. The new National Lighthouse Museum will open nearby at the old Coast Guard base. From here you can either drive or board bus S-40, heading west on Richmond Terrace to the:

SNUG HARBOR CULTURAL CENTER ❷, 1000 Richmond Terrace, Staten Island, NY 10301, ☎ 718-448-2500, Internet: www.snug-harbor.org. *Open daily, 9–dusk. Visitor Center, Botanical Gardens, site, parking free. Fee for individual museums, below. Free tours on Sat. & Sun. at 2. Gift shop. Café. Partially ♿.*

Still a work-in-progress, Snug Harbor represents an ambitious plan to transform an entire 83-acre National Landmark District into a major metropolitan cultural center. While much of it has yet to be realized, there is easily enough here to keep you busy for an hour or two. Originally, this campus-like complex was built in the early 19th century as a retirement home for "decrepit, worn-out sailors;" a rather elegant collection of columned Greek Revival structures facing the Kill Van Kull and Upper New York Bay. Ask for a free map at the Visitors Center before wandering around.

Much of the site is occupied by the **Staten Island Botanical Gardens**, a place of subtle beauty all year round. Within its 50 acres are found natural areas, both fresh and saltwater wetlands, woodlands and meadows, and formal gardens. These include the English perennial border, the pond garden, and the rose, herb, sensory, potager, and white gardens. There are also parterres, a conservatory, and good bird-and-butterfly observations. ☎ *718-273-8200, Internet: www.sibg.org. Open daily during daylight hours.*

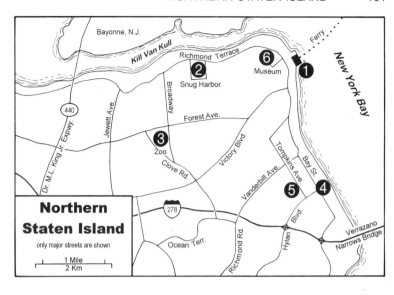

Snug Harbor Cultural Center

Free. Gift shop. Café. Chinese Scholar's Garden open Tues.–Sun. 9–5, admission $5. &.

Behind this is an outdoor theater for summer concerts and, to the east, the **Staten Island Children's Museum** with its hands-on fun activities. Kids can exercise their imaginations at the WKID-TV studio, the Walk-In Workshop, Block Harbor, and the interactive Portia's Playhouse. ☎ *718-273-2060. Open in summer, Tues.–Sun. 11–5; during the school year, Tues.–Sun. noon–5. Admission $4 for everyone 2 years and older. Gift shop.* &.

Changing exhibitions of regional and national significance are featured at the **Newhouse Center for Contemporary Art** in the Main Hall. ☎ *718-448-2500. Open Wed.–Sun., noon–5. Donation requested.* Next door to this is the **John A. Noble Collection**, where maritime life is celebrated through art, photography, models, videos, artifacts, and more. ☎ *718-447-6490. Open Mon.–Fri., 9–2. Donation requested.*

Continue west on bus S-40 to Port Richmond Terminal, and there transfer to an S-53 bus going southeast to the:

STATEN ISLAND ZOO ❸, 614 Broadway, Staten Island, NY 10310, ☎ 718-442-3101, Internet: www.statenislandzoo.org. *Open daily 10–4:45, closed Thanksgiving, Christmas, New Year's. Adults $3, children (3–11) $2, under 3 free; free to all on Wed. after 2. Snack bar, "Zoovenir" shop, pony rides.* &.

New York City's "biggest little zoo" makes a delightful short stop, especially for those with kids in tow. Its world-renowned **Serpentarium** abounds with snakes and other lovable reptiles, while exotic maritime creatures including sharks swim about in the **Aquarium**. The **South American Tropical Forest** offers a boardwalk journey through an exotic forest teeming with life, an ecological theme echoed in the **African Savannah**, a natural habitat simulated in its twilight. For kids, there's the **Children's Center** — a New England farm setting reached via a covered bridge and a duck pond.

Continue south on bus S-53 to School Road, just before the huge bridge, and transfer to the S-51 northbound along Bay St. to Hyland Blvd. and the:

ALICE AUSTEN HOUSE ❹, 2 Hylan Blvd., Staten Island, NY 10305, ☎ 718-816-4506, Internet: www.aliceausten.8m.com. *Open Thurs.–Sun., noon–5. Closed major holidays and Jan.–Feb. Suggested donation $2. Gift shop. Partially* &.

Alice Austen (1866–1952) lived in this cozy Victorian cottage overlooking the Narrows nearly all her life, and it was here that she practiced her remarkable career as an amateur photographer. From 1884 until 1934, she passionately documented social life on Staten Island, in Manhattan, in Chicago, and even in Bavaria. Many of these photos are on display in the restored house, affording visitors a fantastic glimpse into the past.

Northbound bus S-51 heads back to the ferry terminal, or you can stroll west a few blocks to Tompkins Ave., turning north to the nearby:

GARIBALDI-MEUCCI MUSEUM ❺, 420 Tompkins Ave., ☎ 718-442-1608. *Open Tues.–Sun. 1–5. Closed major holidays. Suggested donation $3.*

Giuseppe Garibaldi (1807–82), the hero of the Italian Revolution, lived here in exile in 1850 before returning to the homeland to continue the struggle for unification. This simple farmhouse was the home of his friend, an Italian-American inventor named Antonio Meucci, who developed the first working telephone in 1857. Defrauded by a business partner and unable to finance the development of his invention or the continuation of his provisional patent, he died a broken man in 1889, while another gentleman named Bell patented his own version of the device in 1876. This is why you have probably never heard of Meucci.

From here, northbound bus S-52 or S-78 will return you to the ferry terminal, near which is the:

STATEN ISLAND INSTITUTE OF ARTS & SCIENCES ❻, 75 Stuyvesant Place, one block west of Richmond Terrace, Staten Island, NY 10301, ☎ 718-727-1135, Internet: www.siias.org. *Museum open Mon.–Sat. 9–5, Sun. 1–5; Ferry Collection daily 8–1. Both closed major holidays. Suggested donation for museum: Adults $2.50, seniors & children $1.50; Ferry Collection: Adults $1, children 25¢. Gift shop.*

Located just three blocks west of the ferry terminal, the venerable SIIAS is one of New York City's oldest cultural institutions. Its collections, both permanent and temporary, focus on the fine and decorative arts, the natural sciences, and especially on local Staten Island history. A special treat is the **Ferry Collection**, appropriately installed in the ferry terminal itself, right in the main waiting room. Here you can examine artifacts from the long history of the Staten Island Ferry while enjoying the view.

Staten Island South of the Expressway

S taten Island south of the I-278 expressway looks even less like New York City that does its northern section — and much more like sub-urban New Jersey. Still, there are some real gems to be found lurking among the developments. Enough, in fact, to keep you busy all day.

GETTING THERE:

By Public Transportation: From the tip of Manhattan, a half-hour ride on the Staten Island Ferry brings you to the ferry terminal at the northern end of Staten Island. See page 27 for details. Here board bus number S-74, taking you to the Historic Richmond Town and within walking distance of the Tibetan Museum. The same bus route terminates in Tottenville, just a few blocks from the Conference House. Return to the ferry terminal directly on bus number S-78.

By Car, take I-278 via the Verrazano Narrows Bridge (from Brooklyn) or the Goethals Bridge (from New Jersey) to Staten Island, then head south on Richmond Road (NOT Richmond Ave.!) to Clarke Ave. From here follow signs into the **Historic Richmond Town** parking lot.

Return on Richmond Rd., soon turning left uphill to Lighthouse Ave. and the **Tibetan Museum**.

Continue west on Arthur Kill Rd., then south (left) on Richmond Ave. to Hylan Blvd. Turn right (west) and follow Hylan Blvd. to its end in Tottenville, where you'll find the **Conference House**. From Times Square in Manhattan to the farthest point is about 26 miles by road, a bit less by ferry.

Note that you can also bring your car over on the ferry, for which there is a charge.

PRACTICALITIES:

Avoid making this trip on a Monday or Tuesday, when everything is closed. Note that the Tibetan Art Center is open from April through November, and by appointment the rest of the year. The Conference House is open on Fridays through Sundays only. Check the opening times carefully before venturing forth. Good weather will greatly enhance this trip. Those traveling around by bus rather than private car should invest in a one-day **Metro Card** (see page 19). For further information contact the

Staten Island Tourism Council, One Edgewater Plaza, Whitehall and South streets, Staten Island 10305, ☎ 718-442-4356 or 1-800-573-SINY, Internet: www.ci.nyc.ny.us/statenislandtourism.

FOOD AND DRINK:

There are very few really good places to eat along this route, although fast-food emporiums abound. Some suggestions are:

The Old Bermuda Inn (2512 Arthur Kill Rd. at Bloomingdale Rd., just off NY-440 exit 4, 2 miles northeast of the Conference House) It's only open for dinner, but the superb Continental cuisine served in this intimate 1830 Victorian mansion makes a fine finale to your day. ☎ 718-948-7600. X: lunch, Sun., Mon., Tues. $$$

Goodfella's Old World Pizza (1716 Hylan Blvd., 2 miles south of I-278, at Garreston Ave.) Real brick-oven pizza, plus pastas and salads. ☎ 718-987-2422. $ and $$

There is also a convenient **snack bar** at Historic Richmond Town.

LOCAL ATTRACTIONS:

Circled numbers in text correspond to numbers on the map. Head straight to:

*HISTORIC RICHMOND TOWN ❶, 441 Clarke Ave., Staten Island, NY 10306 ☎ 718-351-1611, Internet: www.historicrichmondtown.org. *Open July–Aug., Wed.–Fri. 10–5, Sat.–Sun. 1–5; rest of year Wed.–Sun. 1–5. Closed Easter, Thanksgiving, Christmas, New Year's Day. Adults $5, seniors, students, and children (6–18) $2.50. Gift shop. Snack bar. Activities. Partially ᵫ.*

You'd never guess that you're actually in New York City as you stroll around this restored village of 17th- to early 20th-century buildings! Costumed craftspeople go about their historic tasks as docents in period dress lead you through the open houses. To date, some 27 structures ranging from the Voorlezer's House of 1695 to public buildings of the late 1800s have been restored, and work continues on others. Don't miss the marvelous **Historical Museum**, where Staten Island's rich heritage from the earliest beginnings right up to recent decades is explored in exceptionally interesting exhibits.

From here you can walk or drive to the nearby:

*JACQUES MARCHAIS CENTER OF TIBETAN ART ❷, 338 Lighthouse Ave., Staten Island, NY 10306, ☎ 718-987-3500. *Usually open Apr.–Nov., Wed.–Sun. 1–5; rest of year by appointment Wed.–Sun.1–5. Closed some major holidays. Adults $3, seniors $2.50, children $1. Special Sun. programs are $3 extra. Call ahead for current info.*

A peaceful Oriental garden surrounds two exotic stone buildings overlooking New York Bay. One of these, resembling a Tibetan lamasery, houses a large collection of Tibetan and other Buddhist art, while the

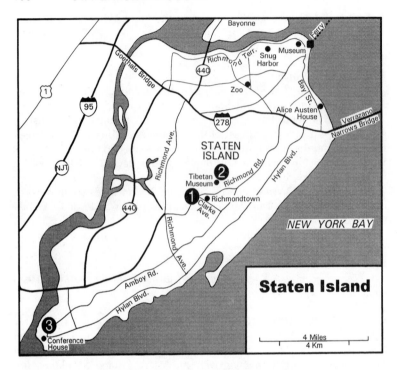

other is a gift shop for related items from the Orient. While Jacques Marchais never traveled to Tibet, she (her real name was Jacqueline!) did own a Manhattan art gallery specializing in these lovely objects.

Bus S-74 continues west to the end of its route at Main St. in Tottenville. From here it's a short walk down Main and west on Hylan to the:

CONFERENCE HOUSE ❸, 7455 Hylan Blvd., Staten Island, NY 10307, ☎ 718-984-6046. *Open Fri.–Sun. 1–4, but call ahead. Adults $2, seniors and children under 12 $1.*

Standing at the foot of Hylan Boulevard is a 1670s stone manor house with period furnishings, a working kitchen, and a beautiful rolling lawn. This was the site, in 1776, of the only peace conference of the American Revolution — a dramatic but unsuccessful meeting between Benjamin Franklin, John Adams, Edward Rutledge, and Britain's Lord Admiral Howe.

Section III

DAYTRIPS IN THE HUDSON VALLEY

New York's Hudson Valley is one of the Northeast's greatest scenic splendors, a place whose beauty launched an entire school of uniquely American landscape painting. Generous as it is in natural glories, it is even richer in history. Discovered by Giovanni da Verranzano in 1524 and later explored by Henry Hudson in 1609, it was first settled by the Dutch in the mid-1600s. Native Americans had of course been here long before that. In 1664 the land came under English rule, and during the Revolutionary War several battles were fought near its banks.

Stretching some 315 miles to the north, the Hudson is actually a tidal estuary from Albany south, being as wide as three and a half miles in places, and as deep as 216 feet. In many ways it is highly reminiscent of Germany's Rhine, especially where it cuts through mountain gorges. The best parts of this dramatic landscape are explored in the 12 daytrips that follow, first going north up the east bank, then up the west bank. By making overnight stops, you could combine several of them into a mini-vacation.

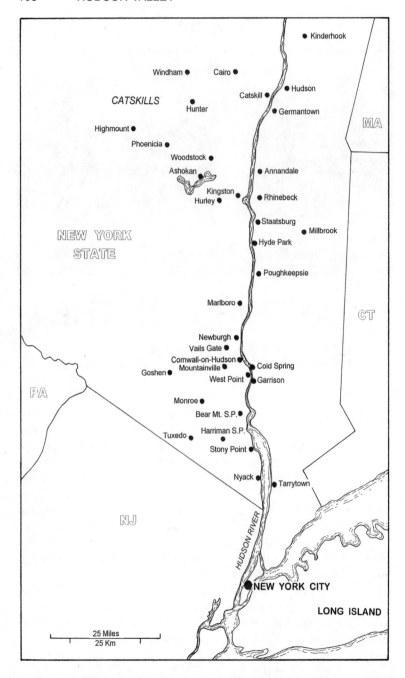

Sunnyside to Tarrytown

Overlooking the widest section of the Hudson River at the point where it is spanned by the majestic Tappan Zee Bridge, the old village of Tarrytown is steeped in history and preserves several of the most intriguing sites from America's past. Its name may derive from the Dutch word *tarwe*, meaning "wheat," or, as Washington Irving conjectured, from the tendency of the early menfolk to tarry too long in the local tavern. In any case, you'll want to tarry too, so allow plenty of time for these treats. This trip combines well with the next one.

GETTING THERE:

By Car, Tarrytown is about 25 miles north of midtown Manhattan. Take the **New York State Thruway** north to Exit 9 at Tarrytown and pick up **US-9** (Broadway) south a mile to Sunnyside, on the right.

Go back to US-9, turn left, and go north 3/4 mile to Lyndhurst, on the left.

By Train: This area is served by frequent commuter trains operated by the Metro-North Railroad from Grand Central Terminal in Manhattan. For schedules ☎ 1-800-638-7646 or 212-532-4900, Internet: www.mta.nyc.ny.us. Unless you don't mind walking a few miles, you'll need a taxi to the sites.

By Boat: New York Waterway offers all-inclusive tours by boat, leaving from Manhattan's Pier 78 at West 38th Street. These operate on weekends from mid-May to early November. They also have a regular ferry service to Tarrytown. For details and reservations ☎ 1-800-533-3779, Internet: www.nywaterway.com.

PRACTICALITIES:

Sunnyside is closed on Tuesdays, weekdays in March, and from January through February. Lyndhurst is closed on Mondays (except holidays) from mid-April through October, and on weekdays from November until mid-April (except for holiday Mondays). For further information contact the sites or the **Westchester County Office of Tourism**, 235 Mamaroneck Avenue, White Plains, NY 10605, ☎ 1-800-833-WCVB or 914-948-0047, Internet: www.westchesterny.com.

FOOD AND DRINK:

Some good choices for lunch in Tarrytown are:

Equus (400 Benedict Ave., about a miles east of the Tappan Zee Bridge)

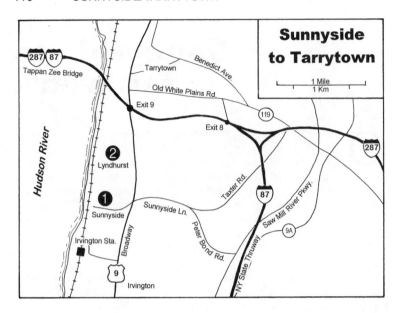

Romantically situated in a stone castle overlooking the Tappan Zee, this French restaurant features contemporary cuisine. Dress well and reserve. ☎ 914-631-3646. $$$

Caravela (53 N. Broadway, US-9, in downtown Tarrytown) Portuguese and Brazilian specialties, especially seafood. ☎ 914-631-1863. $$

Horsefeathers (94 N. Broadway, US-9, downtown Tarrytown) Whether it's a sandwich or a steak dinner. this casual pub is noted for its tasty, home-style cooking. ☎ 914-631-6606. $ and $$

Santa Fe (5 Main St., downtown Tarrytown) A lively place for southwestern cuisine — tacos, fajitas, quesadillas, and the like. ☎ 914-332-4452. $ and $$

Main Street Café (24 Main St., downtown Tarrytown) A wide range of moderately-priced dishes is offered at the locally popular spot. ☎ 914-524-9770. $

There are seasonal cafés at both Sunnyside and Lyndhurst, both with light lunches. Picnicking is also possible at both.

LOCAL ATTRACTIONS:

Circled numbers in text correspond to numbers on the map.

*SUNNYSIDE ❶, West Sunnyside Lane, Tarrytown, NY 10591, ☎ 914-631-8200, Internet: www.hudsonvalley.org. *Open Wed.–Mon. 10–5, closing at 4 in off-season. Closed weekdays in March. Closed Jan.–Feb., Thanksgiving, Dec. 25. Adults $8, seniors (59+) $7, children (6–17) $4. Gift shop. Café.*

Picnic facilities. Partially &.

Washington Irving, the first American to achieve a literary reputation abroad, made his home here in what he described as "a little old-fashioned stone mansion, all made up of gable ends, and as full of angles and corners as an old cocked hat." An apt description of this most picturesque of houses, and an apt dwelling for the author of *The Legend of Sleepy Hollow* and *Rip Van Winkle*. Sunnyside is just as it was in Irving's day, and you can look out over the same views he loved so much, of the Tappan Zee and the beautiful clear pond he called his "little Mediterranean."

From here, you can either drive via Broadway (US-9) or walk a short distance along the Croton Aqueduct Trail to nearby:

LYNDHURST ❷, 635 S. Broadway, Tarrytown, NY 10591, ☎ 914-631-4481, Internet: www.lyndhurst.org. *Open mid-April through Oct., Tues.–Sun. and holiday Mondays, 10–5, last entrance at 4:15; Nov. to mid-April, weekends and holiday Mondays only, 10–4, last entrance at 3:30. Adults $10, seniors $9. students (12–17) $4, under 12 free. Guided tours, self-guided audio or brochure tours. Gift shop. Café. Special events.* &.

This masterpiece of Gothic Revival architecture, maintained by the National Trust for Historic Preservation, was designed by Alexander Jackson Davis for New York City mayor William Paulding and was later owned by merchant George Merritt and finally by railroad speculator Jay Gould, who in 1869 attempted to corner the gold market, setting off the notorious Black Friday panic in the investment community.

The interior is not so much a restoration as a reconciliation among the styles of the three families who lived here. Apparently nothing was ever thrown away, so the place is a treasure house of Victorian elegance. There are Tiffany glass windows, rugs of silk and silver thread, paintings by well-known artists, examples of *trompe l'oeil* decor (wood painted to look like marble, ceilings painted to look like wood), and many other striking details. Its setting on 67 landscaped acres overlooks the spectacular *Tappan Zee, a wide inland sea formed by the Hudson River and spanned by the graceful Tappan Zee Bridge.

Trip 12

More Treats at Tarrytown

Practically next door to the attractions on the previous trip, these treats are among the most exciting to be found within an hour's drive of New York City. Sleepy Hollow, as North Tarrytown is now officially called, is home to a beautifully-restored milling, farming, and trading complex that dates from early Colonial times, and is today operated as a living history site with costumed guides and an operating gristmill. This is also the departure point for tours to Kykuit, the fabulous Rockefeller estate at nearby Pocantico Hills. The Union Church features modern stained-glass windows by Marc Chagall and Henri Matisse, while the Old Dutch Church of 1685 has a suitably atmospheric cemetery recalling Washington Irving's *The Legend of Sleepy Hollow*.

This trip combines well with the previous one, especially if you're staying overnight.

GETTING THERE:

By Car: Take the **New York State Thruway** north to Exit 9 at Tarrytown and pick up **US-9** (Broadway) north about 2 miles to Philipsburg Manor, on the left. Tours of Kykuit depart from here.

Union Church is near Kykuit, about 1.5 miles east of US-9 on NY-448. Tarrytown is about 27 miles north of midtown Manhattan.

By Boat: All-inclusive excursion tours by boat and bus depart Manhattan and Weehawken, NJ in season. ☎ 1-800-533-3779, Internet: www.nywaterway.com for details and reservations.

By Train: Tarrytown is served by frequent commuter trains operated by the Metro-North Railroad from Grand Central Terminal in Manhattan. Get off at the Philipse Manor stop. For schedules call 1-800-638-7646 or 212-532-4900, Internet: www.mta.nyc.ny.us. In season, Metro-North offers all-inclusive rail/van tours, including one to Kykuit.

PRACTICALITIES:

Philipsburg Manor is closed on Tuesdays, weekdays in March, and all of January-February. Kykuit operates from late April until the beginning of November, daily except on Tuesdays. The Union Church is closed on Tuesdays and all of January-March. Reservations are not needed for individuals or groups of less than 10.

For further information contact the sites or the **Westchester County Office of Tourism**, 235 Mamaroneck Avenue, White Plains, NY 10605, ☎ 1-800-833-WCVB or 914-948-0047, Internet: www.westchesterny.com.

FOOD AND DRINK:

See page 109 for restaurants in Tarrytown. In addition, the convenient **Greenhouse Café** in the Visitor Center at Philipsburg Manor offers light lunches from May through October.

LOCAL ATTRACTIONS:

Circled numbers in text correspond to numbers on the map.

PHILIPSBURG MANOR/KYKUIT VISITORS CENTER ❶, Route US-9, Sleepy Hollow, NY 10591, ☎ 914-631-8200, Internet: www.hudsonvalley.org. *Cafeteria. Gift shop.* ₺.

This modern visitors center is the starting point for both visits to the adjacent Philipsburg Manor and for tours by van to Kykuit. Leave your car parked here.

*PHILIPSBURG MANOR ❷, Route US-9, Sleepy Hollow, NY 10591, ☎ 914-631-8200, Internet: www.hudsonvalley.org. *Open April–Oct., Wed.–Mon., 10–5; Nov.–Dec., Wed.–Mon., 10–4; March, weekends only 10–5. Closed Tues., Nov.–Dec., Thanksgiving and Dec. 25. Adults $8. seniors (60+) $7, children (5–17) $4, under 5 free. Partially* ₺.

This Dutch Colonial farm and trade center was one of the headquarters of the Philipse family's 90,000-acre empire on the Hudson. The stone manor house has been restored to its appearance of 1720, and the farm still operates much as it did then: costumed farmers still till the soil, milkmaids tend the cows, and the great millstones of the water-driven gristmill turn wheat into flour. Philipsburg is rich in history and lore. It was here that Major André was captured after conspiring with Benedict Arnold to betray West Point; it was here, with the Headless Horseman hot on his heels, that Ichabod Crane tried but failed to get over the millpond bridge. Today you see much the same landscape that Ichabod saw in his headlong flight, and you can walk over the Headless Horseman Bridge to the Old Dutch Church and cemetery.

*KYKUIT ❸, Pocantico Hills, Bedford Rd., NY-448, Sleepy Hollow, NY 10591, ☎ 914-631-8200, Internet: www.hudsonvalley.org. *Open late April to beginning of Nov., Wed.–Mon. Closed Tues. Tours depart the Visitors Center 9–4 on weekends and 9-3 on weekdays. Adults $20, seniors (60+) $19, children (5–17) $17.* ₺.

The Rockefeller Estate at Pocantico Hills, home to John Sr., John Jr., and Nelson, is renowned for both its beauty and its fabulous art collection. Begun in the early 20th century, Kykuit (pronounced *kigh-cut* and meaning "lookout") has evolved over the years, always as a comfortable home rather than an ostentatious mansion. Terraced gardens overlook the scenic Hudson Valley, and are decorated with modern sculptures by Calder, Marini, and others. More contemporary art, from Picasso to Warhol, can be admired in Nelson Rockefeller's basement gallery. Nelson (1908–79), a major figure in the modern art world, was the long-time

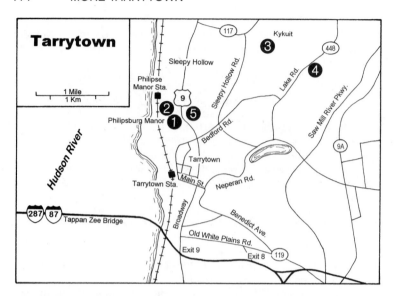

Governor of New York and later Vice-President of the United States. Along with the art and the views, the tour also includes a wonderful collection of antique carriages and automobiles.

UNION CHURCH OF POCANTICO HILLS ❹, Bedford Rd., NY-448, Sleepy Hollow, NY 10591, ☎ 914-332-6659, Internet: www.hudsonvalley.org. *Open Apr.–Dec., Wed.–Fri. 11–5, Sat. 10–5, Sun. 2–5, closed holidays and Jan.–March. Admission $3. Non-denominational services Sun. mornings.* ⟨.

In the sanctuary of this lovely stone church you can go back for a moment to the time of the Old Testament prophets depicted on seven extraordinary windows created by Marc Chagall. The stained glass gives a special translucence to the unmistakable forms and palette of this modern master. There are also two other windows by Chagall, and a beautiful rose window by Matisse, commissioned as a memorial to Abby Aldrich Rockefeller.

Back at the Visitors Center, before you leave town go across Broadway (US-9) to visit the **Old Dutch Church and Sleepy Hollow Cemetery ❺**. Dating from the 1680s, this is thought to be the oldest functioning church in New York State. Its thick stone walls were designed to withstand Indian attacks, while the adjacent cemetery was haunted by a headless horseman — providing the inspiration for Washington Irving's *The Legend of Sleepy Hollow*. The newer part of the cemetery contains the graves of several notable persons, including Washington Irving, Andrew Carnegie, and William Rockefeller.

Garrison, Boscobel, and Cold Spring

A s you venture farther north along the Hudson, you'll leave suburbia behind and enter real countryside. Here you can encounter nature at its most picturesque, renewing your spirits with invigorating walks through lovely landscapes. Your sprits can also be renewed at the gorgeous interfaith Christian Unity Center, at a leading center for the visual and dramatic arts, and by just strolling around two wonderful old riverside villages. And then there's Boscobel, an incredible estate mansion of 1804 that's been fully restored and opened to the public.

GETTING THERE:

By Car, Cold Spring is about 50 miles north of midtown Manhattan. Take the **New York State Thruway** (I-87) north to Exit 9 at Tarrytown and pick up **US-9** (Broadway) north to Graymoor. From there follow **NY-403** into Garrison, then **NY-9D** north to Boscobel. 9D continues beyond this into Cold Spring. For a faster return, take NY-301 east to US-9 and head south.

By Train: Metro-North has frequent commuter trains from Grand Central Terminal in Manhattan to both Garrison and Cold Spring, but you'll need a cab to reach the main attraction, Boscobel.

PRACTICALITIES:

This trip can be made on any day in good weather, even in winter, bearing in mind that Manitoga is closed on weekends from November through March, and that Boscobel is closed on Tuesdays and some holidays, and also from January through March. The Foundry School Museum, a minor sight, is closed on Mondays and Fridays.

For further information, phone the sites directly (or visit their web sites), or contact the **Putnam County Visitors Bureau**, 110 Old Rte. 6, Carmel, NY 10512, ☎ 845-225-0381 or 1-800-470- 4854, Internet: www.visit putnam.org.

FOOD AND DRINK:

Both Garrison and Cold Spring have interesting restaurants; here are a few choices:

Xavier's Restaurant (Highland Country Club Rd., NY-9D, south of NY-403, in Garrison) Contemporary American cuisine served in a luxurious setting. ☎ 845-424-4228. $$$

Hudson House Restaurant (2 Main St. in Cold Spring) Regional

American cuisine, in an historic landmark building right on the Hudson. ☎ 845-265-9355. $$ and $$$

Henry's-on-the-Hudson (184 Main St. in Cold Spring) A casual bistro for light lunches and full meals. ☎ 845-265-3000. $ and $$

Depot Restaurant (1 Railroad Plaza in Cold Spring) Casual dining right by the railroad tracks, indoors or out. ☎ 845-265- 2305. $ and $$

Foundry Café (55 Main St. in Cold Spring) Healthy, regional American cuisine. ☎ 845-265-4504. $

LOCAL ATTRACTIONS:

Circled numbers in text correspond to numbers on the map. You might want to begin with a visit to the:

GRAYMOOR CHRISTIAN UNITY CENTER ❶, US-9, Garrison, NY 10524, ☎ 845-424-3671, Internet: www.atonementfriars.org. *Grounds open daily 8 a.m. to 9:30 p.m. Free. Inquire about services, tours, pilgrimages, weekend retreats, weekly meetings, special programs. Picnic facilities. Gift shop. Largely ♿.*

Here, situated on top of a high hill, commanding a magnificent view, is the monastery of the Franciscan Friars of the Atonement. Pilgrims from around the world come here to attend services, visit the shrines and chapels, and make the **Stations of the Cross** at the Crucifixion Group. The Unity Center is an interfaith conference and retreat facility where people of all beliefs can heed the injunction of Isaiah 2:3: "Come, let us go up the mountain of the Lord."

Just south of Garrison, on NY-9D, is another retreat of sorts, this one a consummate harmony of aesthetics and nature:

MANITOGA ❷, NY-9D, Garrison, NY 10524, ☎ 845-424-3812, Internet: www.manitoga.org. *Trails open year round, weekdays 9–4, and also on weekends from April–Oct., 10–6. Suggested donation $4. Special events.*

Industrial designer Russel Wright spent three decades creating this strangely satisfying natural environment, whose name in the native Algonquin language means "Place of the Great Spirit." Although it appears absolutely natural, it is in fact more a theatrical stage set with a backdrop of carefully placed native trees, ferns, mosses, and wild flowers. Begun in 1942 on land that had been long damaged by logging and quarrying, it was opened to the public in 1975 as a place where all who came could experience an innate kinship with Mother Earth. Several **hiking trails** of various lengths meander through the hilly landscape, each chancing upon unexpected discoveries along the way. Don't miss taking a good look at **Dragon Rock**, Wright's own glass-walled home set on the edge of a water-filled quarry. Tours of this unique building can be made at an additional fee, but advance reservations are essential.

Head north on NY-9D into the delightful riverside community of

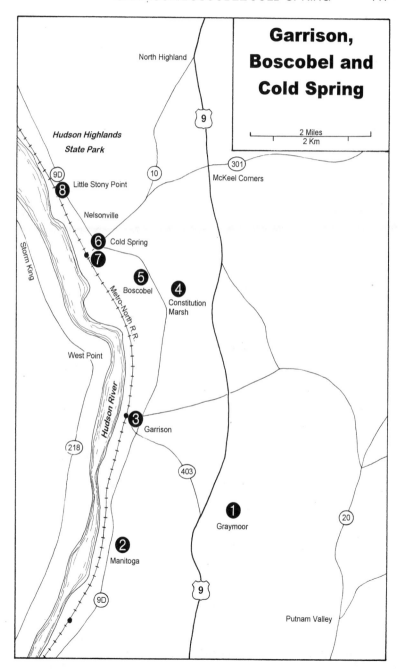

North Highland

Garrison, Boscobel and Cold Spring

2 Miles
2 Km

Hudson Highlands State Park

9

10

301

McKeel Corners

9D

8 Little Stony Point

Nelsonville

Storm King

6 Cold Spring

7

Metro-North R.R.

5 Boscobel

4 Constitution Marsh

West Point

Hudson River

3 Garrison

218

403

1

Graymoor

20

2

Manitoga

9

9D

Putnam Valley

Garrison ❸. Scenically located just across the Hudson River from the West Point Military Academy (see page 138), the hamlet is best known for its **Garrison Art Center**, a complex of century-old buildings housing exhibition galleries and studios dedicated to the visual and dramatic arts. Entrance to the galleries is free, so why not stop by for a look? *Garrison's Landing,* ☎ *845- 424-3960, Internet: www.hvgateway.com/GARRISON. Open daily noon–5.*

Heading north from Garrison on NY-9D, you'll soon come to the **Constitution Marsh Wildlife Sanctuary ❹**, a 200-acre nature preserve operated by the National Audubon Society. Self-guided walks can be taken on trails and boardwalks through this tidal marshland, where literally hundreds of bird species have been spotted, and where wild flowers abound. For a real treat, make an advance reservation in season for a guided canoe trip through a maze of old canals that fill up at high tide — remember that the Hudson River is actually tidal all the way to Albany and is strongly influenced by the Atlantic Ocean. *Indian Brook Rd., off NY-9D, Garrison, NY 10524,* ☎ *845-265-2601, Internet: www.hvgateway.com/marsh. Open daily, 9–dusk. Free.*

Just north of this, on NY-9D, is the:

*BOSCOBEL RESTORATION ❺, 1601 Route 9D, Garrison, NY 10524, ☎ 845-265-3638, Internet: www.boscobel.org. *Open April–Dec., Wed.–Mon., 9:30–5, closing at 4 in Nov.–Dec. Last tour begins 45 minutes before closing time. Closed Tues., Thanksgiving, Christmas, and all of Jan.-March. Adults $8, seniors (62+) $7, children (6–14) $5, under 6 free. Special events.*

Begun in 1804 and a flawless example of New York Federal architecture, Boscobel overlooks a rocky gorge in the Hudson Highlands where the river cuts through the Appalachian Mountain range. This is indeed a *bosco bello*, a "beautiful wood." Boscobel's builder, States Morris Dyckman, wanted the finest of everything for his dream house, and despite his wife's pleas for economy, he spared no expense. This, he told her, would be their "last sacrifice to Folly." Today, you can be glad he had his way.

Both the building and its interior were patterned after the style of Robert Adam — delicate, flowery, pleasing to the eye. The mantels and moldings are exquisitely designed; the furnishings include Ducan Phyfe pieces and much of Dyckman's original china, silver, and library. Outside, across the portico, are carvings resembling graceful draperies of wood. You can also tour the stunning formal rose garden, the orangerie and herb garden, and several original outbuildings, including the "necessary house." There is also a mile-long woodland trail cutting through 30 acres just south of the mansion.

After visiting Boscobel, you will wince to learn that it nearly fell victim to the wrecker's ball in the 1950s. It now stands 15 miles north of its original site, whence it was transported piece by piece and restored with generous support from Lila Acheson Wallace, founder of the Reader's Digest.

Head north a short distance to the scenic village of **Cold Spring** ❻, a jewel of a riverside hamlet that abounds in antique shops, boutiques, inns, and restaurants. Located just across the Hudson from the dramatic Storm King Mountain (see page 140), it also affords some stunning views. Wander down to the river, then around the village, possibly stopping at the **Foundry School Museum** ❼ on Chestnut Street. This small museum, operated by the Putnam County Historical Society, is a treasure house filled with Americana and fascinating exhibits on local history and industry. It's located in a refurbished 170-year-old three-room schoolhouse originally used by the West Point Foundry for their apprentices' and the children's education. The museum features the world-renowned painting *The Gun Foundry* by John Ferguson Weir, and has a reference library with photographs and maps, as well as genealogical and local history information. *63 Chestnut St., Cold Spring, NY 10516,* ☎ *845-265-4010, Internet: www.hvgateway.com/MUSEUM. Open Tues.–Wed. 10–4, Thurs. 1–4, Sat.–Sun. 2–5. Closed Mon., Fri., and Jan.–Feb. Donations accepted.*

For some really good views of the Hudson Valley and Storm King Mountain, head north just beyond Cold Spring to the **Little Stony Point State Park** ❽ on NY-9D just north of NY-301. Jutting out into the Hudson Fjord, its hiking trails provide some memorable vistas to enjoy before your return to the city.

Trip 14

Poughkeepsie and Hyde Park

There's plenty of history to be explored on this daytrip — along with a smattering of art and natural beauty. A truly memorable dining experience is possible, too, if you make arrangements in advance.

Of the main attractions, the Franklin D. and Eleanor Roosevelt National Historic Sites, together with the Roosevelt Library and Museum, constitute a moving memorial to the First Family that saw the nation through the Great Depression and the Second World War. The nearby Vanderbilt Mansion is, among other things, an apt expression of the class interests President Roosevelt was often accused of betraying by his social and economic policies. If you plan your trip far enough ahead and make reservations, you can really make a day of it by having lunch or dinner at the world-renowned Culinary Institute of America.

GETTING THERE:

By Car, take the **Saw Mill River Parkway** north to the Hawthorne Interchange and pick up the **Taconic State Parkway** north to the junction with **I-84**. Go west on this to Exit 13 and continue north on **US-9** towards Poughkeepsie. Take this for about 8 miles to Locust Grove/Samuel F.B. Morse Historic Site. From there follow directions in the text. Poughkeepsie is about 75 miles north of midtown Manhattan.

The easiest return is to get on the Taconic State Parkway where it intersects with US-44, near Innisfree and Millbrook.

PRACTICALITIES:

The major attraction, the Home of Franklin D. Roosevelt and its museum, is open daily except New Year's Day, Thanksgiving, and Christmas. Nearby Val-Kill is closed on weekdays from November through December and March through April, and also every day in January and February. The Vanderbilt mansion is closed on Tuesdays and Wednesdays from November through April. Of the minor attractions, The Samuel F.B. Morse Historic Site is closed from late November through April, and the Innisfree Garden on Tuesdays and Wednesdays and from November through April. The Art Museum at Vassar College is closed on Mondays, Thanksgiving, and Christmas through New Year's Day.

For further information contact the sites directly, or the **Dutchess County Tourism Promotion Agency**, 3 Neptune Rd., Poughkeepsie, NY 12601, ☎ 845-463-4000 or 1-800-445-3131, Internet: www.dutchesstourism.com.

FOOD AND DRINK:

The Culinary Institute of America (433 Albany Post Rd., US- 9, just south of Hyde Park) America's most prestigious cooking school offers memorable meals by its young chefs, served in four distinctly different dining rooms. The **Caterina de Medici Restaurant** serves contemporary and regional Italian cuisine, the **Escoffier Restaurant** features classic French cuisine, the **American Bounty Restaurant** offers regional American cuisine, and the more casual **St. Andrew's Café** has a wide range of contemporary dishes. Dress well and reserve as far in advance as possible, ☎ 845-471-6608, menus on the Internet: www.ciachef.edu. X: Sun., 3 weeks in summer, and Christmas to New Year's. $$ to $$$

Cappucino by Coppola's (568 South Rd., US-9, 4 miles south of Poughkeepsie) This casual Italian bistro features home cooking and a laid-back atmosphere. ☎ 845-462-4545. $$

River Station (1 Water St. in Poughkeepsie) Sandwiches, burgers, steaks, fish, and more in a casual pub overlooking the Hudson. ☎ 845-452-9207. $$

Spanky's (85 Main St. in Poughkeepsie) A fun place for Southern and Creole specialties. ☎ 845-485-2294. $$

Coppola's Italian-American Bistro (535 Albany Post Rd., US- 9, near the F.D.R. site in Hyde Park) American and Italian dishes in a friendly, casual atmosphere. ☎ 845-229-9113. $ and $$

Millbrook Diner (224 Franklin Ave. in the center of Millbrook) A classic diner, with classic Greek and American diner fare. ☎ 845-677-6319. $

LOCAL ATTRACTIONS:

Circled numbers in text correspond to numbers on the map.

SAMUEL F.B. MORSE HISTORIC SITE/LOCUST GROVE ❶, 370 South Rd., US-9, Poughkeepsie, NY 12601, ☎ 845-454-4500. *Open May to Thanksgiving Day, daily 10–4. Last tour at 3:30. Adults $5, seniors (60+) $4, children (6–12) $2.*

Since the Locust Grove property was granted to Colonel Peter Schuyler in 1688, it passed through many hands, including those of Samuel F.B. Morse, the famed artist and inventor of the telegraph (see page 291), who bought it in 1847 and remodeled the house as a Tuscan villa. The dining room addition and the large collection of fine furnishings were the work of the Young family, who owned Locust Grove from 1901 to 1975 and set aside a trust to maintain it as a historic site and wildlife sanctuary.

Today, you can see early telegraph equipment, Morse memorabilia, period furnishings, and changing exhibits from the Young collection of dolls, fans, costumes, books, and assorted Americana. Outside, the 145-acre site is a nature preserve with several easy hiking trails and some lovely views.

To visit the next site, head east on Spackenkill Road (NY-113) for a

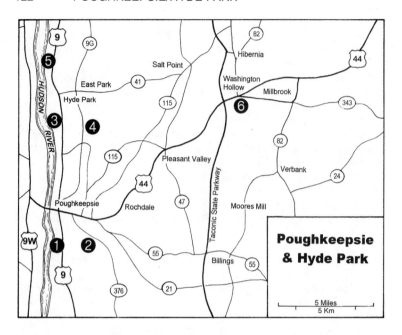

half-mile, turning left onto Wilbur Boulevard. At its end, Hooker Avenue, turn right, then left onto Raymond Avenue for a half-mile. Enter through the stone archway on the right into:

VASSAR COLLEGE/THE FRANCES LEHMAN LOEB ART CENTER ❷, 124 Raymond Ave., Poughkeepsie, NY 12601, ☎ 845-437-5632. *Open Tues.–Sat. 10–5, Sun. 1–5. Closed Mon., Thanksgiving, and from Christmas through New Year's. Free. &.*

Founded by Poughkeepsie brewer Matthew Vassar in 1861, Vassar College was a pioneering experiment in higher education for women. Today it is a coeducational college known for its academic quality and the beauty of its 1,000-acre campus. More than 200 species of trees, some exotic, offer their shade to 100 distinctive buildings designed by such noted architects as James Renwick, Jr. (the 1865 Main Building, after the Tuileries, reportedly planned so that it could be converted to a brewery if females proved uneducable), Marcel Breuer (Ferry House), and Eero Saarinen (Noyes House). The Norman-style chapel has five Tiffany windows, and the great stained-glass window in Thompson Library depicts Elena Lucrezia Cornaro Piscopia receiving the first doctorate awarded to a woman (by the University of Padus in 1678). The $7.2-million Seeley G. Mudd Chemistry Building, opened in 1984, boasts the latest in energy-saving technology and laboratory equipment.

The main focus of your attention, however, is on the stunning new

*Frances Lehman Loeb Art Center designed by Cesar Pelli and opened in 1993. Its permanent collection consists of over 12,500 works, including 19th-century English drawings, 20th-century art, Hudson River landscapes, Rembrandt etchings, and Dürer engravings. Other works date from as far back as ancient Egypt and as up-to-date as what's happening in New York today. Enjoy.

Head north on US-9 through **Poughkeepsie** (pronounced *pooh- KIP-see* and meaning "reed-covered lodge by the little water place" in the native tongue), the seat of Dutchess County, founded in 1683 and currently recovering from years of urban blight. North of it, still on US-9, is the major attraction of this trip:

*HOME OF FRANKLIN D. ROOSEVELT NATIONAL HISTORIC SITE ❸, 519 Albany Post Rd., US-9, Hyde Park, NY 12538, ☎ 845-229-9115, Internet: www.nps.gov/hofr. *Open daily 9–5. Closed New Year's, Thanksgiving, and Christmas. May be closed some days in winter. Tour and museum: Adults $10, children 16 or younger are free. Advance tour reservations ☎ 1-800-967-2283 or http://reservations.nps.gov, recommended for weekend afternoons and fall foliage season. Combination pass for tour, museum, Val Kill site, and Vanderbilt Mansion is available from May through Oct., $18. Book store. Partially ♿.*

Franklin Delano Roosevelt was born in this house on January 30, 1882, and kept it as his family home all his life. With the inimitable recorded voice of Eleanor Roosevelt as a guide, revealing anecdotes about this room or that, you may have the uncanny feeling that you're really visiting the living family, not just the house. You'll see some magnificent furnishings: the beautifully wrought Dresden chandelier and mantel set bought by Roosevelt's father in 1866, fine pieces from Italy and the Netherlands, and a Gilbert Stuart painting of one of F.D.R.'s illustrious ancestors.

Echoes of more recent history are heard in Roosevelt's office, his "Summer White House," where in June 1942 he and Winston Churchill signed the agreement that led to the development of the atomic bomb. Upstairs, you'll find the boyhood room used by Roosevelt and his sons after him. Perhaps the most moving is F.D.R.'s own bedroom, with his favorite photos, Fala's leash and blanket on the chair where the little Scottie always slept, and the books and magazines the president left scattered about on his last visit here in March 1945, shortly before his death.

The name Roosevelt, from the Dutch, means "field of roses." How fitting, then, that in a beautiful garden of roses, surrounded by century-old hemlocks and perennial flower beds, both Franklin and Eleanor now rest. The tombstone is of Imperial Danby, the same white marble used in the Thomas Jefferson Memorial in Washington. A sundial stands just beyond the graves; at its base is a small plaque flush with the ground and hard to see from the walk. Here, still close to his master, lies Fala.

On the same grounds is the *Franklin D. Roosevelt Library and Museum*, near the house. Those who experienced the Roosevelt years will be reminded of many things here as they peruse newsworthy gifts from foreign rulers, oddities (remember the Sphinx?), family heirlooms, photos, naval paintings, ship models, and more. Be sure to go downstairs to see the Ford specially fitted for Roosevelt to drive despite his handicap. The F.D.R. Library was the first presidential library and houses Roosevelt's papers. ☎ *1-800-337-8474, Internet: www.fdrlibrary.marist.edu. Open same time as home above; joint ticketing with tour above.* ♿.

While here, you might want to make a little sidetrip to the nearby:

ELEANOR ROOSEVELT NATIONAL HISTORIC SITE/VAL-KILL ❹, NY-9G, Hyde Park, NY 12538, ☎ 845-229-9115, Internet: www.nps.gov/elro. Located 2 miles east of the F.D.R. home, ask for driving directions. *Open May–Oct., daily 9–5; March–April and Nov.–Dec., Sat.–Sun. 9–5. Closed Jan.–Feb., Thanksgiving, Christmas. Adults $5, under 17 free. Combination ticket with F.D.R. home and museum (above), and Vanderbilt Mansion (below) $18.* ☎ *1-800-967-2283 or http://reservations.nps.gov for advance tour reservations, recommended for weekend afternoons and fall foliage season. Partially* ♿.

Eleanor Roosevelt was a tireless worker for social justice and political reform. During F.D.R.'s 12 years as president, she performed with dignity and grace the difficult role of First Lady to "that man in the White House." It was here at her country retreat, Val-Kill, that she relaxed from the cares of public life and entertained friends, relatives, and a fair contingent of foreign dignitaries. Val-Kill was dedicated as a memorial to Eleanor Roosevelt and opened to the public on October 11, 1984, the centennial of her birth. It reflects both her personal tastes and her work for the wide range of causes she adopted.

Back on US-9, continue north to the:

*VANDERBILT MANSION NATIONAL HISTORIC SITE ❺, 4097 Albany Post Rd., Hyde Park, NY 12538, ☎ 845-229-9115, Internet: www.nps.gov/vama. *Open May–Oct., daily 9–5; rest of year, Thurs.– Mon. 9-5. Closed New Year's, Thanksgiving, and Christmas; and on Tues.–Wed. from Nov.–April. Adults $8, under 17 free. Combination ticket with both Roosevelt sites (above) $18. Admission by tour only; advance reservations suggested for peak period,* ☎ *1-800- 967-2283, http://reservations.nps.gov. Partially* ♿.

A turn-of-the-century palatial mansion, this relic of the Gilded Age is considered to be one of the best examples of the Beaux-Arts style in the country. Designed by the architectural firm of McKim, Mead and White, with interiors by the leading decorators of the time, it was the country home of a grandson of the railroad baron Cornelius Vanderbilt, and it expresses the influence of European art on American wealth in those days. It is filled with fine marble, mahogany woodwork, throne chairs, tapestries, beaded crystal chandeliers, heavily napped rugs (one weighs 2,300 pounds!), and hand-embroidered silk. The glittering opulence impresses, in different ways, everyone who visits the mansion — which, with 59 rooms, 22 fireplaces, and quarters for 60 servants, is considered the most modest of the various Vanderbilt estates.

Enjoy the river views, then follow the map east to the Taconic State Parkway for the drive home. Near the interchange at US-44 is one last stop that might interest you:

INNISFREE GARDEN ❻, Tyrrel Rd., Millbrook, NY 12545, ☎ 845-677-8000, Internet: www.hudsonvalleyonline.com/millbrook/innisfree. From the parkway interchange with US-44, take US-44 toward Millbrook, turning right just before the Cornell Extension Center, onto Tyrrel Rd. *Open May–Oct., Wed.–Fri., 10–4 and weekends 11–5. Free on weekdays, adults $2 on weekends.*

Innisfree explores a design form called a cup garden; its origins are obscure but its roots are in ancient Chinese paintings. The Chinese devised the cup garden to draw attention to something rare or beautiful. They segregated an object, setting it apart by establishing enclosure around it so that it could be enjoyed without distraction. At Innisfree the cup garden concept has become a stroll from one three-dimensional garden picture to another. A cup garden can be an framed meadow, or a lotus pool, or a rock covered with lichens and sedums. At Innisfree, as in Chinese gardens, the restricted station points found in Japanese gardens do not exist. The visitor roams free to discover picture after picture.

Rhinebeck

The trips are getting longer now, but there are enough unusual attractions here in northern Dutchess County to lure even the most jaded of daytrippers. Mansions, scenery, and local history museums, of course; the Hudson Valley is full of them. At how many other places, however, can you experience a World War I dogfight in the sky — or take a flight in a 1920's open-cockpit biplane? Have lunch at what may be America's oldest inn, where George Washington and other notables have dined before you? Or visit a strange castle made completely from scrap materials? This trip is really worth the hundred-mile drive from the city.

GETTING THERE:

By Car, take the **Saw Mill River Parkway** north to the Hawthorne Interchange and pick up the **Taconic State Parkway** north to **US-41**, north of Poughkeepsie. Go west on this to **US-9**, turn right, and head north past the Vanderbilt Mansion (see previous trip) about 4 miles to the Mills-Norrie State Park, entrance on the left. This puts you in the Norrie section of the park; Mills Mansion is about a mile north, off US-9. From here, follow directions in the text. Rhinebeck is about 95 miles north of midtown Manhattan.

By Train: Amtrak provides regular service from Pennsylvania Station in Manhattan to Rhinecliff-Kingston, a scenic ride of less than two hours. From there you would have to take a taxi to whichever sites interested you.

PRACTICALITIES:

This trip requires a bit of advance planning as the opening times of the sites vary considerably. The main attraction, the Old Rhinebeck Aerodrome, is open daily from mid-May through October, but air shows are only held on weekends from mid-June through mid-October. The Mills Mansion is closed on Mondays and Tuesdays, while Wilderstein closes completely from November through April, and is also closed on Mondays through Wednesdays. Montgomery Place is closed on Tuesdays, on weekdays from November through mid-December, and completely from mid-December through March. Wing's Castle is closed on Mondays and Tuesdays, and completely from late December until late May. Obviously, your best choice is on a weekend from late May through October, or at least on a Thursday or Friday in season.

For further information contact the sites directly, or the **Dutchess County Tourism Promotion Agency**, 3 Neptune Rd., Poughkeepsie, NY 12601, ☎ 845-463-4000 or 1-800-445-3131, Internet: www.dutchesstourism.com.

FOOD AND DRINK:

Beekman Arms 1776 Tavern (4 Mill St., center of Rhinebeck) This famous cozy Colonial tavern has been around for centuries, serving hearty regional American fare. ☎ 845-871-1766. $$$

Foster's Coach House Tavern (22 Montgomery St. in Rhinebeck) Sandwiches, salads, burgers and the like, with lots of atmosphere. ☎ 845-876-8052. X: Mon. $ and $$

Mughal Raj (110 Route 9 South, Rhinebeck) Excellent Indian cuisine in an unpretentious setting. ☎ 845-876-4696. $ and $$

Rolling Rock Café (46 Route 9 in Rhinebeck) A bustling place with a wide range of America's favorite dishes. ☎ 845-876-7655. $ and $$

LOCAL ATTRACTIONS:

Circled numbers in text correspond to numbers on the map.

MILLS-NORRIE STATE PARK ❶, Staatsburg, NY 12580, ☎ 845-889-4646. *Open daily all year, daylight hours. No entry fee. Picnicking, hiking trails, fishing, bicycling, cross-country skiing. Fees for golf course, camping, and marina use. Food concession in season. Partially ♿.*

This attractive park on the Hudson offers fine facilities for a day's outing. There are really two parks here, one the Mills Historic Site (see below), and the other the Norrie recreation area. On the grounds of the Norrie section is an environmental educational center run by the Dutchess Community College, housed in a fieldstone structure built on the water's edge around 1935 by the Civilian Conservation Corps. The road through the park is especially scenic.

Just north of this is the:

MILLS MANSION STATE HISTORIC SITE ❷, Old Albany Post Rd., Staatsburg, NY 12580, ☎ 845-889-8851. *Open April–Labor Day, Wed.–Sat. 10–5, Sun. noon–5; Labor Day to late Oct., Wed.–Sun. noon–5; also around Christmas. Adults $3, seniors $2, children under 12 $1. Partially ♿.*

The Mills Mansion was originally a Greek Revival structure built in 1832 by Morgan Lewis, Revolutionary War officer and governor of New York from 1804 to 1807. It was later the home of Ogden and Ruth Livingston Mills, who hired the noted architectural firm McKim, Mead and White to enlarge and remodel it in the Neoclassical style. Mills was a prominent financier, his wife was a member of an established New York political family, and their son served as Secretary of the Treasury under Herbert Hoover. The mansion reflects the lifestyle of America's wealthy and powerful over several generations. The gorgeous marble fireplaces, rich wood paneling, and gilded plasterwork make an appropriate setting for Flemish tapestries, fine artwork, and ornate furnishings in the Louis XV and Louis XVI styles. The grounds are beautifully landscaped and afford a sweeping panorama of the Hudson.

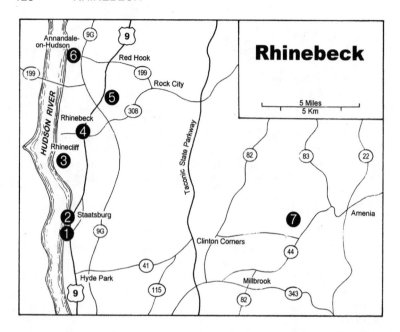

Continue north on US-9 towards Rhinebeck. Just south of the village is another estate worth visiting. To get there, turn left on Mill Road and follow it for 2.2 miles to Morton Road, where you turn right to visit the:

WILDERSTEIN PRESERVATION ❸, 330 Morton Rd., Rhinebeck, NY 12572, ☎ 845-876-4818, Internet: www.wilderstein.org. *Open May–Oct., Thurs.–Sun., noon–4. Last tour at 3:30. House tour: Adults $7, under 12 free. Grounds and trail system are free. Gift shop.*

This fanciful Queen Anne mansion was built completely of wood in 1888 and served several generations of the Suckley family, descendants of the Beekmans and Livingstons. In 1983 it and the 35 acres of scenic land surrounding were donated to a non-profit historic preservation group. The grounds were designed in the Romantic style by Calvert Vaux, one of the designers of New York's Central Park, while the lavish interior is the work of J.B. Tiffany.

Return to US-9 and head north into **Rhinebeck Village ❹**, settled by the Dutch in 1686 on land purchased from the Native Americans. In 1719 German refugees from Europe's religious wars named the town after their former home in the Rhine Valley, parts of which very much resemble the Hudson Valley. At the village center, the junction of US-9 and NY-308, stands the venerable **Beekman Arms Inn**, built around 1766 and said to be the oldest continuously operating hotel in the country. Its tap room is an

A 1917 Fokker Triplane in mock combat over Rhinebeck
(Photo courtesy of Old Rhinebeck Aerodrome)

attractive and popular spot for drinks and dining (see Food and Drink, above). Rhinebeck is a picturesque old town, and you may want to spend some time here shopping, sightseeing, or attending one of the events at the Dutchess County Fairgrounds. For further information, contact the **Chamber of Commerce** booth just across the street from the inn. ☎ 845-876-4778. *Open May–Nov., daily, 10–4.*

Now for the main attraction. From the Beekman Arms, continue north on US-9 past the junction with NY-9G a short way to Stone Church Road, opposite a church. Turn right here and follow signs to the:

*OLD RHINEBECK AERODROME ❺, P.O. Box 229, Rhinebeck, NY 12572, ☎ 845-752-3200, Internet: www.oldrhinebeck.org. *Open mid-May through October, daily 10–5. Airshows mid-June through mid-Oct., Sat.–Sun. at 2 p.m. Admission on non-airshow days: Adults $6, seniors $5, children (6–10) $2, under 6 free. Admission on airshow days: Adults $12, seniors $10, children (6–10) $5, under 6 free. Flights in classic biplane on weekends, $40 per person; rides ticket booth opens at 10 a.m. — first come, first served. All flights are at the pilot's discretion.*

This one-of-a-kind "museum in the sky" is a showcase for the late Cole Palen's collection of vintage aircraft dating from 1900 to 1937. Palen sank everything he had into acquiring and maintaining these rare specimens, which take to the air every weekend in season for a thrilling ***airshow**. The daring young men in their flying machines, sporting aviator garb out of World War I, are aided in takeoffs and landings by a ground crew that apparently knows exactly how to handle planes without brakes or automatic starters, on runways of dirt that slope just enough to give the necessary boost. Before and after the show, you can take a *barnstorming ride in a 1929 New Standard open-cockpit biplane for a thrilling view of the Hudson Valley. The planes, some of which have starred in movie and TV productions, are on display for your inspection every day during the season.

Game for what is probably the most impressive mansion in these parts? If so, continue north on Church Road, becoming Norton Road, then turn left on NY-199 to River Road, CR-103. Here turn right, north, towards Annandale and:

MONTGOMERY PLACE ❻, River Rd., Annandale-on-Hudson, NY 12504, ☎ 845-758-5461, Internet: www.hudsonvalley.org. *Open April–Oct., Wed.–Mon. 10–5; Nov. weekends 10–5; early Dec., weekends noon–5. Guided tours: Adults $6, seniors (60+) $5, children (6–17) $3. Self-guided grounds only, $3. Picnicking permitted. ♿.*

Built in 1805 in the Federal style, this 23-room mansion is the centerpiece of an exquisite 434-acre estate complete with famed gardens, pick-your-own orchards, walking trails, museum, garden shop, and glorious views across the Hudson River to the Catskill Mountains beyond. The prominent Livingston family called it home for nearly 200 years, leaving only in 1985 when it was deeded to Historic Hudson Valley, the organization responsible for most of the sites on the two Tarrytown trips (see pages 109-114). Nearly all of the furnishings are original.

The easiest route back to New York City is to take NY-199 east a few miles to the Taconic State Parkway and head south on it. If time permits, and you're interested, you could get off the Taconic at Clinton Corners and head east on Route 57, the Dutchess Wine Trail, perhaps stopping at the **Millbrook Winery** for a tour and tasting. ☎ *845-677-8383.* Just beyond it, on Bangall Road, is a very strange site. **Wing's Castle ❼**, after over 20 years of construction by artists Peter and Toni Wing, remains very much a work-in-progress. This fantasy home, looking like some imaginary fairytale castle with elements borrowed from worldwide cultures, is constructed entirely from salvaged materials and found junk. The interior is filled with objects even stranger than the building itself, if that is possible. *RR 1, Box 174A, Millbrook, NY 12545.* ☎ *845-677-9085. Open late May to late December, Wed.–Sun. 10–4:30. Adults $5, children $3.*

Columbia County

I t's 120 miles from New York City to the historic town of Hudson, but one singular attraction alone makes the journey all worthwhile. Olana, the home of the renowned 19th-century landscape painter Frederic Edwin Church, is a fantasy castle like no other, a magical trip into the imagination. Add to that one of the most intriguing towns in the area, another historic estate on the river, a charming village, and the home of an early American president, and you've got the makings of a truly fascinating daytrip.

GETTING THERE:

By Car: Take the **Saw Mill River Parkway** north to the Hawthorne Interchange and pick up the **Taconic State Parkway** north towards Albany. At the junction with **NY-199** turn left and proceed west past the junction with US-9 in Red Hook to the junction with **NY-9G**. Just over the Columbia County line, turn left on **Route 6** and follow signs to Clermont, entrance on the right. After visiting there, follow directions in the text. The town of Hudson is about 120 miles north of midtown Manhattan.

PRACTICALITIES:

Avoid making this trip on a Monday or Tuesday, or at any time from mid-October through March — when Olana is closed. Clermont is closed on Mondays, on weekdays from November through mid-December, and completely from mid-December through March. Lindenwald closes on weekdays from November through mid-May. The best times to visit are Wednesdays through Sundays, from April through mid-October.

For further information contact the sites directly, or **Columbia County Tourism**, 401 State St., Hudson, NY 12534, ☎ 1-800-724-1846 or 518-828-3375, Internet: www.columbiacounty.com.

FOOD AND DRINK:

Charleston (517 Warren St. in Hudson) A wide and creative variety of international dishes. ☎ 518-828-4990. X: Tues., Wed. $$

Bradley's Grill (in the St. Charles Hotel, 16 Park Place, Hudson) American cuisine, from a light lunch to a full meal, in a restored historic 1868 hotel. ☎ 518-822-9900. $ and $$

Columbia Diner (717 Warren St. in Hudson) American, Greek, and Italian dishes; home cooked and unpretentious. ☎ 518-828-9083. X: Sun. eve. $

LOCAL ATTRACTIONS:

Circled numbers in text correspond to numbers on the map.

CLERMONT STATE HISTORIC SITE ❶, 1 Clermont Ave., Germantown, NY 12526, ☎ 518-537-4240, Internet: www.friendsofclermont.org. *Historic house open Apr.–Oct., Tues.–Sun. 11–5, and on holiday Mon. 11–5; Nov.–Dec. 15, weekends 11–4. Closed non-holiday Mon. and mid-Dec. through March. Adults $3, seniors $2, children (5–12) $1. Grounds open daily year-round, 8:30–sunset, free. Special events. Gift shop. Picnicking. Hiking trails. Gardens. Cross-country skiing. Partially &.*

Here is the ancestral home of Robert R. Livingston, a member of the Continental Congress, one of the five framers of the Declaration of Independence, and a man with a finger in many another historic pie. As first chancellor of New York State, he administered the presidential oath of office to George Washington, and as minister to France under Thomas Jefferson, he negotiated the Louisiana Purchase. In 1802 he agreed to finance Robert Fulton in the experiments that led to the first commercially practical steamboat. Fulton named the boat *Clermont* in Livingston's honor, and it stopped at the estate on its maiden voyage up the Hudson in 1807.

Originally built in 1730, the house was burned by the British in 1777 in reprisal for Livingston's staunch advocacy of American independence, and rebuilt largely through the determined efforts of Livingston's wife, Margaret Beekman Livingston. Clermont remained in the hands of the Livingston family until 1962, when the State of New York acquired it, restored it to its appearance in 1930, and opened it as a public park and a memorial to one of its first families. Today you can tour the house, stroll through the lovely restored gardens, and picnic on the grounds, enjoying a glorious view over the Hudson to the Catskills rising in the west.

Continue north on NY-9G for about 15 miles. As the Rip Van Winkle Bridge comes into view, watch for the road to Olana, on the right about a mile before the bridge.

*OLANA STATE HISTORIC SITE ❷, Route 9G, Hudson, NY 12534, ☎ 518-828-0135, Internet: www.olana.org. *Open April–May and mid-Oct. through Oct. 31, Wed.–Sun., 10–5; June through mid-Oct., Wed.–Sun. 10–6. Also open on Memorial Day, Independence Day, Labor Day, and Columbus Day. Closed Mon.–Tues. and Nov.–March. Last tour 1 hour before closing. Reservations are not required, but are advised as the number of daily admissions is limited. Adults $3, seniors $2, children $1. Grounds open daily 8–sunset, and are free. Picnicking. Trails. Cross-country skiing. Special events. &.*

"As the good woman said of her mock-turtle soup, 'I made it out of my own head.'" Thus, with what can only be called magnificent understatement, did Frederic Edwin Church describe his 31 years of work on Olana, the striking castle he designed and built on an Italian layout with

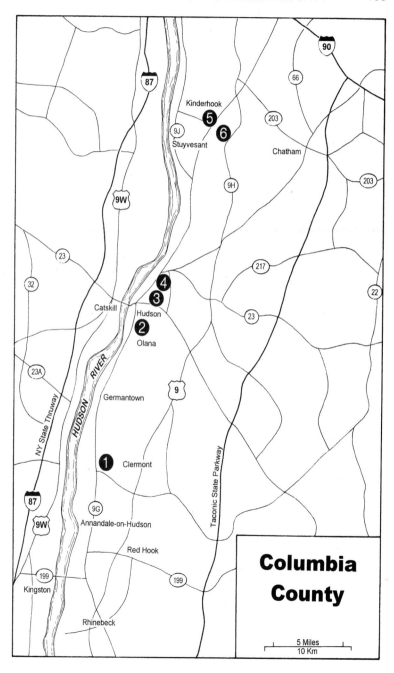

Columbia County

strong Persian decorative elements. Church was a noted painter of the Hudson River school and studied with its founder, Thomas Cole, who first introduced him to the site where Olana now stands. Like the other members of the school, Church painted native American landscapes and Hudson River scenes, but he had a preference for foreign and exotic subjects — a preference aptly reflected in Olana, in contrast to the homey, plain, and very American-looking residence of Thomas Cole across the river in Catskill.

The main portion of Olana was built between 1870 and 1876, with some additions in the 1880s. As Church constantly reworked his paintings, so he constantly fashioned and refashioned Olana, proclaiming it "finished" only in 1891, when he turned its operation over to his son. The **interior**, meticulously preserved just as Church planned it, is a marvel of intricately patterned tiles, gilded arches, vibrant colors, exquisite furnishings from Persia, Kashmir, and other Near Eastern lands. Church's work — some of which adorns Olana's walls, along with two paintings by Thomas Cole — is noted for its delicate rendering of light, and this same sensitivity is displayed in the design and placement of the windows, each framing a scenic view, each capturing a different quality of light.

Church lavished equal attention on his 250 acres of property, which was farmland when he purchased it in the 1860s. Today it is a beautiful **woodland**; each of the thousands of trees selected by Church and planted with a painterly eye for composition. He even created the beautifully contoured lake at the foot of the hill to "balance" the view of the Hudson against the Catskills. Indeed, driving through Olana's grounds is like driving through one of Church's paintings — a romantic landscape conceived in the artist's mind's eye and executed with utmost care on the canvas of the Hudson River Valley.

Return to NY-9G, turn right, and go north briefly to the junction with NY-23. Bear left and continue north to **Hudson** ❸ on what is now 9G/23B (Columbia St.). Soon you will pick up signs to the Firemen's Home. Follow these, continuing a block beyond the point where 9G/23B turns right. The next corner is State Street. Turn right past the library, then bear left on Carroll to the next corner, Short Street. Turn left (this is now Harry Howard Ave.) and proceed to the top of the hill and the Firemen's Home, on the left. Drive to the parking lot at the right of the buildings. In the last building on the left is the:

AMERICAN MUSEUM OF FIREFIGHTING ❹, 117 Harry Howard Ave., Hudson, NY 12534, ☎ 518-828-7695. *Open daily, 9–4:30. Closed major holidays. Free, donations accepted.* ♿.

This museum, operated by the Firemen's Association of the State of New York, contains one of the oldest and largest collections of firefighting equipment and memorabilia in the country. There are thousands of items here, from firehats, badges, banners, and speaking trumpets to paintings, prints, and lithographs. And, of course, the engines, scores of them, stalwart antiques spanning two centuries of firefighting, from the horse-drawn days through the steam era to the early motorized trucks of the 1920s and later. The oldest specimen is the Newsham engine, built in England in 1725; imported to New York in 1731, and in continuous service for the next 154 years. Fittingly, the museum is located in the Firemen's Home, close to some of the men who used the equipment to battle the flames of yesteryear.

While in **Hudson**, you might want to take a look at the historic town itself. Henry Hudson landed here in 1609, but it was not really settled until the 1780s, when the land was purchased by mariners seeking a deep water harbor safe from any threat of attack by the British. It remained a shipping port, famed mostly for its notorious bordellos, gambling parlors, and illicit taverns strung along Diamond Street. Don't look for them now; the street was cleaned up in the 1950s and even its name changed — to Columbia Street. Pity. The thoroughfare you do want to visit, however, is nearby Warren Street, lined with historic houses and literally dozens of antique shops. Stroll along it to the river, where there are some nice views.

Continue north on US-9 for about 11 miles to **Kinderhook** ❺. On the left as you come into town is the **James Vanderpoel House**, an 1819 building in the Federal style, maintained by the Columbia County Historical Society as a museum. In addition to a fine collection of Duncan Phyfe and Chippendale furniture, the museum has materials on local history and documents relating to Martin Van Buren. It's a good place to get directions for a walking tour of Kinderhook, a town frequented by Washington Irving, his fictional creation, Ichabod Crane, and by the pre-treasonous Benedict Arnold, among others. ☎ *518-758-9265. 16 Broad St. Open Memorial Day weekend to Labor Day weekend, Thurs.–Sat., 11–5 and Sun. 1–5. Closed major holidays. Adults $3, seniors (55+) and children (12–18) $2.* The society also operates the **Luykas Van Allen House**, a little south of the town on NY-9H. Built in 1737, it has been restored as a museum of 18th-century Dutch culture and Hudson Valley art. Adjacent to this is the one-room **Ichabod Crane Schoolhouse**, restored to its 1920's appearance and named after Washington Irving's legendary schoolteacher from Kinderhook. ☎ *518-758-9265. Open Memorial Day weekend to Labor Day Weekend, Thurs.–Sat. 11–5, Sun. 1–5. Closed major holidays. Adults $3, seniors (55+) and children (12–18) $2.*

Continue south on NY-9H to the:

MARTIN VAN BUREN NATIONAL HISTORIC SITE ❻, 1013 Old Post Rd., Kinderhook, NY 12106, ☎ 518-758-9689, Internet: www.nps.gov/mava. *Open mid-May through Oct., daily 9–4; rest of year Sat.–Sun. 9–4. Times subject to change, check. Adults $2, under 17 free.*

Van Buren bought this 1797 estate, known as **Lindenwald**, in 1838 during his term as the eighth President of the United States. In 1850 he hired famed architect Richard Upjohn who, while enlarging the home, added a third floor, tower, and porch to complete the new Italianate exterior. The modern conveniences of running water, bathroom and kitchen plumbing, and a kitchen range were also part of the renovation. These items, and much of the President's original furnishings, are seen on the tour.

Van Buren was born in Kinderhook in 1782, the end of the Revolutionary War, and lived until 1862, well into the Civil War. His life spanned the most critical days of the infant nation, and in his cool and competent way contributed more to its development than he is usually given credit for.

Continue south on NY-9H to NY-23 and turn left. This will quickly take you to the Taconic State Parkway, the easiest way back to New York City.

Van Buren's Estate at Lindenwald
(Photo courtesy of Martin Van Buren National Historic Site)

West Point and the Hudson Highlands

One of the most visited sites in New York State is the United States Military Academy at West Point, whose story spans the entire history of this nation — from the Revolution right up to the present. Here, in the spectacular Hudson Highlands, where the great waterway fights its way through the Appalachian Mountains before beginning its leisurely journey to the sea, were molded the careers of some of America's greatest heros. Here also, in the shadow of the mighty Storm King Mountain, is a deep respect for the environment, as is witnessed by two outstanding establishments, the Museum of the Hudson Highlands and the Storm King Art Center. All three add up to an exciting daytrip of discovery.

GETTING THERE:

By Car: Leaving New York City via the **George Washington Bridge**, take the **Palisades Interstate Parkway** north to the Bear Mountain traffic circle. Follow signs for **US-9W** north to West Point. Go a few miles on 9W to the junction with **NY-218** and turn right to Highland Falls and **West Point**. When the road forks, follow the sign on the right to the main gate (Thayer Gate South). The Visitor Center and Museum are just outside the gate. West Point is about 50 miles north of midtown Manhattan.

After visiting West Point, leave via the Washington Gate at the north end and follow directions in the text.

By Bus: ShortLine/Gray Line buses offer daytrip packages to West Point and also to the Storm King Art Center, departing from Manhattan's Port Authority Bus Terminal. ☎ 1-800-243-3935, Internet: www.shortline bus.com.

PRACTICALITIES:

West Point may be visited on any day except Thanksgiving, Christmas, or New Year's Day. The Museum of the Hudson Highlands is closed on Mondays and a few major holidays, while the Storm King Art Center is open daily but closes completely from mid-November through March. Good weather will greatly enhance your enjoyment of this trip.

If you plan to climb Storm King Mountain, be sure to wear suitable shoes.

For further information, contact the sites directly, or **Orange County Tourism**, 30 Matthews St., Goshen, NY 10924, ☎ 845-291-2136 or 1-800-762-

8687, Internet: www.orangetourism.org.

FOOD AND DRINK:

Hotel Thayer (just outside the main gate of West Point) A traditional old hotel with fine dining overlooking the Hudson; American and Continental cuisine. ☎ 845-446-4731. $$$

Schades Restaurant (457 Main St. in Highland Falls, just south of the academy) Sandwiches, pizza, pastas, and full meals in a casual, family-oriented setting. X: major holidays. ☎ 845- 446-2626. $

Painter's Tavern (266 Hudson St. on Cornwall-on-Hudson) Burgers, salads, sandwiches and the like, served amid local art. ☎ 845-534-2109. $

LOCAL ATTRACTIONS:

Circled numbers in text correspond to numbers on the map.

*UNITED STATES MILITARY ACADEMY ❶, West Point, NY 10996, ☎ 845-938-2638, Internet: www.usma.edu. *Grounds open daily, dawn to dusk. Visitor Center open daily 9–4:45, closed Thanksgiving, Christmas, New Year's Day. All facilities and parking free. Self-guided tour, picnic areas, gift shops, restaurant at Hotel Thayer on grounds. Leashed pets only. Commercial guided tours, ☎ 845- 446-4724, not affiliated with academy, leave from Visitor Center daily except on football Saturdays or Graduation Week. Many areas are* &.

West Point, site of the U.S. Military Academy established by an Act of Congress in 1802, figured prominently in the Revolutionary War, though it was never a battleground. It was one of four strategically situated fortifications along the mid-Hudson, and it was here, in 1778, that the great 150-ton chain was laid across the river to Constitution Island to block British ships. It was as commander of West Point in 1780 that General Benedict Arnold made his name a synonym for "traitor" by plotting to betray the Point into British hands.

The Hudson bends sharply here before continuing towards Poughkeepsie, providing fine scenic views at Trophy Point, where you can see some of the 300-pound links of the river chain and a battle monument to the Civil War dead. There are many other monuments and memorials scattered throughout the grounds, including a 9-foot bronze *American Soldier* by Felix Deweldon, designer of the Iwo Jima Flag Raising Memorial. If your timing is right, you can watch the current crop of cadets drilling on The Plain, the same parade ground where Baron von Steuben drilled the ragtag soldiers of the Continental Army.

The **Visitor Center** just outside Thayer Gate is the best place to start your visit. Here you can see displays and videos on cadet training, pick up free maps and brochures for a self-guided tour, or join a guided bus tour. ☎ 845-938-2638. *Open daily 9–4:45, closed Thanksgiving, Christmas, New Year's Day. Gift shop. One-hour guided tours, April–Oct., adults $6, children $3; Two-hour tours May-Oct., adults $8, children $5;*

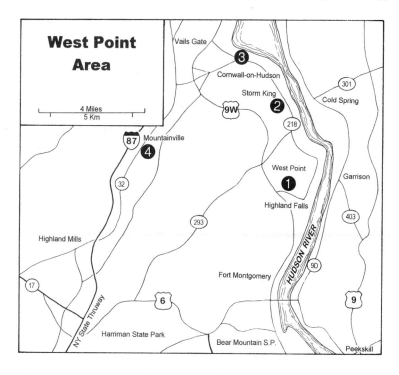

off-season guided tours, Nov.–March, adults $6, children $3. Guided tour info: ☎ *845-446-4724.* ♿.

Nearby is the ***West Point Museum**. "Weapons change," said General George S. Patton, "but man who uses them changes not at all." This quotation is called to mind as you view an imposing array of military arms, flags, uniforms, and memorabilia. There are dioramas of past wars, military miniatures, and weapons from the War with Spain, the Boxer Rebellion, the Civil War, Vietnam, and other conflicts. Other displays include a six-ton World War I tank, George Washington's personal "gentleman's pistols," and Napoleon's sword and pistols. The collection of military battle art is the largest such collection in the United States. ☎ *845- 938-2203. Open daily 10:30–4:15, closed Thanksgiving, Christmas, New Year's Day. Free.* ♿.

Be sure to visit some of the West Point Chapels. **Cadet Chapel**, built in 1910, is an impressive cross-shaped structure in "Military Gothic," with an exceptionally large pipe organ and magnificent stained-glass windows. ☎ *845-938-2308, Open Mon.–Sat. 8–4:15.* **Catholic Chapel**, another fine building, is in the Norman style and is modeled after an abbey in England. ☎ *845-938-8760. Open daily 9–9.* **Jewish Chapel** has a gallery museum that chronicles Jewish participation in America's military history. ☎ *845-938-*

2710. Open Mon.–Fri. 9–4, Sat.–Sun. noon–4. **Old Cadet Chapel**, dating from 1836, has a file with the names of those buried in the adjoining cemetery, including Revolutionary War heroine Margaret Corbin, General Custer, General Winfield Scott, and astronaut Edward White, killed in a space test in 1967. ☎ 845-938-2433. *Open daily 8–4.*

Fort Putnam, a restored Revolutionary War fortification, offers periodic exhibits and a commanding view of West Point and the Hudson River. It was built in 1778–79 to provide protection for Fort Clinton, downriver near what is now the Trailside Museum in Bear Mountain State Park. *Open limited hours between May and September. Ask at the museum, above.*

Visits to **Constitution Island**, across the Hudson from West Point, involve a boat trip for which reservations must be made in advance. The first local fortifications were made here, but were overrun by the British in 1777 and recaptured by the Americans the next year. These, and an historic mansion of 1836, may be seen on the tour. ☎ *845-446-8676 for information and reservations.*

Leave West Point by the northern Washington Gate and continue north on NY-218 to **Storm King State Park** ❷. Although this park is undeveloped and has no facilities, it does provide access to trails leading to the top of the majestic *Storm King Mountain. The climb is not particularly difficult, and the views are spectacular. An important environmental battle raged here in the early 1960s when Con Ed, New York City's unloved supplier of electricity, sought to build a pumped-storage generating plant on a saddle in the mountain, which would have destroyed much of the natural beauty as well as doing serious harm to the river's fish population. With the public up in arms, environmental groups brought legal action and successfully blocked the plans, setting a precedent for future unwanted "developments" around the nation. ☎ *845-786-2701, Internet: www.nys parks.com. Free.*

Continue north into the nearby town of Cornwall-on-Hudson, home of the:

MUSEUM OF THE HUDSON HIGHLANDS ❸, The Boulevard, Cornwall-on-Hudson, NY 12520, ☎ 845-534-7781, Internet: www.hvmarket place.com/museumhh. *Open summer: Mon.–Fri. 11–5, Sat.–Sun. noon–5; winter, Mon.–Fri. 2–5, Sat.–Sun. noon–5. Closed some major holidays. Nature shop. Donation.* ♿.

In a granite gorge on the side of a mountain, surrounded by self-guiding nature trails, stands a prize-winning piece of architecture housing a unique museum with natural history displays, cultural exhibits, local art, and an assortment of live animals native to the region. The walls are adorned with attractive murals, and an exhibit area depicts habitats of the Hudson Valley.

Nearby is **Kenridge Farm**, a 174-acre former horse farm that now serves as a branch of the museum, with an education center, workshops, and an excellent hiking trail. Ask at the museum for directions.

Now follow the map to NY-32 and turn south to Mountainville and the:

*STORM KING ART CENTER ❹, Old Pleasant Hill Road, Mountainville, NY 10953, ☎ 845-534-3115, Internet: www.stormkingartcenter.org. *Open April–late Oct., daily 11–5:30; late Oct. to mid-Nov. 11–5. Sculpture Park remains open until 8 on Sat. from Memorial Day weekend until Labor Day weekend, and on Sun. of holiday weekends during the same period. Closed mid-Nov. through March. Adults $7, seniors $5, students $3, 5 and under free. Tours. Picnic area. Gift shop. Partially ♿.*

More than 120 large-scale contemporary sculptures are on display here in 500 acres of landscaped gardens overlooking Schunnemunk Mountain. The museum, with its elegant cut-stone mansion in the French Norman style, displays a superb collection of sculptures by well-known American and European artists, supplemented by loans from other museums. Among those represented are Calder, Noguchi, Smith, and Nevelson. From the gardens you can look out through five enormous granite Ionic columns to magnificent vistas of rolling foothills. If your thirst for scenic beauty still isn't quenched, you can take a hike through the **Mountainville Conservancy of Storm King Art Center**, encompassing 2,300 acres of Schunnemunk Mountain, about four miles west of here.

To return to New York City, continue down NY-32 to Harriman, where you can get on the New York State Thruway (I-87) — a quick way home.

Trip 18

Bear Mountain and Harriman State Parks

When New Yorkers want to come to the woods to play, this is where they head for. Only 45 miles from Manhattan via a scenic, truck-free parkway, it's very easy to get to and offers — especially in its more rugged southern part — both an enjoyable escape and a chance to learn a little history.

GETTING THERE:

By Car: Leave New York City via the George Washington Bridge and once across, take the **Palisades Interstate Parkway** north into Bear Mountain and Harriman State Parks. Just south of Exit 17 is the Visitor Center. From there, follow directions in the text.

These sites are also accessible via the New York State Thruway (I-87) and the Tappan Zee Bridge.

The farthest point is about 45 miles north of midtown Manhattan.

PRACTICALITIES:

Both parks, especially Bear Mountain, can get a bit crowded on fine weekends in season. If possible, come on a weekday. Good weather is absolutely essential for enjoyment of this trip.

For further information, contact the parks at ☎ 845-786-2701, Internet: www.nysparks.com. You might also check with the **Rockland County Department of Tourism**, 3 Main St., Nyack, NY 10960, ☎ 845-353-5533 or 1-800-295-5723, Internet: www.rockland.org, or **Orange County Tourism**, 30 Matthews St., Goshen, NY 10924, ☎ 845-291-2136 or 1-800-762-8687, Internet: www.orangetourism.org.

FOOD AND DRINK:

In the park there's always the classic:

Bear Mountain Inn (in Bear Mt. Park at US-9W) Both a restaurant and a cafeteria, with the usual American favorites. The inn itself, a stone-and-timber affair, has been here since the 1920s. Rooms available for overnight stays. ☎ 845-786-2731 or 1-800-458-8264. $ and $$

Two other recommended eateries in the vicinity are:

Hudson House (134 Main St. at Franklin in downtown Nyack) A wide variety of creative dishes, indoors or out, in a restored downtown building. ☎ 845-353-1355. X: Mon. $$

Annie's Restaurant (149 Route 9W in Stony Point) A classic fast-food drive in, right out of the 1950s. ☎ 845-942-1011. $

Both parks are ideal spots for a picnic, and there are seasonal food concessions at the more popular sites.

LOCAL ATTRACTIONS:

Circled numbers in text correspond to numbers on the map.

Begin at the **Park Visitor Center** ❶, located on the center island of the Palisades Interstate Parkway just south of Exit 17. Here you can get current information, trail and road maps, guidebooks, snacks, fishing licenses, and some outdoor recreation gear. ☎ *845-786-5003. Open daily except Thanksgiving, Christmas, and New Year's Day, 8–5. Both Bear Mountain and Harriman state parks, on opposite sides of the parkway, charge a vehicle use fee of $6 every day from May to Sept., and on weekends the rest of the year. An Empire Passport, valid for one year and sold at the Visitor Center, covers these charges. Note that several of the sites do not permit pets, and the others are subject to limitations. Inquire before bringing Fido along.*

Just north of this, at Exit 17, is the **Anthony Wayne Recreation Area** ❷ of Harriman State Park. Facilities here include picnic areas with fireplaces, playing fields, plus hiking, biking, and cross-country skiing trails. Located in a wooded valley, this is a good spot for those who don't like things too crowded.

Continue north to the Bear Mountain Traffic Circle and turn right to the inn. You are now in **Bear Mountain State Park** ❸, New York's year-round playground, which covers more than 5,000 acres of the Highlands that gave the Hudson its reputation as the Rhine of America. The popular **Trailside Museum and Zoo,** near the inn, has exhibits on the history and natural history of the area. Other features include shaded picnic groves, nature, hiking, biking, and cross-country ski trails, playing fields, a swimming pool, ice skating, lake and river fishing, and for those with their own boats, a dock on the Hudson.

One of the best mountain drives available near the city is the ride to the top of 1305-foot-high Bear Mountain on *****Perkins Memorial Drive** ❹. Along the way there are continual vistas from scenic overlooks, and historic markers telling of battles that took place directly below. From the **Perkins Tower** atop the mountain you can see (on a clear day) High Point in New Jersey (see page 308), New York's skyscrapers, and, much closer, Anthony's Nose just across the river and Sugar Loaf Hill to the north. There are picnic areas below the tower, and a road leading to the well-photographed overlook above Bear Mountain Inn.

Note that at the Bear Mountain traffic circle you can drive over the **Bear Mountain Bridge** to the east bank of the Hudson and some of the sites described in Trips 11-16. When it was completed in 1924, this was the longest main suspension span in the world. Until then, there were no fixed vehicular crossings of the Hudson south of Albany; all traffic had to use ferries. Today the historic bridge carries not only US routes 6 and 202, but also pedestrians, bicycles, and the famed Appalachian Trail. Just south

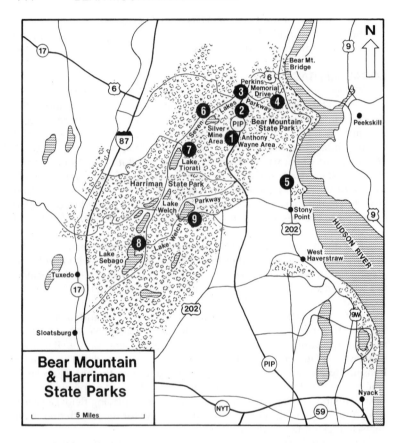

Bear Mountain
& Harriman
State Parks

5 Miles

of the bridge is Iona Island, once a navy base where bombs and ammunition were assembled during both World Wars. In the mid-1960s the Navy gave Iona to the Palisades Interstate Park Commission for development as a recreation area, but nothing came of these plans. It is now a winter sanctuary for the endangered bald eagle. The island itself is closed to the public but can be viewed from the causeway.

At this point you might want to make a little side trip to explore a bit of Revolutionary War history. If so, head south on US-9W for about six miles to the:

*STONY POINT BATTLEFIELD STATE HISTORIC SITE ❺, P.O. Box 182, Stony Point, NY 10980, ☎ 845-786-2521, Internet: www.nysparks.com. *Open mid-April through Oct., Wed.–Sat. 10–5, Sun. 1–5. Also open on Memorial Day, Independence Day, and Labor Day. Usually free, nominal admission for special events. Picnic facilities. Tours.* ♿.

Stony Point Battlefield is the site of a daring midnight assault by the Corps of Light Infantry, under the command of Brigadier General Anthony Wayne, against a British fort on July 15, 1779. Two columns, armed with unloaded muskets and fixed bayonets, encircled the garrison by wading through the waters of Haverstraw Bay from the south and around the peninsula from the north while a center column fired weapons to divert the enemy troops and draw their attention away from the real attack. Within 33 minutes the American victory was complete, and most of the defenders — including the British commander — were captured.

Today, the battlefield has a museum with an audiovisual program and features artillery exhibits along with a model display of the Marshall map, drawn by the British engineer in charge of defenses and discovered by site staff in 1992. In addition, guided tours, weapons demonstrations, an 18th-century camp, interpretive signs, special events, river views, and the oldest lighthouse on the Hudson combine to create a very worthwhile side excursion.

Back in the park area, take US-6 and Seven Lakes Drive west into the heart of **Harriman State Park**. This is much larger (over 46,000 acres) than Bear Mountain and includes more rugged terrain as well as many undeveloped areas. Like Bear Mountain, it offers a wide range of activities and facilities for year-round use.

Continue south on Seven Lakes Drive to the **Silver Mine Area ❻**, a lovely woodland park by a picturesque mountain lake. Paths and picnic areas make it a fine place to spend an afternoon, or to go fishing or boating. The fall foliage is outstanding here. ☎ *845-351-2568. Open daily. Vehicle use fee daily from May–Sept., and on weekends the rest of the year.*

A bit farther down the road is **Lake Tiorati Beach ❼**. This large, clear lake offers a refreshing swim, and little tufts of islands provide intriguing destinations for fishermen. Again, there are picnic tables, hiking trails, and a boat launch site. Fishing and boating are permitted, and there's ice skating in winter when conditions permit. ☎ *845-351-2568. Open daily. Vehicle use fee daily May–Sept., on weekends the rest of the year.*

Continue south on Seven Lakes Drive past lakes Askoti and Skannatati *(fishing only)*, Lake Kanawauke *(picnicking and hiking; vehicle use fee daily May–Sept, weekends rest of year)*, and the junction with NY-106. Just beyond this is **Lake Sebago Beach ❽**. One of the larger beaches in the area, this ia another superb setting, with fine walks and good views all around. Activities here include swimming, sports, games, picnicking, fishing, and boating. There's a place to rent boats, and a food concession — in season, of course. ☎ *845-351-2583. Open daily. Vehicle use fee daily May–Sept., on weekends the rest of the year.*

Finally, a bit to the north on Lake Welch Drive, is **Lake Welch Beach ❾**. This is another large beach area, able to handle the biggest summer crowds. The swimming and boating are excellent, and there's a lovely hedged lawn for sunbathing. Other activities include fishing, picnicking, hiking, and even camping. In winter, weather permitting, there's ice fishing and snowmobiling. Boats may be rented, and there's a food concession. ☎ *845-947-2444. Open daily. Vehicle use fee daily May–Sept. and on weekends the rest of the year. Partially* X.

From Lake Sebago you can continue south to NY-17, which joins the NY State Thruway (I-87) at Suffern. Those leaving from Lake Welch can head east on NY-106 to the Palisades Interstate Parkway, then south. Either route will return you to New York City.

Newburgh

Newburgh, an old Hudson River industrial town, has certainly seen better days, but is still rich in early American history. George Washington had his headquarters here for over a year during the Revolutionary War, and it was here that his orders ending the conflict in 1783 were issued. The sites of these and other Revolutionary events have been preserved by the State of New York, which operates them as living history museums complete with staff in period costumes and re-enactments of past activities.

Still earlier history can be relived at the nearby Gomez Mill House of 1714, the oldest surviving Jewish homestead in North America. Continuously occupied for nearly three centuries, the house, along with its associated mill, ice house, and root cellar, is now open to the public for a unique look at the contributions the former occupants have made to the multicultural history of the Hudson Valley.

For those who can stay overnight or longer, this area makes a fine base for exploring the entire Hudson Valley in even greater depth than daytrips alone can afford.

GETTING THERE:

By Car: The fastest (but not shortest) route is to take the **New York State Thruway** (I-87) north to Exit 17, Newburgh. A shorter and more scenic (but slower) route is to cross the George Washington Bridge and take the **Palisades Interstate Parkway** north to Bear Mountain, then **US-9W** past West Point into Newburgh. You will probably want to return from the last stop at Vails Gate via US-9W and the Parkway.

PRACTICALITIES:

This trip can only be taken from mid-April through October, and then only from Wednesdays through Sundays — plus a few national holidays. At other times all of the sites are closed.

For further information contact the sites directly, or **Orange County Tourism**, 30 Matthews St., Goshen, NY 10924, ☎ 845-291-2136, Internet: www.orangetourism.org.

FOOD AND DRINK:

Free picnic facilities are available at most of the sites. Otherwise, you might try:

Il Cena' Colo (228 Route 52, near junction of NY-300, west of Newburgh) Northern Italian delights, especially the cuisine of Tuscany. ☎

845-564-4494. X: Tues., holidays. $$ and $$$

Yobo Oriental (1297 Route 300, near NY-17K, west of Newburgh. Favorite dishes from all over the Orients — Japan, China, Korea, Indonesia, and Thailand. ☎ 845-564-3848. $$

Raccoon Saloon (1330 Main St. in Marlboro, near Gomez House) Burgers 'n beer, and the like. ☎ 845-236-7872. $

LOCAL ATTRACTIONS:

Circled numbers in text correspond to numbers on the map.

In the fall of 1782, after seven years of war, more than 8,000 soldiers and officers of the Continental Army camped in the Newburgh area to await news of the peace negotiations in Paris. Three of the historic sites on this trip, all administered by the Palisades Interstate Park Commission, tell the story of this long encampment of Washington's army.

From Exit 17 of the Thruway, or from US-9W in Newburgh, go east on Broadway (NY-17K) to Liberty Street and there turn south two blocks to the:

*WASHINGTON'S HEADQUARTERS STATE HISTORIC SITE ❶, corner Liberty and Washington streets, Newburgh, NY 12551, ☎ 845-562-1195, Internet: www.nysparks.com. *Open mid-April through Oct., Wed.–Sat. 10–5, Sun. 1–5. Also open President's Day, Memorial Day, Independence Day, Labor Day, and Columbus Day. Adults $3, NYS seniors $2, children (5–12) $1. Tours. Picnic facilities. Partially ♿.*

The Jonathan Hasbrouck House in Newburgh served as Washington's headquarters from April 1782 to August 1873. Here he issued orders, declined a suggestion that he become America's first king, and in general spent the days none too happily, if you can judge from a letter he wrote on January 10, 1783: "Time will pass heavily on in this dreary mansion in which we are fast locked by frost and snow." The house, begun in 1725 and completed by 1770, is furnished as it might have been when Washington was here. It stands on seven acres overlooking the Hudson. On the grounds is the 53-foot Tower of Victory, erected to commemorate the 100th anniversary of the disbanding of the Continental Army. Nearby is a museum with exhibits and audiovisual displays.

History of an even earlier period, and of a different sort, can be experienced nearby by making a short side trip north about four miles on US-9W to Marlboro. Turn right on Mill House Road to visit the:

GOMEZ MILL HOUSE ❷, 11 Mill House Rd., Marlboro, NY 12542, ☎ 845-236-3126, Internet: www.gomez.org. *Open mid-April to late Oct., Wed.–Sun. 10–4. Adults $3, under 12 free. Special events are usually held on Sundays, check the web site for details.*

After fleeing from the Spanish Inquisition, Luis Moses Gomez in 1714 settled down here near the Hudson, building a fieldstone blockhouse from which he traded with the Native Americans. Over the years this

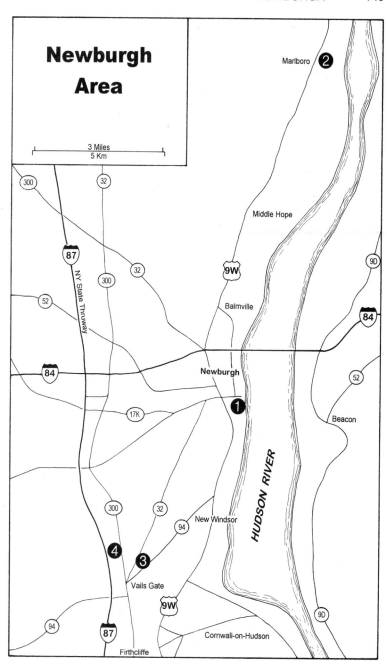

Newburgh Area

3 Miles
5 Km

evolved into the home you see today, reputedly the oldest in the county and actually the oldest existing Jewish residence in America. Later owned by other distinguished families, the 28-acre site has been preserved by their descendants as well as those of Luis Moses Gomez and in recent years opened to the public. Along with the six-room house, the isolated site, surrounded by woods, includes a mill and its dam, a root cellar, an ice house, and more.

Return south on US-9W past Newburgh to the intersection with NY-94. Turn right on 94 and go about two or three miles to Forge Hill and:

KNOX'S HEADQUARTERS STATE HISTORIC SITE ❸, Vails Gate, NY 12584, ☎ 845-561-5498, Internet: www.nysparks.com. *Open Memorial Day through Labor Day, Wed.–Sat. 10–5, Sun. 1–5. Adults $3, NYS seniors $2, children (5–12) $1. Picnic facilities. Special events. Mostly &.*

This elegant 1764 Georgian house of stone and frame construction was the home of John Ellison, merchant-miller. General Horatio Gates used it as his headquarters in the winter of 1782–83, while he was in command of the New Windsor Cantonment. Earlier in the war it sheltered Generals Henry Knox and Nathaniel Greene. A short walk from the house is the **Jane Colden Native Plant Sanctuary**, a beautiful sight in the spring when the wildflowers bloom, and just beyond are the ruins of the 1741 gristmill that made the Ellisons' fortune and a surviving stone bridge that was part of the King's Highway.

Continue briefly on 94 to the junction with NY-32 and NY-300 (Temple Hill Road). Turn right on 300 and go about a mile to the:

NEW WINDSOR CANTONMENT STATE HISTORIC SITE ❹, Vails Gate, NY 12584, ☎ 845-561-1765, Internet: www.nysparks.com. *Open mid-April through Oct., Wed.–Sat. 10–5, Sun. 1–5. Also open on Memorial Day, Independence Day, and Labor Day. Adults $3, NYS seniors $2, children (5–12) $1. Picnic facilities. Re-enactments. Special events. Tours. &.*

The Cantonment is the living history of the Continental Army's final winter encampment (1782–83) of the Revolutionary War. Some 7,000 soldiers and over 500 women and children spent the last months of the war on this site, building over 500 log huts for winter quarters, and waiting for news of peace. Some of the officers, their meager pay long overdue, circulated mutinous documents known as the Newburgh Addresses, calling for the army to take matters into their own hands. General Washington showed a fine political instinct in his personal handling of the situation. His emotional speech in the "Temple" building demonstrated sympathy with their grievances while appealing to their patriotism. In the end the officers unanimously reaffirmed their support for the general and the cause for which they had fought so long. On April 19, 1783, exactly eight years after the "shot heard round the world" was fired at Concord, the Cessation of Hostilities was announced to the army, and the soldiers soon dispersed to their homes in the newly independent United States of

America.

Today at New Windsor Cantonment the daily routine of the Continental Army's last encampment is re-created through "living history" demonstrations, including blacksmithing, woodhewing, cooking, and 18th-century medical practices. Every afternoon uniformed interpreters hold a military drill and demonstrate the firing of Revolutionary War muskets and a cannon in front of the re-created "Temple." At the Visitor Center there is an audiovisual display and exhibits, including an original award created by Washington exclusively for enlisted men, the Badge of Military Merit, predecessor of the Medal of Honor and the inspiration for the Purple Heart.

You could head north on NY-300 to Exit 17 of the Thruway for a fast ride back to New York City, or take a shorter scenic route by going south to Firthcliffe, where you can rejoin US-9W and eventually the Palisades Interstate Parkway.

Trip 20

Central Orange County

There are some unusual sights in this otherwise quiet part of Orange County, and if you come on a weekend between late July and mid-September, you can experience an annual treat the alone makes the trip highly worthwhile.

GETTING THERE:

By Car: Take the **New York Thruway** (I-87) north towards Albany to Exit 15A and pick up **NY-17** north for about 8 miles to the junction with **NY-17A**. Turn left and go about 3 miles west to Sterling Forest and the New York Renaissance Faire.

Continue on 17A to Warwick, turning right on **NY-94**. Go north on this about 6 miles to Florida, where 94 branches off to the right. Go straight and continue on 17A about 4.5 miles to **Goshen**. In Goshen at the junction with NY-17/US-6, 17A becomes NY-207. Continue through the stoplight to the entrance of the Goshen Historic Track; just beyond this is the Harness Racing Museum and Hall of Fame.

Go back to the junction with NY-17/U5-6 (Quickway) and take it east about 10 miles, passing Goosepond Mountain State Park, an unspoiled wilderness tract with hiking trails and bridle paths. Get off the Quickway at Exit 129, Museum Village Rd., and follow signs to the Museum Village of Orange County.

The Museum Village is about 70 miles northwest of midtown Manhattan via Sterling Forest and Goshen. For the return trip, continue east on the Quickway to the Thruway.

PRACTICALITIES:

The Renaissance Faire is held on weekends from late July through mid-September, and also on Labor Day. If you come at that time, you'll probably want to spend most of the day there, limiting time for the other attractions. The Harness Racing Museum is open daily, except Thanksgiving, Christmas, and New Year's Day. Lastly, Monroe's Museum Village is open from May through December, on Wednesdays through Sundays. In each case, you should check first before making the journey.

For further information contact the sites directly, or **Orange County Tourism**, 30 Matthews St., Goshen, NY 10924, ☎ 845-291-2136, Internet: www.orangetourism.org.

FOOD AND DRINK:

Those coming for the Renaissance Faire will find plenty of hearty food and drink; otherwise you might try:

Catherine's (153 W. Main St. in Goshen) Quality dining in an historic building. ☎ 845-294-8707. $$

Oliver's (40 Park Pl. in Goshen) A real English pub conveniently near the racing track. ☎ 845-294-5077. $

LOCAL ATTRACTIONS:

Circled numbers in text correspond to numbers on the map.

Much of pristine **Sterling Forest** ❶ — some 15,000 acres of it — is now a state park, filled with wildlife and rare plants. Parts of it may be visited and used for such pursuits as hiking, fishing, boating, cross-country skiing, ice skating, and the like. Another part of the forest is home to the annual:

*NEW YORK RENAISSANCE FAIRE ❶, 600 Route 17A, Sterling Forest, Tuxedo, NY 10987, ☎ 845-351-5171, Internet: www.renfair.com/NY. *Open on weekends from late July through mid-Sept., and on Labor Day Monday, 10–7. Adults $16.75, children (5–12) $7, under 5 free. Advance sale tickets at discount. Admission includes entertainment. Food and drink concessions. Picnic tables. Artisan crafts on sale. Largely ♿.*

If you think that all the romance has gone out of the world, try shedding your cares and a few centuries at the New York Renaissance Faire, where you can thrill to the spectacle of knights in shining armor jousting on horseback as in days of yore, lend an ear to the strolling minstrels, laugh along with the jesters and mimes, sate yourself on hearty fare and noble drink, fritter away your farthings at the gaming tables, and watch the players strut and fret their hour upon the stage at the Globe Theater. Struth, all this and more, as you like it, in the lovely setting of Sterling Forest. The festival is now in its 24th year, and going strong.

Follow the directions (above) to Goshen, home of the:

HARNESS RACING MUSEUM & HALL OF FAME ❷, 240 Main St., Goshen, NY 10924, ☎ 845-294-6330, Internet: www.harnessmuseum.com. *Open daily, 10–6. Closed Thanksgiving, Christmas, New Year's Day. Adults $7.50, seniors $6.50, children (6–12) $4, under 6 $3.50. ♿.*

The former Good Time Stable has been converted into a museum dedicated to the Standardbred trotters who made this area famous. More than 100 exhibits in the large box stalls and hay chutes capture the flavor of harness racing and tell the story of this quintessential American sport, the great national pastime of the 19th century, still entertaining millions of enthusiastic fans today. There's an original painting of Hambletonian, the Standardbred "daddy of 'em all," as well as Currier and Ives lithographs, wood carvings, bronzes, and statuary. Dioramas and films depict the immortal horses and drivers, and there are lifelike statuettes of the sport's

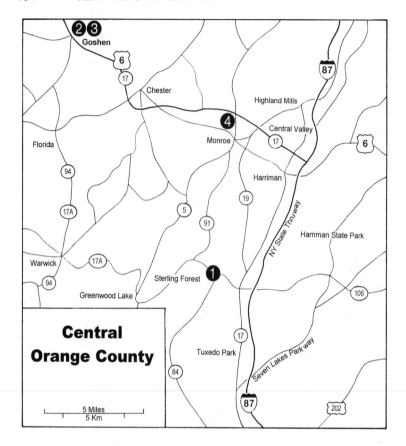

great personalities in the United States Harness Writers Association Living Hall of Fame. You can browse in the Peter D. Haughton Memorial Library or in the Weathervane Shop, which sells horseshoes, jewelry, and all manner of items related to harness horses.

GOSHEN HISTORIC TRACK ❸, 44 Park Place, Goshen, NY 10924, ☎ 845-294-5357. *Open for walking tours all year daily 9–5. Racing in spring and summer; schedule and fees vary (check in advance). Picnicking, refreshment stand, special events all season. Partially &.*

This National Historic Landmark, harness racing's oldest track (1838), still offers races. Even if there are none scheduled on the famous half-mile during your visit, you can see the horses in their stables and watch them go through their paces during the daily workout.

Follow the directions in "Getting There" (above) to Monroe and the:

MUSEUM VILLAGE IN ORANGE COUNTY ❹, Museum Village Rd., Monroe, NY 10950 ☎ 845-782-8247, Internet: www.museumvillage.org. *Open May– June and Sept.–Dec., Wed.–Fri. 10–2, Sat.–Sun. and holidays 11–4; July–Aug., Wed.–Fri. 10–5, Sat.–Sun. and holidays 11–5. Adults $8, seniors $6, children (3–15) $5. Picnic area. Snack bar. Shops. Special events. Partially ♿.*

Here's an outdoor museum that gives you a vivid taste of life in pre-industrial America. At 33 buildings clustered around the Village Green, you can see demonstrations of such indispensable 19th-century skills as weaving, blacksmithing, cobbling, wood carving, sheep shearing, and the making of candles, brooms, soap, cider, and other basics. A collection of steam and gas engines heralds the arrival of 20th-century technology, while a natural history exhibit takes you back to prehistoric times and for once invites you to "please touch" the bones of a well-preserved mastodon.

The Museum Village specializes in such contrasts, with exhibits that remind you how laborious life was before the invention of modern appliances like the vacuum and the Cuisinart, but may also make you long for the simpler days of Dr. Daniel's Housecleaning Fluid and Gargle. Throughout the year there are special events, including antique shows, Christmas shopping and caroling, Halloween tricks and treats, and an annual kite-flying day where you can buy or build your own aerodynamic contribution to the Hudson Valley skies.

Kingston

O ne of the oldest towns in New York State — only New York City and Albany are older — Kingston was first settled by the Dutch in 1652. In 1777 it was the state capital, and later became a transportation hub when the Delaware and Hudson Canal joined the coal fields of Pennsylvania with the Hudson River in 1827. Today its historic past is well preserved as part of the state's Urban Cultural Park Program, which has been instrumental in the revitalization of a once-blighted urban core.

GETTING THERE:

By Car: Take the **New York State Thruway** (I-87) north towards Albany to Exit 19. Follow signs for Kingston; halfway around the traffic circle, exit at Washington Avenue. Go two blocks to North Front Street, turn left, and go four blocks to Fair Street. Park as close to here as possible and follow directions in the text.

Kingston is about 95 miles north of midtown Manhattan.

PRACTICALITIES:

This is really a summer trip, best taken on a weekend or holiday between Memorial Day and Columbus Day. Several of the sights are closed at other times, so check the listings below carefully, and confirm them (they do change!) before making the journey.

For further information contact the sites directly or **Ulster County Tourism**, 10 Westbrook Lane, Kingston, NY 12401, ☎ 1-800-342-5826 or 845-340-3566, Internet: www.co.ulster.ny.us. More local information can be had from the **Kingston Urban Cultural Park**, 308 Clinton Ave., Kingston, NY 12401, ☎ 1-800-331-1581 or 845-331-7517, Internet: www.ci.kingston.ny.us.

FOOD AND DRINK:

Armadillo Bar & Grill (97 Abeel St. in Rondout) Tex-Mex and other Southwestern dishes with a Nuevo Latino twist. ☎ 845-339-1550. $$

Ship to Shore Restaurant (15 West Strand in Rondout) A popular place for burgers, steaks, and of course seafood. ☎ 845-334-8887. $ and $$

Hoffman House (94 N. Front St. in Stockade) Traditional American and British cuisine in a restored 17th-century Dutch house. ☎ 845-338-2626. X: Sun. $ and $$

Deising's (109 N. Front St. in Stockade) Light lunches in a coffee shop and bakery. Creative sandwiches, burgers, salads, soups, and the like. ☎ 845-338-7503. $

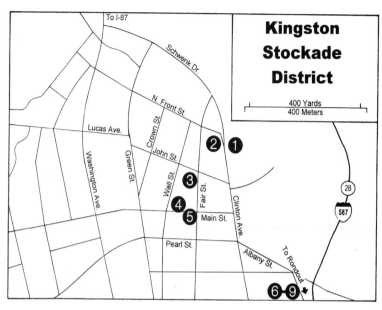

Kingston Stockade District

400 Yards
400 Meters

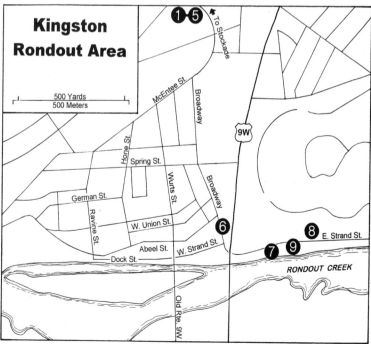

Kingston Rondout Area

500 Yards
500 Meters

SUGGESTED TOUR:

Circled numbers in text correspond to numbers on the map.

Historic Kingston is divided into three distinct areas, two of which are especially appealing to visitors. These are the uptown area known as **Stockade** and the waterfront area known as **Rondout**. The tour begins uptown, after which you drive to the Rondout to continue.

Kingston's **Stockade District** was once just that. Hostilities with the local Native Americans led in 1658 to the construction of a 13-foot-high wall surrounding the small community. Within the next 50 years this was gone, but the area remained the heart of the growing town for the next century or so. Today its streets are lined with historic buildings dating from as far back as the late 1600s, some of which can be visited. Begin your tour at the **Kingston Urban Cultural Park Visitor Center ❶**, were you can get a brochure for a self-guided **Historic Stockade Walking Tour**, learn about Kingston's colorful past as a transportation hub during the early growth of the nation, and see exhibits on local history. ☎ *845-331-9506 or 1-800-331-1518, Internet: www.ci.kingston.ny.us. 308 Clinton Ave. Open May–Oct., daily, 11–5. At other times use the Rondout Visitor Center, below. Free.* ♿.

Your first stop should be the:

*SENATE HOUSE STATE HISTORIC SITE ❷, 296 Fair St., Kingston, NY 12401 ☎ *845-338-2786, Internet: www.nysparks.com. Open mid-April through Oct., Wed.–Sat. 10–5, Sun. 1–5. Adults $3, NYS seniors $2, children (5–12) $1. Picnic facilities. Tours. Re-enactments.* ♿.

The Senate House, administered by the Palisades Interstate Park Commission, holds an important place in the history of New York State. Built by Wessell Ten Broeck in 1676 of rock-cut limestone, with one wall of Holland brick, it was already a century old when the first state legislature convened here on September 9, 1777. On October 7 the legislature adjourned upon learning that British troops were moving up the Hudson towards Kingston, and on October 16 the British landed and set the town afire. The house was damaged in the fire and repaired by its owner, Abraham Van Gaasbeek. Only the porch is "new" — it dates from 1888. There's a lovely rose garden behind the house, and the museum has historical exhibits and a collection of paintings by John Vanderlyn, a Kingston native and a student of Gilbert Stuart's.

Walk down the street to the:

VOLUNTEER FIREMEN'S HALL AND MUSEUM ❸, 265 Fair St., Kingston, NY 12401, ☎ *845-331-0866. Open Apr.–Oct., Fri. 11–3, Sat. 10–4. From June–Aug. also open Wed. & Thurs. 11–3. Donation.*

In 1981 Kingston's seven volunteer fire companies and the Exempt Firemen's Association leased this 1857 fire station of the Wiltwyck Hose Company from the city as a meeting hall. As a labor of love, the members turned the first floor into a museum and opened it to the public. In the parlor you'll find hand-carved black walnut furniture and the inevitable firehouse player piano (it works). Also on display is an extensive collection of antique fire-fighting equipment, memorabilia, and prints. Books and documents testify to the valor of the early firemen and trace the history of fire fighting in Kingston, which began when the city ordered a fire engine from England in 1754. Three years and many fires later, this primitive but functional apparatus arrived and served admirably for two decades, until it went up in smoke when the British burned Kingston in 1777.

Turn right on Main Street to the:

OLD DUTCH CHURCH ❹, Main & Wall Sts., Kingston, NY 12401, ☎ 845-338-6759. *Open year round, Mon.–Fri. 10–2. Free.*

This attractive 19th-century church is home to one of the oldest congregations in America, established in 1659. The church museum holds artifacts and documents of historical interest, including a letter from George Washington. George Clinton, first governor of New York (1777-95), vice-president under Jefferson and Madison, and one of the earliest New York politicians to manipulate election results (in the 1792 gubernatorial race against John Jay), is buried in the cemetery.

Also on Main Street, nearby, is the **Fred J. Johnston Museum ❺**, a treasury of 18th- and early 19th-century furnishings and decorative art. Long a prominent landmark, this 1812 Federal-style house is now open to the public. ☎ *845-339-0720. 63 Main St. Open May–Oct., Sat.–Sun. 1–4. Admission $3.* ♿.

Retrieve your car and follow Clinton Avenue south, making a left on St. James Street, then a right on Broadway. This leads southeast through most of Kingston to the **Rondout Area**, where Rondout Creek meets the Hudson River. This fine example of a 19th-century waterfront was once alive with shipbuilding activities and the transshipment of Pennsylvania coal plus locally-produced construction materials. Its prosperity lasted well into the 20th century, but declined as highways took over from water and rail transport. Today, Rondout is experiencing a renaissance, with numerous tourist attractions. Begin your visit at the main office of the **Kingston Urban Cultural Park Visitors Center ❻**, where you can see exhibits on the waterfront's past and pick up a free walking tour brochure. ☎ *845-331-7517 or 1-800-331-1518, Internet: www.ci.kingston.ny.us. 20 Broadway. Open May–Oct., Mon.–Fri. 9–5, Sat.–Sun. 11–5. Free.* ♿.

Your first stop should be the:

HUDSON RIVER MARITIME MUSEUM ❼, 1 Rondout Landing, Kingston, NY 12401, ☎ 845-338-0071, Internet: www.ulster.net/~hrmm. *Open May–Oct., daily 11–5. Museum entrance: Adults $3, seniors (60+) and children (6–12) $2; Museum, boat ride, and lighthouse visit: Adults $8, seniors and children $7.*

Here is a museum celebrating the rich maritime heritage of the Hudson River, its related industries and recreations. Visitors see a variety of models, artifacts, and antique vessels, along with the bell from the 19th-century steamboat *Mary Powell* and other relics of river life.

The historic ***Rondout Lighthouse** is a highlight of your visit during the summer months, and can be reached via a ten-minute boat ride aboard the liberty launch *Indy 7* for an additional fee (see prices above). *Operates daily in July–Aug. at 12:30, 1:30, 2:30, and 3:30, plus 11:30 on weekends; also weekends and holidays in May–June and Sept.–Oct. at 12:30, 1:30, 2:30, and 3:30.* The Museum Store offers books, souvenirs, and gift items with a nautical flavor. Hospitality is available to transient boaters at a reasonable rate.

Many yachts, sailboats, tugs, launches, cruisers, and coastal liners make Rondout Landing a port of call. The Hudson River cruise ship *Rip Van Winkle* (see below) departs from the adjacent waterfront area. Each year the museum hosts a variety of programs and special events, including the Shad Festival in May, with the day's catch pan-fried before your eyes. There's also the Lighthouse Festival and New Boat Show in June, the Antique and Classic Boat Show in August, and the International Festival in September.

Nearby is the:

TROLLEY MUSEUM OF NEW YORK ❽, 89 East Strand, Kingston, NY 12401, ☎ 845-331-3399, Internet: www.tmny.org. *Open Memorial Day to Columbus Day, noon to 5 on weekends & holidays. Adults $3, seniors and children $2. Visitor center and ride are* ♿.

Landlubbers will appreciate this museum on wheels, an old-time trolley offering a 1.5-mile scenic ride along the Hudson. There's a selection of antique cars on display, as well as more trolley lore in the visitor center.

While here, you might consider taking a cruise:

HUDSON RIVER CRUISES ❾, Rondout Landing, Kingston, NY 12401, ☎ 845-255-6515, Internet: www.hudsonrivercruises.com. *Operates May through Oct. Inquire about current schedules and fares. Meal and beverage service on board.*

Here's a relaxing, delightful way to take in the sights and sounds of the Hudson River Valley on a two-hour cruise aboard the 300-passenger *Rip Van Winkle*. A guide regales you with a capsule history as you glide past wild stretches of shoreline, lavish estates, quaint lighthouses, island castles, and soaring bridges.

Scenic Drives in the Catskills

Three different scenic drives that probe the Catskills are described in this chapter; take your choice. Either of them moves you into the heart of the Catskill Mountains, taking in some truly magnificent scenery and passing many points of interest along the way.

Those lucky enough to stay overnight or longer could, of course, take all three drives, and could also combine the drives with trips 15, 16, or 21 to make a real mini-vacation.

GETTING THERE:

By Car: Since this trip is planned mainly for the enjoyment of the drive itself, the directions are incorporated with the brief descriptions of the principal attractions along the route, given below. It is about 95 miles from midtown Manhattan to Kingston, about 120 miles to Catskill.

PRACTICALITIES:

Remember that this area is in a different weather pattern from New York City. Spring comes late here; by the same token, two or three weeks before the leaves turn in the city they'll be at their peak in the mountains.

For further information about the first route, contact **Ulster County Tourism**, 10 Westbrook Lane, Kingston, NY 12401, ☎ 1-800-342-5826 or 845-340-3566, Internet: www.co.ulster.ny.us. For the second and third routes contact **Greene County Promotion**, Route 23B, Catskill, NY 12414, ☎ 1-800-355-2287 or 518-943-3223, Internet: www.greene-ny.com.

FOOD AND DRINK:

Many of the fancier restaurants serve only dinners; here's some good choices for lunch:

Bear Café (295 Tinker St., Rte. 212, in Bearsville near Woodstock) A popular and very busy place for creative American dishes. X: Tues. ☎ 845-679-5555. $$

La Conca d'Oro (440 Main St. in Catskill) A wide range of Italian dishes. X: Tues., weekend lunches. ☎ 518-943-3549. $$

Last Chance Café (Main St. in Tannersville) It's a restaurant, a café, a food store, and even an antique shop — all in one. X: weekdays from April–June. ☎ 518-589-6424. $ and $$

Bluestone Country Foods (54C Tinker St. in Woodstock) Healthy vegetarian dishes. ☎ 845-679-5656. $

Taco Juan's Mexican Food (31 Tinker St. in Woodstock) Both Mexican and light American favorites. ☎ 845-679-9673. $

Sweet Sue's (Main St. in Phoenicia) Sandwiches, pancakes, eggs, and the like; a great place for brunch. ☎ 845-688-7852. $

Bell's Coffee Shop (387 Main St. in Catskill) A local favorite for typical coffee shop fare. ☎ 518-943-4070. $

Maggie's Krooked Café (Tannersville) Breakfast served all day, plus burgers, sandwiches, salads, and the like. ☎ 518-589-6101. $

Jimmy O'Connor's Windham Mountain Inn (South St. in Windham) This popular Irish pub serves lunch along with the Guinness. ☎ 518-734-4270. $

SUGGESTED DRIVING TOURS:

Circled numbers in text correspond to numbers on the map.

It is possible to combine any two of these driving routes in the same day by going west on one and returning east on the other, in which case the text for the return trip would of course be in reverse order.

ROUTE NY-28 FROM KINGSTON:

Kingston, explored on the last trip, is one of the gateways to the Catskills. From the **New York State Thruway** Exit 19 at **Kingston** ❶, you'll drive west on **NY-28**, but first go three miles south on Old Route 209 to **Hurley** ❷, capital of New York for one month in 1777 after Kingston was burned by the British, birthplace of Sojourner Truth, and a station on the Underground Railroad. Settled since the mid-17th-century, the village is famed for its stone houses, some of which are among the oldest private dwellings in the United States. Here you can visit the **Hurley Patentee Manor**, a Dutch cottage built in 1696 and enlarged in 1745 as an English country mansion. ☎ *845-331-5414. 464 Old Rte. 209. Open mid-July to Labor Day, Wed.–Sun. 11–4. Admission $2.* Once a year, on the second Saturday in July, the town dresses up in 17th-century garb for **Stone House Day**, when the public is invited to tour several privately-owned Dutch stone houses (be sure to look for the witch-catcher in the chimney of the Polly Crispell House). Brochures for a self-guided walking tour are available in town. Another annual event is the colorful **Corn and Craft Festival** on the third Saturday in August, where you can eat corn while perusing local crafts. *For local information contact the Hurley Heritage Society,* ☎ *845-338-1661.*

Returning on Old 209 to NY-28, turn left and go west. Almost immediately you'll enter the **Catskill Forest Preserve** ❸, an enormous tract of almost 700,000 acres where you can hike through some of the wildest, most unspoiled country in the East. Part of the State Forest Preserves, the park stretches across Ulster and Greene counties into Sullivan and Delaware counties; most of the sites on this drive and the next lie within its boundaries.

Proceeding west on NY-28 for several miles, you'll come to the tip of

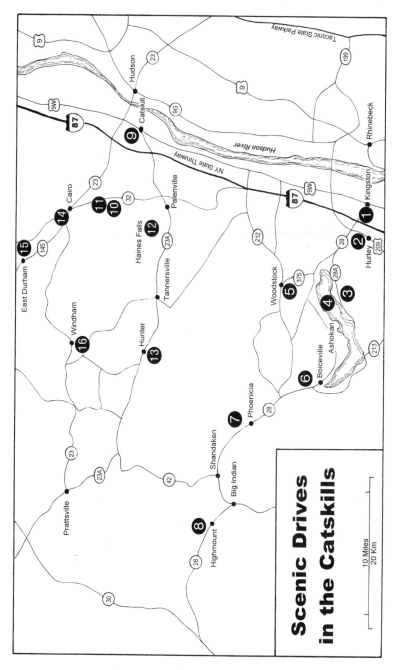

Scenic Drives in the Catskills

the 12-mile-long **Ashokan Reservoir** ❹, whence comes a large proportion of New York City's daily water supply. When the reservoir was first built beginning in 1909, eight communities, thousands of graves, and many miles of roads and railroads had to be either moved or be drowned by the advancing waters — a situation that was not popular with the locals. The underground hydroelectric plant is not open to the public, and there's no picnicking here, but fishing and boating are allowed by permit. Or you can just look: mountains unfold in all directions, cloud formations and reflections in the clear waters are superb. Often when the fall foliage has petered out along the Thruway and across the river, this area is still ablaze with color. You can continue along the north side of the reservoir on NY-28 or, better still, take the more **scenic southern route** around it on NY-28A, which brings you back to 28 on the other side of Boiceville.

Continuing west on NY-28 from the eastern end of the reservoir, you come to the attractive small town of West Hurley. Just beyond is the junction with NY-375. Take this north about 3 miles for a **side trip** to Woodstock.

*Woodstock ❺ has attracted artists, writers, and musicians since 1902, when a wealthy Englishman named Ralph Whitehead established the Byrdcliffe art community. Strongly influenced in his rejection of the industrial world by the writings of John Ruskin, Whitehead purchased over 1,200 acres of farmland just above Woodstock and there built a village where free thinking artists, poets, craftsmen, and the like could live in splendid isolation from the evils of modern society. His authoritarian ways, however, caused many of the artists to establish their own nearby communities, and in the village itself. Musicians came later, and in the late 1960s staged the infamous Woodstock Music Festival — which was actually held on a farm some 60 miles to the west after town officials denied them a permit. Today, Woodstock is populated by all manner of creative types, their hangers-on, and tourists in search of rural Bohemia.

The **Woodstock Artists Association** (*28 Tinker St.*, ☎ *845-679-2940, open Thurs.–Mon.*), **Kleinert/James Art Center** (*34 Tinker St.*, ☎ *845-679-2079, Internet: www.woodstockguild.org, open Fri.–Sun.*), and the **Center for Photography at Woodstock** (*59 Tinker St.*, ☎ *845-679-9957, Internet: www.cpw.org, Open March–Dec., Wed.–Sun.*) are among the largest galleries, with frequent exhibits and events. Other galleries, boutiques, restaurants, cafés, and shops are found on the streets leading from the village center. All types of music are presented, with the **Maverick Concerts** (☎ *845-679-8217, Internet: www.beekman.net/maverickconcerts*) being the oldest of its kind in the nation, playing on weekends from June to early September. Contact the **Woodstock Chamber of Commerce**, ☎ 845-679-6234, Internet: www.woodstock-online.com, or visit their booth just off the Village Green.

Back on NY-28, continue west to **Boiceville** ❻, at the western end of the reservoir. Here you can stop at the **Crackerbarrel Country Store** (☎ *845-657-6540*) to discover all sorts of old-fashioned things you thought were no longer made.

Another 8 or 9 miles on 28 brings you to **Phoenicia** ❼, where you can hike, swim, camp, and find a variety of winter activities at **Romer Mountain Park** (☎ 845-688-7440, *open daily Dec.–March, 10–5*), or board the **Catskill Mountain Railroad** (☎ 845-688-7400, *open late May–Oct., weekends and holidays*) for a scenic 2.8-mile ride along Esopus Creek. While there, visit the **Empire State Railway Museum** in Phoenicia's historic 1899 station. (☎ 845-688-7501, *Internet: www.esrm.com, open weekends Memorial Day to Columbus Day, 11–4*). This is trout country, but fly fishermen aren't the only ones who flock to the creek; the untamed waters makes it a favorite haunt of innertubers. If you haven't brought your own tube, you can rent one from **F-S Tube & Raft Rental** (☎ 845-688-7633, *Internet: www.catskill-park.com*) or **Town Tinker Tube Rental** (☎ 845-688-5553, *Internet: www.towntinker.com*). Note that NY-214 goes north from Phoenicia to Hunter Mountain and NY-23A (see next drive).

About 13 miles west of Phoenicia, still on NY-28, you'll come to **Highmount** ❽, where you can hit the slopes at **Belleayre Mountain Ski Center** (☎ 845-254-5600, *snow phone 1-800-942-6904, Internet: www.belleayre.com*). There's cross-country skiing too, and in summer you can picnic here and take a scenic chairlift ride to the summit.

You're now at the edge of Catskill Park. This drive ends here, but NY-28 goes on through Delaware County to Oneonta.

ROUTE NY-23A FROM CATSKILL:

From the **New York State Thruway** (I-87) Exit 21 you can drive west along this stunning wilderness route through Greene County, legendary home of Rip Van Winkle. Leaving the Thruway puts you in the historic town of **Catskill** ❾, where art enthusiasts can see the **Thomas Cole House** at 218 Spring St. *Presently closed; may reopen.* Cole, the founder of the Hudson River School, lived here from 1836 to 1848 and did some of his most important work in the studio.

Heading west from Catskill to Palenville, NY-23A crosses NY-32, which goes north to Cairo and NY-23 (see next drive). Along the way are many lovely waterfalls and some interesting attractions. Left off 32 is a turnoff for the *Catskill Game Farm ❿, which more than 68 years ago began a conservation project to preserve species endangered in the wild and today has large breeding herds of rare and vanishing animals. There are more than 2,000 furred and feathered creatures representing some 150 species here, including rhinos, giraffes, zebras, cheetahs, and tame deer for the children to pet. This is a far more sophisticated operation than you might expect, and well worth the rather steep admission price. There are also rides, shows, a playground, a café, and a gift shop. *400 Game Farm Rd., off NY-32. ☎ 518-678-9595, Internet: www.catskillgamefarm.com. Open May through Oct., daily 9–6. Adults $13.95, children (4–11) $9.95.* ⓖ.

Just up the road a piece on 32 is **Ted Martin's Reptile Adventure** ⓫. Dozens of species of snakes, turtles, lizards, and alligators are on display, and there are shows and hands-on experiences with the creatures. Both this and the previous attraction could just as well be taken as part of the next drive. *5464 Rte. 32, ☎ 518-678-3557. Open Memorial Day to Labor Day, daily 10–6, and weekends May to Columbus Day. Adults $6.50, children $4.25. Partially ♿.*

Back on 23A, continue west into **Catskill Park** (see previous drive) and on to **Haines Falls** ⑫. The falls, high and beautiful, are off the route a little in Twilight Park. Tucked away in the forest, accessible by trail from the North Lake State Park off 23A in Haines Falls, is New York's highest waterfall, **Kaaterskill**, which James Fenimore Cooper described so vividly in Leatherstocking Tales.

From Haines Falls continue west on 23A to Hunter ⑬, where a tempting array of activities awaits you at the Catskills' second-highest mountain. **Hunter Mountain Ski Area** *(☎ 518-263- 4223, ski phone 800-FOR-SNOW, Internet: www.huntermtn.com)*, a vast three-mountain complex with 49 slopes and trails plus snowmaking facilities that insure over 160 ski days per season, can easily accommodate thousands of skiers an hour. In summer and fall you can take the **Hunter Mountain Sky Ride** for wonderful views of the Catskills. The **Ski Museum**, documenting the history of the sport, is open all year. The well-known **Hunter Mountain Festivals** *(☎ 518-263-4223)* run virtually nonstop from early July through October.

NY-23A continues another 13 miles or so through Lexington to Prattsville, where it merges with the next route, NY-23.

ROUTE NY-23 FROM CATSKILL:

From the **New York State Thruway** (I-87) Exit 21 you again head west from **Catskill** ⑨, through more gorgeous mountain scenery, but now you're north of where you were on the last drive. Soon you will pass Leeds, with the oldest stone bridge in New York (1780), and South Cairo, with its slightly incongruous **Mahayan Buddhist Temple**, an ornate specimen of Chinese architecture, and a serene place that welcomes visitors to its Grand Hall and its 500 golden Buddhas. *☎ 518-622-3619. Open daily 7–7. Donation.*

Approaching **Cairo** ⑭, you'll pass the junction with NY-32, where you can go south to Ted Martin's Reptile Adventure and the Catskill Game Farm, both described on the previous drive.

From Cairo you can make a side trip north about 7 miles on NY-145 to **East Durham** ⑮. Here, on 145, is the **Irish American Heritage Museum**, which features exhibitions on Irish history, culture, literature, and genealogy. Its location is not so strange when you wander around the village and discover that it is practically Ireland's 33rd county, what with its Irish shops, pubs, cultural center, and festival. *☎ 518-634-7497, Internet: irishamericanmuseum.org. Open Memorial Day to Labor Day, Wed.–Sat. 11–4, Sun. noon–4; and Labor Day to Columbus Day, Fri.–Sat. 11–4 and Sun. noon–4. Adults $3.50, seniors and children $2. ♿.*

While in the neighborhood, you might want to have some fun at a nearby water park, **Zoom Flume**, which features giant water slides, a tubing river, rapids, and a pool. There are also some non-watery attractions including a playground, nature trails, and a scenic overlook. *Shady Glen Rd., off NY-145,* ☎ *518-239-4559 or 1-800-888-3586, Internet: www.zoom flume.com. Open June weekends 10–5; July–Labor Day, daily 10–6. Adults $15.95, children (7 and under) $12.95. Partially &.*

Continuing west on 23, wind you way up to **Windham** ⓰, where you'll find a fine downhill skiing facility, **Ski Windham** *(*☎ *518-734-4300 or 1-800-SKI-WINDHAM, Internet: www.skiwindham.com).* There's a classy atmosphere at this once private ski club, which has a 3,050-foot mountain and excellent snowmaking facilities.

NY-23 continues west to Prattsville, where it meets NY-23A, on the previous drive. You can turn left here and make a circle around the heart of Greene County by going east on 23A back to Catskill, or continue west to Prattsville, Oneonta, and beyond.

Section IV

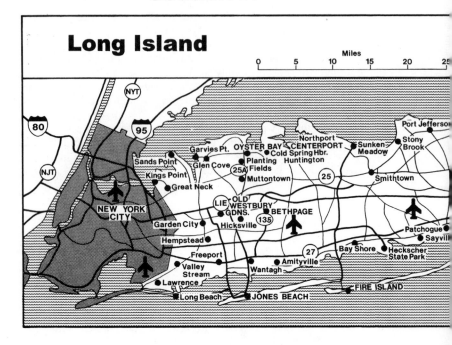

TOURING ON
LONG ISLAND

The next trips take you to that famous 120-mile-long fish-shaped piece of glacial deposit called Long Island, with its innumerable bays, coves, and inlets on Long Island Sound to the north and its beautiful ocean beaches to the south — "that slender riotous island which extends itself due east of New York," as F. Scott Fitzgerald called it, "the old island here that flowered once for Dutch sailors' eyes — a fresh, green breast of the New World."

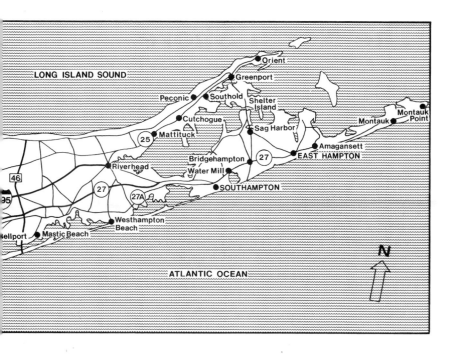

To judge by the way the city empties out and the Long Island Expressway fills up on weekends, many New Yorkers already have their favorite retreats on the island. This section outlines four long drives that take you to all the familiar haunts and suggest some possibilities for exploration off the beaten track. You'll be traveling in a more or less straight line out to the fishtail tip of Long Island, first along the North Shore, then to the North Fork, where historic New England-type towns flourish, then along the South Shore, and finally to the Hamptons and Montauk, with miles of beaches that apparently come and go at the will of the Atlantic Ocean.

Trip 23

*The North Shore

Long Island, occupied on the west by the two New York City boroughs of Brooklyn and Queens, stretches east across Nassau and Suffolk counties, encompassing populous suburbs, thriving seaport towns, quaint villages, and some of the finest beaches to be found anywhere. It is rich in Indian lore and Colonial history, studded with fine architecture, blessed with fertile farmlands and almost limitless recreational opportunities. This first drive, exploring the North Shore, is especially rich in history and includes several of the fabulous estates that the island is famous for. Most of these are fairly close to the city, so you need not venture too far to enjoy the very best.

There is much more here than can be seen in one day, so you'll have to pick and choose according to your interests — or stay overnight. You might even combine all four Long Island drives into one mini-vacation.

GETTING THERE:

By Car: From midtown Manhattan to Stony Brook is about 50 miles, and Riverhead about 80 miles. Leave the city via the **Queens Midtown Tunnel** and the **Long Island Expressway** (I-495). Get off at Exit 30 and take the **Cross Island Parkway** north about a mile, then **NY-25A** east to Great Neck Road. Take that north, becoming Bayview Avenue, to the first attraction. Since this trip is planned mainly for the enjoyment of the drive itself, the directions are incorporated with the brief descriptions of the attractions along the route.

PRACTICALITIES:

Most of the island's shore towns have public beaches but require permits or parking stickers for nonresidents; if you're planning a beach outing, check with the nearest municipality first.

For further information about Long Island, contact the **Long Island Convention & Visitors Bureau**, 330 Motor Parkway, Hauppauge, NY 11788, ☎ 631-951-3440 or 1-877-FUN-ON-LI, Internet: www.licvb.com, or contact the sites directly.

FOOD AND DRINK:

Long Island's North Shore is fairly loaded with good restaurants; here are a few choices:

La Pace (51 Cedar Swamp Rd. in Glen Cove) A longtime favorite for Northern Italian cuisine. X: weekend lunches. ☎ 516-671-2970. $$$

Peter Luger (255 Northern Blvd., NY-25A, in Great Neck) A renowned, elegant steakhouse. ☎ 516-487-8800. $$ and $$$

Bryant & Cooper Steakhouse (2 Middle Neck Rd. in Roslyn) Superb steaks, chicken, and seafood in an upscale setting. Convenient to Old Westbury Gardens. X: weekend lunches. ☎ 516- 627-7270. $$ and $$$

Three Village Inn (150 Main St. in Stony Brook, by the Village Green) Regional American, especially New England, specialties in an 18th-century homestead with a view. ☎ 631-751-0555. $$ and $$$

Louie's Shore Restaurant (395 Main St. in Port Washington) Seafood and steaks right on the bay. ☎ 516-883-4242. $$

DiMaggio's (706 Port Washington Blvd. in Port Washington) Pizza and other Italian specialties. ☎ 516-944-6363. $

Friend of a Farmer (1382 Old Northern Blvd., Main St., in Roslyn) Soups, salads, sandwiches and traditional American fare served in an old barn. ☎ 516-625-3803. $

Canterbury Ales Oyster Bar & Grill (46 Audrey Ave. in Oyster Bay) Fresh seafood, and landlubber choices as well ☎ 516-922- 3614. $

Wyland's Country Café (55 Main St. in Cold Spring Harbor) Light lunches; sandwiches, salads, and the like. ☎ 631-692-5655. $

Tortilla Grill (335 New York Ave. in Huntington) A full range of tasty Mexican dishes. ☎ 631-423-4141. $

SUGGESTED DRIVING TOUR:

Circled numbers in text correspond to numbers on the map.

On this drive, you'll go east on **NY-25A** (Northern Blvd. in Queens), noting the attractions along the route to the north and south.

Just over the Nassau County line from Queens, to the left off 25A in the Great Neck area, is the **U.S. Merchant Marine Academy** ❶ at Kings Point, where you can visit the Memorial Chapel honoring the service's war dead and see exhibits of shipping history in the **American Merchant Marine Museum**. On some Saturdays in the spring and fall, regimental reviews are held on the grounds. The academy is very attractively located, with scenic views across the Sound, and its main administration center, Wiley Hall, was once the country home of automobile magnate Walter P. Chrysler. *Steamboat Rd., Kings Point,* ☎ *516-773-5515, Internet: www.usmma.edu. Grounds open year round except July and federal holidays, daily 9–4:30. Museum open Tues.–Fri. 10–3 and Sat.–Sun. 1–4:30. Free. Largely* ♿.

Continue east on 25A. North of Manhasset, reached via **NY- 101**, is the **Sands Point Park and Preserve** ❷, former Gold Coast estate of Daniel Guggenheim and his son Harry, founder of Newsday. On the grounds are the English Tudor-style Hempstead House, the Irish-influenced Castlegould, and the Normandy-style manor house Falaise. The very, very rich have a knack for picking beautiful spots, and Sands Point is no exception. It has a great view of Long Island Sound and looks across Hempstead Harbor to Glen Cove. **Castlegould**, a stone castle of 1902, now serves as a visitor center and exhibition hall. *95 Middleneck Rd.,* ☎ *516-571-7900.*

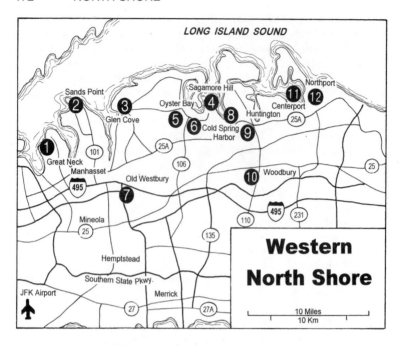

LONG ISLAND SOUND

Sands Point
Oyster Bay
Sagamore Hill
Northport
Centerport
Glen Cove
Cold Spring Harbor
Huntington
25A
Great Neck
Manhasset
101
25A
106
Old Westbury
Woodbury
25
495
110
495
231
Mineola
25
135
Hemptstead
Southern State Pkwy.
JFK Airport
Merrick
27
27A

Western
North Shore

10 Miles
10 Km

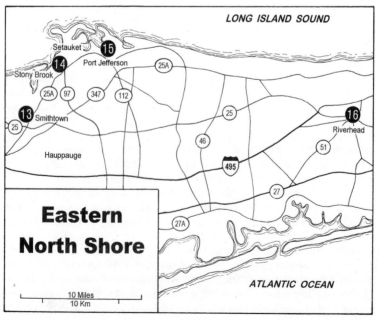

LONG ISLAND SOUND

Setauket
Port Jefferson
25A
Stony Brook
25A
97
347
112
25
Smithtown
25
46
Riverhead
51
495
Hauppauge
27
27A

Eastern
North Shore

ATLANTIC OCEAN

10 Miles
10 Km

Open daily 10–5. Adults $6, seniors (59+) $4, children (3–12) $3. &. Tours of **Hempstead House** *are offered May–Oct., Fri.–Sun. 12:30–4:30. Fee $2.* *Falaise, a world of medieval splendor, also houses memorabilia relating to the adventures of aviator Charles Lindbergh. It may be seen on tours. Tours May–Oct., Wed.–Sun., noon–3. Last tour at 2. Adults $5, seniors $3, under 10 not admitted.*

Continue on to Garvies Point, the next stop, reached by returning to 25A, heading east, and turning north on **NY-107**. Here, at the **Garvies Point Museum and Preserve ❸**, you can see exhibits on the geological formation of the region and its history of Indian settlement as revealed by archaeological finds. You can also follow 5 miles of nature trails through 62 acres of forests, meadows, and high bluffs overlooking boulder-strewn beaches. *Barry Drive, Glen Cove,* ☎ *516-571-8010, Internet: www.516web.com. Open Tues.–Sun., 10–4. Closed some holidays. Adults $1, children (5–12) 50¢. &.*

Now you're ready to charge up Sagamore Hill for a visit to the beloved retreat of America's 26th president, Theodore Roosevelt. The centerpiece of the **Sagamore Hill National Historic Site ❹** in Oyster Bay is T.R.'s family home, restored to the period of 1910-15 to reflect the full range of his presidential and later activities. Completed in 1885, this fine old Queen Anne-style structure incorporates many of Roosevelt's personal desires, including a large piazza with rocking chairs where the family could sit and watch the setting sun, a bay window with a southern view, and enormous fireplaces. You'll see objects collected on his trips around the world, gifts from the famous, family heirlooms, trophies, and personal mementos such as the "Clara-doll" in the playroom and the Teddy bears named after him. "Nothing," said Roosevelt, "can take the place of family life." Near the house is the **Old Orchard Museum**, offering historical exhibits, documents, photographs, and hourly showings of a stirring documentary on the highlights of T.R.'s life. *20 Sagamore Hill Rd., Oyster Bay,* ☎ *516-922-4447. Internet: www.nps.gov/sahi. House open Memorial Day to mid-Sept., daily 9:30–4; mid-Sept. to Memorial Day, Wed.–Sun. 9:30–4. 45-minute tours limited to 14 persons. Museum open all year, daily 9–4:45. Visitor center open daily 9–4:30. All closed on Thanksgiving, Christmas, New Year's Day. Admission: Adults $5, ages 16 and under free. Bookstore. Partially &.*

On the way up to Sagamore Hill, you'll pass several other sites well worth visiting. Some of the finest collections of plantings in the East are to be found at the 400-acre *Planting Fields Arboretum State Historic Park* **❺** with its superb specimens of trees, shrubs, and flowers, particularly lavish displays of rhododendrons and azaleas, and a Synoptic Shrub Collection presenting an A-to-Z sampler of species and varieties best as ornamentals. The rose collection alone contains over 900 plants. On the grounds is **Coe Hall**, a 65-room Elizabethan-Tudor mansion, originally the estate of marine insurance magnate William Robertson Coe. *Planting Fields Road, Oyster Bay,* ☎ *516-922-9201, Internet: www.plantringfields.org. Arboretum open year round daily 9–5, except Christmas; mansion*

Apr.–Sept., daily noon–3:30. Parking $5 per car. Gardens free. House tours: Adults $5, seniors $3.30, children (7–12) $1. Mostly &.

The town of **Oyster Bay** ❻ has several buildings of historic interest. **Raynham Hall** is a 1705 clapboard saltbox with a Victorian wing of 1851. Home of the Samuel Townsend family, it served as headquarters for the Queen's Rangers after Long Island was taken by the British during the American Revolution. *20 West Main St., Oyster Bay.* ☎ *516-922-6806. Open July–Labor Day, Tues.–Sun. noon–5; rest of year, Tues.–Sun. 1–5. Closed Thanksgiving, Christmas, New Year's Day. Adults $3, seniors (65+ and children (6–18) $2.* The **Earle-Wightman House** is another Colonial saltbox, built around 1720. It now contains historical exhibits, town memorabilia, and the collection of the Oyster Bay Historical Society. *20 Summit St., Oyster Bay.* ☎ *516-922-5032. Open Tues.-Fri. 10-2, Sat. 9-1, Sun. 1-4. Closed some major holidays. Adults $1.50, seniors and students $1, under 12 free. Partially &.*

Before continuing along the North Shore, you could go south of 25A and west a few miles to:

*OLD WESTBURY GARDENS ❼, 71 Old Westbury Rd. just below Expressway, Old Westbury. ☎ 516-333-0048, Internet: www.oldwestbury gardens.org. *Open late April through Oct., Wed.–Mon. 10–5; also on Sun. in Nov. and early Dec. Closed Mon. Last admission at 4:15. Gardens only: Adults $8, seniors (62+) $6, children (6–12) $3, under 6 free. House & Gardens: Adults $10, seniors $8, children $6. Gift shop. Plant shop. Café. &.*

Now a National Historic Site, the former estate of financier John S. Phipps contains 8 formal gardens; including the Boxwood Garden, with its ancient giant boxwood and reflecting pool; the Walled Garden, with 2 acres of herbaceous borders and brilliant seasonal flower displays; and the charming Cottage Garden, once the playground of the Phipps children, with a small thatched cottage surrounded by a miniature garden and a fairyland of flowering shrubs. **Westbury House**, a fine Charles II-style mansion built in 1906, contains many priceless antiques and paintings by noted English artists such as Sir Joshua Reynolds and John Singer Sargent. Both the house and grounds are patterned after an English country estate of the 18th century.

Return to 25A and head east to **Cold Spring Harbor** ❽, just over the Suffolk County line. As befits an old whaling town, Cold Spring Harbor has a **Whaling Museum** with a completely outfitted 19th-century American whaling boat with original gear, many tools of the trade, and other artifacts of this bygone era, including a scrimshaw collection of over 400 pieces along with an 1850 diorama. *Main St., Cold Spring Harbor,* ☎ *631-367-3418, Internet: www.cshwhalingmuseum.org. Open Memorial Day to Labor Day, daily 11–5; rest of year Tues.–Sun. 11–5. Adults $2, seniors (64+) $2, students (5–18) $1.50, under 5 free. &.*

A considerably less gargantuan fisherman's target is the focus of attention at the 118-year-old **Cold Spring Harbor Fish Hatchery and Aquarium**, where you can observe trout in various stages of maturation and see exhibits on fish and amphibians native to New York. *Route NY-25A at NY-108, Cold Spring Harbor, ☎ 516-692-6768, Internet: www.islandguide.com/hatchery. Open year round, daily 10–5. Closed Thanksgiving and Christmas. Adults $3, seniors and children (5–12) $1.50, under 5 free. ♿.*

The next stop is **Huntington ❾**, today known chiefly as a commuter suburb and center of precision manufacturing, but a town that still preserves many reminders of its past. The **Huntington Historical Society** maintains the **David Conklin Farmhouse** (c. 1750) at New York Avenue and High St., with period furnishings and displays on local history; the **Kissam House** of 1795, a favorite with antique buffs; and the **Huntington Sewing & Trade School** (1905), with research collections. *2 High St., Huntington, ☎ 631-427-7045. Conklin House open Tues.–Fri. and Sun., 1–4. Kisam House open May–Oct., Sun. 1–4. Adults $2.50, seniors (62+) $2, under 12 $1.*

Huntington's Heckscher Park, a popular spot for picnicking and outdoor concerts, contains the noted **Heckscher Museum of Art**, with a fine permanent collection of paintings and sculpture from the 1500s to the present, from both America and Europe. The 19th-century American landscapes are exceptional. *2 Prime Ave., Huntington, ☎ 631-351-3250, Internet: www.heckscher.org. Open Tues.–Fri. 10–5, Sat.–Sun. 1–5. Closed Mon., Thanksgiving, Christmas. Suggested donation: Adults $3, children (7–17) $1. ♿.*

South of Huntington, on Old Walt Whitman Road opposite Walt Whitman Mall, is the **Walt Whitman Birthplace State Historic Site ❿**, where the "good gray poet" was born in 1819. Whitman spent his boyhood in this charming shingled farmhouse, which has been restored as a museum honoring America's greatest poet. The lower floor contains period furnishings; upstairs are memorabilia and various exhibits. A new Interpretive Center was added in 1997, with exhibition galleries, an orientation film and Walt Whitman's voice on tape, and a Poetry Circle for readings. *246 Old Walt Whitman Rd. West Hills, Huntington Station, ☎ 631-427-5240, Internet: www.nysparks.com. Open late June–Labor Day, Mon. and Wed.–Fri. 11–4, Sat.–Sun. noon–4; rest of year, Wed.–Fri. 1–4, Sat.–Sun. noon–4. Closed holidays. Adults $3, seniors and students $2, children (7–12) $1, 6 and under free. Picnic facilities. Gift shop. Bookshop. ♿.*

A few miles east of Huntington is Centerport, and here, at the tip of Little Neck Point, is an attraction not to be missed:

*VANDERBILT MANSION, MARINE MUSEUM, PLANETARIUM, AND PARK ⓫. *180 Little Neck Rd., Centerport. ☎ 631-854-5555. Open Memorial Day–Labor Day, Tues.–Sun. 10–5; rest of year Tues.–Sun. noon–5. Closed Mon., Thanksgiving, Christmas, New Year's. Adults: $8. seniors and students $6, children $4. Tours $3 extra. Planetarium $3 extra. Gift shop. ♿.*

The Vanderbilt Museum is housed in a mansion built by William K.

Vanderbilt II, a great-grandson of the legendary Commodore Cornelius Vanderbilt. Known as the Eagle's Nest, this opulent 24-room Spanish Revival edifice was a simple six-room country dwelling before it fell under the transforming spell of the Vanderbilt fortune. William K. was an enthusiastic naturalist, sportsman, and collector. Today the exotic art treasures he gathered in his world travels fill the dining room, bedrooms, library, and sitting room. There are several enormous hobby collections and a natural history display of over 17,000 marine and wildlife specimens, many of them quite rare. Outside, you can see panoramic vistas through columns of marble from the ruins of Carthage, Spanish-Moroccan buildings with bell tower and bells dating from 1715, courtyards and mosaic-bordered walks, and landscaped gardens overlooking Northport Bay. Also on the grounds is the **Vanderbilt Planetarium**, one of the largest in the country, which puts on impressive sky shows.

Continuing east, you come to **Northport** ⑫, settled by English Puritans in 1656 on land purchased from the Matinecock Indians. The town has an excellent harbor, and its rich seafaring past is unfolded in the exhibits at the **Northport Historical Museum**, located in the Carnegie Library. *251 Main St., Northport, ☎ 631-757-9859. Open Tues.–Sun. 1–4:30, closed holidays. Donation.* On the tip of a spit of land jutting out into Long Island Sound is **Eaton's Neck Lighthouse**, built in 1798 and still casting its warning beacon almost 18 miles out to sea.

If you continue east on 25A, you'll shortly arrive in **Smithtown** ⑬, where you'll see the famous Bull Statue in a small park in the center of town. The statue commemorates the exploits of one of the early town fathers, Richard Smith, who made a bet with the Indians about how far a man could travel on a bull in a day. Impressed with his demonstration, the Indians granted him all the land he and his mount covered. Researchers are still attempting to determine whether the bull went farther in those days. There are a number of historic buildings in Smithtown, including the Caleb Smith House, where the local historical society makes its headquarters.

Continue on to **Stony Brook**, an old harbor town where you can easily spend a day. The entire village is a bit of a museum piece, having been restored to the Federal period through the generosity of philanthropist Ward Melville in the early 1940s. It's a pleasant place to shop, dine, stroll, or explore the:

*MUSEUMS AT STONY BROOK ⑭, 1208 Route 25A, Stony Brook, ☎ 631-751-0066, Internet: www.museumsatstonybrook.org. *Open Wed.–Sat. 10–5, Sun. noon–5, holiday Mon. 10–5. Closed most Mon., Tues., Thanksgiving, Dec. 24–25, and Jan. 1. Adults $4, seniors (60+) $3, students (6–17) $2, college students with ID $2, under 6 free. Gift shop. &.*

The Museums at Stony Brook are a remarkable historical and cultural complex housing collections of American art and artifacts. The **History**

Museum exhibits costumes, dolls, toys, textiles, and housewares; and has permanent exhibits of finely crafted decoys and miniature period rooms. The **Art Museum** offers changing exhibits of 19th- and 20th-century art, with emphasis on the works of William Sydney Mount (1807–68), a Stony Brook resident and an important figure in 19th-century American art for his portraits and scenes of everyday rural life. The **Carriage Museum** houses over 100 horse-drawn carriages, wagons, and sleighs. There is also a blacksmith shop, a one-room school, a 1794 barn, and a herb garden on the park-like grounds.

Leaving Stony Brook, you can continue east on 25A to **Port Jefferson** ⓯, another attractive harbor town, where the Port Jeff Ferry docks on its daily round trips to Bridgeport, Connecticut all year round. *102 West Broadway, Port Jefferson, ☎ 631-473-0286, in CT. 203-335-2040.* Along the way, in **Setauket**, you'll pass the **Thompson House**, a Colonial saltbox built around 1700, once the home of Long Island historian Benjamin F. Thompson. It has a good collection of early Long Island furniture and a Colonial herb garden. *93 North Country Rd., Setauket, ☎ 631-941-9444. Open Memorial Day to Columbus Day, Fri.–Sun. 1–5. Adults $3, seniors and children $1.50.*

About 15 miles east of Port Jefferson, 25A merges with NY-25. From here you can continue east to Riverhead ⓰, the last stop on this North Shore drive. Another historic town with fine beaches, boating facilities, and deep-sea fishing, Riverhead is the home of the **Suffolk County Historical Museum**, depicting the history of the county and its people in a series of exhibits highlighting early crafts, transportation, whaling, and the Long Island Indian legacy. *300 West Main St., Riverhead, ☎ 631-727-2881. Open Thurs.–Sat. 12:30–4:30. Donation.*

Trip 24

The North Fork

On this drive, you can pick up where you left off on the North Shore, following NY-25 east. As you go beyond Riverhead, the scenery changes from suburban to downright rural, with tiny villages, farms, isolated beaches, and vineyards. The atmosphere here is reminiscent of New England, which is actually not all that far away. In fact, Rhode Island is only some 20 miles as the seagull flies from Orient Point, the last stop on this trip. This is a place for relaxation, with gorgeous land and seascapes, and precious little in the way of regular tourist attractions. Enjoy.

GETTING THERE:

By Car, Riverhead is about 80 miles east of midtown Manhattan, and Orient Point about 105 miles. Take the **Long Island Expressway** (I-495) to its end, then **NY-25** east. Road directions are incorporated into the Suggested Driving Tour, below.

PRACTICALITIES:

Most of the island's shore towns have public beaches but require permits or parking stickers for nonresidents; if you're planning a beach outing, check with the nearest municipality first.

For further information about Long Island, contact the **Long Island Convention & Visitors Bureau**, 330 Motor Parkway, Hauppauge, NY 11788, ☎ 631-951-3440 or 1-877-FUN-ON-LI, Internet: www.licvb.com, or contact the sites directly. Additional information is available from the **North Fork Promotion Council**, P.O. Box 1056, Southold, NY 11971. ☎ 631-298-5757, Internet: www.northfork.org.

FOOD AND DRINK:

Ross' North Fork Restaurant (Route 48, west of Young Ave., in Southold) Contemporary American cuisine from local ingredients, with local wines. ☎ 631-765-2111. X: Jan. to mid-Feb. $$ and $$$

Aldo's (103 Front St. in Greenport) Mediterranean dishes in a small bistro, BYOB. ☎ 631-477-1699. $$

Claudio's (111 Main St. in Greenport) Right at the marina, and run by the same family since 1870! Mostly seafood, but there are steaks as well. ☎ 631-477-0627. X: Jan. to mid-April. $$

Modern Snack Bar (628 Main Rd., NY-25, between Riverhead and Jamesport) An old favorite family diner right out of the 50s. ☎ 631-722-3655. $

Cutchogue Diner (Main Rd., NY-25, in Cutchogue) Yet another old-fashioned diner, with typical diner fare. ☎ 631-734-9056. $

SUGGESTED DRIVING TOUR:

Circled numbers in text correspond to numbers on the map.

The drive begins east of Riverhead, and follows **NY-25** through acres of rolling farmland and fields of potato plants, berry vines, vegetables, and fruit trees. Soon you come to **Aquebogue ❶**, where the North Shore's wine country begins. A good winery to visit here is **Palmer Vineyards**, which offers self-guided tours, tastings in a cozy pub and, of course, sales of its products. *108 Sound Ave., Aquebogue,* ☎ *631-722-9463, Internet: www.palmervineyards.com. Open daily 11–6. Free.* ᕹ.

Pass through **Mattituck ❷**, with its fine harbor and several buildings of historic interest. About three miles east of this is **Cutchogue ❸**, where you will find the **Old House**, the **Old Schoolhouse Museum**, and the **Wickham Farmhouse** clustered around the historic village green. The Old House, built in 1649, is a particularly good example of English Tudor architecture and is furnished with authentic period pieces, as is the Wickham Farmhouse, dating from the early 1700s. The Old Schoolhouse Museum (1840), Cutchogue's first district school, takes you back to the basics of 19th-century education. ☎ *631-734-7122. Open July–Aug., Sat.–Mon. 1–4. Adults $1.50, children 50¢.* Cutchogue is also the home of **Hargrave Vineyards**, one of Long Island's oldest and best-known wineries, where you can taste the results of the Pinot Noir, Chardonnay, and Merlot harvest. ☎ *631-734-5158. Open daily, 11–5.*

Continue east to Southold, passing another fine winery, **Pindar Vineyards** in Peconic. This large operation produces many different varieties, which can be sampled along with a tour. *Main Rd., Peconic,* ☎ *631-734-6200. Open daily except major holidays, 11–6.* ᕹ. Nearby is **Osprey's Dominion Vineyards**, most noted for its Chardonnay and Cabernet Sauvignon wines. Tours and tastings are offered. *44075 Main Rd., Peconic,* ☎ *631-765-6188 or 1-888-295-6188, Internet: ospreydominion.com. Open Mon.–Sat. 10–5, Sun. 12–5. Closed major holidays. Free.* ᕹ.

Southold ❹ is a historic town proud of its past. Its **Indian Museum** has one of the largest and best collections of Indian artifacts on Long Island. *1080 Main Bayview Rd.,* ☎ *631-765-5577. Open July–Aug., Sat.–Sun. 1:30–4:30. Donation.* The restored village green complex has some interesting Colonial and Victorian houses that are maintained by the **Southold Historical Society** and that may be visited. ☎ *631-765-5500, call for current information.*

To the north of the village is the **Horton's Point Lighthouse and Nautical Museum**, facing Long Island Sound. Built in 1857, it is still in service and still sends its beam of light out some 14 nautical miles. The adjacent keeper's dwelling houses a small museum with an eclectic collection of maritime artifacts. Visits to the museum include a tour of the lighthouse. *Lighthouse Rd., Southold.* ☎ *631-765-5500, Internet: www.longislandlight*

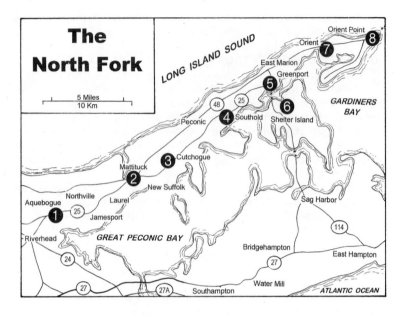

The North Fork

5 Miles
10 Km

LONG ISLAND SOUND

Orient Point ⑧

Orient ⑦

East Marion

Greenport ⑤

GARDINERS BAY

48   25

Peconic   ④ Southold   ⑥   Shelter Island

③ Cutchogue

Mattituck ②

New Suffolk

Sag Harbor

Northville   Laurel

Aquebogue   ⑤   Jamesport

Riverhead

GREAT PECONIC BAY

114

Bridgehampton

East Hampton

24

27

27   27A   Southampton   Water Mill   ATLANTIC OCEAN

houses.com/hortonpoint. *Open Memorial Day to Columbus Day, Sat.–Sun. 11:30–4. Suggested adult donation $2.*

Not far east of Southold is **Greenport** ⑤, an old whaling town often described as "New England on Long Island." Here in addition to fine beaches, great fishing, and some outstanding seafood restaurants, you'll find the **East End Seaport Maritime Museum** with its displays of maritime artifacts, navigational aids, tools, and local history. *3rd St. at the docks.* ☎ *631-477-2100, Internet: www.greenport.com/seaport. Open Memorial Day–Sept., Wed.–Mon. 10–5; also at other times, call. Adults $2, children $1.*

Also in Greenport is the **Railroad Museum of Long Island**, located in an 1892 freight house and displaying various artifacts, photos, and memorabilia of the Long Island Railroad. There are also two pieces of rolling stock and a turntable. The same museum operates a restoration site in Riverhead, where you can see various engines and cars being restored. You might want to stop there on the way home. *Fourth St.* ☎ *631-477-0439, Internet: www.bitnik.com/rmli. Open Memorial Day to Columbus Day, Sat.–Sun. and holidays, noon–5. Adults $1, children 50¢.* ♿.

Greenport is also the docking point for the ferry to **Shelter Island** ⑥, one of Long Island's loveliest and least "touristy" spots. This aptly-named patch of land, seven miles long and six miles wide, was settled in 1652 by New England Quakers fleeing Puritan persecution and is still a peaceful haven today. Situated between the North and South forks, it has a highly irregular coastline pierced by inlets and caressed by coves, with miles of pristine beaches and acres of gently rolling hills. It is also accessible by ferry from Sag Harbor (see page 000). *For more information contact the Shelter Island Chamber of Commerce, P.O. Box 598, Shelter Island, NY 11964.* ☎ *631-749-0399 or 1-800-9-SHELTER, Internet: www.onisland .com/si/chamber. For ferry information from Greenport* ☎ *631-749-0139.*

The next stop is **Orient ❼**, near the eastern tip of the North Fork. Here **Orient Beach State Park** spreads over a 357-acre peninsula on Gardiners Bay, offering excellent swimming and fishing. ☎ *631-323-2440, Internet: www.nysparks.com. Open daily. Parking Memorial Day–Labor Day, $6 per car.* In town, on Village Lane, is the **Oysterponds Museum**, a complex of five museum buildings that have been designated a National Historic District. *1555 Village Lane,* ☎ *631-323-2480. Open Open mid-June to Sept., Sat.–Sun. 2–5, also Thurs. in July–Aug. 2–5. Adults $3, children 50¢.*

From Orient, it's a short hop to **Orient Point ❽**, which is as far east as you can go on the North Fork unless you want to board the Cross Sound Ferry for a 90-minute trip to New London, Connecticut. ☎ *631-323-2525 or 860-443-5281, Internet: www.longislandferry.com.* (There's a smallish island east of Orient Point, Plum Island, but it's used by the government for animal disease experiments and is off-limits to the public — no doubt for good reason.) The ferry service operates daily except Christmas and requires advance reservations if you want to take your car along.

The South Shore

L ong Island's South Shore is a completely different world from its ritzy North Shore. You won't find much in the way of great mansions and estates in this seemingly endless sprawl of middle-class suburbia, but you will find plenty of magnificent beaches and, farther out, protected natural environments where you can take a walk along nature trails. There are also some small but unusual museums, a few bits of preserved history, and a chance to ride a ferry out to Fire Island. So put on your walking shoes, bring a swim suit, and enjoy the day.

GETTING THERE:

By Car: From Manhattan, take the **Queens Midtown Tunnel** and the **Long Island Expressway** (I-495) to the **Grand Central Parkway** (Exit 22A) in Queens. Take this south almost to JFK Airport, then turn east on **NY-27** towards Valley Stream. On this drive you'll use NY-27 and NY-27A as the main routes and reference points. Road directions are incorporated into the site descriptions, below. The farthest point, Hampton Bays, is about 85 miles east of midtown Manhattan.

PRACTICALITIES:

This is really an outdoors trip that should be taken between late Spring and early Fall, and then only in good weather. Try to avoid the weekend crowds, when the Long Island Expressway becomes the world's longest parking lot. The museums and historic sites, mostly minor attractions, have varying schedules, so check out the individual listings of any that appeal to you. If you're going to the beach, don't forget the sunscreen and sunglasses!

For further information about Long Island, contact the **Long Island Convention & Visitors Bureau**, 330 Motor Parkway, Hauppauge, NY 11788, ☎ 631-951-3440 or 1-877-FUN-ON-LI, Internet: www.licvb.com, or contact the sites directly.

FOOD AND DRINK:

You'll find picnic facilities, cafeterias, snack bars, and even restaurants at the beaches. And, of course, fast food everywhere. Other than that, here are a few good eateries:

Rose Cottage (NY-27A, a half-mile east of NY-110, 348 Merrick Rd. in Amityville) Continental cuisine in a chalet-like setting. ☎ 631-691-6881. X: Mon. $$ and $$$

La Grange Inn (499 Montauk Hwy., NY-27A, a mile east of West Islip)

Continental and German cuisine in a restful atmosphere. ☎ 631-669-0765. X: Tues. $$ and $$$

Sansar Indian Cuisine (128 Broadway in Hicksville) A wide range of Indian dishes, including a lunch buffet. ☎ 516-681- 9834. $ and $$

Raay-Nor's Cabin (550 Sunrise Hwy., NY-27, in Baldwin, west of Freeport) A rustic old favorite for country dishes, especially chicken. ☎ 516-223-4886. $ and $$

Bay Shack (Maple Ave. in Bay Shore) Convenient to the Fire Island ferry, this simple place is popular for its various seafoods. $

SUGGESTED DRIVING TOUR:

Circled numbers in text correspond to numbers on the map.

Cross into Nassau County on NY-27 (Southern Belt Parkway), which becomes the Sunrise Highway paralleling NY-27A, Montauk Highway, until the two merge. A few miles southwest of Valley Stream, the first major town you come to is **Lawrence ❶**, where you can visit **Rock Hall**, a Georgian Colonial manor of 1767 filled with artwork and antiques. This is just east of J.F.K. Airport, and can also be reached via Rockaway Boulevard in Queens. *199 Broadway, Lawrence,* ☎ *516-239-1157. Open April–Nov., Wed.–Sat. 10–4, Sun. noon–4. Closed holidays. Free.* From here you may want to continue south across the Atlantic Beach Bridge onto **Long Beach ❷**, a popular resort island with five miles of beach, a three-mile board-walk, and other recreational facilities. ☎ *516-432-6000. Beach pass $5.* &.

Continuing east from Valley Stream, you'll shortly come to **Lynbrook**, and just south of here in East Rockaway's Memorial Park is the **Grist Mill Museum ❸**, with two floors of East Rockaway memorabilia and exhibits on Indian and maritime history. *Wood and Atlantic Avenues, East Rockaway.* ☎ *516-887-6300. Open June–Labor Day, Sat.–Sun. 1–5. Donation.* North of Lynbrook is **Hempstead ❹** where you'll find the **African-American Museum.** Exhibits here explore the history, cultural heritage, and contributions of African-American Long Islanders. *110. N. Franklin St., Hemsptead.* ☎ *516-572-0730. Open year round, Thurs.–Sat. 10–4, Sun. 1–4. Free.* &.

Back on NY-27, continue east to **Freeport ❺**, a fishing and boating center with the famous "Nautical Mile" of **Woodcleft Canal**, a great place to dine on seafood, shop for fresh fish, charter a boat, take a canal excursion, or just shop in the market. Freeport is also the gateway to one of the most popular parks in the Greater New York City area:

*JONES BEACH STATE PARK ❻, Box 1000, Wantagh, NY 11793, ☎ 516-785-1600, Internet: www.nysparks.com. *Open mid-June to Labor Day, daily dawn to midnight; rest of year, daily dawn to dusk. Park and beach are free. Parking $7 from Memorial Day to Labor Day; free the rest of the year. Picnic facilities. Restaurant. Snack bars. Gift shop. Museum. Playground. Showers. Fishing. Golf. Pool.* &.

This is surely one of the nation's great beaches. Stretching along some 6.5 miles of oceanfront, it manages to accommodate even the largest

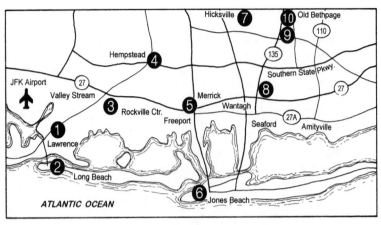

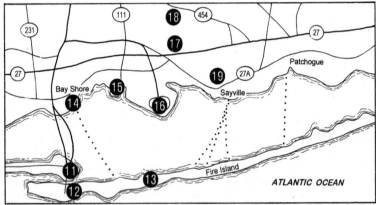

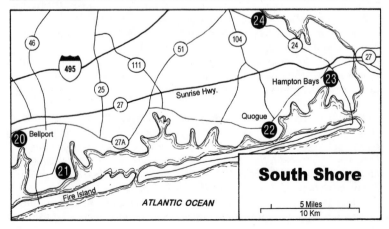

hordes that descend on it on a hot summer's day. Want to get away from the mobs? Just stroll along the water's edge and soon enough you'll be almost all by yourself.

Jones Beach was created in the late 1920s on an isolated, windswept sandbar by the visionary builder Robert Moses, a near-legendary character who changed the face of New York during his long reign as power broker from 1924–68. What he built here is amazing — this is no ordinary beach. From the classic Art Deco bathhouses to the long boardwalk, from the many sports facilities to the signature 200-foot-high tower, there's a lot to feast your eyes on.

The **Jones Beach Outdoor Theater** seats some 14,000 for concerts by name pop, country, and rock entertainers. Jones Beach attracts enormous crowds but by and large knows how to handle them. Getting there is another matter; try to go early on a weekday to avoid the automotive holding pattern on the approach roads on weekends. On the way to Jones Beach from Freeport via Meadowbrook State Parkway, you'll pass a junction with the Loop Parkway, which takes you to several parks and beaches on the east end of Long Beach Island (see above).

A little east of Freeport on 27 is **Merrick**, settled in 1643 and named for its original inhabitants, the Merokian Indians, commemorated by the town's 18-foot Totem Pole. About 2 miles beyond Merrick is Wantagh, another access point for Jones Beach, via the Wantagh State Parkway. From Wantagh, you might want to detour north several miles to **Hicksville ❼** to look at the magnificent doors of **Trinity Lutheran Church**, exact replicas of the 15th-century bronze doors executed by the Florentine sculptor Lorenzo Ghiberti for the east portal of the Baptistery of the Duomo of San Giovanni Battista, a milestone of the Italian Renaissance. Ghiberti's fellow Florentines were so impressed with the doors, whose gold-leaf-embellished panels depict scenes from the Old Testament, that they named them the "Gates of Paradise." *40 West Nicholai St.,* ☎ *516-931-2225. Open daily 9–5. Donation.* ♿. Also in Hicksville, in the Old Heitz Place courthouse and jail, is the **Hicksville Gregory Museum**, an outstanding geology museum with over 4,000 rock and mineral specimens, including a fluorescent display, as well as fossils, seashells, Indian and local history artifacts, and a large Lepidoptera collection. *Heitz Place and May Ave., Hicksville,* ☎ *516-822-7505. Open Tues.–Fri. 9:30–4:40, Sat.–Sun. 1–5, closed holidays. Nominal admission.*

Just east of Wantagh, on Washington Avenue in **Seaford ❽**, is another good place to study natural history, the **Tackapausha Museum and Preserve**, with exhibits on the flora, fauna, and geological formation of Long Island. Several miles of nature trails wind through the preserve's 80-acre glacial outwash plain, where many species of birds nest. ☎ *516-571-7443. Open Tues.– Sat. 10–4, Sun. 1–4, closed holidays. Adults $1, under 12 50¢.* ♿.

From Seaford, it's a short hop north to Bethpage. Nearby, off

Bethpage Parkway, is **Bethpage State Park** ❾, a beautifully groomed facility of almost 1,500 acres, with tennis courts, a regulation baseball diamond, hiking and biking trails, cross-country skiing, and a golfer's paradise of five 18-hole golf courses. *Bethpage Parkway, Farmingdale.* ☎ *516-249-0701, Internet: www.nysparks.com. Parking fee from Memorial Day to Labor Day. Partially &.*

North of the park, on Round Swamp Road, is the:

*OLD BETHPAGE VILLAGE RESTORATION ❿, Round Swamp Rd., Old Bethpage, NY 11804, ☎ 516-572-8400. *Open March–Oct., Wed.–Sun. 10–5; Nov.–Dec., Wed.–Sun. 10–4. Closed some holidays. Last admission one hour before closing. Adults $6, seniors and children (5–12) $4. Tours. Gift shop. Partially &.*

Old Bethpage Village is an outdoor living-history museum with over 30 restored pre-Civil War buildings, a working farm, and costumed inter-preters re-enacting life on rural Long Island from 1815 to 1875, when the Industrial Revolution was beginning to make itself felt.

Return to NY-27 and continue east through Massapequa across the Suffolk County line to Amityville, with many charming restored homes and antique shops. Continuing east a few miles on 27, you'll come to the Robert Moses Causeway, which takes you across Great South Bay to **Captree State Park** ⓫, on the eastern tip of the same off-shore bar as Jones Beach (see above), and linked to it by Ocean Parkway. Captree is an ideal spot for fishermen, who can try their luck off the piers or rent a fishing boat at the dock. *Box 247, Babylon,* ☎ *631-669-0449, Internet: www.nys parks.com. Picnic facilities. Snack bar. Playground. Parking fee charged Memorial Day to Labor Day. &.*

Proceeding south across Fire Island Inlet on the Robert Moses Causeway, you come to **Robert Moses State Park** ⓬, a 1,000-acre stretch of shore with fine beaches, windswept sand dunes, and excellent swimming and fishing areas. The park occupies the western tip of Fire Island, the famous 32-mile-long barrier beach and resort colony. *Box 247, Babylon,* ☎ *631-669-0470, Internet: www.nysparks.com. Open daily, sunrise to sunset. Parking fee $7 charged Memorial Day to Labor Day. Beach. Showers. Picnic facilities. Snack bar. Golf. Marina. Fishing. Mostly &.* The **Fire Island Lighthouse**, east of the park, has been there since 1827 and has saved countless ships from a watery grave along these treacherous shores. At its base is a visitor center and museum, with tours up all 192 steps for a great view. *Burma Rd.,* ☎ *631-661-4876. Open July–Labor Day, daily 9–5. Adults $4.*

Fire Island National Seashore ⓭ (☎ *631-289-4810, Internet: www.nps.gov)* comprises almost 20,000 acres of the island and has three areas open to the public: **Sailors Haven**, with marina, swimming beach, snack bar, visitor center, and nature and interpretive activities; **Watch Hill**, with comparable facilities plus a 26-site campground; and **Smith Point**

West, with visitor center, interpretive activities, and a wheelchair-accessible boardwalk. The extraordinary **Sunken Forest**, a unique ecosystem trapped in a depression behind the dunes at Sailors Haven, displays many unusual plant adaptations and is shrouded in an air of primeval mystery.

The Robert Moses Causeway is one of only two auto routes to Fire Island; the other is the William Floyd Parkway/Smith Point Bridge at the eastern end. However, no roads run the length of the island, and the only way to reach the points in between is to walk or take one of several passenger ferries that run from the South Shore to various points on the island: **Fire Island Ferries** (☎ 631-665-3600) from Bay Shore, serving Saltaire, Kismet, Fair Harbor, Dunewood, and Ocean Beach, with charter trips to Sunken Forest; **Sayville Ferry Service** (☎ 631-589-8980) from Sayville, serving Fire Island Pines, Cherry Grove, and Sunken Forest/Sailors Haven; and **Davis Park Ferry Company** (☎ 631-475-1665) from Patchogue, serving Davis Park and Watch Hill.

From the Robert Moses Parkway, you can pick up NY-27A, Montauk Highway, and continue east to **Bay Shore** ⓮, one of the ferry terminals serving Fire Island. On the way, you'll pass **Sagtikos Manor**, a Colonial mansion dating from the 1690s, home of an aristocratic family, headquarters of British general Henry Clinton during the Revolutionary War, proud recipient of an overnight stay by George Washington in 1790. *Montauk Hwy., Bay Shore*, ☎ 631-665-0093. A short way east, in **Islip** ⓯, is **The Grange**, a re-created Long Island farm village complete with a working windmill.

Continuing east briefly on 27A, you'll come to the junction with the Southern State Parkway, which takes you south to **Heckscher State Park** ⓰, some 1,600 scenic acres facing Great South Bay, with 3 miles of waterfront, picnic facilities, hiking, biking, and cross-country skiing trails, a nature preserve, boat launch, camp sites, and a range of recreational facilities. *Box 160, East Islip,* ☎ *631-581-2100, Internet: www.nysparks.com. Open daily, sunrise to sunset. Snack bar. $7 Parking fee in season.* &.

Just beyond the Southern State junction on 27A is the **Bayard Cutting Arboretum State Park** ⓱, under cultivation since 1887, with a magnificent collection of trees that includes some of the original plantings. The lovely Connetquot River flows by, attracting flocks of aquatic birds, and there are marked nature trails (some of them wheelchair-accessible) through the pinetum, the swamp cypresses, the rhododendron plantings, the wildflower section, and other beautiful areas of this 609-acre horticultural center. In the center of this stands the original Tudor mansion, now a small nature museum. *Box 466, Oakdale,* ☎ *631-581-1002, Internet: www.nys parks.com. Open Tues.–Sun. 10–5 plus legal holidays. Gift shop. Snack bar. Parking fee $7.* &. Just north of the arboretum is **Connetquot River State Preserve** ⓲, almost 3,500 acres crisscrossed by hiking trails and bridle paths, with an old gristmill and a fish hatchery on the grounds. *Box 505, Oakdale,* ☎ *631-581-1005, Internet: www.nysparks.com. Open daily. Parking fee in season.*

Continue eastbound on 27A to the **Long Island Maritime Museum** ⓳ in West Sayville, where you can see some fascinating exhibits on Long Island maritime history, including a turn-of-the-century boatshop, a 1907 restored oyster cull house, the oyster schooner *Priscilla* (1888) and sloop *Modesty* (1923), and a collection of equipment used in lieu of the poetic gifts of Lewis Carroll's Walrus to pry oysters from their beds. *86 West Ave., West Sayville,* ☎ *631-854-4794. Open Wed.–Sat. 10–3, Sun. noon–4. Closed major holidays. Donation.* ♿. Nearby Sayville is a terminal for ferries to Fire Island (see above), as is Patchogue, another few miles east on 27A.

Another 3 miles east of Patchogue is a turnoff for **Bellport** ⑳, an interesting Great South Bay village listed on the National Register of Historic Places. Here you'll find the **Bellport-Brookhaven Historical Society Museum**, a multi-building complex that includes a blacksmith shop, a milk house, the Post Crowell House, the Underhill Studio Museum of Early American Decoration, and the nearby Barn Museum, with an eclectic range of exhibits including marine and nautical displays, gyroscopic instruments designed by the noted American inventor Elmer A. Sperry, Indian artifacts, toys, and more. *31 Bellport Ln.,* ☎ *631-286-0888. Open Memorial Day–Labor Day, Tues.–Sat. 1–4:30. Nominal admission.*

Returning to 27A (local road 80), you can continue east a few miles to the turnoff for **Mastic Beach** ㉑, passing the William Floyd Parkway, which leads across Smith Point Bridge to Fire Island (see above). In Mastic Beach, at 245 Park Drive, is the **William Floyd Estate**, the 250-year-old homestead of Brookhaven-born William Floyd, Long Island's only signer of the Declaration of Independence. ☎ *631-399-2030. Open Memorial Day–Labor Day, Sat.–Sun., 11–4:30. Free.* ♿.

The next stops, about 14 miles east of Mastic Beach, are quaint Quogue and fashionable Westhampton Beach, the former hugging an inlet of Moriches Bay, the latter surrounded by the water, both popular shore resort and recreation areas. In **Quogue** ㉒ is the **Old Schoolhouse Museum**, with artifacts and exhibits on local history displayed in a schoolhouse of 1822. *Quogue St. East,* ☎ *631-653-4111. Open July–Aug., Wed., Fri. 3–5, Sat. 10–noon.*

Another 8 miles farther east on 27A (Montauk Highway, local road 80), where the Shinnecock Canal links Great Peconic Bay and Shinnecock Bay, is the last stop on this South Shore Drive, **Hampton Bays** ㉓, an appealing place for family outings, fishing expeditions, swimming, and sailing.

The fastest way back to New York City is to head north on NY-24 to its junction with the Long Island Expressway (I-495). Along the way, on 24 just north of Hampton Bays, you'll encounter the **Big Duck** ㉔, one of those strange roadside attractions that were so popular in the 1930s and have now mostly disappeared, only to be replaced by bland chain stores and fast-food joints. This 20-foot-high piece of whimsical architecture was built in 1931 by a duck farmer as his poultry stand; today it's a non-profit gift shop operated by a local preservation society. Just looking at it will give you the smile you'll need before facing the Long Island Expressway.

The South Fork: Through the Hamptons to Montauk

The South Fork means the Hamptons, and the Hamptons mean different things to different people. Reams have been written about this string of towns, which have been variously praised as the place to be on Long Island and criticized as being too "trendy." Whether your taste runs to celebrity watching or birdwatching, the fact remains that the Hamptons are beautiful and stately old towns, if a bit hectic at times. You may want to be in the thick of the fast-paced social scene, or visit during the week or in the off-season, but whenever you go, you'll soon see why so many of the famous and not-so-famous have succumbed to the Hamptons' charms.

Sag Harbor is a different sort of place; an old whaling port with much of its Colonial and 19th-century atmosphere left intact to delight today's visitors. And Montauk — the end of the line — appeals to romantics who love the sea, nature, isolation, windswept dunes, and lonely lighthouses.

GETTING THERE:

By Car: From Manhattan, take the **Long Island Expressway** (I-495) all the way to Exit 70, then **Route 111** south to **NY-27** (Sunrise Highway). Head east on 27, crossing the Shinnecock Canal. From there follow directions in the text. The farthest point, Montauk Point, is about 130 miles from midtown Manhattan.

By Train: Most of the towns (but not Sag Harbor) can be reached via the Long Island Railroad, leaving from Manhattan's Pennsylvania Station (lower level) and making stops in Queens. You will need local transportation by cab or bicycle, however. ☎ 718-217-5477, Internet: www.mta.nyc.ny.us/lirr for information.

By Bus: The Hampton Jitney provides a comfortable service from several Manhattan locations. Reservations are needed. For information and reservations ☎ 1-800-936-0440, Internet: www.hamtonjitney.com. Again, you'll need local transportation.

PRACTICALITIES:

Expect huge crowds on weekends in summer; better to come midweek or out of season. Good weather is essential. Be aware that although the beaches are free, parking at them is not. Many require a parking permit, which can be quite expensive for nonresidents. Your best choices for a reasonable fee are Main Beach in East Hampton, Atlantic Beach in Amagansett, and Hither Hills State Park in Montauk.

For further information about Long Island, contact the **Long Island Convention & Visitors Bureau**, 330 Motor Parkway, Hauppauge, NY 11788, ☎ 631-951-3440 or 1-877-FUN-ON-LI, Internet: www.licvb.com, or contact the sites directly. Some local information sources are: **Southampton Chamber of Commerce**, 76 Main St., Southampton 11968, ☎ 631-283-0404, Internet: www.southamptonchamber.com; **East Hampton Chamber of Commerce**, 79A Main St., East Hampton 11937, ☎ 631-324-0362, Internet: www.east hamptonchamber.com; and **Montauk Chamber of Commerce**, P.O. Box 5029, Montauk 11954, ☎ 631-668-2428 or 1-800-773-6427, Internet: www.mon tauk-chamber.com.

FOOD AND DRINK:

The South Fork abounds in good eateries, so you won't go hungry. Here are a few choices:

Gosman's Dock (500 W. Lake Drive in Montauk) This huge restaurant overlooking the harbor has been serving excellent seafood for over 50 years. ☎ 631-668-5330. X: mid-Oct. through April. $$ and $$$

The Grill (29 Newtown Ln. in East Hampton) Everything from salads to burgers to full meals, indoors or out. ☎ 631-324-6300. $$

B. Smith's (Long Wharf at Bay St., Sag Harbor) Southern and Mediterranean influences in a New American cuisine, with a view of the bay. ☎ 631-725-5858. X: Oct.–May, and holidays. $$

Shagwong Restaurant (Main St. in Montauk) An Irish pub with a lively bar scene. ☎ 631-668-3050. $$

Barrister's (36 Main St. in Southampton) A casual place for tasty American dishes, with a covered terrace. ☎ 631-283-6206. $ and $$

La Super Rica (Main & Bay streets, Sag Harbor) A popular spot for Mexican dishes. ☎ 631-725-3388. $ and $$

Lobster Roll (Montauk Hwy, NY-27, between Amagansett and Montauk) An old-fashioned roadhouse that's world-famous for its inexpensive seafood. ☎ 631-267-3740. $ and $$

Golden Pear (99 Main St. in Southampton) High quality sandwiches, pasta dishes, and baked goods, for lunch or dinner. ☎ 631-283-8900. $

Grand Café (66 Newtown Ln. in East Hampton) A favorite place for light lunches. ☎ 631-324-9207. $

SUGGESTED DRIVING TOUR:

Circled numbers in text correspond to numbers on the map.

Begin by following **NY-27A** (Montauk Highway, local route 80) across the Shinnecock Canal to Southampton, passing the **Shinnecock Indian Reservation ❶**, site of the colorful Pow-Wow held every year on Labor Day weekend. ☎ *631-283-6143 for information.* Their trading post offers Native

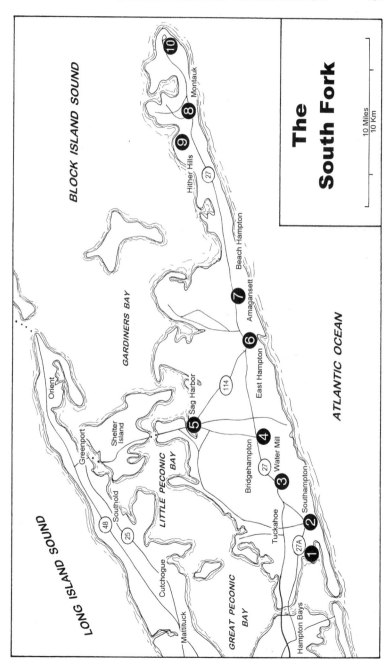

The South Fork

American arts and crafts, has a café, and — being on a reservation – has a tax-free smoke shop. ☎ *631-283-8047, Internet: www.shinnecocktrading post.com.*

A prime shopping district, **Southampton ❷** is actually one of New York's oldest English settlements, having been settled as far back as 1640. By the mid-19th century it had evolved into a resort for wealthy New Yorkers, sprinkled with Victorian and Colonial-style "cottages." It is still considered a place for "old money," although it also offers many cultural and historical attractions. The **Parrish Art Museum** in the center of town has a fine permanent collection of American paintings and sculptures, including many works by William Merritt Chase and Fairfield Porter. It also sponsors an ambitious program of changing exhibits and other events. *25 Job's Ln., Southampton, ☎ 631-283- 2118. Open mid-June to mid-Sept., Mon.–Tues. and Thurs.–Sat., 11–5, Sun. 1–5; rest of year, Thurs.–Sat. and Mon., 11–5, Sun. 1–5. Adults $2, seniors $1, students free. ♿.*

Southampton's long history is traced in the Native American, Colonial, and whaling exhibits at the **Southampton Historical Museum** on Meeting House Lane, a lovely, sprawling frame house built by a whaling captain in 1843 and still filled with period furniture and artifacts. Behind it are restored outbuildings including a one-room school, a blacksmith's and a carpenter's shop, a drug store, a barn, and a wigwam. *17 Meeting House Ln., an extension of Job's Ln., ☎ 631-283-2494. Open mid-June to mid-Sept., Tues.–Sun. 11–5. Adults $3, seniors $2, children $1. Gift shop. Partly ♿.*

The **Halsey Homestead** of 1648 is the oldest saltbox in New York State, and features period furnishings and a Colonial herb garden. *South Main St., a half-mile from Job's Ln. and Main, ☎ 631-283-3527. Open mid-June to mid-Sept., Tues.–Sun. 11–4:30. Adults $2, under 12 50¢.*

East of Southampton, shortly after NY-27A merges with NY-27, is **Water Mill ❸**, originally 40 acres of land granted by the town of Southampton to one Edward Howell in 1644, on condition that "sayd Edward Howell doth promise to build for himself to supply the necessities of the towne, a sufficient mill at Mecoxe." Over the years Howell's mill changed hands many times and provided power for grinding grain, spinning cloth, and manufacturing paper. Today it has been restored as the **Water Mill Museum** and once again grinds grain as it did over three centuries ago. Also here are several innovative exhibits on the history of milling and other vanished arts of the pre-industrial era, all designed to encourage visitor participation. *Old Mill Rd., off NY-27, ☎ 631-726-4626. Open Memorial Day through June, weekends 1–5; July to Labor Day, Mon. and Thurs.–Sat. 10–5, Sun. 1–5. Adults $2, seniors $1.50, children free. Art gallery. Craft shop. Partly ♿.*

Continuing east on 27, you'll come to **Bridgehampton ❹**, sometime hangout of the literati and a stop on the social circuit. At the **Bridgehampton Historical Museum,** you can visit the Corwith House of about 1830, a wheelwright shop, a machine shop, a tractor barn, and the old local jail. *Main St. and Corwith Ave.*, ☎ *631-537-1088. Open mid-June through Labor Day, Thurs.–Sat. noon–4. Donation. Partially &.*

From Bridgehampton you can head north on NY-79. In the picturesque and pleasantly low-key town of **Sag Harbor ❺**, once the fourth-largest whaling port in the world, you'll find many reminders of the Colonial and seafaring past. The **Sag Harbor Whaling Museum**, a Greek Revival mansion (1845) with roof ornamentation of carved blubber spades and harpoons, and a right whale jawbone arching over the doorway, has several rooms devoted to local history in addition to a vast collection of whaling tools and all sorts of strange memorabilia. *200 Main St.*, ☎ *631-725-0770. Open mid-May through Sept., Mon.–Sat. 10–5, Sun. 1–5. Adults $3, seniors $2, children (6–13) $1. Partially &.*

The restored 1787 **Custom House** recalls the days when Sag Harbor was Long Island's principal port of entry. *Main and Garden Sts.*, ☎ *631-692-4664. Open July–Aug., Tues.–Sun. 10–5; May–June and Sept.–Oct., weekends 10–5. Adults $3, seniors and children (7–14) $1.50.* In the late 19th century, after the whaling industry declined, Sag Harbor was the site of a watch casing factory that employed many Jewish workers. **Temple Adas Israel**, a white frame building with striking stained-glass windows, was built in 1898 to serve them and is Long Island's oldest Jewish temple. Above Sag Harbor is North Haven Peninsula, where you can board a ferry *(*☎ *631-749-1200)* to Shelter Island (see page 180). Across from the peninsula, on a spot of land between Noyack and Little Peconic bays, is the **Elizabeth Morton National Wildlife Refuge.** ☎ *631-286-0485. Open daily. Free.*

The Sag Harbor-East Hampton Turnpike (NY-114) takes you to the next stop, perhaps the most beautiful town on Long Island, as rich in history and architecture as it is in society-page functions and designer labels. ***East Hampton ❻** is best seen on a walking tour, provided you can find a place to park. A good starting point is **Home, Sweet Home**, inspiration for the 1820s song of that title and boyhood home of its author, actor and playwright John Howard Payne. Built in the late 17th century, it houses fine collections of American furnishings, a gallery with changing exhibits, and Payne memorabilia. The **Pantigo Windmill** (1804) and a period herb garden are on the grounds. *14 James Ln., across the Village Green from NY-27.* ☎ *631-324-0713. Open Mon.–Sat. 10–4, Sun. 2–4. Closed Nov. 1, Thanksgiving, Christmas, New Year's. Adults $4, ages 2–12 $2.*

Next door is the **Mulford Farm Museum**, a restored farmhouse built around 1680, now a museum of architectural history maintained by the East Hampton Historical Society. The society has its headquarters at the nearby **Osborn-Jackson House**, a 1775 Colonial saltbox with later additions, and also maintains the 1784 Clinton Academy, New York's first preparatory school. ☎ *631-324-6850. Open July–Labor Day, daily 10–5. Adults $2, seniors $1.50, children $1.* There's another historic windmill in East Hampton, the handsome and fully equipped **Hook Mill**, built as a gristmill in 1806 and still up to the old grind. ☎ *631-324-0713. Open July–Aug.,*

Fri.–Sun. 2–4. Adults $1.50, children $1.

The center of East Hampton cultural life is the **Guild Hall**, with changing art exhibits and an interesting program of poetry readings and workshops. ☎ *631-324-0806. Open Memorial Day–Labor Day, daily 11–5; rest of year Wed.–Sat. 11–5, Sun. noon–5. Admission $3.* ♿. Guild Hall's **John Drew Theater** offers year-round entertainment and a particularly fine summer menu of theatrical productions, concerts, and films. Finally, like the other towns along the South Fork, East Hampton (village and town — note that the town includes East Hampton, Amagansett, and Montauk) offers a full range of facilities for fishing, boating, swimming, and other water sports.

Nearby **Amagansett ❼**, just east of East Hampton, is a lovely small town with another good museum of local seafaring history, the **East Hampton Town Marine Museum**. In addition to whaling exhibits, shipwrecks, and a fascinating installation on underwater archeology, there are several displays on methods of commercial and sport fishing. *Bluff Rd. Turn south from 27 on Atlantic Ave., then right on Bluff Rd.* ☎ *631-267-6544. Open July–Labor Day, daily 10–5; June and Sept., weekends 10–5. Adults $4, seniors and children $2.*

The last stop, on the easternmost tip of Long Island far from the madding crowds, is **Montauk ❽**, justly renowned for its excellent fishing — many world-record catches have been hauled from its waters — and striking windswept scenery. In the past, Montauk has survived a couple of major development attempts (in one of the few happy results of the Depression, plans to turn it into a northern Miami Beach crashed along with the stock market, though the tower built by the would-be developer still stands rather incongruously in the heart of town), and despite recent encroachments, it remains relatively unscathed by the real-estate boom and social whirl of the Hamptons.

Montauk was settled in 1655 on land purchased from the Montaukett Indians, and danged if the cowboys didn't follow soon after, turning the place into a big ranch whose major social event was the annual cattle drive from Patchogue. There's a lot of wilderness left at several parks in the area, including **Hither Hills State Park ❾** and the starkly beautiful **Montauk Point State Park ❿**, site of the historic **Montauk Point Lighthouse**, erected by order of George Washington in 1795. Today, it's operated by the Coast Guard, and also houses a museum. You can climb to the top for a ***great view**. ☎ *631-668-2461. Park open all year. Free. Parking fee from Memorial Day to Labor Day $7. Lighthouse,* ☎ *631-668-2544,Internet: www.montauk lighthouse.com, open Memorial Day to Labor Day, Sun.–Fri. 10:30–6, Sat. 10:30–7; spring and fall, weekends 10:30–4:30. Adults $4, children (6–11) $2. Children under 41" tall not allowed in tower.*

You don't usually think about cowboys and Indians when you think of New York, much less about eons-old geological processes, but here at Montauk Point, gazing out into the vast gray Atlantic Ocean, you can almost imagine the birth of a continent and the discovery of a New World.

Montauk Point Lighthouse

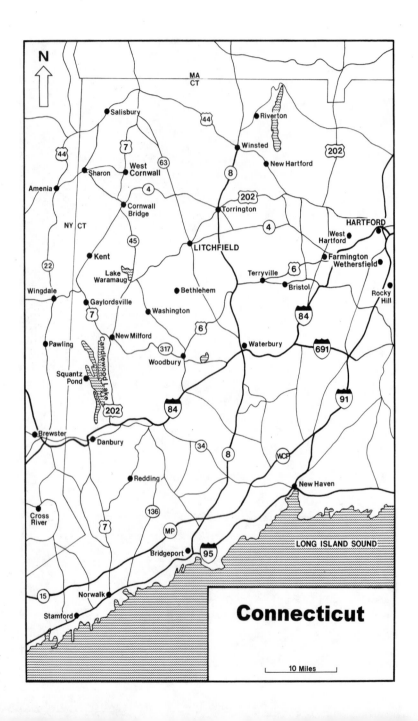

Section V

DAYTRIPS TO
CONNECTICUT

New England begins just a few miles from New York City, and what a different world it is. The first four trips in this section follow the shoreline of Long Island Sound, with several historic port towns and the tang of saltwater and seafaring in the air. The last of these is also home to a great university, whose campus is well worth a trip in itself. To the north, the Litchfield Hills district with its unspoiled Colonial towns, pre-Revolutionary homes, and quietly beautiful countryside beckons. Finally, there is Hartford, the state capital, whose first-class attractions may surprise you.

If you have the time, why not stay overnight — perhaps at a cozy Bed and Breakfast or country inn — and combine two or more of these little excursions?

Trip 27

Greenwich and Stamford

A s you head north on Route I-95, the first towns you'll encounter in Connecticut are Greenwich and Stamford, barely 15 miles northeast of The Bronx. Already, you're in a different world. There are more attractions here than you can see in a single day, so you'll have to pick and choose according to your interests. Most are fairly close to I-95, and some of the major ones can even be easily reached by commuter train from New York — although you'll need a car for others.

GETTING THERE:

By Car: Head northeast on **I-95** to Exit 3 in Connecticut, Greenwich, about 30 miles from midtown Manhattan. Stamford, Exit 8, is a few miles farther on I-95. If you are ending your day at the Audubon Center, the Stamford Museum, or the Bartlett Arboretum, you might prefer to return to New York City via the Merritt Parkway (CT-15) and Hutchinson River Parkway, a more scenic and truck-free route.

By Train: The **Metro-North Railroad** offers frequent commuter service from New York's Grand Central Terminal to both Greenwich, Cos Cob, and Stamford, and service between them. For information ☎ 212-532-4900 or 1-800-METRO-INFO, Internet: www.mta.nyc.ny.us. **Amtrak** provides service on its Northeast Corridor to Stamford, ☎ 1-800-USA-RAIL, Internet: www.amtrak.com.

PRACTICALITIES:

For further information contact the sites directly, or the **Coastal Fairfield County Convention & Visitors Bureau**, 297 West Ave., Mathews Park, Norwalk CT 06850, ☎ 203-899-2799 or 1-800-866-7925, Internet: www.coastalCT.com.

FOOD AND DRINK:

A few of the better choices are:

Amadeus (201 Summer St. in downtown Stamford) Viennese and Continental cuisine in an elegant Old World setting, with schnitzels, tortes and strudels featured. ☎ 203-348-7775. X: weekend lunches, major holidays. $$ and $$$

Il Falco (59 Broad St. in downtown Stamford) A quietly elegant restaurant noted for its fine Italian cuisine. ☎ 203-327-0002. X: weekend lunches, major holidays. $$ and $$$

Manero's (559 Steamboat Rd. in Greenwich) A combination butcher shop, deli, and large restaurant specializing in meat and fish dishes — a local favorite for over 50 years. ☎ 203-869-0049. $$

Atlantis (Greenwich Harbor Inn, 500 Steamboat Rd. in Greenwich) American cuisine overlooking the harbor. ☎ 203-861-1111. $$

Bank Street Brewing (65 Bank St. in Stamford) This casual brewpub offers beef, seafood, and Italian specialties. ☎ 203- 325-2739. $$

Telluride (245 Bedford St. in Stamford) American Southwestern cuisine with South American touches, in a rustic setting reminiscent of Colorado. ☎ 203-357-7679. X: weekend lunch. $$

Lacaye Restaurant (410 Elm St. in Stamford) A simple and unusual place for Haitian home cooking. ☎ 203-358-8008. $

LOCAL ATTRACTIONS:

Circled numbers in text correspond to numbers on the map.

From Exit 3 of I-95 turn right on Arch Street into **Greenwich**, following it to Steamboat Road and continuing a short distance on Museum Drive to the first attraction. For those coming by train, it is a three-minute walk from Greenwich Station down Steamboat Road to the:

BRUCE MUSEUM ❶, One Museum Drive, Greenwich, CT 06830, ☎ 203-869-0376, Internet: www.brucemuseum.org. *Open all year Tues.–Sat. 10–5, Sun. 1–5; closed Mon. and major holidays. Adults $4, seniors & children (5–12) $3, under 5 free. Free to all on Tues. Gift shop.* ♿.

The Bruce Museum bridges the arts and sciences for people of all ages. An unusually wide range of exhibitions cover fine arts, history, environmental sciences, and ethnology. A recent renovation and expansion more than doubled the museum's size. The new Environmental History wing includes a Minerals Gallery, a Wigwam, a Woodlands Diorama, and a Marine Touch Tank. Continually changing art exhibitions offer a range of experiences, from 19th-century American paintings to works from the New York School of the 1980s.

Return on Steamboat Road, passing under I-95, then turn right a block and left onto Milbank Avenue. Head north on this to East Putnam Avenue (US-1) and turn right to the red building on the left, the historic **Putnam Cottage ❷**. Known as Knapp's Tavern during the Revolutionary War, this small house was built around 1690 and is noteworthy for its rare scalloped shingles and huge fieldstone fireplaces. As a stagecoach station along the Boston Post Road, it was a convenient stopping place for Revolutionary leaders, among them General Israel Putnam. "Old Put" was a guest here in 1779 when he discovered a large number of British troops coming up the Post Road. Hurrying from the house, he urged his horse down the side of the cliff and made his escape. The local D.A.R. chapter, which maintains the house as a museum, is responsible for the fine period furnishings and the lovely garden. There is also a restored barn on the grounds. *243 E. Putnam Ave., Greenwich, CT 06830,* ☎ *203-869-9697. Opening hours limited, phone ahead. Adults $2, children under 12 free. Steps into building, difficult for wheelchairs.*

Continue north on US-1. Shortly after the sign for **Cos Cob** is a major intersection and stoplight at Strickland Road. Here a sign directs you to the right; follow it to River Road and the next site, which for those traveling by train is only three blocks from the Cos Cob Metro-North Station.

BUSH-HOLLEY HOUSE ❸, 39 Strickland Rd., Cos Cob, CT 06807, ☎ 203-869-6899, Internet: www.hstg.org. *Open April–Dec., Wed.–Fri. noon–4, Sat. 11–4, Sun. 1–4; Jan.–March, Sat. 11–4, Sun. 1–4. Closed some major holidays. Visitor center free. House tours: Adults $6, seniors and students $4, under 12 free.*

The Bush-Holley House, a National Historic Landmark, is a classic saltbox, circa 1732, located in the Historic Cos Cob district of Greenwich. It is named for its two principal owners: David Bush, a wealthy 18th-century farmer, and Edward P. Holley, a 19th-century farmer-turned-innkeeper.

Often called the "house that never stopped living," Bush-Holley demonstrates the changes that occur with different owners and lifestyles — The Bush family period is represented by an impressive collection of Connecticut antiques.

By 1892, the house had been transformed into a boarding house for struggling artists. First run by Edward P. Holley, it passed on to his daughter Emma Constant, the wife of Elmer Livingston MacRae. MacRae was one of the organizers of the historic 1913 Armory Show in New York City, which introduced modern art to the United States. The Holley Inn became a magnet for artists and writers, attracting the likes of Theodore Robinson, John Twachtman, Childe Hassam, J. Alden Weir, Willa Cather, and Lincoln Steffens.

Displayed in the Bush-Holley House are paintings and etchings by some of the artists who visited what was to be the first American Impressionist summer art colony.

On the grounds is a museum devoted to the works of sculptor John Rogers (1829–1904), who specialized in group studies of slaves, soldiers, and ordinary people. These "Rogers groups" became very popular during the Civil War and remain of interest as vivid records of the period.

Also in the Greenwich area, but north of the Merritt Parkway (CT-15, Exit 28)(check the map location), is a treat for nature lovers, the:

AUDUBON CENTER ❹, 613 Riversville Rd., Greenwich, CT 06831, ☎ 203-869-5272, Internet: www.audubon.org/local/sanctuary/greenwich. *Open all year, daily 9–5, closed major holidays. Adults $3, seniors and children $1.50, free to members of the Audubon Society. Self-guided tours, gift and book shop. No picnicking or pets in nature study areas.* ♿.

Here's the place to go for information on just about every phase of

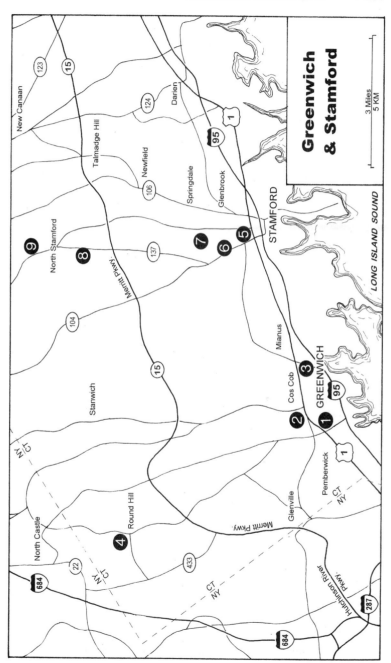

Greenwich & Stamford

3 Miles
5 KM

nature study. Established in 1942, this 522-acre wildlife sanctuary is home to about 90 species of birds, many types of small animals, and a profusion of wildflowers. There are 15 miles of hiking trails through varied habitats, and the visitor center has many excellent interpretive exhibits.

Get back on I-95 and head north to Exit 8, Atlantic Street. Now you're in **Stamford**, a thriving industrial and research center with a population of 108,000 and a score of Fortune 500 companies, blessed with scenic beauty and an eclectic range of attractions that make it equally inviting as a place to live or visit. For those traveling by train, the first attraction is an easy walk from the Stamford Metro-North Station.

*WHITNEY MUSEUM OF AMERICAN ART FAIRFIELD COUNTY ❺, 400 Atlantic St., Stamford, CT 06921, ☎ 203-358-7630. *Open all year, Tues.–Sat. 11–5. Free. Gift shop.* &.

A varied program of major events awaits you at the Fairfield County branch of the prestigious Whitney Museum in New York City (see page 80), founded in 1930 by Gertrude Vanderbilt Whitney to foster the development of American art. Carefully researched and beautifully mounted, the exhibits change every two or three months. Past exhibitions have featured work by Edward Hopper, Alexander Calder, Georgia O'Keeffe, and William Wegman among others.

Head north on Atlantic Street to the intersection with Broad Street. Make a right on Broad and a quick left on Bedford Street. At the corner of Bedford and North streets is the **Hoyt-Barnum House ❻**. The Stamford Historical Society maintains this restored 1699 house, the oldest still standing in Stamford. Originally owned by a blacksmith, the house features four fireplaces, a commanding fieldstone chimney, and period furnishings reflecting life in Stamford over three centuries. *713 Bedford St., Stamford, CT 06903 ☎ 203-323-1183.*

Go east on North Street and turn left onto Strawberry Hill Avenue. Follow this to Colonial Road, making a right to Hope Street. Turn left on Hope and follow it to the:

UNITED HOUSE WRECKING CO. ❼, 535 Hope St., Stamford, CT 06906, ☎ 203-348-5371, Internet www.unitedhousewrecking.com. *Open all year, Mon.–Sat. 9:30–5:30, Sun. noon–5. Free.*

This is the place you've always heard about! For over 40 years, United House Wrecking has built a reputation as "Connecticut's Largest Antiques Emporium." There's a 30-foot-tall statue of "Farmer John" overlooking the property along with countless statues and remnants that welcome you to the main entrance of this unusual establishment.

No two visits are alike here, where truckloads of items are bought and sold each week. A huge 35,000-square-foot building houses antiques, estate furniture, mantels, doors, stained glass, bronzes, paintings, and an seemingly infinite variety of accent pieces. Outdoors, there are several acres of architectural urns, estate gates, fencing, fountains, gargoyles, statues, patio furniture, and hundreds of terra cotta and concrete planters. Visited by thousands all year round, United House Wrecking attracts new home buyers, old home renovators, designers, decorators, collectors, and bargain hunters alike.

Nature lovers may want to visit two more sites, both a bit north of the Merritt Parkway (CT-15). To get there, return to Colonial Road and go west on it back to Strawberry Hill Avenue. Turn north on this and then west on Oaklawn Avenue. At the intersection of High Ridge Road (CT-137), turn right and follow it north under the Merritt Parkway, passing the **Stamford Historical Society Museum** *(☎ 203-329-1183)* at 1508 High Ridge. Here turn left on Scofieldtown Road to the:

STAMFORD MUSEUM & NATURE CENTER ❽, 39 Scofieldtown Rd., Stamford, CT 06903, ☎ 203-322-1646, Internet: www.stamfordmuseum.org. *Open all year, Mon.–Sat. & holidays 9–5, Sun. 1–5; closed Thanksgiving, Christmas, New Year's. Adults $5, seniors and children (5–13) $4, under 5 free. Planetarium shows Sun. at 3 (fee). Nature trails, picnicking, gift shop; concerts, lectures, and special events all year.* ♿.

This fabulous mansion that once belonged to Henri Bendel today looks down upon a picturebook Colonial New England farm, a small gem of a lake dotted with waterfowl, a pool of otters, and miles of trails. The working farm has a restored 1750 barn, grazing oxen, sheep, goats, and pigs, and an exhibit on early rural life.

In the mansion, four galleries offer changing exhibitions on art, Americana, and natural history; along with a permanent exhibit on how four Indian groups adapted their culture to different environments. Seasonal events include Winterfest in January, Maple Sugaring in March, Spring on the Farm in May, and Harvest Day in September.

Finally, go back to High Ridge, turn left, and continue north briefly to Brookdale Road. Turn left here to the:

BARTLETT ARBORETUM ❾, University of Connecticut, 151 Brookdale Rd., Stamford, CT 06903, ☎ 203-322-6971, Internet: www.uconn.edu. *Grounds open all year daily 8:30–sunset; office open all year Mon.–Fri. 9–4. Free. No picnicking, no pets.*

This 63-acre facility of the University of Connecticut features cultivated gardens surrounded by natural woodlands with several ecology trails and a swamp walk. The arboretum specializes in collections of conifers, flowering trees and shrubs, and wildflowers. Many more varieties of plants thrive in the greenhouse, and there's a fine collection of horticultural reference books.

To return to New York City, go back down High Ridge to the Merritt Parkway (CT-15) and take it south; or go back into Stamford and pick up I-95 south.

Trip 28
Ridgefield and Norwalk

Art lovers and those interested in Colonial history will relish a visit to Ridgefield, even though it is a bit out of the way. Just about everyone will enjoy easily-reached Norwalk, with its exquisite Lockwood-Mathews Mansion and the renowned Maritime Aquarium. Norwalk also offers an opportunity for cruises including one to an historic lighthouse, as well as strolling in the trendy SoNo Historic District with its enticing shops, cafés, and unusual eateries.

GETTING THERE:

By Car: Take the **Hutchinson River Parkway** north to Connecticut, where it becomes the **Merritt Parkway** (CT-15). Get off at Exit 39. If you are going to **Ridgefield**, take US-7 north to Wilton, then CT-33 to Ridgefield. You can return on the same route to Norwalk. If you are visiting only the sites in **Norwalk**, go south on US-7 to the intersection with I-95. Do not get on I-95, but continue down the approach road and turn left on West Avenue, going under I-95. The Lockwood-Mathews Mansion is on your right. Return on West Avenue, again going under I-95, until it becomes North Main Street. Turn left on Ann Street to the Maritime Aquarium. You can return to New York City either via I-95 (shorter, heavy truck traffic) or the Merritt Parkway (CT-15)(pleasant, scenic, no trucks).

Ridgefield is about 55 miles northeast of midtown Manhattan, and Norwalk about 45 miles.

By Train: The attractions in Norwalk are within walking distance of the South Norwalk Station, which can be reached by Metro-North's frequent commuter service out of New York's Grand Central Terminal. ☎ 212-532-4900, out of city 1-800-METRO-INFO, Internet: www.mta.nyc.ny.us.

PRACTICALITIES:

The Aldrich Museum is open every day except Mondays, the Lockwood-Mathews Mansion every day except Mondays and Tuesdays, or the months of January and February. The Maritime Aquarium is open every day of the year except Thanksgiving and Christmas Day.

For further information contact the sites directly, or the **Coastal Fairfield County Convention & Visitors Bureau**, 297 West Ave., Mathews Park next to the Lockwood-Mathews Museum, Norwalk CT 06850, ☎ 203-899-2799 or 1-800-866-7925, Internet: www.coastalCT.com.

FOOD AND DRINK:

Norwalk's **SoNo District**, centering on Washington Street and just minutes on foot from the Aquarium, abounds in trendy eateries that are especially lively after dark. Some other suggestions are:

The Inn at Ridgefield (22 West Lane, CT-35, at junction of CT-33) Sophisticated Continental cuisine in a country inn. ☎ 203-438-7323. X: Mon., major holidays. $$$

Silvermine Tavern (194 Perry Ave. in Norwalk. Take Main Ave. to Perry Ave., then 2 miles northwest) This historic 18th-century country inn features wholesome American cuisine in a Colonial dining room or out on the summer terrace. ☎ 203-847-4558. X: Tues. $$ and $$$

Meson Galicia (10 Wall St. in downtown Norwalk, a half-mile north of the Lockwood-Mathews Mansion) Spanish cuisine in an historic old trolley barn. ☎ 203-866-8800. $$

The Brewhouse (13 Marshall St., near the Aquarium in Norwalk) A brewpub with standard American dishes. ☎ 203-853- 9110. $ and $$

LOCAL ATTRACTIONS:

Circled numbers in text correspond to numbers on the map.

ALDRICH MUSEUM OF CONTEMPORARY ART ❶, 258 Main St. (CT-35), Ridgefield, CT 06877, ☎ 203-438-4519, Internet: www.aldrichart.org. *Open all year Tues.–Sun. noon–5, remaining open until 8 on Fri. Tours on Sun. at 2. Adults $5, seniors & students $2, children under 12 and members free. Free to all on Tues. Sculpture garden free. Museum store.* ♿.

Here, in the unlikely setting of Ridgefield — settled in 1709 and still preserving the appearance of an 18th-century New England town — is a serious museum of contemporary art, with changing exhibits of modern and avant-garde works. The sculpture garden is an attractively landscaped outdoor installation of large-scale works by leading artists.

Nearby is the historic:

KEELER TAVERN MUSEUM ❷, 132 Main St. (CT-35), Ridgefield, CT 06877, ☎ 203-438-5485. *Open Wed., Sat., Sun., 1–4. Tours every half-hour; last tour at 3:30. Closed Jan. and holidays. Adults $4, seniors $2, children under 12 $1. Gift shop.*

Considerably more in keeping with Ridgefield's ambience than the Aldrich Museum, this Colonial tavern served as a stagecoach stop and patriot headquarters during the American Revolution and was later converted into a home. During the Battle of Ridgefield in 1777, a British cannonball took up permanent lodging in the wall. Among the subsequent residents was architect Cass Gilbert (1859–1934), designer of the Woolworth Building in New York City, the Supreme Court Building in Washington, D.C., and many other notable structures.

Head south on routes CT-33 and US-7 to Norwalk's attractions (see Getting There, above, for routing):

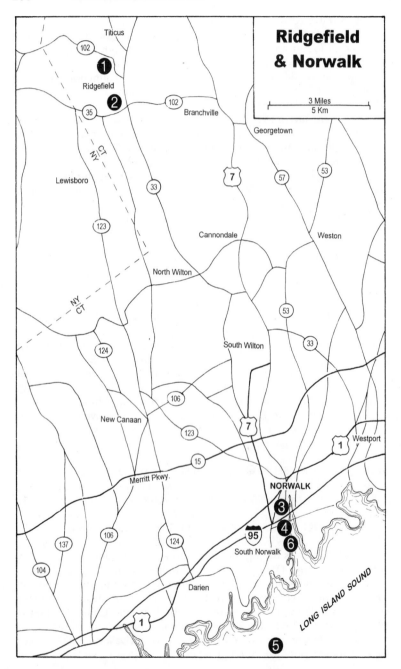

Ridgefield
& Norwalk

3 Miles
5 Km

LOCKWOOD-MATHEWS MANSION MUSEUM ❸, 295 West Ave., Norwalk, CT 06850, ☎ 203-838-9799, Internet: www.lockwoodmathews.org. *Open mid-March through New Year's Day, Wed.–Sun. noon–5. Closed Mon., Tues., Jan.–Feb. Adults $8, seniors and students $5, under 12 free. Tours at 12:30, 1:30, 2:30, and 3:30. Gift shop.*

This Victorian palace was built between 1864 and 1868 by financier and railroad tycoon LeGrand Lockwood, who purchased the finest materials and imported artisans from Europe to create the rich hand-wrought detail found in each of the 50 rooms that surround the octagonal skylit rotunda. At the time, this was probably the most sumptuous private home in America, and a precursor to the grand mansions of the Gilded Age. After Lockwood's death, the mansion was bought by Charles D. Mathews and remained in his family until 1938, when it was sold to the City of Norwalk. Plans to demolish it and erect a new city hall on the site were squelched by a band of concerned citizens who formed a corporation to undertake a major restoration effort and open the mansion as a National Historic Landmark museum.

The tourist information office for this part of Connecticut is in another building on the same property. Just south of here, on the other side of I-95, is the marvelous:

*MARITIME AQUARIUM AT NORWALK ❹, 10 N. Water St., Norwalk, CT 06854, ☎ 203-852-0700, Internet: www.maritimeaquarium.org. *Open all year daily 10–5, until 6 from July–Labor Day. Closed Thanksgiving and Christmas. IMAX movies daily; call for schedules. General admission: Adults $8.75, seniors (62+) $8, children (2–12) $7.25, under 2 free. Combination with IMAX: Adults $13.25, seniors $11.50, children $10. Cruises available in season. Gift shop.* ♿.

Installed in and around a 19th-century factory building on Norwalk's colorful waterfront, The Maritime Aquarium uses the very latest technology to acquaint its visitors with the life of Long Island Sound. An ingenious series of exhibits takes you along a gradual descent from the shallow tidal areas to the depths of the sea. For an unusual sensory experience, you can actually touch some of the living specimens (not the 9-foot sharks!). And don't miss one of the three daily seal feedings. The IMAX theater uses a screen some six stories high and eight stories wide to overwhelm you with fantastic images.

Practically adjacent to the Maritime Aquarium is Hope Dock, from which cruises depart for the **Sheffield Island Lighthouse** ❺ of 1868. The cruise takes 30 minutes each way, and includes a layover on the island of about 90 minutes. A tour of the historic lighthouse is included in the fare, and picnicking is permitted. There are also clam bakes (reserve!) and sunset cruises in summer. Full daily service runs from mid-June to the beginning of September; and limited service from mid-May to mid-June and mid-September to mid-October. *For information* ☎ *203-838-9444, reserva-*

tions at 203-854-4656 or 1-888-547-6863. Fare including tour: Adults $15, seniors $13 on Mon.–Tues. only, under 12 $10, under 3 $5.

Don't leave Norwalk without taking a stroll through the **Historic SoNo District** ❻, practically around the corner from the Aquarium. Just follow Washington Street under the railroad tracks and meander around the neighborhood, filled with shops, galleries, all manner of restaurants, pubs, and cafés. This is a great place to end your day.

Sharks at the Maritime Aquarium
(Photo courtesy of Maritime Aquarium at Norwalk)

Fairfield, Bridgeport and Stratford

As you continue farther up Interstate 95, you'll come to a trio of towns that offer several interesting attractions, including some not ordinarily encountered. Several of these are especially appealing to children, making this an ideal family daytrip.

GETTING THERE:

By Car: It's **I-95** all the way, unless you prefer the somewhat longer but more relaxing **Merritt Parkway** (CT-15). Fairfield is about 55 miles northeast of midtown Manhattan, Bridgeport about 60, and Stratford about 62.

By Rail: All three towns can be reached by Metro-North's frequent commuter service out of New York's Grand Central Terminal. A few of the attractions are within walking distance of the stations, but for most you'll need to take a taxi. ☎ 212- 532-4900, out of city 1-800-METRO-INFO, Internet: www.mta.nyc.ny.us.

PRACTICALITIES:

This is really a fair-weather trip, with many outdoor activities to be enjoyed in season. For further information contact the sites directly, or the **Coastal Fairfield County Convention & Visitors Bureau**, 297 West Ave., Norwalk CT 06850, ☎ 203-899-2799 or 1-800-866-7925, Internet: www.coastalCT.com.

FOOD AND DRINK:

Blue Goose (326 Ferry Blvd. in Stratford) Specializing in meat dishes. ☎ 203-375-9130. $$

Sapporo (520 Sniffens Lane in Stratford) Japanese cuisine right on the Housatonic River. ☎ 203-375-3986. $$

Captain's Cove Restaurant (at Captain's Cove in Bridgeport) Everything from a hot dog to seafood dinners, with seating indoors, on the upper deck, in a gazebo, or on the boardwalk. ☎ 203-335-7104. X: Nov.–Feb. $ and $$

American Steak House (210 Boston Ave., Bridgeport, a half-mile south of Exit 5 of CT-8) A family-friendly cafeteria with a salad bar, à-la-carte items, beer and wine. ☎ 203-576-9989. $

LOCAL ATTRACTIONS:

Circled numbers in text correspond to numbers on the map.

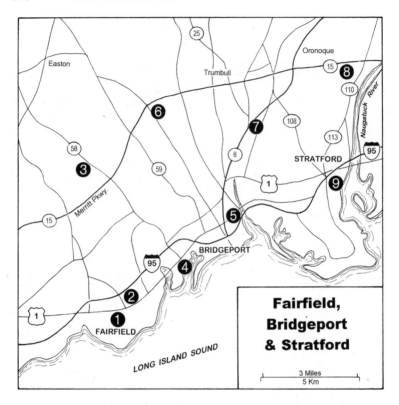

Take 1-95 north to Exit 22 and turn right on Round Hill Road. After crossing US-1, go a block to Old Post Road., turn right, and watch for the **Fairfield Historical Society ❶**, second building on the right. This museum has some fine exhibits, attractively displayed to depict local history. The permanent collections include tools, ornaments, textiles, furniture, ceramics, silverware, paintings, dolls, toys, and maritime memorabilia, along with extensive documentary and genealogical holdings in the research library. The museum is a good place to inquire about sightseeing in Fairfield, which has three historic districts of particular interest: Greenfield Hill, the Old Post Road, and Southport Harbor, a thriving port of entry and shipping center until 1890. *636 Old Post Rd., ☎ 203-259-1598. Open Tues.–Sat. 10–4:30, Sun. 1–4:30, closed holidays. Adults $3, students and under 12 $1.* ♿.

. You may want to continue down Old Post Road through one of Fairfield's historic districts to Sasco Hill Road, turn right briefly, and then go left across a bridge onto Harbor Road for a look at Southport Harbor.

From the Fairfield Historical Society, turn right onto the Old Post

Road. At the first stop sign turn right onto Unquowa Road. Follow through the traffic light at US-1 (Boston Post Road), pass the railroad station on the left and a school on right. Watch for the entrance to the **Connecticut Audubon Society Birdcraft Museum and Sanctuary ❷** on the right. The oldest private songbird sanctuary in the country (1914), Birdcraft was created by Mabel Osgood Wright, founder of the Connecticut Audubon Society, and designated a National Historic Landmark in 1993. The six-acre refuge has a pleasant walking trail and a large pond with a boardwalk observation area. A federal bird-banding station operates in spring and fall. More than 120 species of birds have been attracted to this "birdscaped" property. The museum houses dioramas of Connecticut wildlife, the Frederick T. Bedford collection of African animals, changing exhibits, a gift shop and more. *314 Unquowa Rd., ☎ 203-259-0416, Internet: www.ctaudubon.org/center/birdcraft. Open Tues.–Sun., noon–5. Adults $2, under 14 $1.*

At this point, those interested in birds might want to make a **sidetrip** north to the **Connecticut Audubon Center at Fairfield ❸**. To do this, stay on Unquowa Rd. and proceed under I-95 to Mill Plain Road. Turn right and drive north about 4.5 miles on Mill Plain, which becomes Burr Street. Proceed past the Merritt Parkway underpass and watch for the sanctuary, shortly on the left. The nature center features changing exhibits on state flora and fauna, solar energy applications, a natural history library and, outside in back, a Birds of Prey compound with non-releasable raptors including a Red-tailed Hawk, two Bald Eagles, a Peregrine Falcon and others. The adjacent sanctuary has seven miles of trails winding through 160 acres of woodland, open fields and marshes that are home to more than 100 species of birds, reptiles and mammals, and an abundance of wildflowers, ferns, trees and shrubs. A special feature is a wheelchair-accessible trail for the disabled. *2325 Burr St., ☎ 203-259-6305, Internet: www.ctaudubon.org/center/fairfield. Center open Tues.–Sat. 9–4:30, and also on Sun. noon–4:30 during the spring and fall. The sanctuary is open every day, dawn to dusk. Center free. Sanctuary: Adults $2, children $1. ♿.*

Back in Fairfield, head north on I-95 to Exit 26 in **Bridgeport**. After the ramp bear right on Wordin Avenue to Bostwick Avenue, and turn left following signs to HMS Rose and:

CAPTAIN'S COVE SEAPORT ❹, 1 Bostwick Ave., Bridgeport, CT 06605, ☎ 203-335-1433, Internet: www.captainscoveseaport.com and www.tallshiprose.org. *Tours of H. M. S. Rose daily except when not in port; call for current information and fees. Harbor and Long Island Sound cruises offered on other boats. Craft shops, restaurant (Mar.–Oct.), fish market, afternoon band concerts (Sun.), special events. ♿.*

H.M.S. Rose is a replica of the flagship of Captain James Wallace, an officer of the British fleet stationed off the coast of New England in 1775 under the command of Admiral Samuel Graves. Fortunately for the Revolutionary cause, Graves was a singularly inept officer who made poor use of his forces. His half-hearted attempts to intimidate New England's seafaring towns inspired the colonists to take to their whalers and fishing boats and harass the British fleet. From such humble beginnings sprang the fledgling American navy, which had several early successes, including the capture of a tender from the *Rose*. On your tour of the Rose replica you will learn more about Colonial naval history and the workings of a British frigate.

Afterwards, you'll have an opportunity to take a short **cruise** of the harbor, board the historic *Nantucket* floating lighthouse that once guided ships on the high seas to New York Harbor, visit the craft shops, or dine at the restaurant.

Go back to I-95 and continue briefly to Exit 27 (Lafayette Boulevard). Continue straight off the exit ramp through five lights. Turn left on Main Stret at the fifth light. On the right past the first stop light is:

*THE BARNUM MUSEUM ❺, 820 Main St., Bridgeport, CT 06604, ☎ 203-331-1104, Internet: www.barnum-museum.org. *Open all year; Tues.–Sat. 10–4:30, Sun. noon–4:30. Closed Mon. and major holidays. Adults $5, seniors and students $4, children 4–18 $3, under 4 free. Special exhibitions, gift shop.* ♿.

The Barnum Museum, built in 1893, houses the most significant collection of material related to the extraordinary careers of Phineas Taylor Barnum (1810–91). Exhibit highlights include a five-ring, hand-carved miniature circus; clown costumes and props; and personal mementos of Barnum, General Tom Thumb, and Swedish opera singer, Jenny Lind. The Museum also honors Bridgeport's contributions to the Industrial Revolution and the city's architectural heritage. The Museum features special temporary exhibitions in a new addition designed by the renowned architect, Richard Meier.

Go back on Main to North Avenue. Turn right here and go south briefly to Park Avenue. Turn right on Park and follow it northwest about 2.5 miles to Ninety Acres Park and the:

THE DISCOVERY MUSEUM ❻, 4450 Park Ave., Bridgeport, CT 06604, ☎ 203-372-3521, Internet: www.discoverymuseum.org. *Open Tues.–Sat. 10–5, Sun. noon–5; also open Mon. in July & Aug. Closed major holidays. Adults $7, seniors (64+) & children (3–17) $5.50, under 3 free. Challenger space experience requires advance reservation and costs $3. Gift shop. Food court.* ♿.

A visit to the Discovery Museum is totally interactive. It's a see-hear-touch exploration of the arts and sciences, with more than 100 exhibits on three adventure-filled floors. The duPont Planetarium features an ever-changing look at the night skies, the hands-on galleries have a variety of art and science exhibits, and the fine art galleries host changing exhibitions. The Challenger Learning Center is a computer-operated mission control and space station where you can fly a simulated "space mission."

Continue northwest on Park Avenue to the Merritt Parkway (CT-15) and take it north to Exit 49S. Here take CT-25 south to Exit 5, Boston Avenue. Bear right on Boston after the ramp and go to Noble Avenue. Turn left on Noble and go about a quarter-mile to the:

BEARDSLEY ZOOLOGICAL GARDENS ❼, Noble Ave., Bridgeport, CT 06610, ☎ 203-394-6565, Internet: www.beardsleyzoo.org. *Open all year daily 9–4; closed Thanksgiving, Christmas, New Year's. Adults $6, seniors (62+) & children (3–11) $4, under 3 free. Picnic area, snack bar, gift shop, carousel in season.* &.

More than 200 animals inhabit this 30-acre zoo, Connecticut's largest. Monkeys and birds have the run of a large building, sea lions cavort in an outdoor pool, and farmyard animals mingle with visitors in the children's zoo. Well-tended gardens make Beardsley especially attractive during blooming periods.

Return to the Merritt Parkway (CT-15) and head north on it. Get off at Exit 53S and turn right after the ramp onto CT-110 towards **Stratford**. Watch for the first small road on the right, Main Street. Turn here and continue a half-mile to the **Boothe Memorial Park and Museum ❽**. No one passes this group of unusual, historic buildings for the first time without doing a double-take. Built before and after the turn of the century by Stephen N. and David B. Boothe, descendants of many of the first settlers of Stratford, the complex includes a renovated windmill, a pagoda-like redwood structure with minerals, shells, and fossil displays, a most complete blacksmith shop, a carriage museum, trolley station, and the old Homestead, which is on the National Register of Historic Places. A particular delight for flower fanciers and photographers is the beautiful Jackson and Perkins Trial Rose Garden. *Main St.,* ☎ *203-381-2046. Park open daily 9–5. Museum open June–Oct., Tues.–Fri. 11–1, weekends 1–4. free.* &.

Continue south on Main Street, shortly rejoining CT-110. Proceed to the junction with CT-113, bear right, and continue south on 113 (Main St.), crossing US-1 (Barnum Ave.) and passing under railroad tracks and I-95. Several blocks later, just after Broad Street, is Academy Hill, a small street on the left. Turn here for the **Judson House and Museum ❾**. Built around 1750 on a foundation constructed perhaps over 100 years earlier, this well-preserved house is filled with typical furnishings from the 18th-century. Of special interest are some of the architectural features — the hand-rived shingles on the east gable end of the house, the graceful curved pediment over the doorway, the traditional center stairway, the original wood paneling. The tour takes you through various rooms steeped in an atmosphere of Colonial living. The cellar holds a lower kitchen once used as a slave quarters, equipped with a huge fireplace and a display of period household implements and tools. Behind the Judson House is the **Catharine Bunnell Mitchell Museum**, with carefully researched exhibits tracing the history of Stratford from the period of Indian settlement to about 1830. Both the house and the museum are maintained by the Stratford Historical Society. *967 Academy Hill, Stratford CT 06615,* ☎ *203-378-0630. Open mid-May through Oct., Wed. and Sat.–Sun. 11–4. Adults $2, seniors and students $1.* ♿.

Yale's Harkness Tower

New Haven

Museum fans will revel in this rewarding daytrip to New Haven, as will aficionados of fine architecture. From art to natural history, from musical instruments to old trolley cars, and from Colonial to Contemporary, you'll find quite a range of attractions on and near the lovely campus of Yale University.

New Haven began in 1638 when a group of Pilgrims laid out America's first planned city. Initially independent, it became part of Connecticut as early as 1662. An excellent harbor brought trade and, in 1716, the school that is still New Haven's greatest asset — Yale. Railroads, industry, factories, and immigrants followed in the 19th century, but by the mid-20th this boom turned to blight. Although much of the city has since been revitalized, some problems remain. Happily, the area of interest to tourists — the historic core and adjacent Yale campus — are as beautiful and welcoming as ever.

GETTING THERE:

By Train: Amtrak provides excellent service from New York's Pennsylvania Station and other communities along the Northeast Corridor, ☎ 1-800-USA-RAIL, Internet: www.amtrak.com; while **Metro-North** offers a frequent slower-but-cheaper commuter train service from New York's Grand Central Terminal, uptown Manhattan, The Bronx, Westchester County, and Connecticut, ☎ 212-532-4900, Internet: www.mta.nyc.ny.us/mnr. The New Haven train station is within walking distance of the sights, and there is a local bus.

By Car, New Haven is about 80 miles northeast of New York. Take **I-95** north to Exit 47 and follow Oak St. into downtown New Haven, crossing Church St. and bearing right on N. Frontage Rd. to York St. Turn right here and go several blocks north on York to Elm St., and continue right to the New Haven Green. There are several parking facilities in the area.

PRACTICALITIES:

Avoid coming to New Haven on a Monday, when several major museums are closed. Hours of operation are reduced on Sundays. Check times carefully to coincide with your interests. The best days to see the widest selection of museums are Tuesdays, Wednesdays, and Thursdays. For current details about the Yale University museums phone their **Visitor Center** at 203-432-2300, Internet: www.yale.edu/visitor.

For further information contact the **Greater New Haven Convention &**

Visitors Bureau, 59 Elm St., New Haven, CT 06510, ☎ 203-777-8550 or 1-800-332-7829, Internet: www.newhavencvb.org.

FOOD AND DRINK:

There are plenty of good eateries around the Yale campus, especially in the lower price range. Some choices are:

Union League Café (1032 Chapel St., near the Center for British Art) French cuisine with creative touches, reservations suggested. ☎ 203-562-4299. X: weekend lunch. $$ and $$$

Hot Tomato's (261 College St., just west of The Green) Contemporary Italian cuisine in a smart setting. ☎ 203-624-6331. X: weekend lunch. $$

Louis' Lunch (261 Crown St., a block south of the Center for British Art) The great American hamburger was invented in this tiny diner about a century ago, and they still serve them their way. ☎ 203-562-5507. X: Sun., Mon., dinner on Mon.–Wed. $

Atticus Café (1082 Chapel St., next to the Center for British Art) Light lunches in a bookstore, very literary. ☎ 203-776-4040. $

Claire's (1000 Chapel St., corner of College St., at The Green) Creative vegetarian and kosher fare from around the world — a favorite with Yale students. ☎ 203-562-3888. $

Frank Pepe's Pizzeria (157 Wooster St., a half-mile southeast of The Green, between Chapel and Water streets) A starkly simple place with some of the best pizza in America. X: Tues., lunch on Mon., Wed., Thurs. ☎ 203-865-5762. $

SUGGESTED TOUR:

Circled numbers in text correspond to numbers on the map.

Nearly all of the attractions of New Haven are within comfortable walking distance of **The Green** ❶, a 16-acre plot that has served as the town's common since 1638. In its center are three historic churches, whose present buildings date from around 1815. **Trinity Church**, near Chapel Street, is in the Gothic Revival style, while the **United Congregational Church** is a fine example of the Federal style. The latter contains America's first Hillebrand Tracker organ. Between them stands the **Center Church**, a Georgian beauty whose congregation first worshiped on this site in 1638. Built over an old burial ground, its crypt contains some 137 historic gravestones. *Tours offered Thurs. 11–1:30 and Sat. 11–1; and by appointment,* ☎ *203-787-0121.*

The **Yale University Visitor Center**, along the north side of The Green, offers maps and information for self-guided tours of the campus as well as student-led **guided tours. 149 Elm St.* ☎ *203-432-2300, Internet: www.yale.edu/visitor. Tours Mon.–Fri. at 10:30 and 2, Sat. & Sun. at 1:30. Free.*

For a short do-it-yourself tour that goes past the highlights and takes you to all of the university museums, begin at the **Phelps Gate** along the west side of The Green on College Street. Yale University was founded

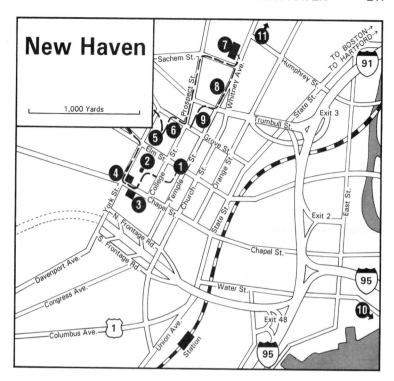

nearby in 1701 as the Collegiate School, but soon (1716) moved to New Haven and later changed its name in honor of its benefactor, Elihu Yale. A member of the Ivy League, it has some 10,000 students and about 4,000 faculty members. America's first Ph.D degrees were awarded by Yale in 1861. Although the campus is predominantly Gothic, there are also significant Georgian buildings, and quite a few outstanding modern structures by today's leading architects.

Enter the campus and pass **Connecticut Hall** on your left. Built in 1752, this is the university's oldest building. Nathan Hale lived here as a student, as did many other famous (and infamous) personages. Straight ahead is the **Harkness Tower ❷**, a 220-foot-tall, highly ornamented bell tower in the Gothic Revival style. Built in 1920, it bears the famous inscription: "For God, for Country, and for Yale." Turn left on High Street to the:

*YALE CENTER FOR BRITISH ART ❸, 1080 Chapel St., New Haven, CT 06520, ☎ 203-432-2800, Internet: wvw.yale.edu/ycba. *Open Tues.–Sat. 10–5, Sunday noon–5. Closed Mon. and major holidays. Free. Gift shop.* ♿.

The largest collection of British art outside Great Britain resides right here in New Haven, housed in a stunning 1977 skylit building that was the last major work by architect Louis Kahn. Amassed over a period of forty years by art patron Paul Mellon, given to Yale in 1966 and later expanded, the paintings, sculptures, prints, and rare books comprise an exciting visual history of life in Britain from the reign of Henry VIII right down to the present. Among the artists represented are Hogarth, Gainsborough, Reynolds, Stubbs, Constable, and Turner.

Right across the street is the:

*YALE UNIVERSITY ART GALLERY ❹, 1111 Chapel St., New Haven, CT 06520, ☎ 203-432-0600, Internet: www.yale.edu/artgallery. *Open Tues.–Sat. 1–5, Sun. 1–6. Closed Mon. and major holidays. Free.* ♿.

North America's oldest college art museum features some 75,000 works ranging from ancient times to the present. It was founded in 1832 and today occupies two handsome buildings: a 1928 structure in the Italian Romanesque style, and a modern 1953 addition by Louis Kahn. Whatever your tastes in art, you'll surely find something of interest here. On the ground floor, a collection of ancient art features a Mithraic temple from Roman Syria; Egyptian, Greek, Etruscan, and Roman sculptures; and a large selection of pre-Columbian artifacts. The first floor is mostly devoted to contemporary works and special exhibits, while Impressionists occupy much of the second floor. Pride of place among these goes to van Gogh's renowned *Night Café, and there are works by Manet, Courbet, Millet, Corot, Degas, Renoir, and Matisse as well. Modern art is represented by such luminaries as Duchamp, Magritte, Stella, Dali, Tanguy, Ernst, Klee, Picasso, Kadinsky, Rothko, and de Kooning.

The third floor has a marvelous selection of medieval, Italian Renaissance, and Flemish Masters paintings. Perhaps the museum's greatest treasure is its *Garven Collection of early American furniture and decorative arts. There are also notable American paintings of the 19th and 20th centuries. Upstairs, the fourth floor is devoted to Asian art from ancient times to the present.

Turn right on York Street, first passing the boldly aggressive **School of Art and Architecture**, a 1964 work by Paul Rudolph noted for its spatial ingenuity, if not its interior comfort. Farther down the street, on the right, stands the **Wrexham Tower**, a duplicate of the historic 16th-century church tower in Wales near which Elihu Yale is buried. Bear left onto the recently revitalized Broadway, home to a thriving retail district that features the famous Yale Co-op store. To the right is **Ezra Stiles College**, designed by Yale graduate Eero Saarinen. The nearby **Payne Whitney Gymnasium** is one of the largest buildings in the world devoted to physical fitness.

Follow the map down Tower Parkway and around to the cathedral-like **Sterling Memorial Library ❺**. With over four million volumes, manuscripts, archives, and even Babylonian tablets, Yale's main library offers plenty to look at. ☎ *203-432-2798. Open Mon.–Thurs. 8:30–midnight, Fri. 8:30–5, Sat. 10–5, Sun. 1 p.m.–midnight; shorter hours in summer. Free.* Even rarer volumes are displayed at the nearby **Beinecke Rare Book and Manuscript Library** ⑥. Translucent marble panels create an unusual lighting effect in this marvelous 1963 structure by Gordon Bunshaft. Inside, visitors can examine an original *Gutenberg Bible, Audubon prints, and changing exhibits. ☎ *203-432-2977. Open Mon.–Fri. 8:30–5, Sat. 10–5; reduced hours in summer. Free.* ⬤.

The **Grove Street Cemetery** has such illustrious permanent residents as Noah Webster, Eli Whitney, and Charles Goodyear, as well as a fine entrance gate. Head north on Prospect Street, turning right on Sachem Street to the:

*PEABODY MUSEUM OF NATURAL HISTORY ⑦, 170 Whitney Ave., New Haven, CT 06511, ☎ 203-432-5050, Internet: wvvw.peabody.yale.edu. *Open Mon.–Sat. 10–5, Sun. noon–5. Closed some major holidays. Adults $5, seniors and children (3–15) $3. Museum shop.* ⬤.

Dinosaurs are the Peabody's specialty, and they've got plenty of them. Among the "terrible lizards" of yore on display are a 67-foot-long brontosaurus, a stegosaurus, and a horned beastie. A wonderful 110-foot-long mural by Rudolph Zallinger depicts the *Age of Reptiles* as it looked some 350 million years ago. Of course there's much more, including all manner of mammals and primates, artifacts of native cultures from the Americas and the Pacific, meteorites, minerals, and various flora and fauna.

Head south on Whitney Avenue to the **New Haven Colony Historical Society** ⑧, a good local history museum featuring exhibits of New Haven's cultural and commercial growth from 1638 to the present. ☎ *203-562-4183. Open Tues.–Fri. 10–5, weekends 2–5. Closed major holidays. Adults $2, seniors and students $1.50, children (6–16) $1. Gift shop.* ⬤.

Heading back towards The Green on Hillhouse Avenue takes you past the intriguing **Yale Collection of Musical Instruments** ⑨. Ever see a Stradivarius? A real one? Or an oud, a koto, a moon guitar, or a stockflote? They're all here, along with harpsichords, virginals, fortepianos, and anything else that makes sweet music. With over 800 instruments from the 16th to the 20th centuries, the collection is rotated so that about a quarter of it is on display at any time. ☎ *203-432-0822. Open Sept. through June, Tues.–Thurs., 1–4. Closed during university recesses. Donation $1.*

ADDITIONAL SIGHTS:

The New Haven area boasts several other attractions, of which the following are especially recommended:

SHORE LINE TROLLEY MUSEUM ⑩, 17 River St., East Haven, CT 06512, ☎ 203-467-6927, Internet: www.bera.org. *Open Memorial Day to Labor Day, daily 10:30–4:30; Apr. & Nov., Sun. 10:30–4:30; May & Sept.–Oct., Dec., weekends 10:30–4:30. Adults $6, seniors (62+) $5, children (2–15) $3. Admission includes unlimited rides. Gift shop. Picnic area. From New Haven, take 1-*

95 east to Exit 51, turn right onto Hemingway Avenue, then left onto River Street.

Nearly a hundred old trolley cars, interurbans, and rapid transit cars either clang their way along three miles of track or reside in the museum area, much to the delight of everyone. Not only can visitors ride them, they can also watch them being restored. Could anything be more fun?

ELI WHITNEY MUSEUM ⑪, 915 Whitney Ave. at Armory St., Hamden, CT 06518, ☎ 203-777-1833, Internet: www.eliwhitney.org. *Open Memorial Day–Labor Day daily 11–4; rest of year, Wed.–Fri. noon–5, Sat. 10–3, Sun. noon–5. Closed Thanksgiving, Christmas, New Year's. Adults $3, seniors & children $2. ♿. From New Haven, continue north on Whitney Avenue past the Peabody Museum and into Hamden.*

Besides inventing the cotton gin, Yale graduate Eli Whitney (1765–1825) pioneered the concept of mass production by being the first to use interchangeable parts in the production of firearms. An amazingly inventive man, he altered the course of American history in more ways than one. This museum, complete with hands-on interactive exhibits, working models, and memorabilia, is devoted to the creative genius of a local lad who certainly made good.

Traveling on the Shore Line Trolley

The Litchfield Hills

On this trip you can take a long ride all the way to the northwest corner of Connecticut, singling out some of the highlights along the route. If you're just out for a scenic drive, you can cover the distance in a day, but if you're interested in spending more time at the various stops, you might want to divide this into two or more trips.

This region, known as the Litchfield Hills, is the quintessential New England, perhaps more consistently pretty than any other spot in all six of those states. Can you really get to know its special charms on a daytrip? Hardly, but the scenic drive outlined here will let you sample some of the best the region has to offer, and perhaps lure you into returning for a longer stay. Happily, the Litchfield Hills abound in quaint old inns, B & Bs, and other desirable lodgings.

There's no denying that this is a lengthy excursion from New York City; the total round trip is a bit over 200 miles. Having a car that's fun to drive helps.

GETTING THERE:

By Car: Take the **Hutchinson River Parkway** north to the junction with **I-684**, then continue on that north to Brewster. Here pick up **NY-22** and continue north about 11 miles towards Pawling. At the junction with **NY-55**, continue north on 22/55 merged for about 6 miles to Wingdale, then turn right (east) on 55 across the Connecticut line to the junction with **US-7** in the quaint village of Gaylordsville. From there follow directions in the text. Litchfield is about 100 miles northeast of midtown Mamhattan.

PRACTICALITIES:

Good weather is a prerequisite for this scenic excursion. Glorious weather would be even better, especially during the fall foliage season. While there are no great cultural sights, the region is rich in low-key historic sites and charming, off-the-beaten-path-type attractions. Some are open year-round, but most close for the winter season. Check individual listings before making your plans as their schedules vary widely, and sometimes change. You will encounter more than a few antique shops, boutiques, country stores, and some unusually good restaurants along the way.

For further information, contact the **Litchfield Hills Visitor Bureau**, P.O. Box 968, Litchfield, CT 06759, ☎ 860-567-4506, Internet: www.litchfield-hills.com. They'll be happy to send you a variety of thorough, informative, lively brochures and a calendar of events for this very eventful region.

FOOD AND DRINK:

Some good places for lunch are:

Tollgate Hill Inn (US-202, Litchfield, 2.5 miles north of The Green, at CT-118) An historic Colonial inn serving sophisticated cuisine in a romantic setting. Reservations, ☎ 860-567-4545. X: Tues. & Wed. off-season. $$$

West Side Grill (43 West St., US-202, Litchfield) The place in town for creative cuisine. Reservations advised, ☎ 860-567- 3885. $$ and $$$

Hopkins Inn (22 Hopkins Rd., near New Preston) Austrian and American specialties overlooking a lake, with outdoor tables in season. Reservations suggested, ☎ 860-868-7295. X: Mon., Jan.–Mar. $$ and $$$

Fife 'n Drum Inn (53 N. Main St., US-7, in Kent) Continental cuisine, Sunday brunches. ☎ 860-927-3509. X: Tues. $$

Aspen Garden (51 West St. in Litchfield, on The Green) A casual place for a wide variety of dishes, all with a Mediterranean influence. Served indoors or on the heated patio. ☎ 860-567-9477. $ and $$

Village Pub & Restaurant (25 West St. in Litchfield, on The Green) A good value in homestyle cooking, especially at lunch. ☎ 860-567-8307. $ and $$

Litchfield Food Company (39 West St., US-202, Litchfield) Great sandwiches and deli specialties. ☎ 860-567-3113. $

Villager Restaurant (Main St., US-7, Kent) A cozy place for simple, home-style lunches. ☎ 860-927-3945. X: evenings. $

SUGGESTED DRIVING TOUR:

Circled numbers in text correspond to numbers on the map.

A few miles north of **Gaylordsville**, on a country road to the left, you can take in a truly lovely sight. *****Bull's Bridge** ❶, one of the two covered bridges in Connecticut still open to automobile traffic, is well over 200 years old. Legend has it that George Washington lost his horse while passing over this span. Beneath it, the Housatonic tumbles over rocks; on its far side is a scenic overlook and parking area. What a fine place for a picnic!

For a village of its size, **Kent** has an extraordinary number of craft shops, galleries, bookstores, and restaurants. It is also home to the *****Sloane-Stanley Museum** ❷ of early American farm implements and tools, brought together by famed author and artist Eric Sloane (1905–85) on land donated by the Stanley tool manufacturing company of New Britain. Captions accompany the tools, which are displayed in a way that demonstrates how they were used. In the early 18th century, Kent was a center of the iron ore industry, and ruins of the old Kent blast furnace are here on the museum grounds, along with a replica of Eric Sloane's studio. ☎ *860-927-3849 or 860-566-3005. Open mid-May through Oct., Wed.–Sun. and holidays 10–4. Adults $3.50, seniors $2.50, children (6–17) $2. Partially* ♿.

Kent Falls State Park ❸ is just a few miles north along US-7. Here Connecticut's loveliest waterfall cascades down several levels to a brook. A wide, winding path leads to the head of the falls, which are particularly

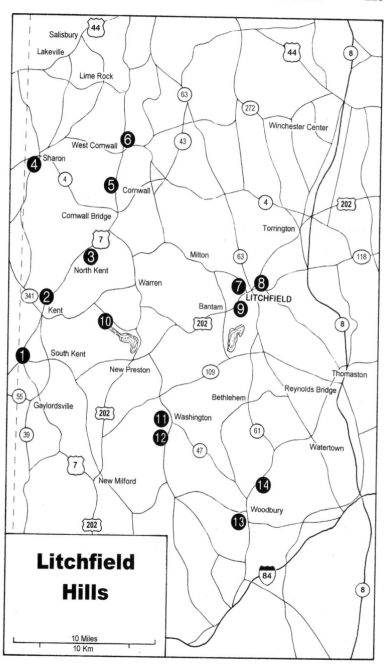

Litchfield
Hills

10 Miles
10 Km

beautiful in spring when the water is high, and in fall when the leaves turn. All around are pine forests with inviting trails for hiking. ☎ *860-927-3238. Open Apr.–Nov., daily 8–sunset. Parking fee $8 ($5 with CT plates) on week-ends and holidays, free other times.* ♿.

From Kent Falls, continue north on 7 for several miles to Cornwall Bridge and the junction with CT-4, passing **Cornwall Bridge Pottery**, where you can watch pots fired in a 35-foot-long wood-burning kiln and inspect the many beautiful items in the showroom. ☎ *860-672-6545, Internet: www.cbpots.com.*

At the junction with CT-4 you have several choices. A left turn onto 4 takes you to **Sharon**, another quintessential New England village with many lovely 19th-century homes and the inevitable green and Congregational church. Here, also, is the **Sharon Audubon Center** ❹. This 684-acre sanctuary of the National Audubon Society is a good place for birdwatching, observation of the spring and fall migrations, or quiet walks through meadows and forests dotted with lakes, ponds, and brooks. The museum and interpretive center has both live and static natural history exhibits, a well as a Children's Discovery Room. ☎ *860-364-0520, Internet: www.audubon.org/local/sanctuary/sharon. Trails open daily dawn to dusk. Center open Mon.–Sat. 9–5, Sun. 1–5, closed major holidays. Adults $3, seniors and children $1.50.*

If you've gone to Sharon, return on CT-4 to Cornwall Bridge and the junction with US-7. Turn left and go north on 7 into **Housatonic Meadows State Park** ❺. This 452-acre park along the rushing Housatonic River is noted for a two-mile stretch of water reserved for fly fishing. Non-anglers will enjoy the beautiful woods and fine hiking trails. ☎ *860-672-3238. Open daily 8–sunset. Free. Partially* ♿.

A little beyond the north end of the park is the postcard-pretty village of **West Cornwall** ❻, where you'll find the second covered bridge over the Housatonic, on Route 128. This one, designed by covered-bridge maven Ithiel Town, has been in continuous use since 1837. West Cornwall is a fine place to stop as there are several interesting crafts shops and eateries near the bridge.

From West Cornwall, go back down 7 through Cornwall Bridge and continue east on CT-4, turning right onto CT-63 and following that south into the lovely little town of *Litchfield ❼. This is New England at its best, and in some ways most typical. Quite a prosperous place in the 18th century, Litchfield went to sleep in the 19th when it was bypassed by the railroad and missed out on the Industrial Revolution. Today it is a beautifully preserved vision of Colonial days, with just enough low-key attractions to keep you busy for a while. At its center, by the junction of US-202 and CT-118, is the picturebook village green and its pristine *Congregational Church** of 1829 — surely one of the most photographed sights in New England. Park as close to here as possible.

Stroll to the south side of **The Green**, where you'll find the **Litchfield History Museum**. Unlike many local museums whose rooms are crammed full of Americana, this one has four spacious galleries where every article on display stands out. The exhibits include furniture, decorative arts, textiles, photographs, and paintings that together tell the story of Litchfield's history. Among the fine collection of paintings by Ralph Earl is a portrait of Mariann Wolcott, daughter of one of Litchfield's most prominent citizens, Oliver Wolcott Sr., who signed the Declaration of Independence, served in the Continental Congress, and was governor of Connecticut in 1796–97. You'll want time to browse here. ☎ *860-567-4501. Open mid-Apr. to Nov., Tues.–Sat. 11–5, Sun. 1–5. Closed major holidays. Adults $5, seniors $3; includes Tapping Reeve House & School, below; children under 14 free. Gift shop. ⅙.*

Go down South Street to the **Tapping Reeve House and Law School**. America's first law school was established here in 1774 by Tapping Reeve, lawyer and jurist. He began by holding classes in the parlor, later moving to the school building next door. Reeve was married to Aaron Burr's sister, and Burr was one of his earliest pupils, the first in a long line of distinguished graduates that included Vice President John C. Calhoun, Horace Mann, three Supreme Court justices, six cabinet secretaries, and 130 members of Congress. The Tapping Reeve House is furnished to the late 18th and early 19th century period, while the Litchfield Law School building houses an exhibit on the school and its graduates. ☎ *860-567-4501. Open mid-April to Nov., Tues.–Sat. 11–5, Sun. 1–5. Closed major holidays. Adults $5, seniors and students $3; includes Historical Museum, above, children 14 and under free. ⅙.*

Across the street is the **Oliver Wolcott Sr. House**, to which, during the Revolutionary War, came Washington, Lafayette, Alexander Hamilton, and the equestrian statue of George III, the latter toppled from its pedestal in Bowling Green, New York City, by the Sons of Liberty, dragged all the way to Litchfield, and melted down into bullets by the women of the town. Farther down South Street is Old South Road, a righthand fork that takes you to the Ethan Allen House, where the famed Revolutionary War hero and leader of the Green Mountain Boys once lived.

Go back to The Green. Here look for a narrow road leading behind the shops on West Street to Cobble Court, a 19th-century cobblestone courtyard ringed by quaint shops. Continue up North Street to a number of other historic spots: the home of Benjamin Tallmadge, a Revolutionary War officer, confidential agent, and aide to George Washington; Sheldon's Tavern, another of Washington's many resting places; the site of the birthplace of Henry Ward Beecher and Harriet Beecher Stowe, whose father, the influential clergyman Lyman Beecher, preached at the earlier Congregational Church; and the site of Miss Pierce's Academy, the first girls' school in the United States, founded by Sarah Pierce in 1792.

Just east of Litchfield, to the left off Route CT-118, is the **Lourdes in Litchfield Shrine** ❽ of the Montfort Missionaries. An outdoor chapel here faces a replica of the grotto at Lourdes, France, where the Virgin Mary is said to have appeared to Saint Bernadette in 1858. To one side, the Way of the Cross starts up a wooded trail that winds to the top of the hill, ending with a flight of steps up to Calvary. ☎ *860-567-1041. Grounds open daily all year, Pilgrimage season May to mid-Oct.; call for schedule of services. Donation.* ☖. By continuing east on CT-118 a little bit and turning right on Chestnut Hill Road, you can visit the **Haight Vineyard and Winery** for tours and complimentary tastings. ☎ *860-567-4045. Open Mon.–Sat. 10:30–5; Sun. noon–5, closed major holidays.*

Head west from Litchfield on US-202. In about two miles you'll come to the **White Memorial Foundation** ❾. Connecticut's largest nature sanctuary, on the shores of Connecticut's largest natural lake, offers 4,000 acres of forest, marshlands, ponds, and streams sheltering a diversity of trees, flowers, ferns, mosses, birds, fish, and wildlife. Some 35 miles of trails provide ample opportunity for hiking, horseback riding, birdwatching, nature study, or relaxed contemplation. Beautiful Bantam Lake offers its shore for picnicking and its waters for fishing. The **Conservation Center** is an excellent natural history museum with an extensive library, a children's room, and displays explaining the varied habitats and ecological systems within the sanctuary. ☎ *860-567-0857. Grounds open daily all year; free. Conservation Center open all year, Mon.–Sat. 9–5, Sun. noon–5, closing earlier in winter. Adults $4, children (6–12) $2.* ☖.

Continue west on US-202 to **Lake Waramaug State Park** ❿. Waramaug, an Indian word meaning "good fishing place," is an apt name for Connecticut's second-largest natural lake, and one of its most beautiful. This 95-acre park located on its northwest shore hosts the annual Women's National Rowing Regatta in May. ☎ *860-868-2592.*

Head south on CT-47 to **Washington** ⓫, home of the **Gunn Historical Museum**. Here's an interesting place, a 1781 house crammed with artifacts reflecting life in Washington in the 18th and 19th centuries — furniture, paintings, toys, dolls and dollhouses, gowns, thimbles, needlework spinning wheels, tools, kitchenware, china, and more. In addition, there are exhibits on the history of Washington since Colonial times. *CT-47 at Wykeham Rd.,* ☎ *860-868-7756. Museum open Thurs.–Sun. noon–4. Donation.*

Continue south on 47 briefly to the junction with CT-199. Turn right and go a bit over a mile to the **Institute for American Indian Studies** ⓬. This is a serious research and educational facility devoted to the history of America's original inhabitants and the study of early cultures. The exhibits include artifacts and art from 10,000 years ago to the present, a furnished longhouse, a replicated 17th-century Algonkian village, a simulated archaeological site, native plant trails, a garden, and a rock shelter. *38 Curtis Rd., off CT-199.* ☎ *860-868-0518, Internet: www.americanindian institute.org. Open Mon.–Sat. 10–5, Sun. noon–5, closed Mon. and Tues. from Jan.–March. Adults $4, seniors $3.50, children (6–16) $2.* ☖.

Continue south on 47 to **Woodbury** ⓭, making a right on Hollow Road to the **Glebe House & Gertrude Jekyll Garden**. This picturesque building, some of it dating from 1690, was part of the glebe (minister's farm) of

Woodbury's first Episcopal priest, John Rutgers Marshall, who took up residence here in 1771. Marshall, like many other Anglicans, was a Tory sympathizer who vigorously opposed American independence and wrote pamphlets attacking the ideas of Thomas Paine. It is sometimes said that Marshall built a secret tunnel in Glebe House to escape in case of trouble, but researchers now believe that this "tunnel," really little more than a basement crawl space, predates Marshall's occupancy. In 1783, when the cause of American independence was won, a group of American clergymen met at Glebe House and elected Samuel Seabury first American bishop of the Protestant Episcopal Church.

Like many of the homes in Woodbury's historical district, Glebe House was built by a local housemaker called Herd (who lived in the nearby red house on Hollow Road, now maintained by the Old Woodbury Historical Society). The gambrel roof and other additions to the central room dates from the 1730s or 1740s. Today, the house has period furnishings, documents relating to the development of the Episcopal Church in America, and features the only garden in the U.S. designed by Britain's most famous 20th-century gardener, Gertrude Jekyll. ☎ *203-263-2855. Open Apr.–May and Sept.–Oct., Wed.–Sun. 1–4; June–Aug., Wed.–Fri. 1–4, Sat. 10–4, Sun. 1–4; Nov. Sat.–Sun. 1–4. Adults $5, children (6–16) $2.* ♿.

Time permitting, you might want to unwind in a nearby natural setting before returning to the hectic city. Head east from Woodbury on US-6 for about two miles to Flanders Road. Turn right here and go about three miles to Church Hill Road, leading to the **Flanders Nature Center** ⓮. This 1,000-acre wildlife sanctuary and outdoor education laboratory offers a choice of two hiking trails through varied terrain and habitats. The wildflower trail is delightful in spring, and the marsh walk is particularly popular with birdwatchers. There are some good exhibits at the trailside environmental center, along with a small natural history museum. ☎ *203-263-3711. Open daily, dawn to dusk. Free.* ♿.

Continuing south on US-6 soon brings you to I-84, which heads west past Danbury and into New York State, where it connects with I-684. Taking the latter south eventually leads into the Hutchinson River Parkway and New York City.

Trip 32

Terryville to Wethersfield

This trip takes you from the eastern Litchfield Hills region of Connecticut into the Farmington Valley just south of Hartford. There's a nice range of interesting museums and historic sites along the entire route, including some rather unusual ones. Then again, you might prefer to spend most of the day at a truly outstanding, old-fashioned family-style amusement park, with one of the very best wooden roller coasters in the entire world. In the same vein, there's a great carousel museum, and to the delight of kids everywhere, a state park filled with thousands of dinosaur footprints from hundreds of millions of years ago.

For those who can stay overnight, possibly in a country inn or friendly B&B, this trip combines beautifully with the previous one to the Litchfield Hills, and the following one to Hartford.

GETTING THERE:

By Car: Take **I-95** northeast to Exit 52 in Connecticut, then **CT-8** north to Exit 39. From here head east on US-6 to Terryville and follow directions in the text. The farthest destination is about 115 miles northeast of midtown Manhattan.

PRACTICALITIES:

Several of the attractions are only open in season, so be sure to check the individual listings carefully, especially if you intend to visit the amusement park. For further information about the Litchfield Hills, contact the **Litchfield Hills Visitor Bureau**, P.O. Box 968, Litchfield, CT 06759, ☎ 860-567-4506, Internet: www.litchfieldhills.com; for Farmington and points north contact the **Greater Hartford Tourism District**, 234 Murphy Rd., Hartford, CT 06114, ☎ 860-244-8181 or 1-800-793-4480, Internet: www.enjoyhartford .com.

FOOD AND DRINK:

Apricots (1593 Farmington Ave., CT-4, in Farmington) Continental cuisine with a river view, indoors or out on the patio in season. Sunday brunch. ☎ 860-673-5405. $$ and $$$

Piccolo Arancio (Farmington Inn, 819 Farmington Ave., CT-4, in Farmington) Contemporary Italian cuisine. ☎ 860-674-1224. X: Fri.–Sat. lunch, Sun., major holidays. $$ and $$$

City Limits (70 Wolcott Hill Rd. in Wethersfield) Hearty Italian dishes in a family-style restaurant. ☎ 860-257-7100. $ and $$

The amusement park offers about a dozen places to eat anything from a hot dog to a full meal. Since Wethersfield is practically in Hartford, you might want to try some of the fine eateries in that capital city. See page 235.

LOCAL ATTRACTIONS:

Circled numbers in text correspond to numbers on the map.
Begin in **Terryville**, home of the unusual:

LOCK MUSEUM OF AMERICA ❶, 130 Main St., Terryville, CT 06786, ☎ 860-589-6359. *Open May through Oct., Tues.–Sun. 1:30–4:30. Adults $3, seniors $2.50, children (4–12) free.* ♿.

If you're ever going to find the key to whatever it is you're looking for, this may be the place. It's a one-of-a-kind collection of more than 22,000 items tracing the American lock industry back to its local beginnings in the early 19th century. There are all kinds of locks and keys for every purpose, from the grim (handcuffs, leg irons) to the utilitarian (trunks, cabinets, safes) to the merely decorative.

Continue east on US-6 and CT-72 a few miles to **Bristol**, where you'll find two more offbeat museums to pique your interest:

NEW ENGLAND CAROUSEL MUSEUM ❷, 95 Riverside Ave. (CT-72), Bristol, CT 06010, ☎ 860-585-5411, Internet: www.thecarouselmuseum.com. *Open Apr.–Nov., Mon.–Sat. 10–5, Sun. noon–5; Dec.–March, Thurs.–Sat. 10–5, Sun. noon–5. Closed major holidays. Adults $4, seniors $3.50, children (4–14) $2.50. Gift shop.* ♿.

Here, in a renovated factory building, is one of the largest collections of carousel art anywhere — a rare treasure that will surely touch the child in you. A tour of the museum includes the famous Bill Brinley's Miniature Circus, and an opportunity to watch (during shop hours) as skilled craftsmen restore rare pieces to their original beauty.

Go north on CT-69 a few blocks to the:

AMERICAN CLOCK AND WATCH MUSEUM ❸, 100 Maple St., Bristol, CT 06010, ☎ 860-583-6070, Internet: www.plads.com/acwmuseum. *Open Apr.–Nov., daily 10–5. Adults $5, seniors $4, children $2.* ♿.

Bristol has been renowned for its clocks since 1790, when Gideon Roberts began making and selling them locally. It is a fitting home for the American Clock and Watch Museum, where more than 3,000 timepieces, from majestic grandfather clocks to Mickey Mouse watches, are on display in clearly labeled exhibits that unfold the history of American horology. Many of the clocks strike hourly, making a joyful noise. Featured is a re-created clock shop from 1825, a Victorian clock store, and a sundial garden. The museum consists of three buildings; the Miles Lewis House

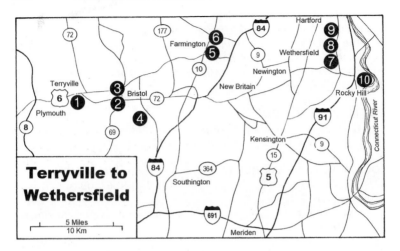

(1801), a fine specimen of the post-Revolutionary mansion house; the Edward Ingraham Memorial Wing (1987); and the Ebenezer Barnes Wing, erected in 1955 using paneling and other materials salvaged from the first permanent residence (1728) in Bristol. In a fireproof vault in the Barnes wing is the Edward Ingraham Library, a comprehensive collection of reference materials on the American clock and watch industries, open to serious researchers by appointment.

For another, completely different kind of attraction — and one that will surely please the kids — turn south from Bristol on CT-229 for a short distance to the:

*LAKE COMPOUNCE THEME PARK ❹, 822 Lake Ave., Bristol, CT 06010, ☎ 860-583-3300, Internet: www.lakecompounce.com. *Open mid-May to mid-June, weekends and some weekdays; mid-June to late Aug., daily; late Aug. to late Sept., weekends; sometimes in Oct. Check current schedule online or by phone. General admission without rides $7.95; all day unlimited rides: Adults $25.95, seniors (60+) and juniors under 52" tall $17.95, age 3 and under free. Shows. Shops. Numerous eateries. Partially ૐ.*

Calling itself "New England's Family Theme Park," Lake Compounce is reputedly America's oldest amusement park, having first opened to the public way back in 1846. Recent additions to its rides include the fastest and longest wooden roller coaster on the East Coast and the only one in the world built on the side of a mountain — and already voted the best wooden coaster on Earth. Other features include the only water park in Connecticut, a white-water rafting ride, an interactive ghost hunt in the dark, several steel roller coasters, and much more. Lake Compounce is a highly successful integration of classic, old-fashioned amusements along with innovative modern rides for today's patrons.

Go back through Bristol, turn right on US-6, and continue east to the junction with CT-10. Turn left and go north briefly to **Farmington**, a picture-perfect New England town of great charm. Watch for the stoplight at Mountain Road, turn right, and proceed to High Street and the:

STANLEY-WHITMAN HOUSE ❺, 37 High St., Farmington, CT 06032, ☎ 860-677-9222). *Open May through Oct., Wed.–Sun. noon–4; Nov.–Apr., Sun. noon–4; closed major holidays. Adults $5, seniors $4, children (6–18) $2.* ♿.

This National Historic Landmark is one of the most beautifully restored Colonial houses in the country. The original portion was built around 1720 and is a good example of the "framed overhang" style popular in England and transplanted by the settlers. Many of the furnishings were made by local craftsmen, and the herb and flower gardens have been planted to reflect 17th- and 18th-century horticultural tastes.

A little farther on Mountain Road, on the left, is a small lane to the:

*HILL-STEAD MUSEUM ❻, 35 Mountain Rd., Farmington, CT 06032, ☎ 860-677-4787, Internet: www.hillstead.org. *Open May–Oct., Tues.–Sun. 10–5; Nov.–Apr., Tues.–Sun. 11–4. Last tour an hour before closing. Adults $7, seniors & students $6, children (6–12) $4.*

A gracious turn-of-the-century mansion, Hill-Stead was built in 1901 for industrialist Alfred A. Pope, an early and prescient connoisseur of Impressionist art. In addition to the fine furnishings, Chinese porcelains, bronzes, and assorted objets, Pope's outstanding collection of paintings by Monet, Degas, Manet, Whistler, and other Impressionist artists is on display here, preserved as he left it by his daughter, Theodate. An interesting figure in her own right, Theodate was one of the first women architects in the United States and counted many artists and writers among her acquaintances. During her years at Hill-Stead, her guests included Mary Cassatt, Henry James, Isadora Duncan, and John Masefield.

Return to US-6 via CT-4 and head east to the junction of CT-9. From here go south, then east (left) on CT-175 into historic **Old Wethersfield**, which may be the oldest English settlement in the state. Here you'll find the:

*WEBB-DEANE-STEVENS MUSEUM ❼, 211 Main St., Wethersfield, CT 06109, ☎ 860-529-0612, Internet: www.webb-deane-stevens.org. *Open May–Oct., Wed.–Mon. 10–4; Nov.–Apr., Sat.–Sun. 10–4. Last tour at 3. Adults $8, seniors (60+) $7, children $4, under 5 free.*

Here are three handsome 18th-century houses restored to reflect the lifestyles of their owners — a merchant, a diplomat, and a tradesman. The oldest of them, the **Joseph Webb House** (1752), was the site of a historic meeting between Washington and Rochambeau in 1781, during which the two generals formulated the strategy that led to the British defeat at Yorktown, the concluding battle of the Revolutionary War. Not only did Washington sleep here, but the bedroom boasts the very same wallpaper that was hung in his honor on that occasion!

The **Silas Deane House** (1766) was the residence of a diplomat who was instrumental in securing French aid for the Revolutionary cause, and who recruited a number of distinguished foreign military officers (Lafayette, Pulaski, von Steuben, De Kalb) to serve with the Continental Army. During the Revolution, Silas Deane was unjustly accused of profiteering, but his reputation was posthumously cleared. His home, built for entertaining on a grand scale, has many unique structural details and a spaciousness unusual in houses of the period.

The last of the buildings, the **Issac Stevens House** (1788), is the least formal, reflecting the simpler tastes of its owner. In addition to the authentic period furnishings (1640–1840) that adorn all three houses, there is an interesting collection of children's toys and ladies' bonnets here.

A little farther down Main, across the street, is the:

KEENEY MEMORIAL CULTURAL CENTER ❽, 200 Main St., Wethersfield, CT 06109, ☎ 860-529-7656, Internet: www.wethhist.org. *Open Tues.–Sat. 10–4, Sun. 1–4. Closed holidays. Admission $3. Visitor Center. Museum shop.* &.

The colorful history of Wethersfield is traced through exhibits in this 1893 structure, along with changing displays of the decorative arts and local art. Closeby is the Old Academy Museum, built in 1804 as a school and now the headquarters of the Wethersfield Historical Society.

Go back on Main to Marsh. Turn right to Broad Street and the:

BUTTOLPH-WILLIAMS HOUSE ❾, 249 Broad St., Wethersfield, CT 06109, ☎ 860-529-0460, Internet: www.webb-deane-stevens.org. *Open May–Oct., Wed.–Mon. 10–4. Admission included with Webb-Deane-Stevens Museum, above, or may be purchased separately.*

From 1720, when this house was built, to 1752, the date of the Webb House (see above), some radical changes in living occurred. The Buttolph-Williams House is a typical "mansion house" of an earlier and more rugged era, giving you a chance to observe the contrast if you visit both. The house has been carefully restored, and the collections of 17th-century pewter, delft, fabric, and furnishings are outstanding. Of special interest is the kitchen, said to be the best preserved, most fully equipped kitchen of its period in New England.

Before leaving Old Wethersfield, you may want to take a walk and see the many other historic buildings — 116 pre-1840 houses within a dozen blocks, as well as a variety of later 19th-century structures — that make this town so attractive. Turn right on Broad Street, passing the village green, and proceed to Maple Street, CT-3. Turn right on Maple briefly to the junction with CT-99, at the light. Turn left and go south on 99 past the junction with I-91 to West St. and a sign for the State Veterans' Hospital. Turn right and watch for:

DINOSAUR STATE PARK ⑩, 400 West St., Rocky Hill, CT 06067, ☎ 860-529-8423, Internet: www.dinosaurstatepark.org. *Grounds open all year daily, 9–4:30, free. Exhibit Center open all year Tues.–Sun. 9–4:30: Adults $2, ages 6–17 $1. Picnicking, hiking and nature trails.* ᕃ.

While excavating a construction site some years ago, a bulldozer operator turned up a stone slab imprinted with curious markings that were soon identified as the three-toed tracks of dinosaurs of the Jurassic Period. Excited paleontologists from the Connecticut Geological Survey and Yale's Peabody Museum watched as workers uncovered over 2,000 prints estimated to be 200 million years old. About 500 of the tracks are enclosed under a geodesic dome, and the rest buried under plastic and sand to protect them from weathering. One area of the 70-acre park has been set aside for visitors who wish to make plaster casts of the tracks to take home (call for instructions and bring your own supplies). In the Exhibit Center you can inspect a life-size model of the animal that best represents the dinosaur whose footprints were found here.

For the return trip, continue on West Street briefly to the junction with I-91. Take 91 south to New Haven, then either CT-15 (Wilbur Cross and Merritt parkways, scenic route with no trucks) followed by the Hutchinson River Parkway south, or 1-95 (faster route) south into New York City.

In the New England Carousel Museum at Bristol

Hartford

Hartford may not be at the top of your destination list; America's Insurance City is hardly that exciting. On the plus side, however, it is blessed with several first-class attractions — and enough minor ones to make this a highly worthwhile excursion. Art lovers will surely enjoy the renowned Wadsworth Atheneum, while literary fans and history enthusiasts will revel in the colorful Mark Twain and Harriet Beecher Stowe houses. Along with its commercial prosperity, Hartford is also the capital of Connecticut, with all the attractions that entails. Having a history that stretches back over 350 years, it offers its share of well-preserved sites.

Yet another refuge from then-oppressive Massachusetts, Hartford — originally a Dutch trading post of 1633 — was settled in 1635 by dissident followers of the Reverend Thomas Hooker, and named after Hertford in England. In 1639 it drew up a constitution, the first ever in the New World, which is why Connecticut calls itself the "Constitution State." Granted a good deal of independence by Charles II in 1662, the colony refused to surrender its charter to an English governor during the notorious Charter Oak incident of 1687.

Hartford's insurance business began in 1794 and has flourished ever since. By the late 19th century the city boasted the highest per capita income in the nation, attracting a talented population and resulting in a rich architectural and cultural heritage that serves it well today.

GETTING THERE:

By Car, Hartford is about 115 miles northeast of New York City. Take I-684 north to Brewster and pick up I-84 east through Danbury and Waterbury to downtown Hartford. Get off at Exit 52 and park in a lot as close to Main Street or the Civic Center as possible. An alternative route is to take I-95 north to New Haven, then I-91 north to downtown Hartford.

After exploring downtown, you might want to use the car to reach the other attractions, instead of a longish walk or bus ride.

By Train: Amtrak provides a limited service to Hartford from New York's Pennsylvania Station, ☎ 1-800-USA-RAIL, Internet: www.amtrak .com, for details.

PRACTICALITIES:

Avoid making this trip on a Monday or major holiday, when several of the best sights are closed. The State Capitol and the Museum of

Connecticut History are closed on weekends and holidays, except that the capitol has tours on Saturdays from April through October. The fabulous Mark Twain House is closed on Tuesdays during the off-season. Hartford throbs with commercial vitality in weekdays; on weekends it is less crowded.

For further information contact the **Greater Hartford Tourism District**, 234 Murphy Road, Hartford, CT 06114, ☎ 860-244-8181 or 1-800-793-4480, Internet: www.enjoyhartford.com. Alternatively, contact the **Greater Hartford Convention & Visitors Bureau**, 1 Civic Center Plaza, Hartford, CT 06103, ☎ 860-728-6789 or 1-800- 446-7810, Internet: www.grhartford cvb.com.

FOOD AND DRINK:

You'll find plenty of places for lunch all along the downtown walking tour, including food courts at State House Square, Civic Center, and The Richardson. Some choice restaurants are:

Gaetano's Ristorante (Civic Center, 2nd level) A casually elegant spot for Northern Italian cuisine. Reservations accepted, ☎ 860-249-1629. X: Sat. lunch, Sun., holidays. $$ and $$$

Max Downtown (185 Asylum St., across from Civic Center) Contemporary versions of American and regional classics. ☎ 860-522-2530. X: Sat. lunch, Sun. lunch. $$ and $$$

Hartford Brewery (35 Pearl St., a block west of the Old State House) A popular brewpub with typical pub dishes and atmosphere. ☎ 860-246-2337. $

Museum Café (in the Wadsworth Atheneum) An unusually good museum restaurant. ☎ 860-728-5989. X: Mon. $

SUGGESTED TOUR:

Circled numbers in text correspond to numbers on the map. Begin your walk at the:

OLD STATE HOUSE ❶, 800 Main St., Hartford, CT, ☎ 860-522-6766, Internet: www.ctoldstatehouse.org. *Open Mon.–Fri. 10–4, Sat. 11–4. Closed some major holidays and last two weeks of Aug. Free. Visitor information center, museums, gift shop, seasonal events.* ⅏.

This elegant Federal structure was the first public commission of Charles Bulfinch (1763–1844), one of America's best early architects. Bulfinch went on to design many other buildings and is perhaps best remembered for bringing the Capitol building in Washington, D.C., to completion in 1830. The Old State House served as Connecticut's state capitol from 1796 to 1878, and as Hartford's city hall from 1879 to 1915. Today it is a National Historic Landmark, museum, and cultural center. A rare Gilbert Stuart full-length *portrait of George Washington hangs in the restored Senate Chamber. **Mr. Steward's Museum** of 1796 is still there, featuring such natural curiosities as a two-headed cow; and there's a fine

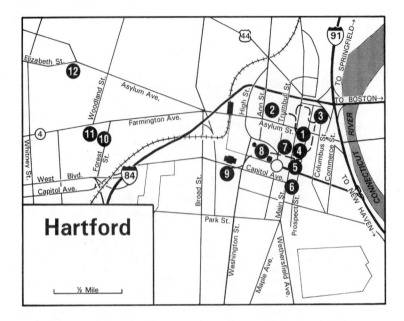

Museum of Connecticut History in the new underground wing. Re-enactments of the famous Amistad trial, held here in the mid-19th century, are performed on occasion.

Stroll north along Main Street, possibly making a little side trip on lively old Pratt Street to the **Hartford Civic Center ❷**. Whether you're here for a convention, entertainment, shopping, or dining, this vast modern complex has it all. An elevated skywalk leads to **CityPlace**, Connecticut's tallest building, a 1984 structure noted for its richly-landscaped atrium. Back on Main Street, **The Richardson** is a marvelous brownstone commercial building of 1877 that was salvaged and recycled as a shopping mall.

Follow the map around to **Constitution Plaza ❸**. These dozen acres of elegant high-rises and landscaped promenades show the effects of urban renewal at its best. Completed in 1964, the plaza combines office space, shopping centers, and parking facilities. Among its features are the boat-shaped elliptical headquarters of the Phoenix Mutual Life, one of the few two-sided buildings on Earth, and the splashless fountain, designed to resists the fiercest provocations from the plaza winds.

Continue around to the **Travelers Tower ❹** of 1919, once the tallest structure in New England. The 527-foot tower was built by the Travelers Insurance Company, a venerable Hartford institution that got its start in 1863 by insuring a Captain James Bolter for $5,000 for a trip from his home to the post office at a premium of two cents. Plenty of other travelers put in their two cents' worth over the years, and the company grew to become one of the giants of the insurance field. *Free tours: mid-May to late Oct., Mon.–Fri. 10–3. Closed holidays.* ☎ *860-277-4208.*

The Travelers Tower stands on a site once occupied by Sanford's Tavern, where in 1687 Sir Edmund Andros, James II's royal governor of New England, demanded the surrender of the original charter granted to the Connecticut colonists by Charles II in 1662. While Andros was engaged in heated debate with the colonists at Sanford's, Captain Joseph Wadsworth took the charter and squirreled it away in the hollow of an ancient white oak, where it remained safely hidden until the colonists succeeded in ridding themselves of the autocratic Andros. The **Charter Oak**, thought to have been more than 1,000 years old, succumbed to a storm in 1856, but the 1662 charter is on display in the Museum of Connecticut History, and the family tree lives on in the white oak on the grounds of the Center Church, just across Main Street.

Immediately south of the tower is the:

*WADSWORTH ATHENEUM ❺, 600 Main St., Hartford, CT 06103, ☎ 860-278-2670, Internet: www.wadsworthatheneum.org. *Open Tues.–Sun. 11–5, closed Mon. and major holidays. Adults $7, seniors & students $5, children $3, under 6 free. Free all day Thurs. and Sat. 11–noon. Gift shop. Café.* ৬.

One of the nation's oldest and best public art museums, the Wadsworth Atheneum has a well-deserved reputation for the excellence and breadth of its collections. More than 50,000 art objects, from ancient Egyptian artifacts to contemporary sculptures, are on display here in spacious galleries occupying five interconnected buildings. There's an extensive selection of paintings representing every major period and style since the 15th century, with some particularly fine works by Monet, Renoir, and other 19th-century French artists. Also noteworthy are the collections of American and English silver, Meissen porcelain, furniture, and period costumes.

Directly south of the Atheneum is **Burr Mall**, a small park dominated by Alexander Calder's massive steel *Stegosaurus*. A little side trip can be made here by continuing south on Main Street to the:

BUTLER-McCOOK HOMESTEAD ❻, 396 Main St., Hartford, CT 06103, ☎ 860-247-8996. *Probable opening times are: mid-May to mid-Oct., Tues., Thurs., and Sun., noon–4. Probable fees: Adult $6, under 18 $2. Call for information.*

This survivor of urban renewal stands in quaint contrast to the glittering office buildings of downtown Hartford. The oldest private home in the city (1782), it has been preserved as a museum of 18th- and 19th-century tastes in furnishings and decorative arts. On display are fine collections of silver, 19th-century American paintings, Chinese bronzes, Egyptian artifacts, toys, and dolls. The annual Victorian Christmas exhibit is a nice way to get into the spirit of the season.

Go back up Main Street. On the left, opposite Travelers Tower, is the **Ancient Burying Ground** ❼, final resting place of some of Hartford's early settlers, with headstones dating back to 1640; look for the epitaph of Dr. Thomas Langrell, who "drowned in the glory of his years, and left his mate to drown herself in tears." Right by the cemetery stands the **Center Church** of 1807, patterned after London's St. Martin's-in-the-Fields, with stained-glass windows by Louis Tiffany. The church occupies the site where the U.S. Constitution was ratified by Connecticut in 1788.

Amble down Gold Street and into **Bushnell Park** ❽. This was the first land in the United States to be claimed for park purposes under eminent domain, and was laid out according to a natural landscape design influenced by the ideas of Hartford native Frederick Law Olmsted. The **Pump House Gallery** in its southeast corner features exhibits by area artists. ☎ *860-543-8874. Open Tues.–Fri. 11–2. Free.* ♿. A popular spot for outdoor concerts and special events, the park is also the home of a restored 1914 Carousel, a real beauty transported here from Canton, Ohio. For fifty cents you can ride one of the 48 brightly-painted hand-carved horses and try for the brass ring. ☎ *860-585-5411. Open May to mid-Oct., Tues.–Sun. 11–5.*

Dominating Bushnell Park is the:

STATE CAPITOL ❾, 210 Capitol Ave., Hartford, CT 06106, ☎ 860-240-0222. *One-hour tours begin at neighboring Legislative Office Building: Sept.–June, Mon.–Fri. 9:15 first tour, 1:15 last tour; July–Aug. Mon.–Fri. 9:15 first tour, 2:15 last tour. Also open Sat. from Apr–Oct., 10:15 first tour, 2:15 last tour. Closed state holidays. Free.* ♿.

Here is Hartford's most impressive building, seat of Connecticut government since 1879, housing the state executive offices and legislative chambers. A great gold-leaf dome presides over this eclectic architectural concoction by Richard Mitchell Upjohn. On the tour you'll see statues, murals, and historic displays featuring bullet-riddled flags, Lafayette's camp bed, and other reminders of Connecticut's past, as well as a plaster model of the Genius of Connecticut, which adorned the capitol spire until it was melted down during World War II.

Just across the street is the **Museum of Connecticut History**, where you can see the original royal charter of 1662, a collection of locally-made Colt firearms, and more. ☎ *860-566-3056. Open Mon.–Fri. 9–4, closed state holidays. Free.* ♿.

From here you can either drive, take a bus, or hike to the:

HARRIET BEECHER STOWE HOUSE ❿, Nook Farm, 77 Forest St., Hartford, CT 06105, ☎ 860-522-9258, Internet: www.hartnet.org/~stowe. *Open June–Columbus Day, Mon.–Sat. 9:30–4, Sun. noon–4; rest of year Tues.–Sat. 9:30–4, Sun. noon–4. Closed New Year's Day, Easter, Labor Day, Thanksgiving, Dec. 24–25. Adults $6.50, seniors (60+) $6, children (6–16) $2.75.*

Nook Farm is an old Hartford neighborhood that attracted a remarkable group of 19th-century writers and intellectuals connected by family ties and bonds of friendship. Among the distinguished company that settled here were women's-rights activist Isabella Beecher Hooker, playwright and thespian William Gillette, Senator Joseph Hawley, and Charles Dudley Warner, editor of the *Hartford Courant* and co-author with Mark Twain of *The Gilded Age*. Today most of Nook Farm has been torn down, but several of the original buildings remain, including the homes of its most famous residents: Harriet Beecher Stowe and Mark Twain.

Author Harriet Beecher Stowe settled into this Victorian "cottage" in 1873, and remained here until her death in 1896. The house certainly reflects the tastes of its owner: the design of the kitchen follows the specifications set forth in the book Stowe wrote with her sister, *The American Woman's Home*; some of her paintings hang on the walls; there are mementos of her career as a writer and reformer, and many original items of furniture, including the tiny desk at which she penned her most important work, *Uncle Tom's Cabin* (1852), a book that aroused popular sentiment against slavery and sold 300,000 copies within a year — a staggering figure in those days.

Whatever you do, don't miss seeing the nearby:

*MARK TWAIN HOUSE ⓫, Nook Farm, 351 Farmington Ave., Hartford, CT 06105, ☎ 860-493-6411, Internet: www.hartnet.org/twain. *Open Memorial Day to Columbus Day and Dec., Mon.–Sat. 9:30–5, Sun. 11–5; rest of year, Mon. and Wed.–Sat. 9:30–5, Sun. noon–5. Closed New Year's Day, Easter, Thanksgiving, Dec. 24–25. Tours last 1 hour last tour at 4. Adults $9, seniors (65+) $8, youths (13–18) $7 children (6–12) $5. Museum shop. Partially ⚬.*

Mark Twain's house, designed by Edward Tuckerman Potter, is a colorful and idiosyncratic reflection of the author's personality, perhaps best appreciated by those who have read his works and know his humor. The south façade is modeled after a Mississippi River steamboat, the dressing room re-creates a riverboat pilothouse, and the etched windows in the upstairs study, where Twain wrote *The Adventures of Tom Sawyer, The Adventures of Huckleberry Finn,* and five other books memorialize his great passions in life — smoking, drinking, and billiards. Twain lived at Nook Farm with his wife and three daughters from 1874 to 1891, when financial difficulties forced him to sell the house and take to the lecture circuit.

Game for more before calling it a day? It's only a hop to the:

CONNECTICUT HISTORICAL SOCIETY ⓬, 1 Elizabeth St., Hartford, CT 06105 ☎ 860-236-5621, Internet: www.chs.org. *Museum open all year, Tues.–Sun. noon–5; library open all year Tues.–Sat. 9–5; both closed Mon. and holidays. Adults $6, seniors (60+) and students $3, children (6-17) $3. Partially ⚬.*

The leading repository of museum materials on state history, the

Connecticut Historical Society has eight galleries of changing exhibits and permanent displays, including two particularly fine furniture collections: the Barbour Collection of Connecticut pieces from the Colonial and Federal periods, and the George Dudley Seymour Collection of 17th- and 18th-century pieces. You can also see Connecticut-made silver, pewter, toys, glassware, pottery, and stoneware. The art of the tavern sign is well represented by more than 70 specimens, suggesting that a fair number of past Connecticut residents were not customers of the Phoenix Mutual Life Insurance Company, which accepted only teetotalers when it was established in Hartford in 1851. The society also maintains a vast library of almost two million historical manuscripts, 100,000 books, 3,500 bound volumes of newspapers and periodicals, extensive genealogical holdings, and assorted maps, prints, and photographs.

The Mark Twain House

Constitution Plaza and The Travelers Tower

Connecticut's State Capitol

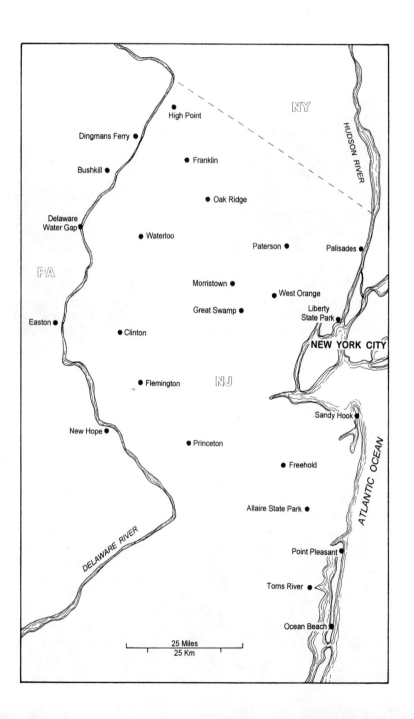

NY

HUDSON RIVER

• High Point

Dingmans Ferry •

• Franklin

Bushkill •

• Oak Ridge

Delaware
Water Gap •

• Waterloo

Paterson •

Palisades •

PA

Morristown •

• West Orange

Great Swamp •

Liberty
State Park •

Easton •

NEW YORK CITY

• Clinton

• Flemington

NJ

Sandy Hook •

New Hope •

• Princeton

ATLANTIC OCEAN

• Freehold

Allaire State Park •

DELAWARE RIVER

Point Pleasant •

Toms River •

Ocean Beach •

25 Miles
25 Km

Section VI

DAYTRIPS TO
NEW JERSEY and
PENNSYLVANIA

These seventeen trips unlock a treasure chest that lies close to New York City and is easily reached. Fourteen of them are in New Jersey, beginning with destinations that are actually within sight of Manhattan — accessible by convenient public transportation as well as by car. Nature has been lavish with the shoreline here, providing miles of white ocean sand, rolling breakers, and fresh unpolluted air. Turning inland, you follow historic trails leading to Revolutionary War battlefields and white mansions from Colonial days. Eventually, you cross the Delaware River into Pennsylvania for the three remaining daytrips, about as far as it's practical to go on a one-day excursion.

The Palisades

D iscovered in 1524 by Giovanni da Verrazano, the Palisades ("fence of stakes") are volcanically-formed basalt cliffs overlooking the Hudson River. In 1900 Congress established the Palisades Interstate Park Commission to protect the cliffs from destruction by quarrying. The park consists of over 80,000 acres of land in New York and New Jersey; the 2,500-acre New Jersey Section, extending about 11 miles from Fort Lee to the New York State Line, is a National Historic Landmark and a National Natural Landmark. Here, minutes from Manhattan, you can stand on cliffs 300 to 500 feet high as you survey a panorama that includes the mighty Hudson, the New York skyscrapers, Long Island, Westchester, and far beyond. Looking straight down, you'll have awesome views of the tops of trees that literally grow up on the sides of the precipice. Below, along the shore, are picnic grounds and boat basins.

This delightful scenic drive, so close to the city and yet so removed from its bustle, begins with a visit to an important Revolutionary War site, then offers several outlooks with panoramic views stretching from Lower Manhattan to the Tappan Zee Bridge at Tarrytown. On the way back you can drive down to the river level to explore the Palisades from below, possibly taking a hike on one of the many trails or having a picnic.

GETTING THERE:

By Car: Take the upper level of the **George Washington Bridge** to the first **Fort Lee** exit, after the exit for the Palisades Interstate Parkway. Bear right and go down the ramp to Hudson Terrace, at the traffic light. Turn right and go about 50 feet past the next light to the **Fort Lee Historic Park** entrance, on the left.

Return towards the bridge and continue north on the **Palisades Interstate Parkway**, making stops at the various sites. Rockefeller Lookout is about 3 miles north, just off the parkway on the right. Alpine Lookout is another 3 miles north on the right; park headquarters is just above, off Exit 2 on the right; and State Line Lookout is off Exit 3, on the right, about 3 miles north of Alpine.

Return south on the parkway to Exit 2, Alpine. From here you can take the undercliff **Henry Hudson Drive** south to several more sites. This drive then climbs up to the parkway Exit 1, from which you return to the George Washington Bridge. **NOTE** that the Henry Hudson Drive is open to cars and bicycles only, during daylight hours only, and only from the first Saturday in April until the last Sunday in October. It may also be closed due to bad weather or rock slides. If it is closed, you can return to the

George Washington Bridge on the parkway instead.

The Palisades Interstate Parkway is open to **passenger cars and motorcycles only**. Commercial vehicles, campers, and trailers are prohibited.

PRACTICALITIES:

Good weather, preferably between April and the end of October, is essential to enjoying this scenic drive, which can be made by passenger car or motorcycle only. The Fort Lee Historic Park, however, can be reached by bus from Manhattan — and it is possible to hike along either the Long Path or the Shore Trail, getting to them by bus from Manhattan, or even on foot across the George Washington Bridge.

Information can be obtained from the **Palisades Interstate Park**, New Jersey Section Headquarters, Alpine Approach Rd., Alpine, NJ 07620, ☎ 201-768-1360, Internet: www.njpalisades.org. Many cultural, educational, and recreational programs take place in the park throughout the year. Call the park headquarters or check their web site for a calendar of events.

FOOD AND DRINK:

Picnic facilities are available at all developed sites, with tables on a first-come, first-served basis. Barbequing is possible at the Alpine, Undercliff, Englewood, and Ross Dock areas only — bring your own stove and fuel and follow the posted rules. There are seasonal concession stands at the Englewood Area and Ross Dock. Other than a picnic, your best bet is the:

Lookout Inn (State Line Lookout, at the north end of the trip) Lunches and snacks are served in this cafeteria, located in a stone chalet built by the WPA in 1937. An information center is also here. ☎ 201-750-0465. $

SUGGESTED TRIP:

Circled numbers in text correspond to numbers on the map. Begin at the:

FORT LEE HISTORIC PARK ❶, Hudson Terrace, Fort Lee, NJ 07024, ☎ 201-461-1776. *Grounds open daily, 8 a.m. to sunset. Visitor Center open March–Dec., Wed.–Sun. 10–5; rest of year weekends only, 10–5. Parking fee $4, charged April.-Oct. Picnicking (no grills or fires). Museum. Bookstore. Mostly င.*

Fort Lee played a disheartening role in the early phases of the American Revolution, when the British were fighting for control of the Hudson. In July 1776, to block them, George Washington ordered the fortification of a number of sites on both sides of the river, including this fort named for General Charles Lee, a mercurial man who envied Washington and whose treason almost handed the British a victory at the Battle of Monmouth later that year. In August a large British force landed on Long Island and drove the American defenders across Brooklyn into Manhattan. Throughout the fall skirmishes raged where skyscrapers now

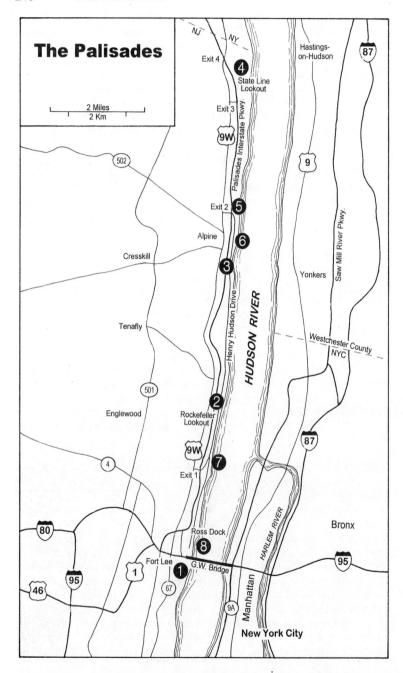

stand, and Washington fell back to Harlem Heights and White Plains. In November the Americans suffered a major defeat at Fort Washington, in what is today upper Manhattan. With its sister fort in British hands, Fort Lee lost its strategic importance and was already being evacuated when a surprise attack forced a hasty fight, resulting in further losses of men and badly needed supplies. That December, as Washington retreated deeper into New Jersey, Tom Paine penned the famous line "These are the times that try men's souls."

Fort Lee Historic Park, administered by the Palisades Interstate Park Commission, commemorates those trying times. The **Visitor Center**, just east of the original fort, features a bookstore and gift shop, historic exhibits, audiovisual displays, and a short film. Outside, two overlooks give spectacular *views of the George Washington Bridge, the New York skyline, and the Hudson River (minus the attacking British armada). Opened in 1931, the *George Washington Bridge** was once the longest such span in the world, and is still easily among the most beautiful. Fourteen lanes of traffic constantly fill its 3,500-foot leap across the Hudson River.

Winding trails take you through the southern part of the 33-acre park to reconstructed **gun batteries** and an 18th-century **soldier's hut** where demonstrations of Colonial life are staged. Of course, momentous battles still rage in this area daily during the rush hour, but it's hard to imagine it as a wilderness outpost of America's war for independence.

A Soldier's Hut at Fort Lee Historic Park

Head north, crossing the bridge approach roads and onto the **Palisades Interstate Parkway**, which leads north past several lookout points. For those interested in **hiking**, the New Jersey Section of the Palisades Interstate Park contains two designated National Recreational Trails, the Long Path and the Shore Trail, both beginning at the George Washington Bridge. The famous **Long Path**, marked by blue squares, winds along the clifftops past Rockefeller, Alpine, and State Line lookouts, crossing into New York State. The **Shore Trail** follows the low route to the New York State Line and is marked with white squares. Six sets of stairs marked by overlapping blue and white squares connect the two trails. Average hiking time is 30 minutes per mile; camping, cooking, and cliff climbing are prohibited, and hikers must be off the trail by dark.

The Palisades Interstate Parkway in about three miles brings you to the **Rockefeller Lookout** ❷. You're across the Hudson from the Riverdale section of the Bronx, just above Manhattan Island. To the right is the George Washington Bridge, and behind it, the New York skyscrapers. Beyond them is the Long Island Sound and Long Island. The hills north of the bridge rise to become Washington Heights, highest point on Manhattan. During the Revolution this was the site of Fort Washington, one of the city's ill-fated defenses. Fort Tryon Park stretches along the clifftops, and at the upper end stands the Cloisters (see page 91), a medieval museum maintained by the Metropolitan Museum of Art.

Underneath the New York end of the bridge at Jeffreys Hook you can just make out the **Little Red Lighthouse**, slated for demolition when the bridge went up, but spared through protests and publicity. Look straight down the side of the cliffs for staggeringly effective views of treetops mingling with gigantic columns of rock. *20-minute parking limit, no fee. One curb, but fair ♿ access to vista points.*

Continue north another three miles to the **Alpine Lookout** ❸. From here, part of the Long Path takes you to the very edge of the cliffs, among the craggy pillars that poured out of the earth and solidified so many eons ago. That's Yonkers across the river. *20-minute parking limit, no fee. Steps and gravelly walk to promontory.*

Three more miles north and you'll be at the **State Line Lookout** ❹. You're now across from Hastings-on-Hudson, and 532 feet tall. The best view is to the north where the Tappan Zee Bridge carries the New York Thruway across three miles of river between Tarrytown and Nyack. The Long Path still clings to the top of the cliffs — why not join it for a hike? While here, you can visit the small chalet, built of chestnut wood and native stone in 1937 by the WPA. There's an information center inside, along with the Lookout Inn cafeteria; and special programs are held here throughout the year. ☎ *201-768-1360. Grounds open daily during daylight hours. Chalet generally open weekdays 10 a.m. to an hour before dusk, weekends 9 to a half-hour before dusk. May be closed on weekdays in the off-season. 1-hour parking limit, no fee. Partially ♿.*

Now it's time to turn around and head south, returning via a different route with an entirely different perspective on the scenery. Take the parkway south to Exit 2, Alpine, there joining **Henry Hudson Drive**. This scenic road descends the cliff and runs along the bottom from here south to Fort Lee, with an climb up at Englewood that connects with the parkway's Exit 1. It is open to cars and bicycles only, from the first Saturday in April until the last Sunday on October. Along the way you'll first come to the:

ALPINE AREA ❻, Base of Alpine Approach Rd., Alpine, NJ 07620, ☎ 201-768-1360, marina ☎ 201-768-9798. *Open daily during daylight hours. Road may be closed in winter. Parking fee April–Oct., $4. Picnicking, hiking, fishing, boat basin, special events. Partially ₲.*

High above this lovely riverfront area hang the great cliffs, with trees growing at all angles from the rock crevices. Manmade embellishments include picturesque pavilions and the historic **Blackledge-Kearny House**, built circa 1750 and believed to have been British General Cornwallis' headquarters during a 1776 invasion of New Jersey. Whether this is true or not, the legend saved it from being torn down in the 1930s, when it became the nation's only historic shrine dedicated to an enemy general. ☎ *201-768-0379. Open April–Oct., weekends and holidays, noon–5; or by appointment. Closed Nov.–March. Tours.*

Trails lead along the riverbank and right up the side of the Palisades. If these seem pretty steep, you might note that during the Revolution, British soldiers climbed them, carrying all their equipment, on their way to capture Fort Lee.

The next stop on the Henry Hudson Drive is the **Englewood Area ❼**. This is the park's largest picnic site, with a boat basin and beach as well as access to the trail system. There is also a refreshment stand, open on Wednesdays through Sundays, from spring through fall. ☎ *201-768-1360. Open daily during daylight hours. Parking fee $4 charged from April–Oct. Mostly ₲.*

The last stop before returning to New York City is at **Ross Dock ❽**, practically beneath the George Washington Bridge. Recently renovated, this scenic riverfront picnic area offers especially nice views along with recreational facilities and access to the trail system. ☎ *201-768-1360. Open daily during daylight hours. Road closed Nov.–March, but there is foot access from the bridge. Parking fee $4 charged April–Oct. ₲.*

Liberty State Park, the Statue of Liberty, and Ellis Island

N ew Yorkers are notorious for never visiting the Statue of Liberty, probably because it's too close to home. Here's your chance to make a real daytrip out of it by going via New Jersey's Liberty State Park, practically next door to both the statue and Ellis Island. The park also features the fabulous Liberty Science Center, a thoroughly modern hands-on museum of discovery, along with a wildlife habitat you can explore, swimming, tennis, fishing, and other sports, picnicking, and such historic sites as the vast CRRNJ train and ferry terminal of 1889.

During the 19th and early 20th centuries this area was a bustling industrial site with extensive freight and passenger transportation facilities for travel by both water and rail. Centuries before then it was already a Lenape Indian encampment, and later was settled by the early Dutch, English and Swedish arrivals. The first ferry service to Manhattan began as early as 1661, and in 1836 the opening of the Morris Canal facilitated travel west to Pennsylvania. Toward the end of the 19th century, the area was developed as a prime site for freight and commuter operations by the former Central Railroad of New Jersey and the Lehigh Valley Railroad. Its proximity to Ellis Island made it the first destination for some eight million immigrants eager to begin their trek into the American heartland. Following World War II, the area was abandoned by both the railroads and industry, and soon fell into decay. Salvation came with the approach of the nation's Bicentennial Celebration in 1976, when the entire area was redeveloped as a state park.

Both the Statue of Liberty and Ellis Island can also be reached by ferry from Lower Manhattan (see page 33), but doing so precludes a chance to enjoy the other attractions at Liberty State Park.

GETTING THERE:

By Car, Liberty State Park is about 10 miles southwest of midtown Manhattan. Take the **Holland Tunnel**, then the **New Jersey Turnpike Extension** (I-78) south to Exit 14B.

Those coming via the George Washington Bridge can take the New Jersey Turnpike (I-95) south to Exit 14, then the Turnpike Extension to Bayonne and Jersey City, getting off at Exit 14B.

By PATH Train: Take a PATH train from along Sixth Avenue in midtown Manhattan, making a connection to **Exchange Place** in Jersey City. There transfer to the **Hudson-Bergen Light Rail** south to Liberty State Park. For PATH information ☎ 1-800-234-PATH, Internet: www.panynj.gov; for Light Rail information ☎ 973-762-5100, Internet: www.njtransit.state. nj.us/hblrail. PATH fare $1, Light Rail fare $1.50, half-fare for seniors and children.

By Ferry: Take the NY Waterway boat from the **World Financial Center** in downtown Manhattan to the **Colgate Ferry Terminal** at Exchange Place in Jersey City, then the Hudson-Bergen Light Rail south to Liberty State Park, as above. NY Waterway also provides service from the World Financial Center to the Liberty Harbor landing, within walking distance of the park (or by Light Rail from Marin Blvd.). For ferry information ☎ 1-800-53-FERRY, Internet: www.nywaterway.com. *Check first as this service may or may not be operational due to reconstruction in lower Manhattan.*

PRACTICALITIES:

Both the Statue of Liberty and Ellis Island are open every day except Christmas. Note that the Liberty Science Center is closed on Mondays from early September through March, and also on Thanksgiving and Christmas. Visitors intending to climb to the crown of the statue must start early as access is limited and there may be very long waiting lines, especially in summer.

FOOD AND DRINK:

There are several cafeterias and snack bars at Liberty State Park, Liberty Science Center, the Statue of Liberty, and Ellis Island. In addition, Liberty State Park has picnic facilities.

LOCAL ATTRACTIONS:

Circled numbers in text correspond to numbers on the map.

LIBERTY STATE PARK ❶, Morris Pesin Drive, Jersey City, NJ 07305-4678, ☎ 201-915-3400, Internet: www.libertystatepark.com. *Open daily 6 a.m. to 10 p.m. Park free. Parking $5. Visitor center, natural area, trails, observation points, picnic area, playground, refreshments, boating, fishing, swimming pool (Memorial Day–Labor Day, fee). Leashed pets only. Mostly ♿.*

Here's a glorious *****view** you'll never forget. After you drive down State Flag Row (arranged in order of induction into the Union), you'll see the Statue of Liberty looming just 1,750 feet ahead. To the left lies Ellis Island, and beyond, the confluence of the Hudson and East rivers. Between them all is Lower Manhattan with its incomparable skyline. The Brooklyn Bridge is prominent, backed by the other bridges across the East River. To your right is the Verrazano Bridge linking Brooklyn with Staten Island. Finally, over the rooftops of Bayonne to the south, is the Bayonne Bridge, completing a giant arc linking three boroughs with New Jersey. The Staten

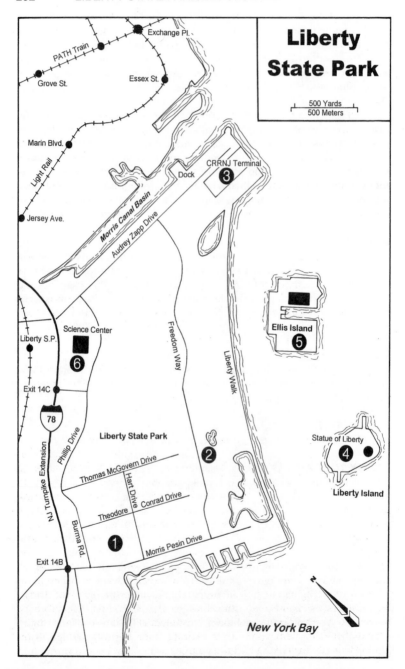

Island Ferry and the popular sightseeing cruisers ply the waters of New York Harbor; tugs, cargo vessels, and, as an occasional bonus, one of the great ocean liners make a never-ending pageant on the waters.

Liberty Walkway, a waterside promenade with ever-changing vistas, leads north past a **nature area ❷** and its interpretive center to the former **Central Railroad of New Jersey Terminal ❸**. Built in 1889 on the site of an earlier terminal, this immense complex includes a ferry dock, a 12-track passenger railroad station, freight and rail yards, maintenance shops, and much more in what was once the greatest concentration of rail facilities in the New York Harbor area. Both commuters from Manhattan and immigrants freshly arrived from Ellis Island used this as a gateway to their homes in New Jersey, and to their new lives west of the city. Service continued until 1967, when the CRRNJ declared bankruptcy. Deserted and falling into ruin, the terminal was rescued in the late 1970s and partially restored as an historic site, with adaptive reuse either in the works or planned for the future.

Just north of the CRRNJ Terminal is the **Morris Canal Basin**, one of the few surviving relics of the great Morris Canal (see page 303) that once linked New York Harbor with the Delaware River and Pennsylvania. This is also the location of the **Circle Line Ferry Dock**, where you can board a ferry to the Statue of Liberty and Ellis Island. *Service operates every day except Christmas, 8:30–4. Round trip to both islands: Adults $8, seniors (62+) $6, children (3–17) $3. For information* ☎ *201-435-9499 or 212-269-5755.*

Purchase your ticket and board the next boat to the:

*STATUE OF LIBERTY ❹, Liberty Island, NY 10004, ☎ 212-363-3200, Internet: www.nps.gov/stli. *Open daily all year 9–5 or 6. Closed Christmas Day. Free. Gift shop. Snack bar. Partially* ♿.

New York Harbor's famous statue was given to America by the people of France in 1886. Created by the famed sculptor Frédéric-Auguste Bartholdi between 1874 and 1884, and mounted on an ingenious internal frame by the noted engineer Gustave Eiffel (of Eiffel Tower fame), it remained in pieces while its American supporters tried to raise enough money for a base. Finally, the newspaper publisher Joseph Pulitzer campaigned in his New York World for funds, promising to publish the names of every donor, no matter how small their contribution. The pennies and dollars poured in, making possible the magnificent pedestal base created by the leading architect, Richard Morris Hunt. The statue was dedicated on October 28, 1886 by President Grover Cleveland.

Visitors who arrive early enough can wait in line to climb all 22 stories up into its **crown** for a stunning view, while those coming later will have to make do with the elevator ride to the top of its pedestal, a still-wonderful and infinitely less exhausting experience. Unless you are physically fit and just love to climb mountains, you'd do better to take the elevator and get a ***view** that is in many ways more exciting since it encompasses all of Lower Manhattan and not just Brooklyn.

Miss Liberty's engrossing history is told in the **Statue of Liberty Exhibit** inside the pedestal base, where you'll see full-scale replicas of its face and foot along with the original 1886 torch and much-altered flame. Videos, photos, prints, and oral histories bring to life the dramatic story of how the statue came to be, and what its image has come to mean to millions of people around the world.

Return to the ferry dock and board the next boat to the:

*ELLIS ISLAND NATIONAL MONUMENT ❺, Ellis Island, New York, NY 10004, ☎ 212-363-3200, Internet: www.nps.gov/elis. *Open daily 9–5, closed Christmas Day. Free. Audio Tour: Adults $3.50, seniors and students $3, children (under 17) $2.50. Cafeteria.* ㅊ.

The immigrant experience and the peopling of America is the theme of the Ellis Island Immigration Museum, housed in the original buildings of the nation's most famous port of entry. Some 12 million people — the ancestors to nearly half of all living Americans — passed through this facility between 1892 and 1954 on their way to the American Dream. Their emotionally-charged story is told through artifacts, displays, a 30-minute video, and in the very walls of the Great Hall itself.

Return by ferry to Liberty State Park, possibly visiting its fabulous:

LIBERTY SCIENCE CENTER ❻, 251 Phillip St., Liberty State Park, Jersey City, NJ 07305-4699, ☎ 201-200-1000, Internet: www.lsc.org. *Open April–Labor Day, daily 9:30–5:30; rest of year, Tues.–Sun. 9:30–5:30. Closed Thanksgiving and Christmas Day. Admission to exhibits only: Adults $9.50, seniors (62+) and children (2–18) $7.50; to IMAX show: Adults $8.50, seniors and children $6.50; to 3-D laser show: adults, seniors and children $3.50. Various discounted combination tickets available. Cafeteria. Science shop.* ㅊ.

From touch tunnels to tarantulas, science equals fun at this thoroughly modern, interactive, state-of-the-art museum. Opened in 1993, it is the metropolitan New York area's only major "hands-on" science education center, presenting the joy and excitement of individual discovery in an unintimidating way. Adding to the fun is one of the nation's largest IMAX theaters, surrounding its audience with a domed screen over eight stories high, a 3-D laser show, and virtual reality experiences.

Northern Monmouth County

Just south of New York City, overlooking its bay, lies an area rich in natural beauty, historic sites, panoramic vistas, and much more. The northern part of New Jersey's Monmouth County offers one of the strangest lighthouses you'll ever see as well as another one that is the nation's oldest to remain in use. The Sandy Hook Unit of the Gateway National Recreation Area has beaches, a nature center, historic locations, and a former military post for you to explore. Inland, there's an authentic 1890's farm where the old ways are carried on by volunteers in period dress, and several historic houses dating from the 1700's.

By staying overnight, you can combine this trip with the previous one as well as with the next two, making a mini-vacation within a close range of New York.

GETTING THERE:

By Car, head south on the **New Jersey Turnpike** (I-95) to its intersection with the **Garden State Parkway** at Woodbridge. From there, take the parkway south to Exit 117 and pick up **NJ-36** southeast through Keansburg, passing signs for **Keansburg Amusement Park & Runaway Rapids** (☎ 1-800-805-4FUN, Internet: www.keansburgamusementpark.com), a place for family fun. A few miles later, exit at the sign to Atlantic Highlands Business District. Continue toward the municipal harbor. Just before the water, turn right on Ocean Boulevard and go about a mile and a half to the top of **Mount Mitchill** and park.

Continue on Ocean Boulevard and rejoin NJ-36 southeast to Highlands. Just before Highlands Bridge, turn right on Portland Road and take an immediate right onto Highland Avenue. Proceed uphill to **Twin Lights** entrance, on the left. The access road is steep and narrow, so be careful.

Go back to NJ-36, turn right, cross Highlands Bridge, and follow signs into **Sandy Hook Unit, Gateway National Recreation Area**.

Either retrace the route back to New York or follow the directions in the text if you would also like to visit **Longstreet Farm**.

The farthest point of this trip is about 50 miles from midtown Manhattan.

PRACTICALITIES:

Sandy Hook, the major attraction, is open every day except New Year's, Thanksgiving, and Christmas. While the Twin Lights site is open on the same schedule, its museum is closed on Mondays and Tuesdays in the off-season.

For further information contact the **Monmouth County Department of Economic Development & Tourism**, 31 East Main St., Freehold, NJ 07728, ☎ 732-431-7470 or 1-800-523-2587, Internet: www.visitmonmouth.com.

FOOD AND DRINK:

This is a great trip for a picnic as most of the sites have facilities, usually with a great view of the bay. Along the route you'll find the usual fast-food outlets, but for dinner you might want to try the:

Hofbrauhaus (301 Ocean Blvd. in Atlantic Highlands) German and American specialties in a Bavarian setting, high above the ocean. ☎ 732-291-0224. Open evenings only. $$

LOCAL ATTRACTIONS:

Circled numbers in text correspond to numbers on the map.

At 263 feet above sea level, Atlantic Highland's **Mount Mitchill** ❶ is the highest point along the Atlantic Coast from Maine to Florida, and offers views of distant New York, Sandy Hook, and the Atlantic Highlands Municipal Harbor. Mount Mitchill County Park is a nice place to stop and picnic while enjoying the sights.

Continue on to the:

TWIN LIGHTS STATE HISTORIC SITE ❷, Lighthouse Rd., Highlands, NJ 07732, ☎ 732-872-1814, Internet: www.visitmonmouth.com. *Grounds open daily all year 9–dusk; museum open daily Memorial Day to Labor Day, 10–5; and on Wed.–Sun. the rest of the year, 10–5. Closed New Year's Day, Thanksgiving, Christmas. Donation. Self-guided tour, picnic facilities. Leashed pets only. Partially* &.

Twin Lights, on the Navesink Highlands, has been the site of a lighthouse since 1828. The present structure was built in 1862 and became America's first electrically powered seacoast lighthouse in 1898. The next year Guglielmo Marconi conducted the first practical demonstration of wireless telegraphy by transmitting the America's Cup race results from Twin Lights to the *New York Herald* newspaper, some 15 miles away. The museum chronicles these and other significant chapters in the history of American seafaring; in addition to a replica of Marconi's wireless, there are specimens of Jersey-built boats, a lighthouse lens exhibit, and the one remaining station of the old U.S. Life Saving Service, which merged with the Revenue Cutter Service in 1915 to become the U.S. Coast Guard. From the twin towers of the lighthouse you can enjoy a ***panoramic view** of the Atlantic and New York Harbor

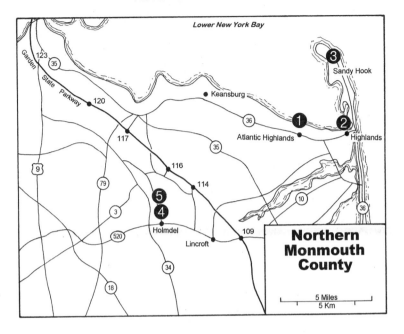

SANDY HOOK UNIT ❸, Gateway National Recreation Area, P.O. Box 530, Highlands, NJ 07732, ☎ 732-872-5970, Internet: www.nps.gov/gate. *Park open daily all year sunrise to sunset; Visitor Center open daily 10–5 except Thanksgiving, Christmas, and New Year's. Beach parking fee: Memorial Day weekend to Labor Day $8 per car on weekdays, $10 on weekends and holidays, free other times of year. Ranger-led and self-guided tours; swimming at guarded beaches, lifeguards on duty from Memorial Day weekend through Labor Day; picnicking; surf fishing at designated areas, night fishing by permit; hiking and nature trails; refreshments (April–October), restrooms. Leashed pets in some areas. Partially ⅋.*

The **Gateway National Recreation Area** was created by Congress in 1972 as one of the nation's first major urban park areas. It opened in 1974 under the management of the National Park Service, which has spearheaded a vigorous effort to preserve the area and reverse the environmental degradation that has taken place over the centuries since the Algonquin Indians roamed these shores. It consist of four units: the Jamaica Bay, Breezy Point, and Staten Island units in New York, and Sandy Hook in New Jersey. Together they serve as a refuge in the heart of the megalopolis for many species of flora and fauna, including *Homo Sapiens*.

The **Sandy Hook Unit** extends over an arm of land that has had strategic importance in the defense of New York Harbor since Colonial times. At the **Spermaceti Cove Visitor Center** there are exhibits about the U.S. Life Saving Service with a 9-minute video, natural history displays, and a bookstore. From the **Sandy Hook Museum** in Fort Hancock's guardhouse you can take guided tours on weekends from 1–5. You can also visit the Sandy Hook Proving Ground, where U.S. Army weapons were tested from 1874 until 1919. Sandy Hook boasts the oldest operating *lighthouse (1764) in the U.S., and the peninsula's fragile sand dunes shelter a great variety of plant and animal life. The famed holly forest is a perennial attraction; over 300 species of birds have been sighted in the area, including the endangered osprey.

Sandy Hook is still under development, and the National Park Service is continually experimenting with new programs. It is wise to check hours and scheduling in advance if you are interested in a particular attraction or activity. Millions of people visit the park each year; you may want to plan your trip for spring, fall, or winter, when it is less crowded.

Time and strength permitting, you might want to continue on to a few other nearby attractions. To do this, continue south from Sandy Hook to Sea Bright, then turn right on Route 520 past Red Bank, the Parkway, Lincroft, and Holmdel. Turn right, north, on NJ-34 and go about a half-mile to the first right, Roberts Road. Take this about 1.5 miles, bearing left on Longstreet Road, and the entrance to:

HOLMDEL PARK & LONGSTREET FARM ❹, Longstreet Rd., Holmdel, NJ 07733 ☎ (park) 732-946-2669, (farm) ☎ 732-946-3758, Internet: www.mon mouthcountyparks.com. *Park open daily, 8 a.m. to dusk, free. Farm open Memorial Day to Labor Day, daily 9–5; rest of year 10–4. Farmhouse open March–Dec., weekends only, noon–3:30. Free. Partially ♿.*

Holmdel Park, with its arboretum, hiking and fitness trails, picnic and play areas, ponds and streams, is an ideal place to end your day in northern Monmouth County. Its star attraction, the *Longstreet Farm, is worth the journey in itself. This authentic working farm has been restored to its 1890's condition and is manned by park employees and volunteers in period costume. You can enjoy a rare slice of out agricultural heritage as you visit the farmhouse of 1775, the many out-buildings, the crop fields, and of course the animals. Phone ahead or check the web site for information about the special activities that are held throughout the year.

Another nearby feature, on Longstreet Road just north of the park entrance, is the **Holmes-Hendrickson House** ❺ of 1754. This Dutch-style house contains fine examples of mid-18th-century furnishings along with displays of home crafts and early farm life. ☎ 732-462-1466, Internet: www.monmouth.com/~mcha. Open May–Sept.; Tues., Thurs., Sun. 1–4, Sat. 10–4. Adults $2, seniors $1.50, children (6–18) $1.

Return to Roberts Road and turn left, then right onto Crawfords Corner Road. At Red Hill Road turn left to Exit 114 of the Garden State Parkway for your trip back to New York.

Southeastern Monmouth County

A restored 19th-century industrial village, a preserved narrow-gauge steam railroad, a Victorian retreat on the sea, an historic old town, and a Revolutionary War battlefield are your options on this excursion into the past. With perfect timing you could probably "do" all five in a day, but a more relaxed approach would be to settle for two or three, according to your interests.

For those staying overnight, this trip combines beautifully with the following one to the Jersey Shore.

GETTING THERE:

By Car: Take the **Garden State Parkway** south to Exit 98 and pick up **I-195** west toward Trenton, *or* take the **New Jersey Turnpike** south to Exit 7A and pick up I-195 east. From I-195 take Exit 31 (Squankum). Go north on **Rte. 574** a short distance, then east on **Rte. 524** (under the Interstate) and into the park.

Return to the Garden State Parkway and go north to Exit 100. Pick up **NJ-33** east and take it about 4 miles to Ocean Grove.

For Freehold and Monmouth Battlefield, go west on NJ-33 into Freehold, then take **Rte. 522** west into the park. The shortest route back to New York is to take US-9 north to the Garden State Parkway, then the New Jersey Turnpike.

Allaire is about 65 miles from midtown Manhattan.

PRACTICALITIES:

This is really a summer trip, to be taken between early May and late September. Go on a weekend if you can, because that's when the Historic Allaire Village opens its buildings to visitors, and when the Pine Creek Railroad runs its steam trains. Please check before you go, however, as schedules are flexible and some attractions are open at other times. Although the trip goes right to the sea, you probably won't have time for a dip.

For further information contact the **Monmouth County Department of Economic Development & Tourism**, 31 East Main St., Freehold, NJ 07728, ☎ 732-431-7470 or 1-800-523-2587, Internet: www.visitmonmouth.com. For information about Ocean Grove, contact the **Ocean Grove Tourism Bureau**, Box 277, Ocean Grove, NJ 07756, ☎ 732-774-4736 (mid-May through mid-October).

FOOD AND DRINK:

Allaire State Park and the Monmouth Battlefield have both picnic facilities and snack bars offering light meals (in season). For restaurants, you'll have to go to Ocean Grove or other nearby communities. Some good choices are:

Old Mill Inn (Old Mill Rd., Spring Lake Heights, at Ocean Rd. between NJ-35 and NJ-71) Steaks and regional American cuisine with a view, overlooking the old mill pond. Sunday brunch. ☎ 732-449-1800. $$

La Nonna Piancones (804 Main St. in Bradley Beach) A casual place for contemporary Italian cuisine. ☎ 732-775-0906. X: Sun. lunch. $$

Raspberry Café (58 Main St. in Ocean Grove) Soups, sandwiches and light meals in an attractive, simple café. ☎ 732-988-0833. $

Sampler Inn (28 Main St. in Ocean Grove) A cafeteria with wholesome home cooking; an Ocean Grove landmark since 1917. ☎ 732-775-1905. X: Nov.–Apr. $

LOCAL ATTRACTIONS:

Circled numbers in text correspond to numbers on the map.

ALLAIRE STATE PARK ❶, P.O. Box 220, Rt. 524, Farmingdale, NJ 07727, ☎ 732-938-2371, Internet: www.allairevillage.org. *Open daily all year, 8 to dusk. Visitor Center open Memorial Day–Labor Day, daily 10–4; rest of year weekends 10–4. Buildings open Memorial Day to Labor Day, Wed.–Sun. 10–4; Labor Day to mid-Nov., weekends 10–4. Building tours $1.50. Parking fee (Memorial Day–Labor Day only), weekends and holidays $3 per car. Picnic facilities, canoeing, nature center, fishing, riding and hiking trails, camping, winter sports, snack bar. Leashed pets only in park, no pets in campsites. Some facilities are ﾎ.*

In 1941 the family of newspaperman Arthur Brisbane deeded 800 acres of land to the people of New Jersey for use as a "historical center and forest park reservation." Since then the park has grown to cover some 3,000 acres of the New Jersey coastal plain. Its attractions include the fascinating **Historic Allaire Village**, whose buildings are open on weekends from May through October and are often the scene of special events. In the late 1700s Allaire was the site of a furnace and forge where iron was smelted from the "bog ore" produced by decaying vegetation. In 1822 James P. Allaire purchased the ironworks to supply his foundry in New York City and built a bustling industrial community of over 400 people. With the discovery of higher-grade Pennsylvania ore and the increasing use of coal, Allaire declined, and the ironworks shut down in 1848. Today, the village has been beautifully restored; and you can visit a furnace, a carpenter's shop, a blacksmith's, a bakery, a general store, and other original buildings where staff dressed in the work clothes of the 1830s demonstrate the old trades. This is a fascinating experience for young and old alike.

The ***Pine Creek Railroad ❷** is a must for just about every visitor. All

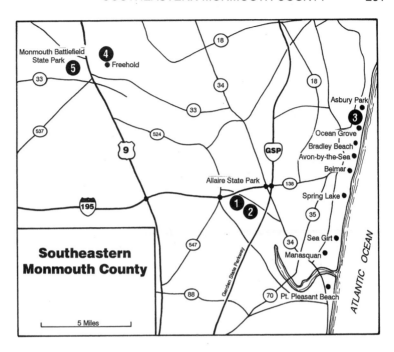

aboard! for a trip back in time on New Jersey's only live steam narrow-gauge railroad. You'll ride in antique cars pulled by a coal-burning loco-motive (veteran diesel engine sometimes employed) of the kind that was used to push back the frontiers of the American West. Adjacent to the sta-tion is an open work area where many old locomotives and cars are being painstakingly restored by volunteers. *Allaire State Park,* ☎ *732-938-5524. Operates daily in July and Aug., noon–4:30; weekends noon–4:30 in May–June and Sept.–Oct. Fare $2.50 per person.*

OCEAN GROVE ❸. *Tourist season Memorial Day to weekend after Labor Day. Beach fees $4.50. Beach picnics, swimming, fishing, boardwalk activi-ties. No pets on beaches.* **Ocean Grove Tourism Bureau**, *Box 277, Ocean Grove, NJ 07756,* ☎ *732-774-4736 (mid-May through mid-Oct.), or* **Chamber of Commerce**, ☎ *1-800-388-4768. An Internet site to check is: www.ocean grovenj.com, also www.oceangrove.com. Boardwalk is ⅃.*

This attractive small town, noted for its Victorian architecture, serves as a setting for religious and cultural programs, Bible meetings, evangeli-cal talks, and recitals. A National and State Historic Site, it was founded in 1869 for Methodist camp meetings. The **Ocean Grove Auditorium**, built in 1894, seats 6,500 persons and is the focal point of the town. Preachers and evangelists use its big stage on Sundays, while famous entertainers and musicians perform on other days. The **Centennial Cottage**, an authentic Ocean Grove seashore vacation home, has been completely restored to its 1870s appearance and is operated as a period museum. *Corner of Central Ave. and McClintock Street,* ☎ *732-774-1869. Open July–Aug., Mon.–Sat., 11–3.*

Freehold ❹, the seat of Monmouth County, was founded in 1715 and is close to the spot where George Washington and his army defeated the British under General Clinton at the Battle of Monmouth on June 28, 1778. Among the places of historic interest are:

MONMOUTH COUNTY HISTORICAL ASSOCIATION MUSEUM & LIBRARY, 70 Court St., Freehold, NJ 07728, ☎ 732-462-1466, Internet: www.mon mouth.com/~mcha. *Museum open all year Tues.–Sat. 10–4, Sun. 1–4; library open all year Wed.–Sat. 10–4. Adults $2, seniors $1.50, children $1.*

Founded in 1898, the Historical Association is dedicated to preserving Monmouth County's heritage. Its headquarters, a beautiful three-story Georgian structure built in 1931, is the setting for one of the country's best regional museums. Fine examples of period furnishings and Americana are well displayed. The floor devoted to "attic artifacts" is especially popular with kids. The library is primarily for research and includes a genealogical and historical reference section. In addition to the museum, the association maintains four historic buildings in Monmouth County, one of which is right here in Freehold.

COVENHOVEN HOUSE, 150 West Main St., Freehold, NJ 07728, ☎ 732-462-1466. *Open May through Oct., Tues., Thurs., Sun. 1–4, Sat. 10–4. Adults $2, seniors $1.50, children $1.*

Maintained by the Monmouth County Historical Association, this Georgian house was built in the mid-18th century by William A. Covenhoven, a successful local farmer, and is furnished according to a 1790 inventory of his estate. In 1778, just before the Battle of Monmouth, the house served as headquarters for British General Sir Henry Clinton.

MONMOUTH BATTLEFIELD STATE PARK ❺, 347 Freehold-Englishtown Road, Freehold, NJ 07726, ☎ 732-462-9616. *Park open daily 8–dusk, Visitor Center daily 9–4. Picnicking facilities, playground, refreshments, hiking and riding trails, nature center. Admission free. Partially ♿.*

The largest single battle of the Revolutionary War was fought here on June 28, 1778, with an indecisive outcome. In the midst of the carnage there appeared a heroine, one Mary Ludwig Hays, who carried pitchers of water to the stricken soldiers and became forever known as "Molly Pitcher." Her story, and that of the battle, is re-created with an audiovisual show and an electric relief map in the **Visitor Center** near the entrance. While there, you can pick up a map and explore the 1,500-acre battlefield itself, perhaps stopping at the **Craig House** of 1710, and at a reproduction of what is thought to be Molly's Well.

The Jersey Shore: Barnegat Peninsula

S ome of the best seaside attractions within easy driving range of New York City are on the Jersey Shore, just 70 or so miles south of the city. Making a daytrip here allows you to sample the various beaches and decide which appeal to you most for a real vacation later on. The three destinations covered on this excursion each have their own personality, from bustling amusement parks to isolated sand dunes. Toms River, on the return route, has some interesting museums and a nearby nature center that are worth a visit.

For those able to stay overnight, this trip combines well with the previous one to Southeastern Monmouth County.

GETTING THERE:

By Car, Point Pleasant Beach is about 70 miles south of midtown Manhattan. Take the **New Jersey Turnpike** (I-95) south to the **Garden State Parkway** at Woodbridge. From there continue south on the parkway to Exit 98, and pick up **NJ-34** southeast to the junction with **NJ-35**. Continue southeast on 35 into Point Pleasant Beach. From here go south on 35 about 10 miles to Seaside Heights and Seaside Park. Island Beach State Park lies just south of this.

Take **NJ-37** west from Seaside Heights for about seven miles to Toms River. Just beyond this you can get on the Garden State Parkway for the drive home.

PRACTICALITIES:

Although you *could* make this trip at any time, chances are you'll enjoy it more between Memorial Day and Labor Day — when the beaches are open and the many amusements in full swing. Island Beach State Park and the mainland attractions are open all year round.

Come prepared for the beach, and don't forget the sunscreen lotion and sunglasses. All of the towns charge a nominal fee to use their beaches. Parking near the beachfront is metered (quarters only), and there are parking lots. Free parking is usually some distance from the water.

For further information on **Point Pleasant Beach** contact the **Greater Point Pleasant Chamber of Commerce**, 517A Arnold Ave., Point Pleasant Beach, NJ 08742, ☎ 732-899-2424. For **Bay Head** ☎ 800-4-BAYHED. For **Seaside Heights** ☎ 732-793-1510 or 1-800-SEASHOR, Internet: www.seaside-heights.nj.us. For the **entire area** contact the **Toms River/Ocean County**

Chamber of Commerce, 1200 Hooper Ave., Toms River, NJ 08753, ☎ 732-349-0220.

FOOD AND DRINK:

Besides the numerous inexpensive eateries along the boardwalk, and perhaps a beach picnic at Island Beach State Park, these are some of the better places for a good meal:

Grenville by the Sea (345 Main Ave., NJ-35, in Bay Head) Creative cuisine in an historic 1890's hotel. Affiliated with a New Jersey winery, so don't order beer. ☎ 732-892-3100. X: Mon. $$ and $$$

Jack Baker's Wharfside (101 Channel Dr. in Pt. Pleasant Beach, half-mile east of NJ-35) Enjoy seafood overlooking Manasquan Inlet. ☎ 732-892-9100. $$

Barmores Shrimp Box (75 Inlet Dr., Pt. Pleasant Beach, half-mile east of NJ-35 via Broadway) A relaxed, casual place for freshly-caught fish, dinner only. ☎ 732-899-1637. $$

Old Time Tavern (Dove Mall, north of jct. of NJ-37 and NJ-166, in Toms River) Steak, seafood, pasta, pizza, and the like in a casual family restaurant. ☎ 732-505-5307. $ and $$

King's Wok (1226 NJ-166, just south of NJ-37 in Toms River) Szechuan, Hunan, and Cantonese specialties. ☎ 732-286-1505. $

LOCAL ATTRACTIONS:

Circled numbers in text correspond to numbers on the map.

POINT PLEASANT BEACH ❶, Greater Point Pleasant Area Chamber of Commerce, 517A Arnold Ave., Point Pleasant Beach, NJ 08742, ☎ 732-899-2424. A web site to check is www.pointpleasantbeachnj.com. *Beach season Memorial Day to Labor Day. One-day beach fees: weekdays, adults $5, children $1.50; weekends, adults $6, children $1.50. Swimming, deep-sea fishing, boat rentals, waterskiing, rides, amusements, boardwalk activities, special events. No pets on beaches. Boardwalk is* &.

This Atlantic Ocean bungalow colony has two miles of white sandy beaches and a bustling boardwalk lined with arcades, rides, stores, and restaurants. The town is home port to a fleet of commercial fishing vessels, but folks out for pleasure rather than business will find plenty of action in these waters, either on their own or in numerous fishing tournaments throughout the season. The Off-Shore Grand Prix, one of the major powerboat races in the United States, attracts large crowds every July, and in September the Seafood Festival offers delicacies from the deep as well as an art show.

Don't miss **Jenkinson's Aquarium**, a state-of-the-art facility with all sorts of exotic life forms that swim, crawl, walk, or fly. There's a petting tank, a live coral reef, a fossil room, and more. *Boardwalk and Parkway,* ☎ 732-892-0600, Internet: www.jenkinsons.com. *Open June–Aug. Daily 10–10, rest of year daily 10–5. Closed Christmas and New Year's. Adults $6.50, seniors and*

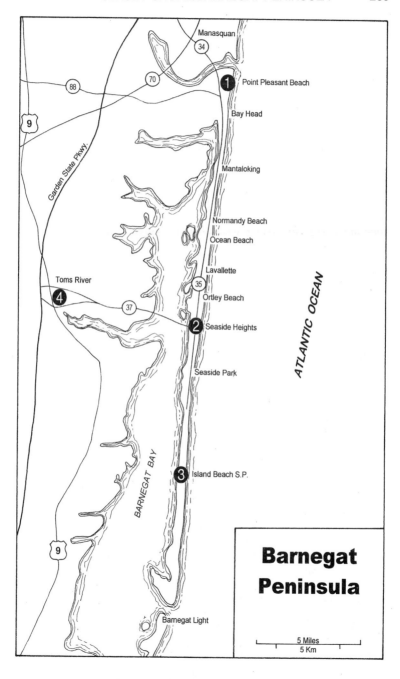

Barnegat Peninsula

ages 3–12 $4.50.

Head south through the popular summer resort communities of Bay Head, Mantoloking, Normandy Beach, Lavallette, and Ortley Beach to:

SEASIDE HEIGHTS ❷, Seaside Business Association, P.O. Box 98, Seaside Heights, NJ 08751, ☎ 732-793-1510 or 1-800-SEASHOR, Internet: www.sea side-heightsnj.org. *Tourist season late May to mid-Sept. Beach fees. Some free parking on west side of town. Swimming, fishing, crabbing, surfboat rental, water skiing, jet skiing. Free entry to amusement park, fees per activity. No pets on beach. One-day beach use fees: Fri.–Sun. $5; Mon.–Tues., $3; Wed.–Thurs. free. Beach access ⟨⟩ available free, ☎ 732-793-4646 in advance.*

Fun and games for the whole family abound on this beautiful three-mile beachfront and mile-long boardwalk, crammed with some of the best rides, games of chance, snack bars, restaurants, and shops to be found along the Jersey Shore. The **Ferris Wheel** offers great views of it all. One of the nation's finest hand-carved wooden merry-go-rounds, the *****Historic Dentzel/Looff Carousel**, has been charming people for over 80 years. Water Works, a water park with slides, rides, and a pool offers plenty of fun. *Open daily, Memorial Day to Labor Day,* ☎ 732-793-6488.

There are fireworks on July 4 and every Wednesday night, and numerous special events throughout the season. Call in advance to get this year's schedule.

Continue south through the more sedate **Seaside Park**, which has its own boardwalk and amusement pier, to:

ISLAND BEACH STATE PARK ❸, P.O. Box 37, Seaside Park, NJ 08752, ☎ 732-793-0506. *Open daily all year, daylight hours; summer hours 8–8. Parking fee. Guided nature tours, swimming, surf fishing (by permit), picnicking (no facilities provided), surfing, beach strolling, scuba diving: all permitted in designated areas only. Life guards, bathhouses, storage lockers, snack bars from mid-June through Labor Day. No pets in swimming areas, leashed pets only elsewhere. Some facilities are ⟨⟩.*

One of the few remaining natural barrier beaches and by far the best along the Jersey Shore, this narrow 10-mile strip of land is a lovely spot to picnic and enjoy the sights and sounds of the ocean. Two nature areas offer acres of dunes dotted with holly clumps and briar thickets, and there's a recreation area for more active pursuits along with a self-guided nature trail. The southern tip of the park is just a stone's throw from the landmark Barnegat Light on Long Beach Island. Please remember that the dunes and beach grass are crucial to the island's fragile environment; walk and drive only in designated areas.

Toms River ❹, back on the mainland, makes a convenient stop before heading back to New York. This thriving community, rich in memories of the Revolutionary War, is home to the **Ocean County Museum**. Housed in a 19th-century Victorian structure, it features displays of early industries, county history, and memorabilia of the dirigibles that once operated from nearby Lakehurst Naval Air Station until the famous Hindenburg disaster occurred there in 1937. *26 Hadley Ave., Toms River, NJ 08754,* ☎ *732-341-1880. Open Tues. and Thurs., 1–3, and Sat. 10–3. Donation $2.*

Also nearby is the **Cattus Island Park** with its scenic bay views, abundant bird life, nature center, and some 14 miles of hiking trails. *1170 Cattus Island Blvd. (via Fischer Blvd. off NJ-37, follow signs), Toms River, NJ 08753,* ☎ *732-270-6960. Park open daily dawn to dusk, environmental center daily 10–4. Free. Partially ⅃.*

Seaside Park

Trip 39

Flemington

B argains, fun, and a strong sense of America's past go together in Flemington, New Jersey's factory outlet town *par excellence*. First settled in 1756 by Samuel Fleming on land originally owned by William Penn, this friendly small town has a remarkably well-preserved core with historic buildings dating as far back as the mid-18th century. In fact, some 60% of its structures are on the National Register of Historic Places. In the late 1800s Flemington became a center for the production of fine pottery and glassware, as it still is, and a hub of railroad activity with some 54 trains a day by 1889. Today, its lovely old center is surrounded by a formidable array of factory outlets, shops, and restaurants. The railroad still runs on steam; only now it carries tourists and shoppers out for a few hours of nostalgic fun. A recent addition to Flemington's attractions is the utterly fantastic Northlandz — surely worth the trip in itself, especially if you have kids in tow or are still one at heart.

GETTING THERE:

By Car, take the **New Jersey Turnpike** south to Exit 14, Newark Airport, then **I-78** west to Exit 30. Head south on **I-287** to Exit 17, then take **US-202** south to Northlandz ❶, on your right two miles north of Flemington.

Continue south to **Flemington**. In town, at the traffic light just before the Flemington Mall, turn right to Main St., just ahead. Turn right on Main, crossing railroad tracks, and park on a side street or in a lot.

Come back down Main St. to Church St. and turn right to **Liberty Village**. The Black River and Western Railroad station is by the main Liberty Village parking lot.

To reach the fairgrounds, go back through town on Church St. to **NJ-31** and drive north about 1.5 miles.

Flemington is about 65 miles southwest of New York's Times Square.

PRACTICALITIES:

Most of the shops, and Northlandz, are open daily all year round. The railroad operates on weekends and holidays from Easter through December, and also on Thursdays and Fridays in July and August. For further information contact the **Flemington Information Center**, Ramada Inn on US-202, P.O. Box 903, Flemington, NJ 08822, ☎ 908-806-8165. Some Internet sites are: www.flemington-nj.com and www.flemington.net.

FOOD AND DRINK:

There are plenty of places to eat in Flemington, including the usual fast-food suspects near the 202/31 traffic circle. Among the better choices are:

Rattlesnake Southwestern Grill (208 Rte. 202/31, 1.5 miles south of the traffic circle) Southwestern American cuisine for lunch or dinner. ☎ 908-788-7772. $$

Upper Crust Tea Room (146 Main St.) Light meals, luncheons, and teas in a Victorian setting. ☎ 908-788-9750. X: Sun. $ and $$

Linda's Eatery (Liberty Village) A cafeteria with comfort food, especially turkey dishes. Indoor/outdoor seating. ☎ 908- 284-9100. $

LOCAL ATTRACTIONS:

Circled numbers in text correspond to numbers on the map.
Why not begin this trip with its most unusual sight? Stop first at:

*NORTHLANDZ ❶, 495 Rte. 202 South, Flemington, NJ 08822, ☎ 908-782-4022, fax 908-782-5131, Internet: www.northlandz.com. *Open Mon.–Fri. 10–4; Sat.–Sun. 10–6. Closed Christmas. Indoor tour: Adults $13.75, seniors 62+ $12.50, children 2–12 $9.75. Snack bar. Gift shop. Outdoor miniature steam train rides.* ໄ.

More than just the largest model train layout on Earth, this is really a fantasy world of almost surrealist proportions. Surely the result of a very, very fertile imagination — or a mad model railroader — Northlandz is superficially realistic but actually quite weird. It simply has to be seen to be believed. Mountains tower three stories high as trains — as many as 125 of them — speed across improbable bridges up to 40 feet long, then plunge into tunnels, emerging in wildly narrow canyons. The entire walk through its many scenes and levels is a full mile in length, opening occasionally into exhibitions of rare dolls, art, and even an impressive theater with a 2,000-pipe organ that is played several times a day. Outside, there is an operating one-third scale steam railway that takes visitors on journeys through the woodland site. You'll have fun at Northlandz, and so will the kids!

Continue down US-202 into town. Historic Flemington is centered on Main Street around the imposing **Union Hotel** ❷ of 1877, a four-story brick structure with a mansard roof and gingerbread porches. Many famous media people stayed there during the notorious 1935 "Trial of the Century" that took place across the street in the former **Hunterdon County Courthouse** ❸, a Greek Revival building of 1828. It was here that Bruno Hauptmann was convicted and sentenced to death for the kidnaping and murder of Charles Lindbergh Jr., the infant son of the pioneer aviator.
Nearby, at 114 Main Street, is the **Doric House** ❹, a Greek Revival structure dating from 1846. Built as a home, it has been restored. Turn right on Mine Street and right again on Park Avenue. A left on Bonnell Street takes you past **Fleming's Castle** ❺ at number 5, a simple Colonial home that must have seemed like a palace in those primitive days. Built in 1756 by the

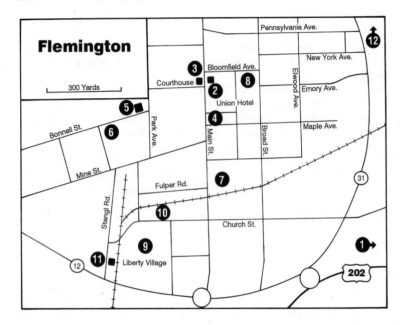

town's founder as an inn, it is the oldest house in Flemington and has been preserved by the Daughters of the American Revolution. Across the street, between numbers 56 and 60, is the small **Case Cemetery** ❻, where the area's first settlers are buried along with their friend, Indian Chief Tuccamirgan.

Factory outlets in town tend to be located up and down Main Street and along the nearby side streets. Large color-coded directories with maps will guide you to the stores. Some of the most famous of these are in the **Flemington Cut Glass Complex** ❼ beginning at Main and Church streets. The first and largest factory outlet in the U.S. for crystal and glass, this series of stores also offers a wide assortment of cookware, gifts, home decorations, and fixtures. Another pioneer in this kind of retailing is the **Flemington Fur Company** ❽ on Spring Street, a block east of the Union Hotel, which has been serving customers from all over the country since 1921.

Liberty Village ❾ and **Turntable Junction** ❿ are two adjacent shopping "villages" of reproduction Colonial-style buildings attractively arranged around open commons. Located two blocks west of Main Street on either side of Church Street, they contain some 70 factory outlet shops featuring all kinds of famous-brand merchandise at discount prices, cafés, and restaurants. Like the shops in town, those in Liberty Village and Turntable Junction are open every day except Easter, Thanksgiving, Christmas, and New Year's; usually from 10–6 or 9; and are largely ♿. *Liberty Village* ☎ *908-*

782-8550, Internet: www.chelseagca.com.
    Nearby is the:

BLACK RIVER & WESTERN RAILROAD ⓫, P.O. Box 200, Ringoes, NJ 08551, ☎ 908-782-6622, Internet: www.brwrr.com. *Vintage steam or diesel trains operate Sat., Sun., and holidays from Easter through Dec., running one-hour round trips between Flemington and Ringoes. During July and August they also run on Thurs. and Fri. There are also trips between Ringoes and Lambertville. Call for current schedules. Adults $8, children 3–11 $4, under 3 free.*

Visit the Ringoes Station, built in 1854 by the Flemington Transportation Company and restored by the Black River & Western. Ringoes Station has a souvenir car, snack bar, and picnic grove.

The **Flemington Fair and Speedway** ⓬, on NJ-31 just north of the town, offers the chance to experience a typical small country fair with all of its agricultural roots intact. Begun in 1856, the **Fair** runs from the Tuesday before Labor Day through Labor Day. Its **Speedway**, one of the best motor racing tracks in the northeast, has auto racing events on Saturdays from May through October. *For information on either,* ☎ *908-782-2413.* ♿.

Inside Northlandz

Trip 40

*Princeton

F ounded in 1696 by Quakers who called it "Prince's Town," Princeton is
one of the most pleasant towns anywhere for casual strolling. Its
streets are lined with well-preserved 18th- and 19th-century houses
recalling a major battle of the Revolutionary War, the brief times when this
was the nation's capital, and the many famous people who lived here over
the years. Its major attraction is, of course, the University, which can easily take hours to explore.

GETTING THERE:

By Car, take the **New Jersey Turnpike** south to Exit 9, then turn right
towards New Brunswick on **NJ-18** and shortly pick up **US-1** south. Follow
this to the Princeton exit, turning right on **Route 571** (Washington Rd.) into
town. Park as close to Nassau St. (NJ-27) as possible; there are several lots
just north of this. Princeton is about 55 miles southwest of Times Square.

By Train: New Jersey Transit trains leave Pennsylvania Station in New
York City at least hourly for the 70-minute ride to Princeton, making stops
at Newark and other towns en route. Take any train marked for Trenton
and change at **Princeton Junction** to a shuttle train that goes directly to the
station on campus, within walking distance of the sights. Bargain round-
trip tickets are available. ☎ 973-762-5100, Internet: www.njtransit.
state.nj.us for details.

Amtrak offers limited service to Princeton Junction on their Northeast
Corridor line, with NJT connections to campus, as above. ☎ 1-800-USA-
RAIL, Internet: www.amtrak.com for details.

PRACTICALITIES:

Avoid making this trip on a Monday or major holiday, when the most
interesting sights are closed. Operating hours are reduced on Sundays.
Some of the minor out-of-town attractions have more limited hours;
check the individual listings if you're interested in seeing them.

For further information contact the **Chamber of Commerce of the
Princeton Area**, 216 Rockingham Rd., Princeton, NJ 08540, ☎ 609-520-1776,
fax 609-520-9107, Internet: www.princetonchamber.org.

FOOD AND DRINK:

Princeton has a wide selection of eateries in every price range; with
an emphasis on eclectic cuisines and student budgets. A few choices are:

Le Plumet Royal (20 Bayard Ln., NJ-206 near Nassau St.) Contemporary
French cuisine in a Colonial-era inn. Sunday brunch. Dress nicely and

reserve, ☎ 609-924-1707. $$$

Lahiere's (11 Witherspoon St. at Nassau St.) A local favorite since 1919, serving French, Continental, and American cuisine. Dress well and reserve, ☎ 609-921-2798. X: Sun. $$ and $$$

Triumph Brewing Company (138 Nassau St.) A micro-brewery serving six varieties of suds along with some wildly creative dishes. ☎ 609-924-7855. $$

Teresa's Pizzetta Caffe (19 Palmer Square East) Modern Italian cuisine, including creative pizzas, in an attractive, casual trattoria. ☎ 609-921-1974. $ and $$

Hoagie Heaven (242 Nassau St.) All sorts of sandwiches. ☎ 609-921-7723. $

LOCAL ATTRACTIONS:

Circled numbers in text correspond to numbers on the map.

PRINCETON UNIVERSITY ❶-❼, Princeton, NJ 08544, ☎ 609-258-1776, Internet: www.princeton.edu. *Orange Key Guide Service conducts free campus tours lasting about an hour. They depart from the Frist Campus Center ❶, see map; Mon.–Sat. at 10, 11, 1:30, and 3:30; Sun. at 1:30 and 3:30. Groups should make advance reservations. No tours on Sat. afternoons during home football games, or from mid-Dec. to early Jan. Summer hours may vary, check first. Most of the campus is ♿.*

Tours, led by undergraduates, include visits to Nassau Hall, the University Chapel, and Prospect Gardens. You can also take self-guided tours, first stopping at the **Tour Office ❶** for a map and guide pamphlets. Among the attractions are:

Nassau Hall ❷. Built in 1756 and twice rebuilt after fires, this was the original home of what was then called the College of New Jersey. The college was founded in 1746 under a royal charter from King George II and first located in Elizabeth, then in Newark. In 1756 it moved to Princeton when the town offered £1,000 and a tract of land, but it did not officially adopt its present name until 1896. In addition to housing the entire college at that time, Nassau Hall also served as a barracks for both Continental and British troops during the Revolution, as a meeting place for the first legislature of the State of New Jersey, and as the capitol of the United States from June through November of 1783. It was named in honor of King William III of the House of Orange-Nassau, which also explains Princeton's colors. The Faculty Room, which you may visit, contains Charles Willson Peale's famous painting of Washington at the Battle of Princeton along with portraits of King George II, King William III, and those of a number of illustrious graduates including presidents James Madison and Woodrow Wilson. *Usually open on Sun.–Fri., afternoons until 5, and on Sat. 9–5.*

University Chapel ❸ was completed in 1928 to replace an earlier one that had burned down. Services are held in a variety of faiths, including

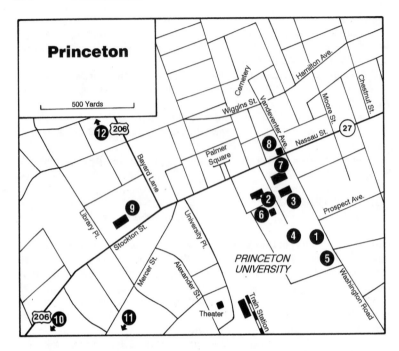

Protestant, Catholic, Orthodox, and Jewish. Modeled after the chapel of King's College in Cambridge, England, it has four great stained-glass windows representing Love, Truth, Endurance, and Hope. Among the figures depicted are John Witherspoon, the University's sixth president and the only clergyman to sign the Declaration of Independence.

Prospect Garden ❹ surrounds the Florentine-style Prospect House, a mansion of 1849 that became the residence of the University's presidents in 1878 and is now a dining and social facility for the faculty. After its gardens were demolished by a rampaging football crowd in 1904, Princeton's then-president Woodrow Wilson had an iron fence erected to enclose the five acres, and Mrs. Wilson laid out the flower garden in approximately its present form. It contains a vast array of trees, bushes, plants, and flowers; from common domestic varieties to the most exotic. Some of the trees predate the house, and at least one example of each variety is labeled with its botanical and common name.

The **Natural History Museum** ❺, Guyot Hall, contains archaeological, biological, and geological specimens. Among its treasures are skeletons of a saber-toothed tiger, a giant pig, a three-toed horse, and a baby dinosaur. The building's exterior is decorated with some 200 carvings of flora and fauna, both those extinct and those still with us. ☎ *609-258-4102. Open Mon.–Fri. 9–5. Free.* &.

*The Art Museum ❻, McCormick Hall. Picasso's 1971 sculpture, Head of a Woman, stands in front of this modern museum building. Inside, the absolutely first-rate collections range all the way from Egyptian, Greek, and Roman antiquities to contemporary American painting and sculpture. Between these are medieval works of art including a stained-glass window from Chartres, Renaissance paintings, Oriental art, some major works of the French Impressionists, and fine photography. If you like art, you'll love this museum. ☎ 609-258-3787, Internet: http://webware.Princeton.EDU/art mus. Open Tues.–Sat. 10–5, Sun. 1–5. Closed Mon. and major holidays. Admission $3. ♿.

The Putnam Sculptures, a collection of some 22 modern sculptures, is scattered all over the campus, both indoors and out. It includes works by Calder, Epstein, Lipchitz, Moore, Nevelson, Noguchi, Picasso, and Segal among other 20th-century masters.

Firestone Library ❼, the home of more than four million books, is the central research library for the University. Its holdings are especially rich in materials relating to the American Revolution. You might want to visit its Exhibition Gallery, to the right of the main entrance.

Princeton Town, whose historic core lies just north of the campus, has a number of attractions of its own, including:

BAINBRIDGE HOUSE ❽, 158 Nassau St., Princeton, NJ 08542, ☎ 609-921-6748, Internet: www.princetonol.com/groups/histsoc. Open Tues.–Sun., noon–4. Donation. Guided tours of Princeton Sun. 2 p.m. or by appointment; adults $6, seniors $4, ages 6–12 $3. ♿.

Built in 1766, this was the birthplace of Commodore William "Old Ironsides" Bainbridge, who commanded the USS Constitution during the War of 1812. Now the headquarters of the Historical Society of Princeton, the house features a museum with changing exhibitions, a library, photo archives, and a museum shop. Maps and other information for self-guided tours of the town are available here.

Just a few blocks west of this is Morven ❾. Once the home of Richard Stockton, a signer of the Declaration of Independence, this brick house of 1755 reportedly served as headquarters for British General Cornwallis in 1777, was visited by Washington, and from 1953 until 1981 was the official residence of New Jersey's governors. 55 Stockton St., ☎ 609-683-4495. Tours on Wed. 11–2 or by appointment. Closed July and Aug. The present governor lives down the road at Drumthwacket ❿, a restored 1835 mansion that may be visited. 354 Stockton St., ☎ 609-683-0057. Tours on Wed., noon–2, call ahead to confirm. Closed Jan., Feb., Aug.

About a mile or so out of town, on Mercer Street, is the Princeton Battlefield State Park ⓫, where George Washington won a decisive victory over the British on January 3, 1777. Princeton, of course, was loyal to the Crown, and as a result got itself looted after the hostilities. On the property is the Thomas Clarke House, a Quaker farmhouse of 1770. Furnished as it would have been during the Revolutionary War, it also exhibits artifacts of the battle. *500 Mercer Rd.,* ☎ *609-921-0074. House open Wed.–Sat. 10–noon and 1–4, Sun. 1–4. Free.*

Five miles north of Princeton via US-206 (Bayard Lane) stands **Rockingham** ⓬. While waiting for the signing of the peace treaty with England, the Continental Congress convened at Princeton. General Washington was invited to attend and made his headquarters at nearby Rockingham, using the Blue Room as his study. Here, in November 1783, he wrote his "Farewell Address to the Armies." You can visit his study and step out as he must have on the balcony, but you won't see the same terrain he saw, for the restored building has been moved from its original site. *108 Route 518 at River Rd., Rocky Hill, NJ 08540,* ☎ *609-921-8835. Open Wed.-Sat. 10–noon and 1–4, Sun. 1–4. Free.*

Nassau Hall

West Orange and Montclair

Thomas Alva Edison, the "Wizard of Menlo Park," spent what were arguably his most creative years in West Orange. Born in 1847, his inventive mind led him to establish a laboratory in Newark, NJ, which was moved to Menlo Park in 1876, and later to West Orange in 1887. It was here that he developed the motion picture camera, the Edison disc phonograph, a dictation machine, generators, storage batteries, a line of household appliances, and much more. Edison's laboratory, a virtual invention factory employing some 200 assistants, has been preserved by the National Park Service as a memorial to the great man. Here you can examine his creations, learn how he revolutionized the process of development, and also visit his nearby mansion and 15-acre estate.

The trip also includes a wildlife preserve with great views extending to the New York skyline, an important art museum that focuses on American creativity, and an 18th-century Federal mansion. Other nearby attractions include the birthplace of President Grover Cleveland, and an unusual zoo. By staying overnight, you can easily combine this trip with others in the vicinity.

GETTING THERE:

By Car, West Orange is about 20 miles west of midtown Manhattan. Take either the **Garden State Parkway** south to Exit 145 *or* the **New Jersey Turnpike** south to Exit 15W, and pick up **I-280** west. Follow I-280 west to Exit 10, making a right at the end of the exit ramp. Go to the end of the street, making a left onto Main Street. Follow this for a half-mile to the **Edison National Historic Site**. From there, follow directions in the text.

PRACTICALITIES:

Avoid coming on a Monday or Tuesday, when the major attraction is closed. The Montclair Art Museum is closed on Mondays and major holidays. Check the individual listings for the other attractions if you intend to include them on your trip.

FOOD AND DRINK:

There are numerous eateries in both West Orange and Montclair. Here are some of the better choices:

The Manor (111 Prospect Ave., Rte. 577, a mile north of I-280 Exit 8B) Reservations are needed for this elegant restaurant set amid gardens.

Classic American cuisine. ☎ 973-731-2360. X: Sat. lunch. $$ and $$$

Highlawn Pavilion (Eagle Rock Ave. in Eagle Rock Reservation) Quality American cuisine in an historic building overlooking the area. ☎ 973-731-3463. X: Sat. lunch, Sun. lunch. $$ and $$$

Pals Cabin (265 Prospect Ave., just north of I-280 Exit 8B) A rustic country place with familiar American favorites. ☎ 973-731-4000. $$

Blue Sky Café (398 Bloomfield Ave. in Montclair) Innovative dishes in a bustling, casual place. BYOB. ☎ 973-746-2553. $$

LOCAL ATTRACTIONS:
Circled numbers in text correspond to numbers on the map.

*EDISON NATIONAL HISTORIC SITE ❶, Main St. and Lakeside Ave., West Orange, NJ 07052, ☎ 973-736-0550, Internet: www.nps.gov.edis. *Open for tours Wed.–Fri. 12:30–4, weekends 10–4. Closed Thanksgiving, Christmas, New Year's Day. Adults $2, under 17 free.* ♿.

Every American who can should make this pilgrimage to the laboratory of the man whose imagination and ingenuity dramatically changed the world. Thomas Alva Edison (1847–1931) came to West Orange in 1887, after he had invented the lightbulb in Menlo Park. This is where he perfected the motion picture camera and the phonograph, among other creations. You have an opportunity to get close to the man himself as you pass through his library and the old lab, where his coat hangs in its accustomed place and his tools lie ready at the workbench. Another feature is a reproduction of the **Black Maria**, the world's first building constructed as a motion picture studio, in which silent movies were produced from 1893 until 1903.

Ask at the Visitor Center by the lab about visits to nearby **Glenmont ❷**, Edison's home, which has recently been restored. The number of visitors to this are restricted, so passes for the tours are given on a first-come basis only. Edison bought the elegant Victorian house furnished, but added many characteristic personal touches of his own. Glenmont is about a mile from the laboratory complex, so you'll have to drive there.

Follow the map to **Eagle Rock Reservation ❸**, a 400-acre hill with two popular lookout points that afford a good view of the local landscape and the distant New York skyscrapers. Besides the view, there's a wildlife preserve here, a picnic area, and trails to hike.

Descend to South Mountain Avenue and take it north to the intersection of Bloomfield Avenue in Montclair, where you'll find:

THE MONTCLAIR ART MUSEUM ❹, 3 South Mountain Ave., Montclair, NJ 07042, ☎ 973-746-5555, Internet: www.montclair-art.com. *Open Tues.–Sat. 11–5, Sun. 1–5. Closed Mon. and major holidays. Adults $5, seniors and students $4, under 12 free. Free to everyone on Sat. from 11–2. Main floor is* ♿.

The Montclair Art Museum presents changing exhibitions from its

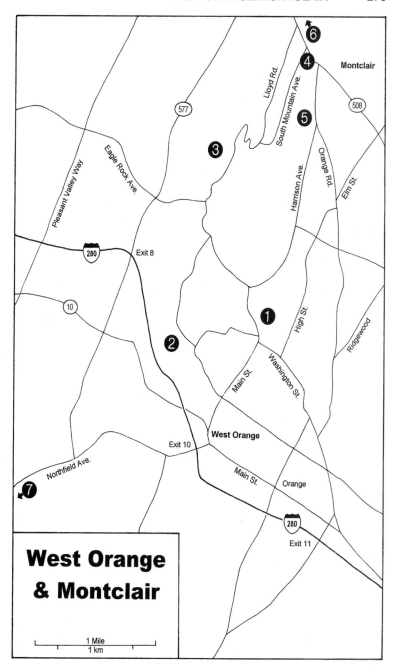

West Orange & Montclair

1 Mile
1 km

own collection as well as loan works. The museum is renowned for its fine collections of American art along with Native American art and artifacts, encompassing more than 15,000 objects. Over 1,000 works represent American painting from the mid-18th century to the present, with particularly strong holdings of the Hudson River School, 19th-century portraits, American Impressionism, the American Scene, Modernism, and 20th-century African-American art. Artists represented include Asher B. Durand, George Inness, Thomas Eakins, William Merritt Chase, John Singer Sargent, Arshile Gorky, Robert Motherwell, Morgan Russell, Romare Bearden, Mel Edwards, and others.

Just a few blocks away, on Orange Road, stands the:

ISRAEL CRANE HOUSE ❺, 110 Orange Rd., Montclair, NJ 07042, ☎ 973-783-1717. *Usually open Sept.–June, Wed. 1–4, Sun. 2–5, other times by appointment; call ahead to be sure it's open. Closed July & Aug. Nominal admission.*

Headquarters of the Montclair Historical Society, this handsome Federal mansion was built in 1796 by Israel Crane, a successful businessman and a descendant of the founding family of Montclair (originally called Cranetown). A civic group saved the house from demolition in 1965 and moved it from Old Road to its present site. It is beautifully furnished in the varying styles of the period 1740–1840, and there are lovely herb and pleasure gardens on the grounds. Visitors can watch and participate in open-hearth cooking and see a variety of historic skills demonstrations including weaving, quilting, lacemaking, tinsmithing, blacksmithing, and basketry.

In the Victoriana House at 108 Orange Road are the Historical Society office and a research library with materials on Colonial and local history. Israel Crane's general store has been re-created in the Country Store museum and Gift Shop, located in a house built in 1818 by Nathaniel Crane.

ADDITIONAL ATTRACTIONS:

Heading northwest on Bloomfield Avenue for about three miles brings you to Caldwell and the:

GROVER CLEVELAND BIRTHPLACE ❻, 207 Bloomfield Ave., Caldwell, NJ 07006, ☎ 973-226-0001. *Open Wed.–Sat. 9–noon and 1–5, Sun. 1–5. Closed holidays and when caretaker is away (call ahead). Free. Partially ♿.*

The Old Manse of the Caldwell First Presbyterian Church was just five years old when Grover Cleveland was born there in 1837. It's a homey place, furnished in the late 19th-century style and maintained as a memorial to the only U.S. President to be born in New Jersey, though he lived in it for only four years. Personal mementos, pictures, and letters from the famous are displayed in wall cases.

One other attraction, this one south of I-280 Exit 8, on Northfield Avenue in the South Mountain Reservation, might interest you:

TURTLE BACK ZOO ❼, 560 Northfield Ave. between Prospect Ave. and Cherry Lane, West Orange, NJ 07052, ☎ 973-731-5800. *Open April–Oct., Mon.–Sat. 10–5, Sun. and holidays 10:30–6; Nov. daily 10–4:30; rest of year weekends only, 10–4:30. Closed New Year's Day, Thanksgiving, Dec. 24–25 and 31. Adults $7, seniors and children (2–12) $3, a dollar less from Nov.–March. Snack bar. Picnic facilities. ♿.*

Hundreds of animals, many native to New Jersey, are featured in this 16-acre zoo, along with a 19th-century miniature train that you and the kids can ride. There's also a petting zoo and an animal nursery.

The Great Swamp

It's hard to believe that a genuine wilderness as large as the Great Swamp exists a mere 25 miles from Manhattan's skyscrapers, but it does. Here is an opportunity to visit three environmental centers, hike miles of primitive trails through a primeval past, observe natural habitats from boardwalks raised above the marshes, learn a bit more about nature, and in general have a thoroughly engrossing experience on an easily accomplished and inexpensive daytrip.

That the Great Swamp still exists at all is really a miracle, as in the late 1950s it almost became the site of a yet another major airport for New York City. Concerned citizens worked relentlessly to align political forces and raise the millions of dollars needed to purchase land and create the National Wildlife Refuge, as well as the two county-run facilities on either side of it.

There are several other attractions in the immediate vicinity of the Great Swamp, including the Museum of Early Trades and Crafts in Madison, the USGA Golf House, and the US Equestrian Team Headquarters. For those able to stay overnight, this trip combines well with the following ones to Morristown and Clinton.

GETTING THERE:

By Car, the easiest route is to take I-80 west to Exit 43, then I-287 south to Exit 30A at Basking Ridge. From there follow North Maple Avenue south into Basking Ridge, turning left on South Maple Avenue and left again on Lord Stirling Road to the Somerset County Environmental Education Center.

An alternative route from New York is to take I-78 west to Exit 36, then head north towards Basking Ridge, following the map to Lord Stirling Road and the Environmental Center.

From there, follow directions in the text.

PRACTICALITIES:

Trails and most facilities in the Great Swamp are open daily, although the headquarters is usually closed on weekends. The Museum of Early Trades and Crafts is closed on Mondays.

Waterproof footgear or old sneakers are strongly recommended for the damp trails. Those visiting from May through September should use an insect repellant and protective clothing as mosquitoes, ticks, and flies may be numerous.

A pair of binoculars would be very handy for observing wildlife closeup. Don't forget your camera!

For further information contact the **Skylands Tourism Council**, ☎ 1-800-4SKYLAND or 908-496-8598, Internet: www.njskylands.com.

FOOD AND DRINK:

There are several restaurants and fast-food outlets in the communities adjacent to the Great Swamp, among which are:

The Grain House at the Olde Mill Inn (US-202 & Maple Ave., off I-287 at Exit 30B, Basking Ridge) American cuisine in a tree-shaded converted barn of 1768, part of an historic inn. ☎ 908-221-1150. $$ and $$$

Fresh Fields Café (641 Shunpike Rd., at Green Village Rd., Hickory Square Mall, in Chatham) Creative American cuisine, with a focus on seafood. ☎ 973-377-4072. X: Sun. lunch, Mon. $$ and $$$

L'Allergria (9-11 Prospect St., near Main St., in Madison) Fine Northern Italian cuisine in an atmospheric setting. Reservations suggested. ☎ 973-377-6808. X: Sat. lunch, Sun. lunch, holidays. $$ and $$$

3 Central (3 Central Ave., near Main St., in Madison) Creative Italian dishes in the center of town. BYOB. ☎ 973-514-1333. X: Sat. lunch, Sun. lunch, holidays. $$

Note that picnicking is not allowed within the National Wildlife Refuge.

LOCAL ATTRACTIONS:

Circled numbers in text correspond to numbers on the map.

SOMERSET COUNTY ENVIRONMENTAL EDUCATION CENTER ❶, 190 Lord Stirling Rd., Basking Ridge, NJ 07920, ☎ 908-766-2489, Internet: www.park.co.somerset.nj.us/lspark. *Center open daily 9–5, closed holidays. Trails open daily dawn to dusk. Free.* ♿.

William Alexander (1726–83), known as Lord Stirling, was a Major General in the American Revolution who built Fort Lee (see page 245) and commanded Continental troops in the Battle of Monmouth (see page 262). Before that, he created an estate with an elegant Georgian mansion and many outbuildings right on the western edge of the Great Swamp. This land now belongs to Somerset County as the 897-acre **Lord Stirling Park**, and is reserved solely for environmental and equestrian activities.

At the heart of the park is the Somerset County Environmental Education Center, which features an **orientation exhibit** covering the 200-million-year history of the Great Swamp, a nature art gallery, classrooms, an auditorium, and more. The entire building is heated and cooled by solar power. It also offers 8.5 miles of **trails**, including 2.5 miles of **boardwalk** allowing easy access to the wetter portions of the park. Naturalists are available to answer questions and provide information.

With a good understanding of the swamp, you can now proceed into its wilder sections. Continue east on Lord Stirling and White Bridge roads to the:

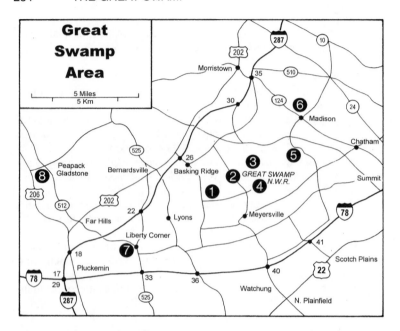

GREAT SWAMP NATIONAL WILDLIFE REFUGE ❷–❹, Pleasant Plains Rd., Basking Ridge, NJ 07920, ☎ 973-425-1222, Internet: www.fws.gov/nj/grs. *Open daily all year, dawn to dusk. Headquarters open Mon.–Fri. 8–4:30, also on some weekends in spring and fall. Free. Visitors allowed in designated areas only. No bicycles or horses on trails. Picnicking, camping, and alcohol prohibited. Pets are allowed only in parking areas. Self-service information booth at the Wildlife Observation Center. Waterproof shoes recommended, insect repellant and protective clothing advisable May–Sept.* ♿.

About 25,000 years ago, the Wisconsin Glacier reached its southernmost point of advance, looked around and retreated, leaving the Great Swamp in its wake. In 1708 the Delaware Indians deeded a huge tract of land including the Great Swamp to the English in exchange for a barrel of rum, 15 kettles, four pistols, four cutlasses, assorted goods and sundries, and £30 sterling. Various attempts to log and farm the area proved unprofitable over the next two centuries. In 1959 a new airport for New York was proposed for the site, but the North American Wildlife Foundation launched a successful campaign to block the project. The 3,000 acres purchased as a result of their efforts were donated to the Department of the Interior in 1960 and became the nucleus of today's 7,375-acre refuge.

The Great Swamp is home to a great variety of flora and fauna, including swamp woodlands, hardwood stands, marshlands, over 200 species of birds, and numerous mammals, fish, reptiles, and amphibians. Among the latter are the rare bog turtle and blue-spotted salamander. Since 1968 the eastern half of the refuge has been designated a **Wilderness Area**. Man-made structures and motorized equipment are prohibited, and the public is restricted to good old foot travel on more than eight miles of trails. The western half is a **Wildlife Management Area** where various habitats are maintained to promote bio-diversity.

Head north a short distance on Pleasant Plains Road to the **Refuge Headquarters ❷**, where you can obtain current information and get yourself oriented.

Return to White Bridge Road and follow the map to the **Wildlife Observation Center ❸** on Long Hill Road. There's a self-service information kiosk here, as well as restrooms, blinds, trails, and an elevated boardwalk trail running into the swamp.

From here to the east lies the Wilderness Area, which can be experienced by hiking a short distance on a primitive path starting at the **Orange Trail Parking Area ❹**.

Turn south on New Vernon Road, leaving the Wildlife Refuge, and follow the map to the:

GREAT SWAMP OUTDOOR EDUCATION CENTER ❺, 247 Southern Blvd., Chatham, NJ 07928, ☎ 973-635-6629, Internet: www.parks.morris.nj.us/asp/parks. *Open daily, 9–4:30. Free.* ♿.

Operated by the Morris County Park Commission, this facility on the eastern wilderness edge of the Great Swamp offers a varied program of activities, guided tours and workshops, and maintains two miles of trails, an observation blind, and an elevated boardwalk through woods, fields, swamps, and marshes.

That's the end of the Great Swamp. To visit the next attraction, continue north on Southern Boulevard and then Green Village Road to Madison and the:

MUSEUM OF EARLY TRADES AND CRAFTS ❻, Main St. & Green Village Rd., Madison, NJ 07940, ☎ 973-377-2982. *Open Tues.–Sat. 1–4, Sun. noon–5. Closed major holidays. Adults $3.50, children (under 13) $2.*

Explore the lives, tools, and products of 18th- and 19th-century New Jersey craftspeople through exhibits and hands-on discoveries. Artisan demonstrations, lectures, traditional crafts workshops, historical performances, craft festivals, kids' clubs, and much more await visitors of all ages. The building itself, a superb example of the Richardson Romanesque Revival style, is a turn-of-the-century gem and the cornerstone of Madison's Historic District.

From here, you can return to New York by either taking NJ-24 north to I-287, then I-80 east to the city; or NJ-24 south to I- 78, then east to the city.

ADDITIONAL ATTRACTIONS:

Should you tire early of the swamp and have little interest in old tools, you might try one of these alternative attractions, both a bit west of the Great Swamp:

U.S. GOLF ASSOCIATION GOLF HOUSE ❼, Liberty Corner Rd. (Rte. 512), 2 miles east of US-202, Far Hills, NJ 07931, ☎ 908-234-2300. *Open Mon.–Fri. 9–5, weekends 10–4. Free.* ♿.

In 1972 the United States Golf Association moved from New York into the red-brick Georgian Colonial estate once owned by the W.J. Sloane family of Far Hills. All of the building is now a museum that charts the history of golf from its origins to the present day. Fascinating displays depict the evolution of golfing equipment, the rules of the game, and clothing worn on the links. You will also see trophies, photographs, pictures of golf courses, and clubs and balls used by today's champions. There is a valuable golfing reference library, and a gift shop that sells golf-related memorabilia and artwork.

Returning on Route 512 through Far Hills to Gladstone brings you to the:

U.S. EQUESTRIAN TEAM HEADQUARTERS ❽, Pottersville Rd., Gladstone, NJ 07934, ☎ 908-234-1251, Internet: www.uset.com. *Open Mon.–Fri. 8:30–4:40, closed major holidays. Call for weekend events and current activities. Free. Partially* ♿.

This is an extraordinary treat for horse lovers. Here you can watch the U.S. riding teams train for international competitions. The horses work out in the morning, and rehearsals for the contests include dressage, show jumping, three-day eventing, and driving. A special treat is a visit to the ornate stable of 1916, one of the largest and most lavish in the nation.

Morristown

N estled among the rolling hills in the center of northern New Jersey, Morristown has a remarkable history, and a broad range of sites to celebrate it. Once the military capital of the American Revolution where George Washington and his troops spent two cold winters, it was also a center of the Industrial Revolution, and later a favorite refuge for New York's emerging millionaires during the Gilded Age. Much of its storied past is preserved both in the Morristown National Historical Park and in the mansions and gardens that surround it. Here's a chance to explore one of New Jersey's most interesting communities.

GETTING THERE:

By Car, Morristown is about 45 miles west of midtown New York City. Take **I-80** west from the George Washington Bridge to Exit 43, then **I-287** south to Exit 36, Morristown. From the exit ramp turn left on Ridgedale to Morris Ave., then left again on Morris Ave., crossing I-287 and passing the Ford Mansion to Washington Place. Here turn left to the parking lot behind the mansion. The route is well marked with brown signs directing you to **Washington's Headquarters**. At the Historical Museum pick up a brochure for a self-guided tour through the rest of the park.

Continue west across I-287 through the center of Morristown. From the main square take Washington St., then make a left on Western Ave., followed by another left at Ann St. that leads steeply uphill to **Fort Nonsense**.

Return to Western Ave. and follow south to **Jockey Hollow**.

Return to the center of Morristown and take US-202 (Speedwell Ave.) north to **Historic Speedwell**, on the right.

Retrace your route south on Speedwell to the Morristown Green and bear right onto Bank St. for 2 blocks. Turn left on Macculloch Ave. for 2 blocks to **Macculloch Hall**.

Continue east for 2 blocks and turn left onto Madison St., which becomes Elm St. At Morris St. turn right, under the railroad trestle, then go a short block past it to Olyphant Place. Turn left here to **Schuyler-Hamilton House**.

Return to Morris Ave., turn left, and continue across 1-287 past Washington's Headquarters. Shortly come to a 3-way split. Staying in right-hand lane, you can go left around the jughandle following sign for U-Turn, then passing the Governor Morris Inn to **Acorn Hall**, on the right.

Continue back on Morris Ave. At the 3-way split, bear right through a stoplight onto Columbia Road. Go uphill and turn left at first light onto

Normandy Heights Rd., then make an immediate left to the **Morris Museum.**

From the museum turn left on Normandy Heights Rd. and continue to Whippany Rd. Turn left on Whippany and proceed briefly to Hanover Ave. Turn left on Hanover and go a short distance to the **Frelinghuysen Arboretum** on the left.

For the **Fosterfields Historical Farm**, return to Morristown Green and head west on Washington St., becoming Route 510. A right turn on Kahdena Rd. takes you to the farm, on the left.

PRACTICALITIES:

Good weather will greatly enhance your enjoyment of this trip. Note that most of the attractions have rather limited opening times, so you'll have to check the individual listings carefully before deciding on which day to make the trip. In any case, you won't be able to see them all in one day. For further information contact the **Historic Morris Visitors Center**, 6 Court St., Morristown, NJ 70960, ☎ 973-631-5151, Internet: www.morris tourism.org, or the **Skylands Tourism Council**, P.O. Box 329, Columbia, NJ 07832, ☎ 1-800-4SKYLAND or 908-496-8598, Internet: www.njskylands.com

FOOD AND DRINK:

Rod's 1890 (1 Convent Rd., in the Madison Hotel, follow NJ-124 1.5 miles east of I-287 Exit 35) A Victorian ambiance in a rural setting, with American cuisine. Reservations suggested. ☎ 973-539-6666. $$ and $$$

Calaloo Café (190 South St., in downtown Morristown) A busy, lively place with American cuisine, especially seafood and pasta dishes. ☎ 973-993-1100. X: holidays. $$

LOCAL ATTRACTIONS:

Circled numbers in text correspond to numbers on the map.

MORRISTOWN NATIONAL HISTORICAL PARK ❶–❸, Washington Place, Morristown, NJ 07960, ☎ 973-539-2085, Internet: www.nps.gov/morr. *Open all year daily 9–5. Closed Thanksgiving, Christmas, New Year's Day. No park entry fee; combination admission to Historical Museum and Ford Mansion $4 for age 17 and over. Free parking. Brochures for self-guided auto tour of the park are available at the Historical Museum and Visitor Center. Leashed pets only. Mostly &.*

Created by an Act of Congress in 1933, Morristown National Historical Park occupies some 1,600 acres that played a crucial role in the Revolutionary War. Twice, in 1777 and again in 1779–80, the Continental Army wintered here under conditions of extreme hardship. Washington chose Morristown because it is protected on the east by swamp lands and by the Watchung ridges, which afforded an excellent vantage point for keeping watch on the large British force in New York City. But these strategic advantages were almost outweighed by the bitter cold weather,

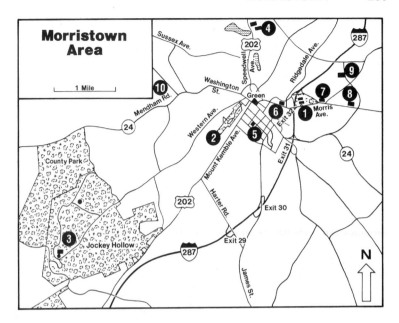

chronic shortages of food and clothing, and by outbreaks of disease — perhaps harsher enemies than the British. Though no battles occurred at Morristown, the two winter encampments were in many ways the greatest test of Washington's leadership and the courage of his men.

Begin your tour in the **Historical Museum** at ****Washington's Headquarters** ❶, which displays Washington memorabilia, period weapons, and a 104-pound link of the chain that was stretched across the Hudson from West Point to Constitution Island to block British warships. A 20-minute film recalls the harsh winter of 1779–80 and shows the dramatic contrast between the lives of the officers and those of the ordinary soldiers, while a new exhibit describes the impact of this large army on the small community of Morristown.

Just beyond the museum stands the **Ford Mansion**, which served as General Washington's headquarters. Fully restored to its 1780 condition, it may be seen on guided tours that begin at the museum. This gracious Colonial house was built by Jacob Ford, Jr. between 1772 and 1774, and was one of the grandest homes in Morristown at the time. When the Revolution began, Ford opened a gunpowder mill to supply the patriot army, in which he became a colonel. He took sick and died during the ill-fated New Jersey "Mud Rounds" campaign in the winter of 1776. Two years later his widow squeezed herself, her three children, and any belongings she valued (some of the patriots were prone to pilfering) into two rooms and offered the rest of the house to General Washington for use as his headquarters. Here he spent one of the worst winters of the 18th century, when no less than 28 blizzards blasted Morristown and compounded the miseries of his men; here he met with foreign dignitaries, including the young Marquis de Lafayette bringing welcome news of French support; and here he fired off an endless stream of letters pleading provisions for the army from Congress and the states.

The next stop on the tour is **Fort Nonsense** ❷, a hill about a mile and a half away that offers a commanding view of the surrounding countryside. Legend has it that Washington ordered the hill fortified to keep his troops occupied and take their minds off their troubles (which included a smallpox epidemic) during the first encampment of 1777. In fact, the fort had great strategic value and was the site of a beacon that was part of an alarm system stretching all the way to the Hudson Highlands. Today, the foundation outlines of the earthworks and redoubt are marked with stone blocks. A series of wayside exhibits describe the role of the surrounding geography in the struggle for independence.

A few miles south of Fort Nonsense is **Jockey Hollow** ❸, site of the 1779–80 encampment. Here Washington's troops felled some 900 acres of timber to build huts and keep themselves in firewood. Washington issued strict specifications for the construction of the huts, which were to be well drained and ventilated to avoid the outbreak of disease that had decimated his troops at Valley Forge two years earlier. By January 1780, nearly 1,200 huts housed some 10,000 men, making Jockey Hollow the sixth-largest city in the United States. There are replicas of the soldiers' huts at Sugar Loaf Hill and markers throughout the hollow noting the locations of the various brigades. Sugar Loaf Hill, in particular, recalls the hardships of the Continental Army: in 1780 the troops of the Pennsylvania Line, stationed here, put down a mutiny by the First Connecticut Brigade; the following year they themselves mutinied, demanding back pay and redress of their many grievances. Near Sugar Loaf Hill is the Grand Parade, a large field where the troops drilled when not confined to their huts by snowdrifts.

Also in Jockey Hollow is the **Wick House**, which served as headquarters for Major General Arthur St. Clair in 1779–80. This house was owned by Henry Wick, a prosperous farmer, and is very different from the Ford Mansion in its homey, comfortable air. Adjacent to the house is an apple orchard and herb garden, reminiscent of those that brought sustenance to the Wick family.

HISTORIC SPEEDWELL ❹, 333 Speedwell Ave., Morristown, NJ 07960 ☎ 973-540-0211, Internet: www.speedwell.org. *Open May–Oct., Thurs. and Sun., 1–5. Adults $5, seniors $4, students (5–18) $3, under 4 free. Free parking at entrance. No pets, no smoking or photographing inside buildings. Vail House is partially* ♿.

Historic Speedwell preserves the site of two major technological innovations that helped fuel America's Industrial Revolution in the early 19th century. Judge Stephen Vail, self-made man and family patriarch, built the **Speedwell Iron Works** next to his Homestead Farm here along the Whippany River. In 1818–19 this foundry cast most of the machinery for the S.S. *Savannah*, the first transatlantic steamship. Later, in 1837, his son Alfred began a collaboration with the artist and inventor Samuel F. B. Morse, and in January 1838 the first successful demonstration of Morse's electromagnetic telegraph took place in the cotton factory, where some of the original wiring may still be seen nailed to the wall. The message that day was "A patient waiter is no loser," courtesy of Judge Vail. "What hath God wrought" came six years later.

A National Historic Site organized in 1966, Speedwell consists of nine buildings, including the Vail House, the cotton factory, a water-powered wheelhouse, a granary, a carriage house, and three historic houses relocated from various parts of Morristown to avoid demolition. There are comprehensive displays on the development of both the steamship engine and the telegraph, a guided tour of the fully-restored Vail House with its original paintings by Morse, a gift shop, and a self-guided tour of the entire complex.

MACCULLOCH HALL ❺, 45 Macculloch Ave., Morristown, NJ 07960 ☎ 973-538-2404, Internet: www.machall.org. *Open Sun., Wed., and Thurs., 1–4. Adults $4, seniors and students $3, under 12 free.* ♿.

George Macculloch, the originator of the Morris Canal (see page 303), built this handsome Federal mansion between 1806 and 1815, and it remained the home of his descendants until the middle of the 20th century. Filled with an eclectic assortment of the American and Europeans decorative arts from the 18th and 19th centuries, it is most noted for its collection of famous cartoons by Thomas Nast, who lived across the street. This 19th-century illustrator created the universal image of Santa Claus that everyone knows so well, gave the Democratic Party its donkey, and helped toppled the corrupt political regime of Boss Tweed in New York City. Another treasure in the house is the original portrait of George Washington by Rembrandt Peale. Macculloch Hall is also noted for its historic garden.

SCHUYLER-HAMILTON HOUSE ❻, 5 Olyphant Place, Morristown, NJ 07960, ☎ 973-267-4039. *Open all year, Sun. 2–4. Adults $4, seniors $3, students $2, under 12 50¢.*

This Colonial house and its garden was the setting for the courtship of Betsy Schuyler by Alexander Hamilton, then a colonel in the Continental Army, stationed in the nearby Ford Mansion as part of General Washington's staff. The house has period furnishings and is maintained by the local chapter of the D.A.R.

ACORN HALL ❼, 68 Morris Ave., Morristown, NJ 07960 ☎ 973-267-3465, Internet: www.acornhall.org. *Open Mon. and Thurs. 10–4, Sun. 1–4. Adults $5, seniors $4, students $2, under 12 free. Partially* ♿.

This beautifully preserved Victorian house (1853) is the headquarters of the Morris County Historical Society. The scrollwork embellishments on the exterior are a good indication of what to expect inside. There are many priceless furnishings, including a Rococo Revival parlor set, a printed velvet rug identical to one displayed at London's Crystal Palace Exhibition in 1851–52, and some porcelains given to Commodore Perry, a relative of the second owner, when he opened Japan to Western trade in 1854.

Acorn Hall takes its name from the majestic, centuries-old red oak that stands near the driveway. The Home Garden Club of Morristown has restored the grounds to re-create a **period garden** of extraordinary variety and beauty, well worth the trip in itself.

MORRIS MUSEUM ❽, 6 Normandy Heights Rd., Morristown, NJ 07960 ☎ 973-538-0454, Internet: www.morrismuseum.org. *Open all year, Tues.–Sat. 10–5, Sun. 1–5. Adults $6, seniors and children $4.* ♿.

This wonderful museum, in an imposing red-brick mansion, holds just about everything from fossils to live animals, fine and decorative arts to archaeology, old-time toys to computers. The museum sponsors a lively program of concerts, lectures, workshops, and special events; and there are lots of activities geared towards kids, including a special room for preschoolers.

FRELINGHUYSEN ARBORETUM ❾, 53 East Hanover Ave., Morristown, NJ 07960, ☎ 973-326-7600, Internet: www.parks.morris.nj.us. *Grounds open daily 8–sunset, visitor center open Mon.–Sat. 9–4:30, Sun. noon–4:30. Donation requested. Hiking trails, nature programs, concerts, special events. No pets. Partially* ♿.

The Morris County Park Commission has its headquarters here in an 1891 country estate, a lovely specimen of Victorian architecture that also houses a fine horticultural library. Elaborate gardens, flowering shrubs, and brilliant displays of roses make the grounds worth visiting at almost any time of the year. There are 127 acres of forest and gardens crisscrossed by well-marked trails.

FOSTERFIELDS LIVING HISTORICAL FARM ❿, 75 Kahdena Rd., off Rt. 510 West, Morristown, NJ 07960, ☎ 973-326-7645, Internet: www.parks.morris.nj.us. *Open April–Oct., Wed.–Sat. 10–5, Sun. noon–5. Mansion tours Thurs.–Sun, 1–3:30. Adults $4, seniors $3, children (6–16) $2. Tours of Willows Mansion $1 additional. Partially* ♿.

Step back in time to the years between 1880 and 1910 on this historic farm, once owned by a grandson of Paul Revere. There's a 19th-century mansion to explore, exhibits on period farming, and a self-guided tour of the farm itself where you'll meet old-time breeds of horses, cows, pigs, sheep, chickens and other living creatures, and see demonstrations of 19th-century farming methods.

Clinton

With its mixture of Colonial and Victorian buildings nestled by the placid banks of the Raritan River, Clinton easily ranks among New Jersey's more attractive small towns. What makes it especially interesting for daytrippers, however, is the restored museum village with its red mill of 1812, an art center, the appealing shops along Main Street, and a number of colorful restaurants including an old stagecoach inn from 1743. Clinton is not nearly as overexposed or commercialized as some of the other preserved old towns in the region, and certainly makes a pleasant respite from urban life.

This trip can easily be combined in the same day with the one to Flemington (see page 268).

GETTING THERE:

By Car: Take the **New Jersey Turnpike** south to Exit 14, *or* the **Garden State Parkway** south to Exit 142A. From either, pick up **I-78** west to Exit 15, the second exit for Clinton. Turn right from the ramp onto West Main Street, go about a quarter-mile, and turn left at the Clinton House Inn to the **Hunterdon Historical Museum**, just before the bridge.

Cross the Raritan River to the **Hunterdon Museum of Art**, just opposite the museum village, on Center Street.

Return to Main Street and turn left through the shopping area for about a block. Turn left on Leigh Street and follow it out of town to **NJ-31**. From here you can head south back to I-78, or head north to the two state parks and New Hampton.

Continue north on NJ-31 to **Spruce Run State Park** *or* turn right onto Route 513, which leads through High Bridge to the **Voorhees State Park**.

For the **Township of Lebanon Museum**, continue north on NJ-31 past the Hampton turnoff, then turn right on Musconetcong River Road to New Hampton.

The farthest point is about 70 miles east of midtown Manhattan.

PRACTICALITIES:

Fine weather is essential for enjoyment of this scenic trip. The major attraction is open from April through October only, and never on Mondays. Avoid coming on a major holiday, when the art museum is closed. A useful web site is: www.njskylands.com/tnclinton.

FOOD AND DRINK:

Clinton has a number of eateries, mostly located along Main Street.

There are also seasonal concessions at both state parks, both of which feature picnic facilities.

LOCAL ATTRACTIONS:

Circled numbers in text correspond to numbers on the map.

HUNTERDON HISTORICAL MUSEUM ❶, 56 Main St., Clinton, NJ 08809, ☎ 908-735-4101. *Open April–Oct., Tues.–Sat. 10–4, Sun. noon–5. Adults $4, seniors $3, children (6–16) $1, under 6 free. Concerts and special events throughout the season. Partially* ♿.

You don't have to be an antiquarian to enjoy the ***Old Red Mill** and reconstructed village set in a 10-acre park complete with waterfall and 150-foot limestone cliffs. Life in bygone times is re-created in the mill, where the waterwheel still turns as it did in the days when grain, flax-seed, limestone, graphite, and talc were processed here. You can also visit a blacksmith's shop, a turn-of-the-century general store and post office, an 1860 little red schoolhouse, a log cabin, old lime kilns, a herb garden, and the gift shop.

The landmark Red Mill was first built in 1812 to process wool, and was later enlarged to accommodate new enterprises such as grist milling, talc grinding, and peach-basket production. Its distinctive roofline dates from the addition of new machinery in 1908. In 1960 the mill was purchased by a local group, painted red, and put to new use as a historical museum. In the years since then other nearby structures were saved and added to the site as a "living history" museum.

Exit the museum and stroll across the picturesque iron bridge from 1870 to the:

HUNTERDON MUSEUM OF ART ❷, 7 Lower Center St., Clinton, NJ 08809, ☎ 908-735-8415. *Open all year, Tues.–Sun. 11–5, closed major holidays. Donation.* ♿.

In a beautifully-renovated 1836 gristmill, hand-hewn beams and wide-plank floors enhance exhibitions of work created primarily by contemporary New Jersey artists. Fine arts and crafts are shown in four galleries. The museum also sponsors lectures, workshops, studio classes, and concerts throughout the year.

Stroll along Main Street with its variety of interesting shops and eateries, then take off for:

SPRUCE RUN STATE PARK ❸, One Van Syckels Rd., Clinton, NJ 08809, ☎ 908-638-8572, Internet: www.state.nj.us/dep/forestry/parks/spruce. ♿.

This State recreation area just north of Clinton surrounds a reservoir and offers picnic areas with grills and shelters, boating, swimming, fishing, camping, and a range of winter sports. There are also miles of hiking, biking, and jogging trails. Special consideration was given to wheelchair accessibility in the design of Spruce Run.

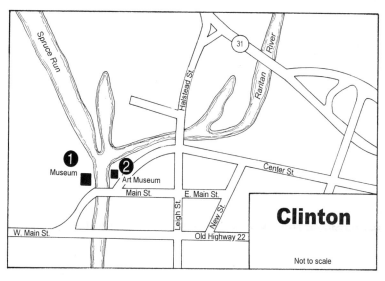

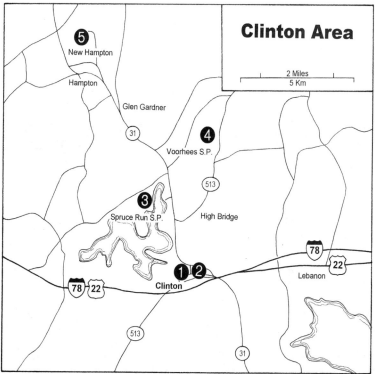

Alternatively, you might visit:

VOORHEES STATE PARK ❹, 251 County Rd. (Route 513), Glen Gardner, NJ 08826, ☎ 908-638-6969, Internet: www.state.nj.us/dep/forestry/ parks/voorhees. *Partially* ♿.

A smaller and less "civilized" park, Voorhees has picnic areas, hiking trails, a scenic overlook, and a playground for children. Camping is also possible, as are fishing, hunting, winter sports, and mountain biking. A special feature is the **Observatory** operated by the New Jersey Astronomical Association, which offers public skywatching programs all year round. ☎ 908-638-8500 for schedules and other information.

Finally, you might continue north to the:

TOWNSHIP OF LEBANON MUSEUM ❺, Musconetcong River Rd., Hampton, NJ 08827, ☎ 908-537-6464. *Open all year, Tues. and Thurs., 9:30–5, Sat. 1–5. Free. Craft classes, lectures, quilt exhibit, and art show. Main floor is* ♿.

Put on your pinafores, hitch up your suspenders, pack your McGuffey's Readers, and grab your slates — you don't want to be late for the Museum at New Hampton, a 19th-century schoolhouse with a vintage, no-nonsense, Three-R's classroom featuring original books, old-style desks, and a potbellied stove. The building, constructed in 1823 as a one-room school, was enlarged in the 1870s, and the second floor is now used for changing exhibits, as well as permanent displays of Indian artifacts, farm tools, and Hunterdon County milk bottles.

The Old Red Mill and the Hunterdon Museum of Art

Paterson

Paterson is certainly no beauty spot, but it does have a fascinating heritage that just might compel a visit, especially if you have an interest in America's Industrial Revolution and the social changes that followed in its wake. This is where it all began in the late 18th century when the enormous waterpower potential of the Great Falls was first harnessed. Much of its 19th-century industrialization has survived intact and may be explored on self-guided walking tours, along with the impressive Great Falls themselves. The lives of the people are remembered, too, both the workers at the American Labor Museum, and the industrialists at Lambert Castle.

GETTING THERE:

By Car, Paterson is about 20 miles west of midtown New York City. Take **I-80** west from the George Washington Bridge to Exit 57B and follow Main St. north into Paterson. Turn left on Market St., then right on Spruce St. to the Visitor Center at the **Great Falls**.

From the falls, cross the Passaic River on Wayne Ave. and turn left on Front St. briefly to Preakness Ave. Turn right, proceed a few blocks to Union Ave., and turn right again. Shortly, at West Broadway, turn left. At the third light make a sharp right onto Barbour St., then the second left onto Mason Ave. The **American Labor Museum** is on the left at Norwood St.

Lambert Castle lies just south of I-80, Exit 57. Take NJ-19 south towards Clifton, turning west on Valley Rd. into the Garret Mountain Reservation.

Buses depart New York City's Port Authority Bus Terminal and points in New Jersey frequently for Paterson, where they stop at the Paterson Bus Terminal on Broadway, near the Great Falls.

Trains operated by New Jersey Transit leave Hoboken (connection to midtown Manhattan via PATH trains) frequently for Paterson, whose train station is within walking distance of the Great Falls by following Market St. west and Spruce St. north.

Those coming by bus or train will probably not be able to visit the American Labor Museum or Lambert Castle unless they take taxis there — or don't mind a very long hike.

PRACTICALITIES:

Note the opening times of each attraction before venturing out to Paterson, and call ahead to confirm them. The Great Falls are spectacular after a period of rain, but less so following a dry spell. For further information contact the **Great Falls Visitor's Center**, 65 McBride Ave., Paterson, NJ 07501, ☎ 973- 279-9587 or 1-888-GRT-FALLS.

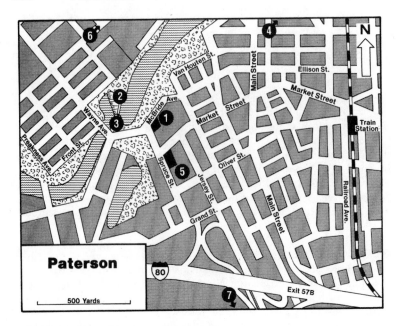

FOOD AND DRINK:

There are several fast-food outlets, and several small ethnic eateries within a few blocks of the Great Falls. You might also consider a picnic there.

LOCAL ATTRACTIONS:

Circled numbers in text correspond to numbers on the map.

GREAT FALLS HISTORIC DISTRICT ❶, 65 McBride Ave., Paterson, NJ 07501, ☎ 973-279-9587 or 1-888-GRT-FALLS, Internet: www.patersongreatfalls.org. *Visitor Center open Apr.–Sept., Mon.–Fri. 9–4, Sun. noon–4, offers a free brochure and map for do-it-yourself walking tours. Guided tours for groups by appointment only, may be customized to suit special interests.* ♿.

Two hundred feet wide and 77 feet high, the **Great Falls ❷ of the Passaic River can be counted on for a spectacular display in any season, provided there has been sufficient rain. They were visited in 1778 by George Washington, the Marquis de Lafayette, and Alexander Hamilton. Attracted by the tremendous power of the falls, Hamilton later became one of the founders of the **Society for Useful Manufactures (S.U.M.)**, which established Paterson in 1791 as the first planned industrial city in the newly- independent United States. Pierre L'Enfant, planner of Washington, D.C., designed raceways (now renovated) for the various mills, and

Paterson grew rapidly. In 1835 Samuel Colt began manufacturing his revolvers here; then the silk boom made Paterson into America's "Silk City." The iron industry was turning out Rogers locomotives at a great rate by the 19th century, and the aeronautics industry came to town after World War I.

Changing technologies gradually made the mills and factories of the Great Falls district obsolete; today it is designated a National Historic Landmark preserving an important chapter in American industrial history. You can walk along the old cobbled streets, see the houses of workmen and mill owners, and visit the Paterson Museum. A footbridge over the falls affords a magnificent view. The **Hydroelectric Plant** ❸ of 1914, one of the oldest in America, has been recently renovated and is once again "on line," generating electricity for the people of Paterson. And, should you get hungry, there's the **Farmer's Market** ❹ just a few blocks away, along with a good selection of ethnic restaurants.

PATERSON MUSEUM ❺, Thomas Rogers Building, 2 Market St., Paterson, NJ 07501, ☎ 973-881-3874. *Open all year, Tues.–Fri. 10–4, Sat.–Sun. 12:30–4:30, closed Mon. and holidays. Adults $2, under 18 free.* ⌖.

Organized in 1925, the Paterson Museum began rather humbly as a collection of rocks and artifacts dug up by local residents and donated to the public library. Growing steadily in size and scope, it was relocated in 1982 into the restored Thomas Rogers Locomotive Erecting Shop (1873) in the Great Falls Historic District. In addition to an exceptional collection of rocks, minerals, and gems, there are archaeological and natural history displays along with exhibits that show Paterson's evolution as a textile and manufacturing center. You can also see the shell of the 14-foot prototype **submarine** built in 1878 by John P. Holland, an underwater pioneer, and a slightly later model, Holland's Fenian Ram, intended by its designer to sink the British navy, thereby winning freedom for Ireland. There is also a magnificent collection of **Colt revolvers** and, outside, some locally-built steam locomotives.

AMERICAN LABOR MUSEUM ❻, Botto House National Landmark, 83 Norwood St., Haledon, NJ 07580 ☎ 973-595-7953, Internet: community.nj.com//cc/labormuseum. *Open all year Wed.–Sat. 1–4, closed major holidays except Labor Day. Adults $1.50, children under 12 free.*

America is a nation of immigrants, built by the sweat and toil of men, women, and children from all over the world. Interestingly, the American Labor Museum in Haledon is one of the very few institutions in the United States dedicated to the history of working people — their lives on and off the job, their culture, their organizing struggles, their aspirations. The museum building itself is a peculiarly apt symbol: in 1908, after emigrating from Italy and laboring 12 hours a day, 6 days a week, for 15 years in New Jersey's textile mills, Pietro and Maria Botto built this house, 12 rooms of their own with garden, the American Dream come true. They installed a grape arbor and bocce court in the garden and ran the house as a kind of social center for fellow Italian immigrants. In 1913, when more than 24,000 workers struck the Paterson silk mills, the Bottos offered their house as a gathering place, and for six historic months it was the scene of meetings, rallies, strategy sessions, and stirring oratory from some of the champions of the cause, including Elizabeth Gurley Flynn, John Reed, Big Bill Haywood, and Upton Sinclair. The Paterson strike was a turning point in the battle for the 8-hour day and other labor reforms.

Through its varied collections, exhibits, ethnic celebrations, lectures, seminars, and workshops, the American Labor Museum re-creates these events and the texture of working people's lives around the turn of the century. For those interested in delving further, there are extensive pictorial and archival materials in the library, open by appointment.

For a rare slice of ordinary life during the decades of this country's industrial transformation, or for a rare visit to a historic site in New Jersey where George Washington did not sleep, go to the American Labor Museum.

LAMBERT CASTLE MUSEUM ❼, Passaic County Historical Society, Valley Rd., Paterson, NJ 07503, ☎ 973-881-2761. *Open Wed.–Sun., 1–4. Closed Mon., Tues., and major holidays. Adults $1.50, seniors $1, children under 15 free. Partially ♿.*

Catholina Lambert (1834–1923) emigrated from rural England at the age of 17 and eventually made a fortune as one of Paterson's major silk mill owners. In 1892 he built this castle on Garret Mountain, overlooking the gritty city, and filled it with a vast collection of American and European paintings and sculptures. After his death it was sold to the city and today serves as headquarters for both the Passaic County Parks Department and the Passaic County Historical Society.

Most of the art is long since gone, but enough remains in the period rooms to get a good sense of the opulent lifestyle to which a wealthy industrial magnate could aspire in the late Victorian era. The main draw here, however, is the changing exhibitions of local history, featuring paintings, photographs, decorative arts, textiles, clothing, and other materials.

The Village of Waterloo, Wild West City, and Lake Hopatcong

O f all the restored historic villages within daytrip range of New York, Waterloo is arguably the most enjoyable. From an authenti- cally reconstructed Indian settlement of 1625 to the cheerful ambiance of the Towpath Tavern next to the locks on the Morris Canal, Waterloo offers a broad scope of experiences covering nearly three cen- turies of America's heritage. It is also home to a world-famous music festi- val held each summer, with offerings from top rock stars to the Metropolitan Opera.

Other nearby attractions include Wild West City, where the wild west of the 1880's comes to life again, and scenic Hopatcong State Park with its historic lake.

GETTING THERE:

By Car, Waterloo is about 60 miles west of midtown New York City. Take **I-80** west of the George Washington Bridge to Exit 25 (Stanhope/Newton) and head north on **US-206**. Follow "**Waterloo Village**" signs through the International Trade Center. The Village is 2 miles from I-80.

For **Wild West City**, return to US-206 and turn north (left) for a short distance to the site, on the right.

For **Hopatcong State Park**, return to I-80 and go east a few miles to Exit 28. There proceed to the stoplight, turn left, and go about a half-mile to the lake.

PRACTICALITIES:

Fine weather is essential for this trip. Note the opening dates of each attraction carefully, as some are closed from mid-fall until mid-spring and on either weekdays or weekends in spring or fall. You can confirm the opening times and special events by phoning or by visiting their web sites. For further information contact the **Skylands Tourism Council**, P.O. Box 329, Columbia, NJ 07832, ☎ 1-800-4SKYLAND or 908-496-8598, Internet: www.njskylands.com

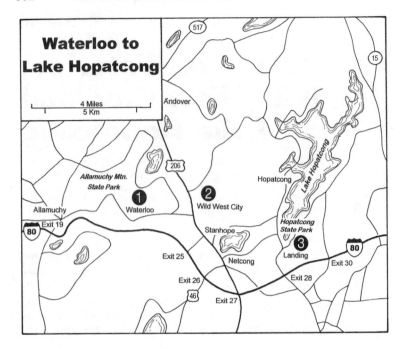

FOOD AND DRINK:

Snacks, full meals, and refreshments are available at all of the sites. Especially recommended places include:

Black Forest Inn (249 US-206, a mile north of I-80 Exit 25, Stanhope) German and Continental cuisine in an Old World setting. ☎ 973-347-3344. X: Sat. lunch, Tues. $$

Towpath Tavern (in Waterloo Village, by the canal) Full lunches, snacks, beverages, wine, and beer served in an historic building overlooking the canal and river. X: weekdays before Memorial Day. $

LOCAL ATTRACTIONS:

Circled numbers in text correspond to numbers on the map.

*THE VILLAGE OF WATERLOO ❶, Stanhope, NJ 07874, ☎ 973-347-0900, Internet: www.waterloovillage.org. *Open April, Wed.–Fri. 10–3; May–June, Wed.–Fri. 10–4, Sat.–Sun. 11–5; July–Oct., Wed.–Fri. 10–4, Sat.–Sun. 11–5; Nov., Wed.–Fri. 10–4. Adults $9, seniors $8 children (6–15) $7. Horse-drawn wagon tours on weekends and holidays, Adults $4, seniors and children $3. Restaurant and snack bar. Gift shop. Partially ♿.*

Originally inhabited by the Lenape Indians, the land around what is now Waterloo was attractive to early settlers because of its fertile soil, water power, timber, and iron ore. By 1760, an iron-making community called Andover Forge developed on the site of the present village. In 1778 the ironworks was confiscated from its pro-British owner and used to produce armaments for the Revolutionary Army. The name was later changed to Waterloo in honor of Wellington's defeat of Napoleon at Waterloo, Belgium, in 1815.

Prosperity came in 1831 with the opening of the **Morris Canal**, which carried boats more than a hundred miles across northern New Jersey from Phillipsburg on the Delaware to New York Bay. Lying at a junction of the canal where boats were lifted across the mountain on an inclined plane, Waterloo became a busy inland port, and later an important railway depot. All of this came to an end in 1901 when a new rail route was developed; the now-obsolete canal ceasing operations in 1927. An attempt to develop Waterloo into an exclusive lakeside community was foiled by the stock market crash of 1929. After World War II, the site was taken over by a foundation and restorations begun, opening to the public in 1964.

There are over 20 original buildings that may be visited on the self-guided walking tour. Dating from the Colonial, Federal, and Victorian periods, these include several furnished houses, a general store, a stagecoach inn, a working blacksmith's shop, an operating saw mill and grist mill, a farmstead and barn, a woodworking shop, an apothecary, the Canal Museum, and the Indian Museum. The old trades are demonstrated by skilled artisans in period costumes, who will gladly answer your questions.

One of Waterloo's major attractions is an authentically re-created *Lenape Indian Village on an island in the lake. Guides in Indian dress explain how Native Americans lived here in the early 17th century, and of course are a big hit with young children. This is considered to be the finest reconstructed Indian village in the northeast.

You might want to finish your tour with a visit to the Towpath Tavern, where you can enjoy snacks or drinks next to the locks of the canal.

Nearby, back on US-206, is:

WILD WEST CITY ❷, Route 206, Netcong, NJ 07857, ☎ 973-347-8900, Internet: www.WildWestCity.com. *Open daily mid-June to Labor Day, 10:30–6; weekends May to mid-June and Labor Day through Columbus Day. (weekdays for groups only). Adults $7.50, seniors $5.25, children (2–12) $6.75; train, stagecoach, or pony rides $1.50 each. Group rates and birthday party packages available. Gift shop. Snacks, meals, refreshments. Special events.*

Here's a convincing replica of Dodge City in the 1880s, with 22 live action shows a day on Main Street. Pan for gold, visit the petting zoo, try the pony rides, ride the miniature train, and watch the famous gunfight at OK Corral. Top off the day by swinging into the Golden Nugget Saloon for a meal and a show.

Just a few miles from here, on the way back to New York, is the:

HOPATCONG STATE PARK ❸, Lakeside Blvd., Landing, NJ 07850, ☎ 973-398-7010, Internet: www.state.nj.us/dep/forestry/parks/hopatcg.htm. *Grounds open Memorial Day–Labor Day, daily 8–8; rest of year, daily 8–4:30. Beach open Memorial Day–Labor Day, daily 10–6. Parking fee from Memorial Day-Labor Day. Swimming, fishing, picnic facilities, playgrounds. No alcohol, no hunting. Leashed pets only, no pets at beach. Snack bar. Partially &.*

Lake Hopatcong is New Jerseys's largest lake and one of its most popular resort areas. Originally created in the early 19th century as a water source for the Morris Canal (see page 303), it is 900 feet above sea level and nine miles long, with 40 miles of shoreline. The lake's southwestern end is the site of the scenic, 113-acre **Hopatcong State Park**, a good place to get your feet wet, have a picnic, or just relax before returning to the Big City. While there, you might want to check out the **Historical Museum** in the old Morris Canal locktender's house. Exhibits there cover local Native American life, the building of the canal, the great era when Hopatcong was a tourist mecca, and the former amusement park on its shores. Call ahead for opening schedule. ☎ 973-398-2616, Internet: www.hopatcong.org/museum. *Free.*

In the Lenape Indian Village

New Jersey's Northwest Skylands

New Jersey's Route 23 heads northwest from suburbia through the mountains to the highest point in the state, overlooking the junction of New Jersey, New York, and Pennsylvania on the Delaware River. Along the way you'll be treated to a variety of attractions, most of which are especially good for children and their families. First, there's the classic Fairy Tale Forest, followed by a tour through a mine deep below the earth, along with a mineral museum and a place where you can go prospecting on your own. The Space Farms Zoo, dating from the 1920s and one of New Jersey's original roadside attractions, continues to fascinate young and old alike. End the day with a sweeping view of Pennsylvania's Pocono Mountains and New York's Catskills from the summit of High Point State Park, or hiking through a natural gorge in the Stokes State Forest. For those lucky enough to stay overnight, this trip combines well with both the previous and the next one.

GETTING THERE:

By Car, the nearest point on this trip is about 40 miles from midtown New York City, and the farthest about 75 miles. From the George Washington Bridge take **I-80** west to Exit 53, there turning north on **NJ-23** to Oak Ridge. From here follow the directions for each attraction.

PRACTICALITIES: ·

Fine weather is essential for this trip. Note the opening dates of each attraction carefully, as some are closed from mid-fall until mid-spring and on either weekdays or weekends in spring or fall. You can confirm the opening times and special events by phoning or by visiting their web sites. For further information contact the **Skylands Tourism Council**, P.O. Box 329, Columbia, NJ 07832, ☎ 1-800-4SKYLAND or 908-496-8598, Internet: www.njskylands.com

FOOD AND DRINK:

Both the Fairy Tale Forest and the Space Farms Zoo offer the kind of food that children love best. Adults might prefer the:

Roadside Restaurant (NJ-23, near junction of NY-94, in Hamburg) A wide selection of comfort foods and Italian dishes in a casual, comfy setting. ☎ 973-702-8801. X: Tues., major holidays. $ and $$

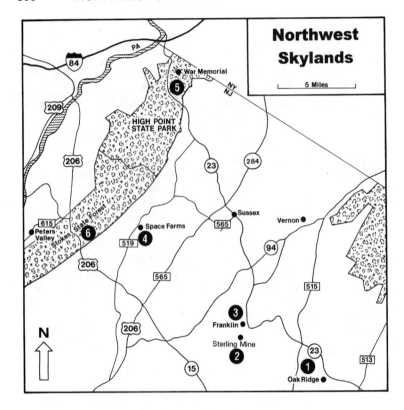

Picnic facilities are available at the Fairy Tale Forest, Space Farms Zoo, High Point State Park, and Stokes State Forest.

LOCAL ATTRACTIONS:

Circled numbers in text correspond to numbers on the map.
From NJ-23, turn left on Oak Ridge Road to the:

FAIRY TALE FOREST ❶, 140 Oak Ridge Rd., Oak Ridge, NJ 07834, ☎ 973-697-5656, Internet: www.fairytaleforest.com. *Open late May to mid-June, weekends 11–5; mid-June to early Sept., Tues.–Sun. 11–5; late Sept.–late Oct., weekends 11–5; late Nov. to late Dec., every evening, 5 p.m. to 9. Closed major holidays. Weekday admission: Adults $7, children $6; weekends: Adults $8, children $7. Gift shop. Restaurant. Picnic tables. Special events.* ⚬.

First opened in 1957, Fairy Tale Forest has long been a landmark for children and their families. Its old-fashioned charms had faded by the 1990s, but then in 1997 a magic touch was applied by new proprietors, bringing back to life its clean, simple fun for a new generation.

Children can hardly wait to enter this enchanted woodland filled with scenes and characters from their favorite stories. Hand-crafted life-size characters inhabit the castles, cottages, and gingerbread houses that dot this eight-acre storybook land. The kids can visit Rapunzel's tower, the Old Woman's shoe, Goldilock's cabin, Jack's beanstalk, and more; renewing their acquaintance with Little Red Riding Hood, Snow White, Humpty Dumpty, Little Miss Muffet, contrary Mary, and other fairytale notables along the way. They can also ride a merry-go-round and a fire engine, or dig for treasure in the Rainbow Shaft. Hot Diggity's Grill has the foods that children love most, and there are special events like magic shows.

Return to NJ-23 and head north a few miles to Route 517, turning left on this to Ogdensburg. Turn right on Passaic St., then left on Plant St. to the:

STERLING HILL MINING MUSEUM ❷, 30 Plant St., Ogdensburg, NJ, 07439 ☎ 973-209-7212, Internet: www.sterlinghill.org. *Open April–Nov., daily 10–5; also on weekends in March and Dec., 10–5. Closed Easter and Thanksgiving. Daily tours in July–Aug. at 11, 1, & 3; otherwise on weekdays at 1 and weekends at 11, 1 & 3. No 3 p.m. tour in winter. Adults $9, seniors $8, children under 17 $6. Mine interior is cool: bring jacket or sweater and wear suitable shoes. Museum. Gift shop.* &.

Take a fascinating journey deep into the earth while exploring the subterranean labyrinth of a former zinc mine, the last underground mining operation in the state. All along the way you'll encounter re-creations of mining scenes, past and near-present, with spectacular fluorescent minerals as a special treat.

Return on 517 and head north on NJ-23 briefly, then follow signs to the:

FRANKLIN MINERAL MUSEUM ❸, Evans St., Franklin, NJ 07416, ☎ 973-827-3481, Internet: www.franklinmineralmuseum.com. *Open April–Nov., Mon.–Sat. 10–4, Sun. 11–4. Closed Easter and Thanksgiving. Museum: adults $4, seniors $3.50, children through grade 12 $2. Prospecting: adults $5, seniors $4, children $2.50. Combination ticket available. Guided tours, gift shop. Museum is &, but not dump.*

There are some 300 different minerals on display here, almost all of them from the Franklin-Ogdensburg area, the beneficiary of a unique sequence of geological events that began about a billion years ago. In the course of these unimaginable eons, several major periods of mountain building produced the world's richest zinc ore body, along with 26 minerals not found anywhere else on Earth. Recently (in the last million years or so, that is), glaciation, erosion, and weathering have continued the process of mineral formation, and new specimens are still being discovered.

The Franklin Mineral Museum contains permanent and traveling collections, as well as what may be the most spectacular display of fluorescent minerals to be found anywhere. The replica mine simulates the operations of the New Jersey Zinc Company, which donated all of the equipment and materials used in the reconstruction. The museum also administers the **Buckwheat Dump**, where you can prospect on your own and take home a bagful of minerals. You're welcome to bring your own gear, or rent or purchase ultraviolet lamps and other equipment at the gift shop.

Return to NJ-23 and continue north to Sussex. At the junction with Route 565, turn left, following signs to Space Farms. Shortly make a right-angle turn and continue straight ahead to Route 519, turning left and proceeding to the:

SPACE FARMS ZOO & MUSEUM ❹, 218 Route 519, Beemerville Rd., Sussex, NJ 07461, ☎ 973-875-8000, Internet: www.spacefarms.com. *Open May through Oct., daily 9–5. Adults $8.95, seniors $7.95, children under 12 $4.50. Picnic area, playground, miniature golf, restaurant, gift shop. Grounds somewhat hilly but manageable for wheelchairs, buildings ↺.*

The denizens of Space Farms are not extraterrestrials, but over 500 native North American mammals, birds, and reptiles, along with a few exotic species from foreign parts, all collected by the Space family. The Spaces have been operating the 400-acre farm since 1927 and pride themselves on their tradition of "tender, loving care in tune with nature." In addition to viewing the animals in their natural habitat, you can visit the museum buildings and see Grandpa Ralph Space's remarkable collection of Americana — antique cars, toys, dolls, clocks, muskets, inventions, gadgets, Indian artifacts, and everything but the kitchen sink (that's in Grandma Space's restaurant, serving short-order specialities with an old-fashioned touch).

Go north on Route 519 about five miles to NJ-23, then north on 23 another few miles to:

HIGH POINT STATE PARK ❺, 1480 State Route 23, Sussex, NJ 07461, ☎ 973-875-4800. *Open daily all year, daylight hours. Admission Memorial Day to Labor Day: $5 per car weekdays, $7 weekends and holidays. Entrance to monument is free when tollbooth is open, otherwise $1 per person (NJ seniors 62+ free). Picnicking, refreshments, swimming and bathhouse, hiking and nature trails, boating, fishing, camping (fee), cross-country skiing, ice skating, ice fishing, snowmobiling, sledding, dog sledding. Leashed pets only. Beach and restrooms ↺.*

The highest point in New Jersey (1,803 feet) lies in this beautiful 14,000-acre park. From the top of the 200-foot **War Memorial** that marks the spot, you can see the Delaware River, the Poconos, the Catskills, and the juncture of three states — New York, New Jersey and Pennsylvania. The 80-mile view is especially magnificent in laurel time and in the fall. Part of the **Appalachian Trail** winds through High Point, and spring-fed Lake Marcia provides a refreshing dip.

Alternatively, from the Space Farms you can head south on Route 519 for about six miles to US-206, then north on 206 about three miles into:

STOKES STATE FOREST ❻, 1 Coursen Rd., Branchville, NJ 07826, ☎ 973-948-3820. A useful Internet site is: www.njskylands.com/pkstokes. *Open daily all year. Free admission to park; Memorial Day to Labor Day admission to Stony Lake day use area $5 per car weekdays, $7 weekends and holidays. Picnicking, playground, swimming and bathhouse, boating, camping (fee), fishing, hiking and nature trails, bridle paths, cross-country skiing, ice skating, ice fishing, sledding. Stony Lake, picnic areas, and newer buildings are* &.

This park of over 15,000 acres on the Kittatinny Ridge offers some of the finest scenery in New Jersey. Don't miss the **Tillman Ravine**, a natural gorge in the southern corner of the park, or the 1,600-foot-high **Sunrise Mountain**, with superb views of the surrounding landscape.

High Point borders **Stokes** on the south, and you can drive from one to the other on interconnected park roads, taking a scenic route along the crest of the mountain. Ask for maps at park offices.

Peters Valley Crafts Center, described on the next trip, is very close to Stokes State Forest. If you prefer to include it on this trip instead, head north on 206 to the junction with Route 521. Turn left here and go about a mile to the junction of Route 615, then turn left again and go about two miles to Peters Valley, near Layton.

Trip 48

Delaware Water Gap

This glorious one-day excursion meanders in and out of the 35-mile-long Delaware River Gap National Recreation Area, taking you through some of the best scenery in the Northeast. Along the way you can visit some spectacular waterfalls, a crafts community, a restored 19th-century village, and numerous other attractions. For the most part, busy and commercialized roads are avoided. It is an especially nice trip to take during the fall foliage season, and — if you can stay overnight — combines well with the previous two trips.

GETTING THERE:

By Car, Delaware Water Gap is about 80 miles west of midtown New York City, while the leisurely drive through the National Recreation Area adds another 50 miles or so in all. Take **I-80** west from the George Washington Bridge all the way to Exit 1, the last exit in New Jersey, just before the Delaware River. Get off here and follow the road under the highway to the **Kittatinny Point Visitor Center**, where you can get a free map and current information about the National Recreation Area as well as have a good view of the Delaware Water Gap.

PRACTICALITIES:

Good weather is essential for this outdoor trip, which is best made between April and November. Be sure to wear comfortable walking shoes, and consider bringing a picnic lunch.

For further information contact the **Delaware Water Gap National Recreation Area**, Bushkill, PA 18324, ☎ 570-588-2451, Internet: www.nps.gov/dewa, or the regional tourist offices: **Pocono Mountains Vacation Bureau**, 1004 Main St., Stroudsburg, PA 18360, ☎ 570-424-6050 or 1-800-762-6667, Internet: www.poconos.org; or **Skylands Tourism Council of New Jersey**, P.O. Box 329, Columbia, NJ 07832, ☎ 908-496-8598 or 1-800-4SKYLAND, Internet: www.njskylands.com.

FOOD AND DRINK:

You'll have wonderful opportunities for a **picnic lunch** on this daytrip. Bushkill Falls offers full facilities, along with a snack bar. Additionally, the Delaware Water Gap National Recreation Area has picnic facilities at both Dingmans Falls and Kittatinny Point, and at various other scenic spots throughout the entire 35-mile area.

Adequate eateries in this heavily-touristed region can be found at

Delaware Water Gap, Stroudsburg, along US-209, and in New Jersey at Peters Valley and Walpack Center.

SUGGESTED TOUR:

Circled numbers in text correspond to numbers on the map.

Begin your tour at the **Kittatiny Point Visitor Center** ❶ of the **Delaware Water Gap National Recreation Area**, where you can find out all about the other attractions, see the exhibits, join a ranger-led discussion program, and watch an introductory video.

Stretching for 40 miles along the banks of the Delaware River, these 70,000 largely unspoiled acres hold a wealth of scenic and recreational opportunities. The most spectacular sight is the **Delaware Water Gap** itself, where over countless millennia, the Delaware River carved a path between the Kittatinny Ridge in New Jersey and the Pocono Mountain Plateau in Pennsylvania. The gap, about 900 feet across at river level, widens to span a mile at the crest, making a dramatic cleft in these ancient mountains, which were once as high as the Rockies. There are three marked gap overlooks; one on the site of the old Kittatinny House, a popular resort hotel destroyed by fire in 1931, one at Point of Gap, and one at Arrow Island. Wildlife abounds here; and you can hike along marked trails graded for difficulty, including a 25-mile section of the Appalachian Trail. Activities in various parts of the National Recreation Area include picnicking, swimming, camping, fishing, boating, canoeing (rentals available outside the park), hiking trails, nature trails, bicycling, rock climbing, ice skating, cross-country skiing, snowmobiling; all in designated areas only. Some facilities are manageable for wheelchairs. *Columbia, NJ 07832,* ☎ *908-496-4458, Internet: www.nps.gov.dewa. Open daily May to mid-Sept., on weekends only the rest of the year.*

Return to 1-80 and head west across the toll bridge into Pennsylvania. Take the first exit and turn right to **Shawnee-on-Delaware** ❷, an old resort with some modern attractions. If you happen to have kids in tow, you might want to stop at **Shawnee Place**, a play-and-water park geared to active youngsters from 2 to 13. ☎ *570-421-7231, Internet: www.shawneemt.com. Open mid-June to Labor Day, daily 10–5. Admission $12, adult spectators $8, seniors $6, under 40" tall $6.*

Continue on a narrow, winding road into the Pennsylvania side of the National Recreation Area. After about nine miles you'll come to US-209, a busy highway lined with commercial establishments. A left turn quickly brings you to the **Pocono Indian Museum** ❸, where the history of the Delaware Indians is brought to life through unique displays of artifacts. Here you can walk through a real bark house, and see thousand-year-old pottery as well as a more recent scalp. *PA-209, Bushkill, PA,* ☎ *570-588-9338. Open daily 9:30–5:30. Adults $4, seniors (62+) $2.50, children (6–16) $2.*

Heading north on PA-209, you'll soon come to the well-marked left turn for a most delightful attraction:

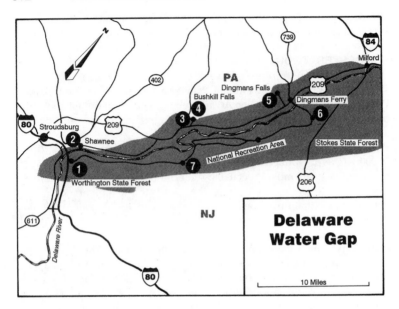

*BUSHKILL FALLS ❹, Bushkill Falls Rd., Bushkill, PA 18324, ☎ 570-588-6682, Internet: www.visitbushkillfalls.com. *Open April–Oct., daily 9–dusk. Adults $8, seniors $7, children 4–10 $2, under 4 free. Picnic area and grills, nature trails, Native American exhibit, wildlife exhibit, fishing, paddle boat rentals, miniature golf, shops, snack bar. Partially &, but not falls.*

Bushkill Falls, the "Niagra of Pennsylvania," has been a classic tourist attraction since 1904, when the Peters family first opened their natural haven to the public. Few changes other than trail improvements have been made in the decades since. This is a wonderful escape into an earlier time when a stunning waterfall in a near-primeval setting was all it took to keep folks happy.

From the entrance, there are four trails to and around the falls. The easiest of these goes to a scenic overlook at the top of the 100-foot-high ***Main Falls**, can easily be done in 15 minutes, and involves no climbing. The **Popular Route** takes you to the bottom of the main falls and up the other side to some upper falls before returning about 45 minutes later. This can be extended by including the **Pennell Falls Trail**. Serious hikers will enjoy the gorgeous **Bridal Veil Falls Trail**, which winds through the boulder-strewn gorge past all eight waterfalls and takes about two hours, including roughly 200 feet of vertical ascent. All of the trails end at the snack bar and old-fashioned pavilion, where you can enjoy lunch or drinks. There are several other attractions, including a Native American exhibit, miniature golf, and paddle boats on a pond.

Continue north on US-209 for about 12 miles to Dingmans Ferry, where you can turn left to **Dingmans Falls** ❺. This is located within the National Recreation Area and may be visited at any time during daylight hours. The **Visitor Center** offers an audiovisual show, nature exhibits, and information. From the parking lot, a half-mile-long nature trail leads through a picturesque gorge dotted with stands of hemlock and rhododendron to the Pocono's highest waterfalls, **Dingmans**, and the aptly-named **Silver Thread Falls**. *Visitor Center open May–Oct., daily 9–5,* ☎ *570-828-7802, Internet: www.nps.gov/dewa. Partially* &.

Return to Dingmans Ferry and turn right on PA-739-S, crossing the toll bridge over the Delaware into the New Jersey side of the National Recreation Area. Continue on to the:

PETERS VALLEY CRAFTS CENTER ❻, 19 Kuhn Rd., Layton, NJ 07851, ☎ 973-948-5200, Internet: www.pvcrafts.org. *Store and gallery open daily in season, weekends off-season. Studio visits on weekends, call for schedule. Store is* &.

Located on the edge of the National Recreation Area, Peters Valley is a year-round residential community where skilled artisans are invited to live and work in exchange for teaching workshops in their various specialties. Workshops have covered such topics as hand-forged tools, the lost-wax process of ceramic shell casting, contemporary teapots, kiln building, goldsmithing, enameling, electroforming and electroplating, landscape and portrait photography, quilting, collage art, handbound books, knotting and coiling, embroidery, silk painting, rustic furniture, and joinery. The gallery and store feature work by resident craftspeople and other nationally-known artists.

A road through the National Recreation Area leads south for about 12 miles to:

MILLBROOK VILLAGE ❼, Old Mine Rd., Millbrook, NJ, ☎ 908-841-9531, Internet: www.millbrookvillage.tripod.com. *Grounds open daily, village open early May to mid-Oct., Wed.–Sun. 9–5. Partially* &.

A small hamlet that developed around a mill built in 1832, Millbrook flourished during the mid-19th century. By the early 1900s, however, it fell into an irreversible decline. What you see today is a skillful re-creation of a late-19th-century rural community, peopled by guides in period costume who demonstrate the crafts of yesteryear. It is located within the National Recreation Area and is operated by the National Park Service.

Continue south through the park for another 11 miles to I-80 for the drive home.

Trip 49

New Hope

A rtists, writers, actors, musicians, and other creative types have been attracted to the charms of New Hope ever since the early 1900s, forming what amounts to a colony on the banks of the Delaware. In more recent times, hordes of tourists have followed, lured by both the arty atmosphere and the very real attractions the town has to offer.

New Hope began to flourish in the 1720s as a ferry town. It was known as Coryell's Ferry during the Revolutionary War, when the local people aided the Continental Army. The mills operated by Benjamin Parry in the late 18th century and the opening of the Delaware Canal in 1832 made the town a bustling commercial center for a time. Its prosperity was extended in the 1890s by the arrival of the railroad, and again by its growing fame as an art colony.

Today, besides the numerous galleries, boutiques, restaurants, cafés, riverside setting, and historic sites, New Hope offers a wonderfully preserved stretch of the canal complete with rides on a mule-drawn barge, and excursions by steam train into the nearby countryside.

Those staying overnight might consider combining this trip with ones to nearby Flemington (page 268) or Princeton (page 272).

GETTING THERE:

By Car, New Hope is about 65 miles southwest of midtown New York City. Take the **New Jersey Turnpike** south to Exit 14, Newark Airport, then **I-78** west to Exit 30. Head south on **I-287** to Exit 17, then take **US-202** south towards Flemington. Continue south on 202 across the Delaware River and pick up **PA-32** south for about a mile, which becomes Main St. in New Hope. Metered parking is available on the side streets, and there are several commercial parking lots.

PRACTICALITIES:

Summer weekends bring mobs of tourists; you'll be much better off coming on a weekday, preferably from May through October. Decent weather will enhance this almost-entirely outdoor trip.

New Hope hosts several annual events including the Auto Show in August and the Arts & Crafts Festival in October. For local information contact the **New Hope Borough Information Center**, South Main and Mechanic streets, New Hope, PA 18938, ☎ 215-862-5880, Internet: www.newhopepa.com. Regional information is obtainable from the **Bucks County Visitors Bureau**, 152 Swamp Rd., Doylestown, PA 18901, ☎ 215-345-4552 or 800-836-2825, Internet: www.buckscountycvb.org.

FOOD AND DRINK:

One of the prime reasons to visit New Hope is to dine well. Not cheaply, but well. Here are some suggestions:

La Bonne Auberge (at Village 2, a mile west on Mechanic St.) It's open for dinner only, a bit hard to find, and very expensive, but the classic French cuisine is as good as you'll find anywhere in these parts. Reservations and jacket required. ☎ 215-862-2462. X: Mon., Tues., some holidays. $$$+

Odette's (South River Rd., PA-32, 4 miles south of New Hope) Set by the canal and the river, Odette's has long been a favorite for stylish, elegant Continental dining in a bistro atmosphere. Sunday brunch. Reservations suggested, ☎ 215-862-2432. $$$

Martine's Fine Food (7 East Ferry St. near Main) A romantic hideaway with an interesting, eclectic menu. ☎ 215-862-2966. $$

Havana (105 South Main St.) Creative, contemporary dishes served indoors or out. Very popular. ☎ 215-862-9897. $$

Lambertville Station (11 Bridge St., just south of the bridge, Lambertville, NJ) Creative American cuisine in a restored Victorian railroad station. X: Sun. lunch. ☎ 609-397-8300. $$

Cock 'n' Bull (Peddler's Village, PA-263 off US-202, Lahaska, PA) Traditional American fare in a Colonial-style setting. Sunday brunch. ☎ 215-794-4010. $$

Spotted Hog (Peddler's Village, US-202 at Street Rd., Lahaska, PA) Standard American fare in a casual country setting. ☎ 215-794-4030. $$

LOCAL ATTRACTIONS:

Circled numbers in text correspond to numbers on the map.

PARRY MANSION ❶, South Main and West Ferry streets, New Hope, PA 18938, ☎ 215-862-5652. *Open May to mid-Dec., Fri.–Sun. 1–5. Adults $5, seniors and students $4, ages 1–12 $1.*

Benjamin Parry, a wealthy lumbermill owner, built this mansion in 1784, and it remained in the family until 1966, when the New Hope Historical Society purchased it. As a result of the remarkable continuity over five generations, it was restored to reflect the various decorative changes experienced by the Parrys themselves over the years. You can see whitewash yield to wallpaper, candles to oil lamps, and the craze for Victoriana to more severe modern tastes.

*MULE BARGE ❷, New Hope Canal Boat Co., 149 S. Main St., New Hope, PA 18938, ☎ 215-862-0758, Internet: www.canalboats.com. *Operates April through Oct., weather permitting. Departures daily May–Oct. at 12, 1:30, 3, and 4:30; in April on Fri., Sat., and Sun. at 12:30 and 3. Adults $7.95, children under 12 $6.50.* ♿.

Here's a chance for a relaxing, hour-long ride on the historic Delaware Canal through New Hope and the surrounding countryside.

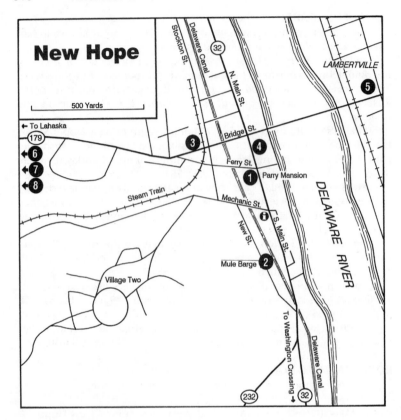

During most of the season a barge musician and historian are aboard to entertain and inform you. Bring your camera, forget your problems, enjoy the ride.

*NEW HOPE & IVYLAND RAILROAD ❸, 32 West Bridge St., New Hope, PA 18938, ☎ 215-862-2332, Internet: www.newhoperailroad.com. *Operates weekends Jan.–late Apr.; Thurs.–Sun. mid-Apr.-late Apr.; Fri.-Sun. late Apr.–mid-June; daily mid-June–early Nov.; Fri,–Sun. early Nov.–mid-Nov.; specials late Nov.–Dec. 25; daily Dec. 26-Dec. 31. Fares: Adults $9.50, seniors $8.50, children 2–11 $5.50, under 2 $1.50. Special evening dinner trains, Sunday brunch trains, and BYOB wine-and-cheese trains. Schedules and fares subject to change; check first. &.*

This nine-mile, 50-minute narrated round trip by vintage steam train takes you from the restored New Hope Station of 1891 across the trestle to which Pearl White was tied in the 1914 silent movie classic, *The Perils of Pauline,* and on through woodlands and countryside to Lahaska before returning. The 1920's passenger coaches are usually pulled by a 1925 Baldwin 2-8-0 locomotive, although other engines may be substituted. The New Hope & Ivyland is one of the only steam railroads in the country that allows people the rare opportunity to *ride in the locomotive while it's pulling the train! Ask at the ticket office about this special treat. There's a small display of railroad history, as well as a gift shop, at the New Hope Station.

Other attractions in New Hope include Coryell's Ferry Boat Rides ❹ on the Delaware River aboard a 65-foot Mississippi-style river boat. *Departures every 45 minutes starting at noon, daily in season. Trips last 30 min. Tickets sold at Gerenser's Exotic Ice Cream, 22 S. Main St.,* ☎ *215-862-2050.* The same shop also sells tickets for Colonial Walking Tours that bring New Hope's Revolutionary past back to life. If you're in town after dark, you might want to take one of the eerie Ghost Tours arranged by a psychic investigator. ☎ *215-957-9988.* New Hope is also famous for its quality art galleries, antique shops, and boutiques of all kinds; and has a broad choice of inns, restaurants, and cafés.

Another enjoyable diversion is to stroll across the bridge to Lambertville ❺ in New Jersey, which has a lower-key atmosphere but many of the same type of attractions as New Hope.

Heading west from New Hope on Route US-202, the old Colonial road linking New York with Philadelphia, soon brings you to the New Hope Winery ❻, where you can taste some of their 30-odd varieties. ☎ *215-794-2331 or 800-592-WINE, Internet: www.newhopewinery.com.* A few miles farther on is the famous:

PEDDLER'S VILLAGE ❼   4 miles west of New Hope on US-202, Box 218, Lahaska, PA 18931, ☎ 215-794-4000, Internet: www.peddlersvillage.com. *Shops open daily except Thanksgiving, Christmas, New Year's.*

This is the star attraction of Lahaska, a village first settled around 1700 by Quakers from England. Originally a collection of barns and chicken coops, Peddler's Village has evolved into 42 acres with 70 specialty shops, eight restaurants, and a country inn arranged as a Colonial village around a common complete with a gazebo and a pond. All kinds of crafts, antiques, and unusual items can be found here; and there are frequent country festivals and special events to entertain you. Its newest attraction is the magnificent Grand Carousel Ride, a beautifully restored 1922 carousel from the famed Philadelphia Tobaggan Company, which you can ride. ☎ *215-794-8960. Museum: Adults $3, seniors $2.75, children $2. Museum and carousel ride: $3.50, children $2.50. Ride only: $1.50, infants free.*

Lahaska has many other shops as well, especially the upscale Penn's Purchase Manufacturer's Outlet Village and the 12 antique dealers in the Antique Courte.

For another nearby attraction, continue two miles west on US-202, then two miles south on PA-413 to the **Buckingham Valley Vineyards** ❽. Free wine tastings and self-guided tours are offered at Bucks County's first winery. *Open March–Dec., Tues.–Sat. 11-6, Sun. noon–4; Jan.–Feb., Thurs.–Sat. 11–5, Sun. noon-4.* ☎ *215-794-7188, Internet: www.pawine.com.*

The Canal Boat Ride at Easton's Hugh Moore Park

The Two Rivers and their Canals

Pennsylvania's canal era was brief but glorious, and left behind a legacy that can still be enjoyed today. For nearly a century, from around
1830 until the 1920s, Easton was an important junction of two river
systems and three canals. From here the 72-mile-long Lehigh Canal ran
northwest to the coal mining regions of Mauch Chunk and White Haven,
the Delaware Canal some 60 miles south to Bristol, and the inefficient,
quirky, and lamented Morris Canal (see pages 253 and 303) 107 miles east
to New York Harbor. While only traces of the latter remain (New Jersey
tried to rid itself of even the memory!), portions of the Delaware and
Lehigh canals have been fully restored and today carry tourists on mule-
drawn boats, plying them with entertaining tales along the way.

Easton, the focus of this daytrip, is also home to Binney & Smith, mak-
ers of those colorful crayons. Children will love their Crayola Factory here,
a special facility made for creative fun. The same building contains the
National Canal Museum, an essential stop for those experiencing the
canal boat ride. Finally, people who enjoy gourmet dining in romantic
riverside getaways can indulge themselves on the way back, putting a perfect end to a memorable day out.

If you can spend more than a day, why not stay overnight and combine this trip with the ones to Clinton (page 293), New Hope (page 314), or
Flemington (page 268)?

GETTING THERE:

By Car, Easton lies about 78 miles west of midtown Manhattan. Take
the **New Jersey Turnpike** south to Exit 14, *or* the **Garden State Parkway** south
to Exit 142A. From either, pick up **I-78** west to Exit 22, just beyond the
Delaware River at Easton, PA. Follow signs southwest a few blocks to
Centre Square and its Two Rivers Landing. From there follow the directions in the text.

PRACTICALITIES:

This watery tour is strictly a summer affair, to be made any day from
Memorial Day to Labor Day, on Tuesdays through Sundays from early May
to Memorial Day, and on weekends in September. Although the Canal
Museum and the Crayola Factory operate all year round, it won't be as
much fun without the canal boat ride.

Those intending to finish the day off with a riverside dinner should make reservations ahead of time or risk possible disappointment.

For further information, contact the **Two Rivers Chamber of Commerce**, 1 South 3rd St., Easton, PA 18044, ☎ 610-253-4211.

FOOD AND DRINK:

Easton offers little more than the usual fast-food outlets, coffee shops, and pizzerias. You might instead pack a picnic lunch to enjoy at Hugh Moore Park. On the way back, however, you will pass a number of enticing, first-rate riverside restaurants — a wonderful way to end the day. Some suggestions are:

Chef Tell's Manor House (1800 River Rd., PA-32, in Upper Black Eddy) The famous TV chef offers eclectic fare along with the standards, all served up in a lovely setting. Sunday brunch. Reservations, ☎ 610-982-0212. $$$

Golden Pheasant Inn (763 River Rd., PA-32, in Erwinna) Classic French cuisine in gorgeously romantic dining rooms. Dinner only, plus Sunday brunch. Reserve, ☎ 610-294-9595. X: Mon. $$$

Cuttalossa Inn (PA-32 in Lumberville) Dine in a 1750 inn on the river, with views of a 30-foot waterfall. American cuisine served indoors and out on the patio. Lunch and dinner. Reservations suggested, ☎ 215-297-5082. X: Sun. $$ and $$$

Black Bass Hotel (3774 River Rd., PA-32, in Lumberville) This 18th-century riverside inn offers contemporary American cuisine, with an outdoor veranda in good weather. Lunch and dinner. Reservations suggested, ☎ 215-297-5770. $$ and $$$

LOCAL ATTRACTIONS:

Circled numbers in text correspond to numbers on the map.

Begin at Easton's **Centre Square** ❶, whose Soldiers' and Sailors' Monument stands on the site of the Old Courthouse of 1765, erected on land rented from the Penn family for the sum of one red rose a year. The town was founded in 1752 by Thomas Penn, a son of William Penn, and shows the elder Penn's influence in its grid layout built around a "Great Square." Its location at the confluence of two great rivers made it an important commercial center from the earliest times, and its industries flourished with the coming of the canals and the later development of railroads. A short stroll around the area reveals many historic houses from those pioneer times. Adjacent to the square is the:

TWO RIVERS LANDING ❶, 30 Centre Square, Easton, PA 18042, ☎ 610-515-8000, Internet: www.crayola.com/factory and www.canals.org. *Canal Museum & Crayola Factory open Memorial Day to Labor Day, Mon.–Sat 9–6, Sun. 11–6; rest of year Tues.–Sat. and holiday Mon. 9:30–5, Sun. noon–5. Closed Easter, Thanksgiving, Christmas, and early Jan. Capacity limited, admission on first-come, first-serve basis. Reservations for groups of 10 or more only. Admission to both attractions $8, seniors 65+ $7.50, under 3*

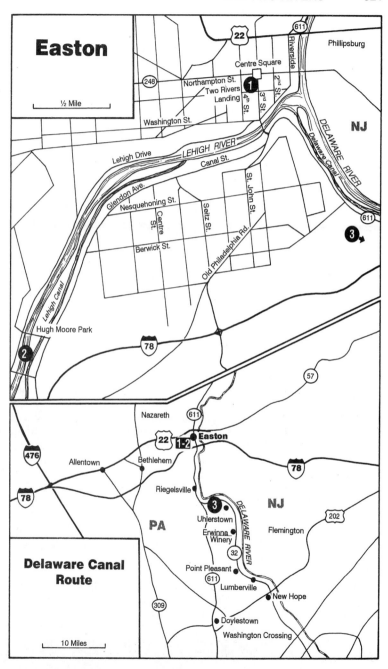

Easton

½ Mile

Centre Square

22

611

Phillipsburg

Riverside

248

Northampton St.

Two Rivers
Landing

1

2nd St.

4th St.

3rd St.

NJ

DELAWARE RIVER

Washington St.

Delaware Canal

LEHIGH RIVER

Lehigh Drive

Canal St.

Glendon Ave.

Nesquehoning St.

St. John St.

Seitz St.

Centre St.

3

611

Berwick St.

Old Philadelphia Rd.

Lehigh Canal

Hugh Moore Park

78

2

57

Nazareth

611

476

22

Easton

1-2

Allentown

Bethlehem

78

78

Riegelsville

3

DELAWARE RIVER

NJ

202

PA

Uhlerstown

Flemington

Erwinna
Winery

32

**Delaware Canal
Route**

Point Pleasant

611

Lumberville

New Hope

309

Doylestown

Washington Crossing

10 Miles

free. ♿.

Two quite separate attractions make up the Two Rivers Landing, both covered by the same admission. In addition, there is a **Visitors Center** on the ground floor. The **Crayola Factory**, on the second floor, is full of interactive displays telling you — and your kids — all about those colorful crayons so familiar to childhood. There is also a replica factory where you can watch vats of brightly-colored liquid being transformed into crayons, and studios where visitors can exercise their creative impulses with crayons, computer graphics, and other art media.

On the third floor is the **National Canal Museum**, where the history of America's canals is told in great detail. Along with actual artifacts, there are old photographs, models, and a video show. A visit here will surely whet your appetite for the next attraction!

From here, drive south on South Third Street almost to the bridge, then turn right on Washington Street and Lehigh Drive, following the latter along the river and crossing a bridge onto the island park. The route is well marked with signs to:

HUGH MOORE PARK/*CANAL BOAT RIDE ❷, P.O. Box 877, Easton, PA 18044, ☎ 610-515-8000. *Park open year-round, dawn to dusk. Free. Canal Boat rides early May to early June, Tues.–Fri. 9:45–2:20, weekends 1:30–4; early June to Labor Day, Mon.–Sat. 10:30–5, Sun. 12:45–5; Sept., weekends 1:30–4. Adults $6, seniors $5.50, children 3-15 $4. Fare includes admission to historic Locktender's House. Boat and Bike rentals. Hiking and biking trails, towpath, picnic facilities, fishing, playground. Shop and snack bar. Ride and parts of park are* ♿.

Climb aboard the canal boat Josiah White for a leisurely ***mule-drawn ride** along a restored section of the Lehigh Canal. Led by a costumed interpreter, the cruise lasts between 45 and 60 minutes, but takes you back well over a century in time to a quieter, gentler era. Begun in 1817 to bring anthracite coal from northeastern Pennsylvania some 150 miles to the coastal cities, the canal declined after the development of railroads but continued limited operations until a disastrous flood in 1942. Along with the ride you can also visit a restored locktender's house and view other fascinating artifacts of 19th-century industry.

Exit via a small bridge to Glendon Avenue, turn left and follow Canal Street to Route PA-611 South. This heads south towards New Hope (see page 314), running alongside the:

DELAWARE CANAL STATE PARK ❸, 11 Lodi Hill Rd., Upper Black Eddy, PA 18972, ☎ 610-982-5560. *Open daily during daylight hours. Free. Hiking, mountain biking, cross-country skiing on towpath, canoeing on watered sections of canal. Picnic facilities.*

Stretching some 60 miles from Easton south to Bristol, the Delaware Canal linked the Lehigh Canal with the Philadelphia area from the early

19th century until being abandoned during the 1930s. It is still in good condition and is fully watered in selected sections. The entire length is now a state park, albeit a rather narrow one, with a restored towpath for hiking, biking, and cross-country skiing. Adjacent to the park is River Road (PA-611 and PA-32), a slow, winding two-lane thoroughfare passing through magnificent scenery.

Along the way you'll discover lovely villages noted for their country inns, romantic restaurants, antique shops, and other low-key attractions. Pass through Riegelsville and Kintnersville, bearing left onto PA-32. Here the road narrows as it squeezes between majestic cliffs and the canal. Below Uhlerstown are several points of interest, including Tinicum County Park and the **Sand Castle Winery**, where you can taste the vinifera vintages on cellar and vineyard tours. *755 River Rd., behind the Golden Pheasant Inn,* ☎ *610-294-9181 or 800-722-9463, Internet: www.sand castlewinery.com. Open daily.*

At **Point Pleasant** visitors can experience the Delaware on canoes, rafts, or tubes. *Daily from May–Sept. Bucks County River Country,* ☎ *215-297-5000.* Just below here is **Lumberville**, a bit of Colonial charm set alongside the river and canal. Its country store has been around since 1770, and offers sandwiches for waterside picnics, bicycle rentals, and a variety of unusual goods. There are public outdoor tables by the locks, and you can walk along the towpath. A footbridge leads across the Delaware to New Jersey and the **Bull's Island Section**, ☎ *609-397-2949,* of the Delaware & Raritan Canal State Park, a haven for picnickers, birds, and birders alike.

Continue south to the intersection with US-202. Immediately south of it is *New Hope, whose canal boat trips, steam train rides, and other attractions are described on pages 315-317.

You can return directly from here to New York by taking US-202 north past **Flemington** (see page 268), connecting with I-78 near Somerville, NJ.

Index

Special interest attractions are listed under their category headings.
Abbreviations: NYC means New York City, CT, NJ, NY & PA refer to states; NHS means National Historic Site, SHS State Historic Site, SHP State Historic Park.

Amagansett, NY 194
AMUSEMENT PARKS:
Keansburg Amusement Park, NJ 255
Lake Compounce Theme Park, Bristol CT 230
Seaside Heights NJ 266
Shawnee Place, Shawnee-on-the-Delaware PA 311
Zoom Flume Water Park, East Durham NY 166-167
Aquariums – see Zoos
ART MUSEUMS:
Aldrich Museum of Contemporary Art, Ridgefield CT 205
Alternative Museum, NYC 49-50
Art Museum, The, Princeton NJ 275
Brooklyn Museum of Art, NYC 96-98
Bruce Museum, Greenwich CT 199
Cooper-Hewitt National Design Museum, NYC 81
Frances Lehman Loeb Art Center, Poughkeepsie NY 123
Frick Collection, NYC 78-79
Guggenheim Museum SoHo, NYC 49
Heckscher Museum of Art, Huntington NY 175
Hunterdon Museum of Art, Clinton NJ 294
Jacques Marchais Center of Tibetan Art, NYC 105
Kykuit, Sleepy Hollow NY 113
Metropolitan Museum of Art, NYC 80-81, 91-92
Montclair Art Museum, Montclair NJ 278-280
Museum for African Art, NYC 49
Museum of Modern Art, NYC 70
Museums at Stony Brook, NY 176-177
Newhouse Center for Contemporary Art, NYC 101

New Museum of Contemporary Art, NYC 49
Parrish Art Museum, Southampton NY 192
Solomon R. Guggenheim Museum, NYC 81
Storm King Art Center, Mountainville NY 141
Wadsworth Atheneum, Hartford CT 237
Whitney Museum Fairfield County, Stamford CT 202
Whitney Museum of American Art, NYC 80
Yale Center for British Art, New Haven CT 217-218
Yale University Art Gallery, New Haven CT 218

Basking Ridge NJ 283-285
Bay Shore NY 187
BEACHES:
Fire Island National Seashore, NY 186
Harriman State Park, NY 145-146
Island Beach State Park, NJ 266
Jones Beach State Park, NY 183-185
Long Beach, NY 183
Ocean Grove NJ 261
Orient Point State Park, NY 181
Point Pleasant Beach, NJ 264
Robert Moses State Park, NY 186
Sandy Hook, NJ 257
Seaside Heights, NJ 266
Bear Mountain State Park, NY 142-145
BOAT RIDES:
Canal Boat Ride, Easton PA 322
Captain's Cove Seaport, Bridgeport CT 212
Circle Line Ferry, Jersey City NJ 253
Circle Line Sightseeing, NYC 62
Coryell's Ferry, New Hope PA 317
Cross Sound Ferry, Orient Point NY 181

Fire Island Ferries, Bay Shore NY 187
Hudson River Cruises, Kingston NY 160
Mule Barge, New Hope PA 315-316
Pier 17, NYC 36
Port Jeff Ferry, Port Jefferson NY 177
Shelter Island Ferry, Greenport NY 180
Shelter Island Ferry, Sag Harbor NY 193
Staten Island Ferry, NYC 27, 99, 104
Tarrytown, NY 109, 112
Bridgehampton NY 192-193
Bridgeport CT 212-214
Bristol CT 229-230
Brooklyn NY 93-98
Bushkill PA 311-312

Cairo NY 166
CANALS:
Delaware Canal, New Hope PA 315-316
Delaware Canal State Park, PA 322
Lehigh Canal, Easton PA 322
Morris Canal, Stanhope NJ 303
Morris Canal Basin, Jersey City NJ 253
Woodcleft Canal, Freeport NY 183
Catskill Mountains, NY 161-167
Catskill NY 165
Centerport NY 175-176
CHILDREN'S ACTIVITIES:
American Museum of Natural History, NYC 83
Children's Zoo, NYC 77
Crayola Factory, Easton PA 320-322
Discovery Museum, Bridgeport CT 213
Fairy Tale Forest, Oak Ridge NJ 306
Jenkinson's Aquarium, Point Pleasant Beach NJ 264
Liberty Science Center, Jersey City NJ 254
Maritime Aquarium at Norwalk, CT 207
New York Renaissance Faire, Sterling Forest NY 153
Northlandz, Flemington NJ 269
Seaside Heights Boardwalk, NJ 266

Shawnee Place, Shawnee-on-the-Delaware PA 311
Space Farms Zoo, Sussex NJ 308
Staten Island Children's Museum, NYC 102
Wild West City, Netcong NJ 303
Zoom Flume Water Park, East Durham NY 166-167
Clinton NJ 293-294
Cold Spring Harbor, NY 174-175
Cold Spring NY 115, 119
COLLEGES & UNIVERSITIES:
Columbia University, NYC 88-89
New York University, NYC 50
Princeton University, Princeton NJ 273-275
U.S. Merchant Marine Academy, Kings Point NY 171
U.S. Military Academy, West Point NY 137, 138-140
Vassar College, Poughkeepsie NY 122-123
Yale University, New Haven CT 216-219
Connecticut 196-240
Cutchogue NY 179

Delaware Water Gap, NJ & PA 310-313

East Durham NY 166
East Hampton NY 193-194
Easton PA 318-322
ESTATES & MANSIONS:
Also see Historic Houses, Historic Sites
Boscobel Restoration, Garrison NY 118
Coe Hall, Oyster Bay NY 173-174
Hill-Stead Museum, Farmington CT 231
Home of Franklin D. Roosevelt NHS, Hyde Park NY 123-124
Kykuit, Sleepy Hollow NY 113
Lambert Castle Museum, Paterson NJ 300
Lockwood-Mathews Mansion, Norwalk CT 207
Lyndhurst, Tarrytown NY 111
MacCulloch Hall, Morristown NJ 291
Martin Van Buren NHS, Kinderhook NY 135-136
Mills Mansion SHS, Staatsburg NY 127

Montgomery Place, Annandale-on-Hudson NY 130
Olana SHS, Hudson NY 132-134
Old Westbury Gardens, Old Westbury NY 174
Parry Mansion, New Hope PA 315
Sagamore Nill NHS, Oyster Bay NY 173
Sagtikos Manor, Bay Shore NY 187
Sands Point Park & Preserve, NY 171-173
Vanderbilt Mansion, Centerport NY 175
Vanderbilt Mansion NHS, Hyde Park NY 124
Wilderstein Preservation, Rhinebeck NY 128

Fairfield CT 210-211
Farmington CT 231
FARMS:
Fosterfields Living Historical Farm, Morristown NJ 292
Grange, The, Islip NY 187
Longstreet Farm, Holmdel NJ 258
Mulford Farm Museum, East Hampton NY 193
Philipsburg Manor, Sleepy Hollow NY 113
Stamford Museum & Nature Center, Stamford CT 203
Festivities 22-23, 38, 42, 72, 79, 153, 162, 166, 271, 301
Fire Island NY 186-187
Flemington NJ 268-271
Freehold NJ 262

GARDENS:
Also see Estates & Mansions
Bayard Cutting Arboretum State Park, Oakdale NY 187
Brooklyn Botanic Garden, NYC 98
Conservatory Garden, NYC 82
Frelinghuysen Arborteum, Morristown NJ 292
Gertrude Jekyll Garden, Woodbury CT 226-227
Innisfree Garden, Millbrook NY 125
Kykuit, Sleepy Hollow NY 113
Manitoga, Garrison NY 116
Old Westbury Gardens, Old Westbury NY 174
Planting Fields Arboretum SHP, Oyster Bay NY 173

Prospect Garden, Princeton NJ 274
Staten Island Botanical Gardens, NYC 100
Garrison NY 115-118
Goshen NY 153-154
Greenport NY 180
Greenwich CT 198-200

Harriman State Park, NY 142, 145-146
Hartford CT 234-240
Hempstead NY 183
High Point State Park, NJ 308
HISTORIC HOUSES:
Also see Estates & Mansions, Historic Sites, History Museums
Acorn Hall, Morristown NJ 291-292
Alice Austen House, NYC 102
Bush-Holley House, Cos Cob CT 200
Butler-McCook Homestead, Hartford CT 237
Buttolph-Williams House, Wethersfield CT 232
Centennial Cottage, Ocean Grove NJ 262
Clermont SHS, Germantown NY 132
Conference House, NYC 106
Covenhoven House, Freehold NJ 262
Earle-Wightman House, Oyster Bay NY 174
Ford Mansion, Morristown NJ 289-290
Fred J. Johnston Museum, Kingston NY 159
Garibaldi-Meucci Museum, NYC 103
Glebe House, Woodbury CT 226-227
Gomez Mill House, Marlboro NY 148-150
Grover Cleveland Birthplace, Caldwell NJ 280
Halsey Homestead, Southampton NY 192
Harriet Beecher Stowe House, Hartford CT 238-239
Holmes-Hendrickson House, Holmdel NJ 258
Home, Sweet Home, East Hampton NY 193
Hoyt-Barnum House, Stamford CT 202

Hurley Patentee Manor, Hurley NY 162

Judson House & Museum, Stratford CT 213-214

Lower East Side Tenement Museum, NYC 42-43

Mark Twain House, Hartford CT 239

Merchant's House, NYC 50

Morven, Princeton NJ 275

Putnam Cottage, Greenwich CT 199-200

Raynham Hall, Oyster Bay NY 174

Rock Hall, Lawrence NY 183

Rockingham, Rocky Hill NJ 276

Schuyler-Hamilton House, Morristown NJ 291

Stanley-Whitman House, Farmington CT 231

Sunnyside, Tarrytown NY 110-111

Tapping Reeve House, Litchfield CT 225

Thompson House, Setauket NY 177

Webb-Deane-Stevens Museum, Wethersfield CT 231-232

Willian Floyd Estate, Mastic Beach NY 188

HISTORIC SITES:

Also see Historic Houses, History Museums

Castle Clinton, NYC 32

Clermont SHS, Germantown NY 132

Edison NHS, West Orange NJ 278

Eleanor Roosevelt NHS/Val-Kill, Hyde Park NY 124

Ellis Island National Monument, NY 254

Federal Hall, NYC 30

Fort Lee Historic Park, NJ 245-247

Fraunces Tavern, NYC 27

Goshen Historic Track, NY 154

Grant's Tomb, NYC 90

Great Falls Historic Distrct, Paterson NJ 298-299

Historic Speedwell, Morristown NJ 290-291

Home of Franklin D. Roosevelt NHS, Hyde Park NY 123-124

Knox's Headquarters SHS, Vails Gate NY 150

Martin Van Buren NHS, Kinderhook NY 135-136

Mills Mansion SHS, Staatsburg NY 127

Morristown National Historic Park, NJ 288-290

Monmouth Battlefield State Park, NJ 262

Nassau Hall, Princeton NJ 273

New Windsor Cantonment SHS, Vails Gate NY 150-151

Olana SHS, Hudson NY 132-134

Princeton Battlefield State Park, NJ 275-276

Sagamore Hill NHS, Oyster Bay NY 173

Samuel F.B. Morse Historic Site, Poughkeepsie NY 121

Senate House SHS, Kingston NY 158

Statue of Liberty, NY 253-254

Stony Point Battlefield SHS, NY 144-145

Twin Lights SHS, Highlands NJ 256

Vanderbilt Mansion NHS, Hyde Park NY 124

Walt Whitman Birthplace SHS, Huntington Station NY 175

Washington's Headquarters SHS, Newburgh NY 148

HISTORY MUSEUMS:

Also see Estates & Mansions, Historic Houses, Historic Sites

Bainbridge House, Princeton NJ 275

Bellport-Brookhaven Historical Society, NY 188

Bridgehampton Historical Museum, NY 192-193

Brooklyn Historical Society, NYC 96

Connecticut Historical Society, Hartford CT 239-240

Custom House, Sag Harbor NY 193

Earle-Wightman House, Oyster Bay NY 174

East Hampton Historical Society, NY 193

Eli Whitney Museum, Hamden CT 220

Fairfield Historical Society, CT 210

Foundry School Museum, Cold Spring NY 119

Fraunces Tavern Museum, NYC 27

Grist Mill Museum, Lynbrook NY 183

Gunn Historical Museum, Washington CT 226

Huntington Historical Society, NY 175

Israel Crane House, Montclair NJ 280

James Vanderpoel House, Kinderhook NY 135

Keeler Tavern Museum, Ridgefield CT 205

Keeney Memorial Cultural Center, Wethersfield CT 232

Litchfield History Museum, CT 224-225

Monmouth County Historical Assoc., Freehold NJ 262

Museum of Connecticut History, Hartford CT 238

Museum of the City of New York, NYC 82

Museums at Stony Brook, NY 176-177

New Haven Colony Historical Society, CT 219

Northport Historical Museum, NY 176

Ocean County Museum, Toms River NJ 267

Old Rhinebeck Aerodrome, Rhinebeck NY 129-130

Old Schoolhouse Museum, Cutchogue NY 179

Oysterponds Museum, Orient NY 181

Southampton Historical Museum, NY 192

South Street Seaport, NYC 35-36

Staten Island Institute, NYC 103

Suffolk County Historical Museum, Riverhead NY 177

Hudson NY 132-135

Hudson Valley, NY 107-167

Huntington NY 175

Hurley NY 162

Hyde Park NY 120, 123-124

Kent, CT 222-224

Kinderhook NY 135-136

Kingston NY 156-160

Liberty State Park, Jersey City NJ 250-254

LIGHTHOUSES:
Eaton's Neck Lighthouse, Northport NY 176

Fire Island Lighthouse, NY 186

Horton's Point Lighthouse, Southold NY 179

Little Red Lighthouse, NYC 248

Montauk Point Lighthouse, NY 194

National Lighthouse Museum, NYC 100

Rondout Lighthouse, Kingston NY 160

Sandy Hook Lighthouse, Highlands NJ 258

Sheffield Island Lighthouse, Norwalk CT 207

Twin Lights, Highlands NJ 256

Litchfield CT 224-226

Long Island, NY 168-195

Madison NJ 285

Manhattan, NYC, NY 25-92

Mansions – see Estates & Mansions

MARITIME INTEREST:
Captain's Cove Seaport, Bridgeport CT 212

East End Seaport Maritime Museum, Greenport NY 180

East Hampton Town Marine Museum, Amagansett NY 194

Horton's Point Nautical Museum, Southold NY 179

Hudson River Maritime Museum, Kingston NY 159-160

Intrepid Sea-Air-Space Museum, NYC 59-62

Long Island Maritime Museum, West Sayville NY 187-188

Sag Harbor Whaling Museum, NY 193

Snug Harbor Cultural Center, NYC 100-101

South Street Seaport, NYC 35-36

U.S. Merchant Marine Academy, Kings Point NY 171

Whaling Museum, Cold Spring Harbor, NY 174

Monroe, NY 155

Montauk NY 194

Montclair NJ 278-280

Morristown NJ 287-292

MUSICAL INTEREST:
Carnegie Hall, NYC 59

Jones Beach Outdoor Theater, Wantagh NY 185

Lincoln Center, NYC 84

Woodstock NY 164

Yale Collection of Musical Instruments, New Haven CT 219

NATIVE AMERICAN LIFE:
Indian Museum, Southold NY 179
Institute for American Indian
  Studies, Washington CT 226
Lenape Indian Village, Stanhope
  NJ 303
National Museum of the American
  Indian, NYC 32
Pocono Indian Museum, Bushkill
  PA 311
Shinnecock Indian Reservation,
  NY 190-192

NATURE CENTERS:
Audubon Center, Greenwich CT
  200-202
Audubon Society Birdcraft
  Museum & Sanctuary, Fairfield
  CT 211
Bartlett Arboretum, Stamford CT
  203
Catskill Game Farm, Palenville NY
  165
Cattus Island Park, Toms River NJ
  267
Connecticut Audubon Center,
  Fairfield CT 211
Constitution Marsh Wildlife
  Sanctuary, Garrison NY 118
Elizabeth Morton National Wildlife
  Refuge, Sag Harbor NY 193
Flanders Nature Center,
  Woodbury CT 227
Garvies Point Preserve, Glen Cove
  NY 173
Great Swamp National Wildlife
  Refuge, Basking Ridge NJ
  284-285
Great Swamp Outdoor Education
  Center, Chatham NJ 285
Heckscher State Park, East Islip NY
  187
Manitoga, Garrison NY 116
Mills-Norrie State Park, Staatsburg,
  NY 127
Museum of the Hudson
  Highlands, Cornwall-on-
  Hudson NY 140
Sharon Audubon Center, Sharon
  CT 224
Somerset County Environmental
  Education Center, Basking Ridge
  NJ 283
Stamford Museum & Nature
  Center, CT 203
Tackapausha Museum & Preserve,
  Seaford NY 185

Ted Martin's Reptile Adventure,
  Palenville NY 165
White Memorial Foundation,
  Litchfield CT 226
Newburgh NY 147-151
New Haven CT 215-219
New Hope PA 314-317
New Jersey 243-313
New York City NY 17-106

**NEW YORK CITY
ATTRACTIONS:**
American Museum of Natural
  History 83
Brooklyn Bridge 34, 94
Brooklyn Heights 93-96
Brooklyn Museum of Art 96098
Carnegie Hall 59
Cathedral of St. John the Divine
  87-88
Central Park 75-80, 82-85
Chelsea 65
Chinatown 37-42
Chrysler Building 73
Cloisters, The 91-92
Columbia University 88-89
East Village 44, 50-51
Empire State Building 64
Fifth Avenue 66-71
Flatiron Building 65
Foley Square 38-39
Fraunces Tavern 27
Frick Collection 78-79
George Washington Bridge 91
Grand Central Terminal 72-73
Greenwich Village 44. 50-55
Intrepid Sea-Air-Space Museum
  59-62
Lincoln Center 84
Little Italy 42
Lower East Side 42-43
Metropolitan Museum of Art
  80-81, 91-92
Museum of Jewish Heritage 33
Museum of Modern Art 70
Museum of the City of New York
  82
National Museum of the American
  Indian 32
NYC Festivities 22-23
NYC Public Transportation 18-20
NY Public Library 62
NY Stock Exchange 30
Radio City Music Hall 71
Riverside Church 90
Rockefeller Center 70-71
St. Patrick's Cathedral 71-72

SoHo 44, 48-50
Solomon R. Guggenheim Museum
    81
South Street Seaport 35-36
Staten Island 99-106
Staten Island Ferry 27
Statue of Liberty 33, 253-254
Times Square 56-59
TriBeCa 44-48
Trinity Church 31
United Nations Headquarters 73
Whitney Museum of American Art
    80
World Financial Center 33
World Trade Center, site of 33
New York Renaissance Faire, Tuxedo
    NY 153
New York State 17-195
Northport NY 176
Norwalk CT 207-208

Ocean Grove NJ 261-262
Old Westbury NY 174
Orient NY 181
Oyster Bay NY 173-174

Palisades Interstate Park, Alpine NJ
    244-249
Paterson NJ 297-300
Pennsylvania 310-313, 314-323
Phoenicia NY 165
Port Jefferson NY 177
Poughkeepsie NY 120-123
Princeton NJ 272-276

RAILFAN INTEREST:
    Black River & Western RR, Ringoes
        NJ 271
    Catskill Mountain RR, Phoenicia
        NY 165
    Central RR of NJ Terminal, Jersey
        City NJ 253
    Grand Central Terminal, NYC
        72-73
    New Hope & Ivyland RR, New
        Hope PA 316
    New York Transit Museum, NYC
        96
    Northlandz, Flemington NJ 269
    Pine Creek RR, Farmindale NJ
        260-261
    Railroad Museum of Long Island,
        Greenport NY 180
    Shore Line Trolley Museum, East
        Haven CT 219-220
    Trolley Museum of New York,
        Kingston NY 160

RELIGIOUS INTEREST:
    Cathedral of St. John the Divine,
        NYC 87-88
    Eastern States Buddhist Temple,
        NYC 39-42
    Graymoor Christian Unity Center,
        Garrison NY 116
    Jewish Museum, The, NYC 81-82
    Little Church Around the Corner,
        NYC 64-65
    Lourdes in Litchfield Shrine,
        Litchfield CT 225-226
    Mahayan Buddhist Temple, Cairo
        NY 166
    Museum of Jewish Heritage, NYC
        33
    Ocean Grove NJ 261-262
    Old Dutch Church, Kingston NY
        159
    Riverside Church, NYC 90
    St. Bartholomew's Church, NYC
        72
    St. Mark's in the Bowery Church,
        NYC 51
    St. Patrick's Cathedral, NYC 71-72
    St. Paul's Chapel, NYC 34
    Shrine of St. Elizabeth Seton, NYC
        27
    Temple Adas Israel, Sag Harbor NY
        193
    Trinity Church, NYC 31
    Trinity Lutheran Church, Hicksville
        NY 185

**RESTORED HISTORIC
VILLAGES:**
    Allaire Village, Farmingdale NJ 260
    Historic Richmond Town, NYC 105
    Hunterdon Historical Museum,
        Clinton NJ 294
    Millbrook Village, Millbrook NJ
        313
    Museum Village in Orange
        County, Monroe NY 155
    Old Bethpage Village Restoration,
        Old Bethpage NY 186
    Philipsburg Manor, Sleepy Hollow
        NY 113
    Village of Waterloo, Stanhope NJ
        302-303
    Wild West City, Netcong NJ 303

REVOLUTIONARY WAR SITES:
    Fort Lee Historic Park, NJ 245-247
    Fort Putnam, West Point NY 140
    Fort Tryon Park, NYC 91

Fraunces Tavern, NYC 27
Monmouth Battlefield State Park, Freehold NJ 262
Morristown NHP, Morristown NJ 288-290
New Windsor Cantonment SHS, Vails Gate NY 150-151
Princeton Battlefield State Park, NJ 275-276
Senate House SHS, Kingston NY 158
Stony Point Battlefield SHS, NY 144-145
Washington's Headquarters SHS, Newburgh NY 148
Rhinebeck NY 126, 128-130
Ridgefield CT 204-205

Sag Harbor NY 193
SCENIC DRIVES:
Bear Mountain, NY 143-146
Catskill Mountains, NY 161-167
Delaware Canal, PA 322-323
Delaware Water Gap, NJ & PA 310-313
Litchfield Hills, CT 221-227
North Fork, Long Island, NY 178-181
North Shore, Long Island, NY 170-177
Palisades, The, NJ 244-249
South Fork, Long Island, NY 189-195
SCIENCE MUSEUMS:
American Museum of Natural History, NYC 83
Bruce Museum, Greenwich CT 199
Dinosaur State Park, Rocky Hill CT 233
Discovery Museum, Bridgeport CT 212-213
Hicksville Gregory Museum, Hicksville NY 185
Liberty Science Center, Jersey City NJ 254
Natural History Museum, Princeton NJ 274
Peabody Museum of Natural History, New Haven CT 219
Sleepy Hollow NY 112-114
Smithtown NY 176
Southampton NY 192
Southold NY 179
Stamford CT 202-203
Stanhope NJ 302-303

Staten Island NY 99-106
Stony Brook NY 176-177
Storm King Mountain, NY 119, 140
Stratford CT 213-214

Tarrytown NY 109-114
Terryville CT 229
Toms River NJ 266-267
Tourist Information Offices 16, 24
Tuxedo NY 153

United Nations Headquarters, NYC 73
Universities – see Colleges & Universities
UNUSUAL MUSEUMS:
African-American Museum, Hempstead NY 183
American Clock & Watch Museum, Bristol CT 229-230
American Labor Museum, Haledon NJ 299-300
American Merchant Marine Museum, Kings Point NY 171
American Museum of Firefighting, Hudson NY 134-135
American Numismatic Society, NYC 91
Barnum Museum, Bridgeport CT 212
Boothe Memorial Park & Museum, Stratford CT 213
El Museo del Barrio, NYC 82
Forbes Magazine Galleries, NYC 51
Franklin Mineral Museum, Franklin NJ 307
Harness Racing Museum, Goshen NY 153-154
Hispanic Society of America, NYC 91
Hudson River Maritime Museum, Kingston NY 159-160
Irish American Heritage Museum, East Durham NY 166
Lock Museum of America, Terryville CT 229
Lower East Side Tenement Museum, NYC 42-43
Madame Tussaud's Waxworks, NYC 58
MarketSite, NYC 58
Morris Museum, Morristown NJ 292
Museum of American Financial History, NYC 31

Museum of Early Trades & Crafts, Madison NJ 285

Museum of the Chinese in the Americas, NYC 39

Museum of the Hudson Highlands, Cornwall-on-Hudson NY 140

Museum Village in Orange County, Monroe NY 155

National Canal Museum, Easton PA 322

National Museum of the American Indian, NYC 32

New England Carousel Museum, Bristol CT 229

New York Transit Museum, NYC v96

NYC Police Museum, NYC 32

Old Schoolhouse Museum, Quogue NY 188

Old State House, Hartford CT 235-236

Paterson Museum, Paterson NJ 299

Shore Line Trolley Museum, East Haven CT 219-220

Sloane-Stanley Museum, Kent CT 222

Sterling Hill Mining Museum, Ogdensburg NJ 307

Township of Lebanon Museum, Hampton NJ 296

Volunteer Firemen's Museum, Kingston NY 159-159

Water Mill Museum, Water Mill NY 192

West Point Museum, West Point NY 139

Whaling Museum, Cold Spring Harbor NY 171

Yale Collection of Musical Instruments, New Haven CT 219

Vails Gate NY 150-151

Wantagh NY 183-185

West Orange NJ 277-278, 280

West Point NY 137-140

Wethersfield CT 231-232

Windham NY 167

WINERIES:

Buckingham Valley Vineyards, Buckingham PA 318

Haight Vineyard & Winery, Litchfield CT 226

Hargrave Vineyards, Cutchogue NY 179

Millbrook Winery, Millbrook NY 130

New Hope Winery, New Hope PA 317

Osprey's Dominion Vineyards, Peconic NY 179

Palmer Vineyards, Aquebogue NY 179

Pindar Vineyards, Peconic NY 179

Sand Castle Winery, Erwinna PA 323

Woodstock, NY 164

ZOOS & AQUARIUMS:

Beardsley Zoological Gardens, Bridgeport CT 213

Central Park Wildlife Center, NYC 77

Cold Spring Harbor Fish Hatchery & Aquarium, NY 175

Jenkinson's Aquarium, Point Pleasant Beach NJ 264

Maritime Aquarium at Norwalk, CT 207

Space Farms Zoo & Museum, Sussex NJ 308

Staten Island Zoo, NYC 102

Trailside Museum & Zoo, Bear Mountain NY 143

Turtle Back Zoo, West Orange NJ 281

Daytrips

• OTHER AMERICAN TITLES •

Daytrips NEW ENGLAND

By Earl Steinbicker. Discover the 50 most delightful excursions within a day's drive of Boston or Central New England, from Maine to Connecticut. Includes Boston walking tours. Revised 2nd edition, 320 pages, 60 maps. ISBN: 0-8038-2008-9.

Daytrips WASHINGTON, D.C.

By Earl Steinbicker. Fifty one-day adventures in the Nation's Capital, and to nearby Virginia, Maryland, Delaware, and Pennsylvania. Both walking and driving tours are featured. 368 pages, 60 maps. Revised 2nd edition. ISBN: 0-8038-9429-5.

Daytrips PENNSYLVANIA DUTCH COUNTRY & PHILADELPHIA

By Earl Steinbicker. Completely covers the City of Brotherly Love, then goes on to probe southeastern Pennsylvania, southern New Jersey, and Delaware before moving west to Lancaster, the "Dutch" country, and Gettysburg. There are 50 daytrips in all. 288 pages, 54 maps. ISBN: 0-8038-9394-9.

Daytrips HAWAII

By David Cheever. Thoroughly explores all the major islands – by car, by bus, on foot, and by bicycle, boat, and air. Includes many off-beat discoveries you won't find elsewhere, plus all the big attractions in detail. Revised 2nd edition, 288 pages, 56 maps. ISBN: 0-8038-2019-4.

Daytrips SAN FRANCISCO
& NORTHERN CALIFORNIA

By David Cheever. Fifty enjoyable one-day adventures from the sea to the mountains; from north of the wine country to south of Monterey. Includes 16 self-guided discovery tours of San Francisco itself. 336 pages, 64 maps. ISBN: 0-8038-9441-4.

In Production: Daytrips QUÉBEC by Karen Desrosiers. 48 One-day self-guided adventures in and from Québec City and Montréal, exploring the best parts of the entire province. Includes a French-Canadian menu translator and travel glossary. 320 pages, 52 maps, B&W photos, ISBN: 0-8038-2032-1

Daytrips

• EUROPEAN TITLES •

Daytrips SPAIN & PORTUGAL

By Norman P.T. Renouf. Fifty one-day adventures by rail, bus, or car – including many walking tours, as well as side trips to Gibraltar and Morocco. All the major tourist sights are covered, plus several excursions to little-known, off-the-beaten-track destinations. Revised 2nd edition, 382 pages, 51 maps. ISBN: 0-8038-2012-7.

Daytrips IRELAND

By Patricia Tunison Preston. Covers the entire Emerald Isle with 55 one-day self-guided tours both within and from the major tourist areas, plus sections on shopping. Expanded 2nd edition, 400 pages, 57 maps. ISBN: 0-8038-2003-8.

Daytrips FRANCE

By Earl Steinbicker. Describes 48 daytrips – including 5 walking tours of Paris, 24 excursions from the city, 5 in Provence, and 14 along the Riviera. Expanded 5th edition, 304 pages, 60 maps, and a menu translator. ISBN: 0-8038-2006-2.

Daytrips ITALY

By Earl Steinbicker. Features 40 one-day adventures in and around Rome, Florence, Milan, Venice, and Naples. Walking tours of the main cities are included. 4th edition, 288 pages, 45 maps, and a menu translator. ISBN: 0-8038-2004-6.

Daytrips LONDON

By Earl Steinbicker. Explores the metropolis on 10 one-day walking tours, then describes 45 daytrips to destinations throughout southern England, with excursions to the Midlands, West Country, and Wales – all by either rail or car. Expanded 6th edition, 352 pages, 62 maps. ISBN: 0-8038-9443-0.

Daytrips GERMANY

By Earl Steinbicker. 60 of Germany's most enticing destinations can be savored on daytrips from Munich, Frankfurt, Hamburg, and Berlin. Walking tours of the big cities are included. Expanded 5th edition, 352 pages, 67 maps, and a menu translator. ISBN: 0-8038-9428-7.

Daytrips HOLLAND, BELGIUM & LUXEMBOURG

By Earl Steinbicker. Many unusual places are covered on these 40 daytrips, along with all the favorites plus the three major cities. 3rd edition, 272 pages, 45 maps, and a bilingual menu translator. ISBN: 0-8038-2009-7.

Daytrips SWITZERLAND

By Norman P.T. Renouf. 45 one-day adventures in and from convenient bases including Zurich and Geneva, with forays into nearby Germany, Austria, and Italy. 320 pages, 38 maps. ISBN: 0-8038-9417-7.

In Production:

EXTRAORDINARY PLACES . . .
Close to London

by Elizabeth Victoria Wallace. Features some unexpected treasures for more adventurous travelers.

RED LIONS & WHITE HORSES . . .
A Journey Through England's Culture and History by Way of its Pubs, Beer and People
by Andrew Whyte.

HASTINGS HOUSE
Book Publishers
2601 Wells Ave., Suite 161, Fern Park, FL 32730
☎ orders toll-free (800) 206-7822
Internet: www.daytripsbooks.com
e-mail: Hhousebks@aol.com

ABOUT THE AUTHOR:

E ARL STEINBICKER is eminently qualified to help visitors (and residents!) discover America's premier metropolis, having lived in Manhattan for over 30 years and having explored nearly all of its nooks and crannies. Although he now resides in Pennsylvania, he makes frequent visits to see how his beloved city is doing.

Earl is a born tourist who believes that travel should be a joy, not an endurance test. For over 35 years he has been refining his carefree style of daytripping while working first as head of a firm specializing in promotional photography and later as a professional writer. Whether by private car or public transportation, he has thoroughly probed the most delightful aspects of places around the world – while always returning to the comforts of city life at night. A strong desire to share these experiences has led him to develop the "Daytrips" series of guides, which he continues to expand and revise. Recently, he has been assisting other authors in developing additional "Daytrips" books, further expanding the series.